WOMEN AND VICTIMIZATION

WOMEN AND VICTIMIZATION

Contributing Factors, Interventions, and Implications

TK Logan, Robert Walker,
Carol E. Jordan, and Carl G. Leukefeld

American Psychological Association
Washington, DC

Published by
American Psychological Association
750 First Street, NE
Washington, DC 20002
www.apa.org

To order
APA Order Department
P.O. Box 92984
Washington, DC 20090-2984
Tel: (800) 374-2721; Direct: (202) 336-5510
Fax: (202) 336-5502; TDD/TTY: (202) 336-6123
Online: www.apa.org/books/
E-mail: order@apa.org

In the U.K., Europe, Africa, and the Middle East, copies may be ordered from
American Psychological Association
3 Henrietta Street
Covent Garden, London
WC2E 8LU England

Typeset in New Century Schoolbook by Stephen D. McDougal, Mechanicsville, MD

Printer: Sheridan Books, Ann Arbor, MI
Cover Designer: Aqueous Studio, Bethesda, MD
Technical/Production Editor: Harriet Kaplan

The opinions and statements published are the responsibility of the authors, and such opinions and statements do not necessarily represent the policies of the American Psychological Association.

Library of Congress Cataloging-in-Publication Data

Women and victimization : contributing factors, interventions, and implications / TK Logan . . . [et al.].—1st ed.
    p. cm.
    Includes bibliographical references and indexes.
    ISBN 1-59147-316-0
    1. Abused women—Rehabilitation. 2. Abused women—Mental health. 3. Abused women—Drug use. 4. Mental illness—Risk factors. 5. Substance abuse—Risk factors. 6. Resilience (Personality trait) I. Logan, TK

    RC569.5.F3A38 2006
    362.82'92—dc22   2005010462

British Library Cataloguing-in-Publication Data
A CIP record is available from the British Library.

Printed in the United States of America
First Edition

This book is dedicated to the thousands of women who have volunteered their time, their thoughts and emotions, and their bodies to research on physical health, mental health, substance abuse, and victimization—often without reward or compensation. Without their willingness to share their experiences, there would be no social science, merely biases, beliefs, and misconceptions.

Contents

Preface

Victimization is a significant public health problem for women. It contributes to injury, health and mental health disability, and substance abuse. Individuals as well as society incur enormous economic and social costs as a result of partner violence and sexual assault victimization of women. The social salience of the issue is evident. However, the great diversity and sheer volume of research on violence against women and associated factors is overwhelming.

One might ask, "Why write another book on victimization, trauma, and related problems? Hasn't enough been written on this topic?" After all, there are thousands of research articles, books, book chapters, advice to clinicians, and other materials on violence against women. Yet it is precisely this fact, in part, that provided the impetus for this book.

In the Indian parable of the blind men and the elephant, each of several blind men touches a body part of the animal and, having had only a partial "view," describes an animal very different from the others based on that part of the elephant he had experienced. None was able to describe the elephant as it really was, for all were unable to comprehend the entire form of the elephant. Only by assembling the various parts in the proper order would a true picture of the animal be revealed.

This desire to see the big picture motivated us to write this book. The diversity of disciplines that have studied violence against women and its consequences, along with the extraordinary range of topics within this general category, make it difficult for clinicians, teachers, trainers, students, researchers, and policymakers to find a coherent representation and review of the phenomena associated with violence against women, particularly intimate partner violence and sexual assault victimization. More important, there is no single source that draws together these divergent findings from research to show how each of the many factors relate to a coherent whole.

This book is an attempt to begin assembling the "elephant"—an attempt to develop a broader perspective on interpersonal victimization among women by examining and integrating the literature across various disciplines. With that overall goal in mind, we have three specific objectives: (a) to integrate research from multiple disciplines on factors that contribute to intimate partner violence and sexual assault victimization, mental health, and substance use among adult women; (b) to provide conceptual and research background on why women may interpret and respond to interpersonal victimization experiences very differently; and (c) to identify implications for future research as well as to identify implications for interventions based on the integration of the pertinent literature.

Integration of the Literature

In addition to the sheer volume of studies, research is often developed with separate "silos" of knowledge where the narrow viewpoint of one set of studies leaves out important variables studied by other scientists. Separate streams or silos of research are critical in understanding specific phenomena being studied. In fact, often it is not clear which factors or variables are important to include without studies that target and examine specific problems. Also, methodologically it is difficult to include or control for every single important factor. However, this specialization or more narrow focus of research can result in partial descriptions of the phenomenon under study that, like those of the blind men, miss the bigger picture and the fundamental reality. The silos of specificity need to be linked to improve the understanding of complex problems such as violence against women. Without integration, it is difficult to see how all these various study findings fit with each other, how they support or differ from each other, and where future research should be directed. In addition, separate research agendas can lead to interventions that treat each issue separately instead of providing a framework for integrated interventions. Thus, the review in this book is an attempt toward trying to make some sense out of various domains of research on violence against women by integrating studies into a coherent framework. It is hoped that this integration of literature will also introduce readers to concepts and research areas that they may not have been aware of previously to help in interpreting research findings as well as planning future studies and interventions.

Individual Differences in Interpretation and Response to Victimization

In addition to integrating the literature, this review embeds the question, "Why do some women exhibit negative outcomes in response to interpersonal victimization, whereas others do not seem to experience the same lasting effects on their psychological or social well-being—even when exposed to a similar event?" The answer has to do with how women interpret a traumatic event as well as how "well-being" or "effects" are assessed. For example, take the question, "Why do some women develop serious mental health consequences in response to victimization, and others seem less susceptible to ill effects?" Studies that only target mental health as the outcome of victimization (e.g., depression or posttraumatic stress disorder [PTSD]) may find that many victims do not respond with depression or PTSD, which may make them seem unaffected by the abuse—a disturbing and confusing finding. However, when the spectrum of outcomes is broadened to include other factors, the picture becomes more complete. In other words, some women may dodge the proverbial bullet of depression or PTSD but experience substance abuse and serious physical health problems. Other women may be relatively unaffected by the victimization experience using any outcome standard.

It is also important to consider that there are individual differences in the interpretation of stressful events. An example of how interpretations of different stressful life events can affect outcomes can be seen in Suzy Kellett's story as recounted on the Internet (*THRIVEnet Story of the Month—December 1999*, 1999).

Suzy Kellett's story began in August 1975, the month she gave birth to quadruplets and the month her husband walked out, leaving her alone to cope with four infants with no income to pay the rent and other bills.

> Everyone felt sorry for her. People would have understood if this 31-year-old mother had drifted into self-pity, complaining how unfair life had been to her. She would be fully justified feeling bitter about her husband and blaming him for her plight. But Suzy says, "I never allowed myself to wonder how my life would be if I only had one [child]. I knew that wouldn't be productive. I had the fabulous four. I had to accept what was real." (*THRIVEnet Story of the Month—December 1999,* 1999, ¶2)

Thus, life circumstances that might have devastated one person may influence another in a profoundly different way. This difference in response to stressful events depends, in part, on how events are interpreted.

One way of understanding the complexities of individual differences in the interpretation and response to victimization is to use the principles of chaos theory as a metaphor to capture the complex, interrelated, and unpredictable outcomes to seemingly similar experiences. The traditional Newtonian way of understanding events is to assign a proportionate value to contributing factors as a way of predicting a comparable proportion of outcomes (Kauffman, 1993). Hence, if one tragic event results in some depression for an individual, then three events should result in proportionately greater depression. The simple addition of many contributing factors should predict greater proportionate harm to a person than would a single factor. However, when examining the complexities of interpersonal victimization and its related problems, it becomes apparent that a more complex and interactive model must be used. When looking at large populations, an increase in the number of contributing factors generally results in more negative psychological, social, and physical consequences; however, with smaller groups or individuals, these probabilities lose predictive strength. Other personal factors can offset major vulnerabilities. Conversely, some individuals may experience major negative consequences with seemingly few contributing factors. Hence, a mechanistic application of the various risk factors described in the literature can result in a mistaken view of the response to interpersonal victimization for women.

At the individual level, chaos theory posits that there are limits of predictability because outcomes may have sensitive dependence on initial but undiscovered conditions (Kellert, 1993). If we look at chaos theory as applied to the different outcomes of similar victimization experiences, we might discover that those women who recover more quickly or who have less severe sequelae have some initial experience, seemingly unrelated to the victimization experience, that may be important in the response to a later traumatic event. That is, small factors, often excluded from research designs, may play powerful roles in shaping outcomes. So, one woman exposed to a trauma may develop both depression and anxiety, whereas another woman, similar in age, race, ethnicity, and socioeconomic status, may not develop any negative long-term consequences. It may be that the second woman had an experience early in life that helps her cope with stress. Say, for example, she had a caring role model during her early formative years, whereas the other woman had no such role model. An unexamined, seemingly small experience or characteristic can have great influence on outcomes over time. In other words, the experience of having a caring role model during the formative years of development can be an "initial condition" and, over time, the individual outcomes can be sensitively dependent on this factor. This example of chaos theory, although used in a metaphorical way, exemplifies the notion that there are many behaviors, factors, experiences, and characteristics that might influence final outcomes that often are not even measured in individual research studies. Thus, our second objective in this book is to provide, by drawing together research from many disciplines, conceptual and research background on why women interpret and respond to partner violence and sexual assault victimization experiences very differently.

Implications for Research and Practice

Our last objective in this book is to discuss implications for research and interventions. Selected concerns are summarized within each chapter, with particular attention to relevant gaps in research literature. In addition, chapters 6 and 7 examine clinical intervention and justice system outcomes, and these reviews lead to a discussion of implications for future research in these respective areas. The final chapter includes a discussion of global concerns arising from this review of the literature. We hope that the identified gaps in research and in applications to practice will contribute to future research agendas and the development of policy and practice standards.

This book is especially relevant for interventions, in part because treatment practitioners often work within diagnostic windows that include only medical and clinical conditions. This review of literature will sensitize practitioners to the wider dimensions of problems that may contribute to their clients' functioning and that may need to be addressed—if not in treatment, at least through referrals to the justice system, other social services, and case management. The factors associated with victimization go far beyond the concept of "dual diagnosis" or co-occurring conditions. As will be seen throughout this review, multiple conditions coexist or give rise to each other over time, and competent clinical preparedness should include anticipating these complex conditions. The case studies presented at the beginnings of chapters 2 through 5 will highlight both the importance and the complexity of various factors that contribute to and interact with victimization, mental health, and substance abuse for practitioners. It is likely that many practitioners will identify with the cases presented because they were developed by combining elements of real cases from the experiences of several of the authors. Thus, we hope that this book will be an important resource for practitioners interested in improving the health and well-being of women.

WOMEN AND VICTIMIZATION

1

Introduction and Overview

In this chapter, we present a broad overview of several key research domains that form the scaffolding for the review of the literature in subsequent chapters. We define the terms used throughout the literature and throughout the book. Finally, a conceptual model is provided that will grow in complexity and detail in succeeding chapters. This conceptual model was used to organize and guide our thinking about the vast literature we reviewed, and we hope that it will help the reader to do so as well.

As mentioned in the Preface, this book offers a review of key findings from a wide array of research pertaining to victimization, mental health, and substance abuse among women, but it does not attempt a systematic critique of the extant literature or attempt to quantify results from various sources into larger scale findings as a meta-analysis would. Rather, this review has selected literature from peer-reviewed journals, published reports, and books that contribute to the understanding of partner violence and sexual assault victimization among adult women and related factors as organized by a heuristic conceptual model developed specifically for this review. Where possible, we have used the consensus literature in this review rather than selecting highly controversial or idiosyncratic studies. Hence, the principal criterion for inclusion is a study's overall contribution to the field of interpersonal victimization and related factors, rather than its inherent methodological or analytical strengths. Further, although this book includes literature on cultural factors, the literature reviewed is primarily about diverse cultures within the North American (United States and Canada) majority. For example, the findings about Hispanics were predominantly about Hispanics in the United States rather than Hispanics in other countries. Thus, the research findings described in this book should be understood within this context and limitation. In addition, not every relevant research article was cited, and not every concept was covered. The intent of this book is to begin consolidating research findings from a wide array of studies and disciplines to integrate and broaden the view of interpersonal victimization, mental health, and substance use among women, using a heuristic conceptual model (described later in the chapter).

Another important distinction is that in selecting the literature for this review, the emphasis was on studies of the experiences of adult women rather than those of children. The literature on both topics—adult and childhood experiences—is vast, and thus the review had to be limited to keep the information manageable. However, although primarily centered on adult experiences of interpersonal victimization, much of the research on adult victimization also suggests that childhood abuse is an antecedent to adult abuse, and the literature does not always distinguish between childhood and adult abuse experiences. In other words, it was not always clear whether health or mental health problems are associated with childhood or adult victimization experiences or with some combination of the two. Thus, although not the target of this review, some of the literature included in this review does discuss research on childhood victimization.

A third important caveat is that in using a cross-disciplinary synthesis, subtle methodological and terminology differences may have been compromised out of a need to conflate findings and relevance to the field. In addition, this book uses three key terms, *victimization*, *stress*, and *trauma*, that are closely related and that at times may be used interchangeably based on the terminology used in the various research studies included in the review. The term *victimization*, as used in this book, predominantly refers to physical, sexual, or emotional abuse by an intimate partner as well as sexual assault by any perpetrator. The term includes discrete assault incidents as well as repeated or sustained assaults over long periods of time. The term *stress* describes the broader category of chronic threat to a person's well-being or safety that results from or may be exemplified by victimization experiences. The term *trauma* is used in the literature in many ways to include both the event, as in traumatic events, and the biopsychosocial reactions to the event, as in posttraumatic stress disorder. Trauma is essentially an injury, and following the logic used in this book, it is an injury related to victimization or to victimization stress. Although the three terms are related, their subtle distinctions are blurred in the literature, and this book is no exception to the ambiguity, because it is a review of the current literature. Conceptually, however, victimization is seen as a variant or type of stressor that may result in the experience of trauma. Thus, trauma is understood as a consequence of extreme stress.

In addition, the term *victim*, as used in this book, refers to women who have experienced interpersonal victimization, particularly intimate partner violence and sexual assault victimization. The literature on violence against women often uses the terms *victim* and *survivor* interchangeably, with some disciplines favoring one over the other. The term *survivor* is often used in the literature to focus on women's strengths in coping with a trauma. The use of the term *victim* in this book is not meant to imply that women who have interpersonal victimization experiences are not survivors or that they do not have important strengths. The term *victim* was simply chosen to provide a consistent terminology across the literature reviewed and should be thought of as interchangeable with *survivor*.

Overview of Key Research Domains

Victimization

Numerous studies have found that victimization experiences for women are not rare or unusual occurrences. For example, the National Violence Against Women (NVAW) survey was done using random-digit dialing for households with a telephone in all 50 states and the District of Columbia to examine victimization experiences (Tjaden & Thoennes, 2000a). Once a residential household was reached, eligible adults were identified, and in total, 8,000 men and women were surveyed. Results indicated that approximately 52% of women surveyed reported having been physically assaulted, and almost 18% reported being victims of an attempted (3%) or completed rape (15%) at some point in their lives. In addition, in a 1-year period, almost 2 million women were physically assaulted, and 302,091 women were forcibly raped. The survey also found that childhood abuse experiences among women were pervasive; 40% of women reported being physically assaulted by a caretaker, and 9% reported being raped by any perpetrator before age 18. Although these statistics are consistent with or greater than those of previous victimization surveys (Craven, 1997; Tjaden & Thoennes, 2000a), these estimates most likely underestimate victimization prevalence because the survey excluded women who were homeless, women living in institutions or group facilities, and those without a phone in their household, who may be the women at highest risk for victimization (Tjaden & Thoennes, 2000a).

The NVAW survey found that most violence against women is perpetrated by intimate partners, with the majority of women over the age of 18 who were victimized reporting they were physically assaulted (72%), raped (62%), or stalked (60%) by an intimate partner (Tjaden & Thoennes, 2000a). For the NVAW study, the term *intimate partner* included a husband, boyfriend, cohabitating partner, ex-husband, or ex-boyfriend. In comparison, only about 16% of the women surveyed reported any victimization by an acquaintance, 15% reported any victimization by a stranger, and 6% reported any victimization by a relative other than a spouse.

The term *victimization* is used extensively throughout this book and primarily refers to adult experiences of partner violence and sexual assault victimization, but also includes childhood victimization when applicable. In other words, studies incorporating childhood victimization are included in this review when they are important to the understanding of how previous victimization experiences influence and interact with adult victimization. Each form of victimization is considered separately in the descriptions that follow.

Physical Assault

Physical assault includes throwing objects, pushing, grabbing, shoving, slapping, kicking, biting, hitting, burning, attempting to harm with a fist or an object, choking, beating, and using a knife or a gun in a threatening or malicious way (Crowell & Burgess, 1996; Straus & Gelles, 1990). As stated earlier, victimization experiences of women are not statistically rare events. By some estimates, 4.4 million women have been physically abused by a partner, and 1.7 million of these women have experienced severe abuse (Plichta, 1996). Browne (1993) reported that one in three women will be assaulted by an intimate partner during her lifetime. Furthermore, a recent study reported one in five couples in the United States experienced at least one episode of intimate partner violence in the year preceding the survey (Schafer, Caetano, & Clark, 1998), a figure consistent with earlier research on intimate violence (Straus & Gelles, 1990). Women also experience assaults by other types of perpetrators. For example, the NVAW study found 11.5% of women reported acquaintance assault, 10.6% reported stranger assault, and 7% reported a nonspouse relative assault as an adult (Tjaden & Thoennes, 2000a).

Whereas male victims are more likely to be assaulted by strangers, women are more likely to be physically assaulted by intimate partners (Tjaden & Thoennes, 2000a). Compared with 8% of men, 25% of women reported lifetime intimate violence victimization, and 1.5% of women and 0.9% of men reported past-year intimate partner violence victimization (Tjaden & Thoennes, 2000b). Furthermore, male violence toward women is more often repeated and is more likely to result in injury and death than female violence toward men (Bachman & Saltzman, 1995; Browne, 1993; S. Sorenson, Upchurch, & Shen, 1996). Although this trend is decreasing, women are victims of intimate partner homicide at a rate approximately 8 times higher than men and are assaulted by intimates with a weapon at a rate approximately 7 times higher than men (Craven, 1997). Also, female victims are more likely to sustain injury than male victims, with almost 33% of women who were raped being physically injured compared with 16% of men, and about 40% of women who were physically assaulted being injured compared with 25% of men (Tjaden & Thoennes, 2000a). Women are also more likely to be injured in assaults committed by intimates than in assaults committed by strangers (Bachman & Saltzman, 1995; Tjaden & Thoennes, 2000a). These figures probably underestimate the number of women with intimate violence-related injuries or treatment needs, however, because partner violence victimization is largely undiagnosed as a potential cause of women's injuries or health-related problems (Abbott, John, Loziol-McLain, & Lowenstein, 1995; Hamberger, Saunders, & Hovey, 1992; Stark & Flitcraft, 1996).

As mentioned previously, childhood and adolescent abuse experiences are examined as risk factors for adult partner victimization rather than as a primary focus. In this light, it is important to recognize that childhood experiences contribute significantly to adult experiences, and continuity of problems is particularly evident with abuse. There is difficulty in interpreting the literature on child abuse, however. For example, studies use various age cutoffs when trying to measure child abuse (Goldman & Padayachi, 2000). Studies that define childhood as ending at the age of 14 years may show very different rates of childhood victimization than studies defining childhood as ending at 18 years. Within these definitional limitations, there are national estimates that about 12.4 children in every 1,000 experienced child abuse or neglect and that children age 11 or younger have the highest likelihood of being abused or neglected (U.S. Department of Health and Human Services [USDHHS], 2003). In part, the adult mental health and related sequelae of abuse often are already apparent in childhood; abused children are at risk for having more problems in school, more mental health problems, and more behavioral problems such as delinquent behavior, substance use problems, and pregnancy (Kelley, Thornberry, & Smith, 1997; Malinosky-Rummell & Hansen, 1993).

Sexual Assault

Sexual violence includes physical force or threats that result in sexual intercourse or other sexual acts such as vaginal, anal, or oral penetration that are referred to as *sexual assault* and *rape* (Bachman & Saltzman, 1995; Randall & Haskell, 1995; Russell, 1990). The NVAW survey found that of women reporting a rape since age 18, 6.5% were raped by a relative other than a spouse, 16.7% were raped by a stranger, 21.3% were raped by an acquaintance, and 61.9% were raped by an intimate partner (Tjaden & Thoennes, 2000a). Elliott, Mok, and Briere (2004) compared women who reported having sexual contact with someone as a result of threats or physical force after turning 18 years old. This study found that women who reported adult sexual assault reported more trauma symptoms than women who did not report adult sexual assault, even though the incident reported happened an average of 14 years earlier.

Some research has shown that between 43% and 55% of women experiencing physical assault by an intimate partner also experience sexual assault by that partner (J. Campbell & Soeken, 1999b; Eby, Campbell, Sullivan, & Davidson, 1995; Wingood, DiClemente, & Raj, 2000). Meyer, Vivian, and O'Leary (1998) found that women who were severely physically abused by their partners reported the highest rates and frequencies of sexual coercion (55%) compared with nonabused (20%) and moderately abused (27%) women. They also found that these women experienced more forced sex (11%) compared with moderately abused women (2%) and nonabused women (0%). Furthermore, women who were raped by an intimate partner were more likely to experience multiple sexual assaults (Koss, Dinero, Seibel, & Cox, 1988; Riggs, Kilpatrick, & Resnick, 1992), with one study finding 65% of women assaulted by an intimate partner reporting multiple sexual assaults compared with 14% of women assaulted by acquaintances and 9% assaulted by strangers (Mahoney, 1999). In fact, Mahoney (1999) found that almost 20% of women reporting sexual assaults by intimate partners reported more than 10 separate sexual assaults in a 6-month period. Among women who are raped by an abusive intimate partner, frequency and duration of sexual abuse by an intimate is associated with long-term impacts on both physical and mental health (Culbertson & Dehle, 2001; Riggs et al., 1992; Ullman & Siegel, 1993), but some studies found that women physically and sexually abused by an intimate partner are less likely to seek help than women sexually assaulted by strangers or acquaintances (Koss et al., 1988; Mahoney, 1999; Ullman & Filipas, 2001).

As with the data on physical violence victimization, sexual violence toward women often begins during childhood. Sexual abuse of girls is far more prevalent than of boys (Lodico, Gruber, & DiClemente, 1996). Studies have found that between 17% and 33% of women from a general population have reported sexual abuse ranging from unwanted sexual experience to rape as children (J. Anderson, Martin, Mullen, Romans, & Herbison, 1993; Finkelhor, Hotaling, Lewis, & Smith, 1990; Gorey & Leslie, 1997). B. Saunders, Kilpatrick, Hanson, Resnick, and Walker (1999) found that 8.5% of women in a national probability sample had experienced at least one completed rape before age 18. Most of the rapes were perpetrated by relatives, boyfriends, husbands, or known nonrelatives, and only a few were stranger rapes (11.4%) The study estimated that 8.33 million U.S. women have a history of a completed rape in childhood or adolescence (B. Saunders et al., 1999). In a similar vein, the NVAW survey found that of the respondents who reported any lifetime rape victimization experience, 21.6% were younger than 12 years when their first rape occurred, and of women raped before age 18, 38.8% were raped by a relative other than a spouse, 46.7% were raped by an acquaintance, 15.0% were raped by an intimate partner, and only 14.3% were raped by a stranger (Tjaden & Thoennes, 2000a). Schubot (2001) found in a random sample of high school students from one rural state that between 11.8% and 14.9% of young women had experienced date rape. Fisher, Cullen, and Turner (2000) conducted a large survey of female college students and found that 10.1% reported being raped and 10.9% reported attempted rape before starting that college year. These authors also found that 2.8% of women had been raped or had experienced attempted rape during the college year. The majority of the perpetrators who raped or attempted rape during the college year of the survey were classmates (39.5%), friends (29.2%), and intimate partners (19.1%).

Psychological Abuse

Psychological or emotional abuse commonly co-occurs with physical and sexual violence (Crowell & Burgess, 1996; Dutton, Goodman, & Bennett, 1999; Follingstad, Rutledge, Berg, Hause, & Polek, 1990; Sabourin, Infante, & Rudd, 1993). There is a high overlap of physical and psychological abuse, with some studies reporting that up to 99% of women who experienced physical abuse by a partner have also experienced psychological abuse (Follingstad et al., 1990; Stets, 1990; Straus, Hamby, Boney-McCoy, & Sugarman, 1996). Straus et al. (1996) found a high correlation between psychological aggression, physical assault, and sexual coercion.

Other research on psychological abuse has delineated several dimensions or types. For example, Follingstad and DeHart (2000) found three types of psychological abuse, including threats to physical health; control over personal freedom; and destabilization of a victim's sense of reality by intimidation, degradation, isolation, or control. Marshall (1999) clustered psychological abuse into two main groups: (a) overt, which included dominating (verbally dominating in conversation and verbal tone), indifference (acting as if the partner does not matter, ignoring the partner), monitoring (constant checking and control of the partner's actions), and discrediting (telling others the partner is crazy or making her look bad to others); and (b) subtle, which included undermining (making her feel as if she has problems or cannot take care of herself or making her feel guilty), discounting (keeping things from her, discouraging her from pursuing her interests, acting as if he does not care what she does and then becoming angry), and isolation (isolating her from friends and family).

Stalking

Stalking, which had long been ignored in the literature on victimization, has received increased attention in the past few years. Although stalking can and does occur from a variety of sources, such as strangers, acquaintances, and relatives, it has also been noted as a variant of intimate partner violence (Burgess et al., 1997; Coleman, 1997; Kurt, 1995; Logan, Leukefeld, & Walker, 2000;

Spitzberg & Rhea, 1999). For example, Logan et al. (2000) found that 27% of a sample of young adults had experienced stalking after breaking up with an intimate partner and that stalking was significantly associated with physical and psychological abuse during the relationship. Another study of 757 women with protective orders against an intimate partner found that about half of the women (54%) reported being stalked by that partner (Logan, Shannon, & Cole, in press). Other studies have also shown a relation between physical and sexual violence with stalking (Cole, Logan, & Shannon, in press; Logan, Shannon, & Cole, in press). The NVAW survey found that most of the women who reported being stalked by a husband or ex-husband (81%) also reported physical assault by that partner, and about one third (31%) reported sexual assault as well (Tjaden & Thoennes, 1998).

Research also indicates that stalkers of intimate partners are more likely to be violent than stalkers of nonintimates (Palarea, Zona, Lane, & Langhinrichsen-Rohling, 1999). One study found that stalkers targeting current or past intimate partners, compared with other stalkers, were more likely to threaten the victim, threaten the victim's property, and be violent against her and her property (Palarea et al., 1999). In addition, intimate partner stalkers were more likely to follow through on threats of violence than stalkers of other types of victims (Palarea et al., 1999). Tjaden and Thoennes (2000b) reported that injury rates were 4 times higher among women stalked by intimate partners compared with women stalked by strangers and acquaintances. That study is consistent with the findings of another study that concluded women who reported stalking by a violent intimate partner also reported more severe violent victimization by that partner compared with women with violent partners who did not report stalking (Logan, Shannon, & Cole, 2005). Female victims of partner violence who are stalked by an intimate partner experience more severe mental health problems compared with women with partner violence experiences who do not experience stalking (Logan, Shannon, & Cole, 2005; Mechanic, Uhlmansiek, Weaver, & Resnick, 2000).

The relevance of stalking behavior for this review of victimization is evident in the persistent and threatening nature of the behavior, which points toward a high lethality risk and greater mental health consequences for women (J. Campbell, 1995; McFarlane et al., 1999; Mechanic et al., 2000). Stalking may be punctuated with rare but intensely violent acts, thus making the threat all the more pervasive.

Physical Health Consequences of Victimization

The most serious consequence of victimization is death. In the United States, approximately one third to one half of female murder victims are killed by an intimate partner (Felder & Victor, 1997; Moracco, Runyan, & Butts, 1998; Puzone, 2000). Other health consequences of victimization are significant, and these are evident in acute injury-related problems and in longer term conditions that result in pain and even impaired ability to function for some women (Resnick, Acierno, & Kilpatrick, 1997). In fact, Sharps and Campbell (1999, p. 163) concluded that violence against women constitutes "a major health problem that is at an epidemic level" in the United States. Greenfeld et al. (1998) reported that during 1994, hospital emergency department personnel treated an estimated 1.4 million people for injuries from confirmed or suspected intimate partner violence. Tjaden and Thoennes (2000a) indicated that about one third of women who were injured during a rape or physical assault required medical care. Girls and women accounted for 39% of the hospital emergency department visits for violence-related injuries in 1994 but 84% of the persons treated for injuries inflicted by intimates (Greenfeld et al., 1998). In another example, Coker, Smith, McKeown, and King (2000) briefly surveyed women who attended family practice clinics and found that more than half (55%) had experienced at least one lifetime incident of intimate partner violence, and 20% were currently experiencing intimate partner violence. Thus, many women utilizing the health care system are also experiencing partner violence victimization, although it is often not assessed or reported.

Violence against women has also been associated with economic costs for victims and society at large. A rape incident, for example, has been estimated to cost approximately $86,500 and an assault incident has been estimated to cost approximately $9,350 in lost productivity, medical care, mental health care, social services, property loss or damage, and quality of life[1] (T. Miller, Cohen, & Wiersema, 1996). The National Center for Injury Prevention and Control (2003) reported that costs of intimate partner violence exceeded $5.8 billion in 1995, with the largest proportion of that amount derived from health care, which accounts for about two thirds of the total costs. A more recent publication updated those costs to 2003 dollars and estimated that intimate partner violence costs society in excess of $8.3 billion (Max, Rice, Finkelstein, Bardwell, & Leadbetter, 2004). Wisner, Gilmer, Saltzman, and Zink (1999) identified a group of women enrolled in a large health plan who were referred by a primary care physician to a mental health provider for treatment of partner violence ($n = 126$) and compared them with a random sample of women ($n = 1,007$) in the system to examine health care costs. Results showed that women with partner violence histories were younger, had more hospitalizations and more general clinic use, used more mental health services, and had more out-of-plan referrals. They also noted that costs to the health plan were 92% greater for the women with partner violence histories compared with the random sample of women.

Because of the high social and personal costs of victimization, the health problems posed by intimate partner violence are immense. Mental health problems are also a significant issue for women, especially for those who have experienced sustained victimization.

Mental Health Consequences of Victimization

Mental health problems are highly prevalent for women with interpersonal victimization histories (Kendler et al., 2000; Logan, Walker, Cole, & Leukefeld,

---

[1]These costs would be higher today, because the estimates were made based on the value of a dollar several years ago.

2002; Resnick et al., 1997). As used in this book, the term *mental health problems* primarily refers to mood, affective, anxiety, and related disorders. Although persons with major thought disorders can have victimization experiences, there is limited research support for a causative relationship between victimization and psychosis compared with the research support for the association of victimization and the mood–affective disorder spectrum.

When the rates of victimization and mental health are examined, mental health problems are more frequent and more severe for women with victimization histories than for women without such histories. For example, Plichta (1996) found that 26.7% of women with child physical abuse histories and 32.7% of women with child sexual abuse histories reported that they had been diagnosed with a depression or anxiety disorder compared with 12.7% of women without a child abuse history. Plichta also found this trend for women reporting intimate partner violence, with 31.9% of women reporting intimate partner violence also reporting a diagnosis of depression or an anxiety disorder compared with 14% of women not reporting intimate partner violence. Additionally, reports of anxiety or depression diagnoses were made by 14.1% of women not reporting victimization, by 24.4% of women with other crime experiences, and by 45.6% of women reporting rape (Plichta, 1996).

Comorbidity or co-occurrence of mental disorders is also relevant to the understanding of victimization and contributing factors to victimization. Research literature throughout the late 1980s and 1990s provided evidence of extensive co-occurrence of mental disorders (Kessler et al., 1994; Klerman et al., 1996; Maser & Cloninger, 1990). In spite of growing interest in co-occurring disorders and multiple diagnoses, both the *Diagnostic and Statistical Manual of Mental Disorders* (3rd ed., rev. [DSM–III–R]; American Psychiatric Association, 1987) and the *Diagnostic and Statistical Manual of Mental Disorders* (4th ed. [DSM–IV]; American Psychiatric Association, 1994) call for using only the single diagnosis that best explains a patient's complaints rather than many potentially overlapping diagnoses (Maser & Cloninger, 1990). To encourage the parsimonious use of diagnoses, the *DSM*s use exclusionary as well as inclusion criteria for disorders. Although the multiaxial system encourages a more complex diagnostic picture, exclusionary criteria tend to limit exploration of multiple diagnoses. A result of this diagnostic method is a possible limitation on the identification of co-occurring disorders among clinical populations. However, extensive co-occurrence has been found with disorders that relate to victimization, including anxiety disorders with depression; affective disorders with personality disorders; and substance use with mood disorders, anxiety disorders, personality disorders, dissociative disorders, and mania (Flynn, Craddock, Luckey, Hubbard, & Dunteman, 1996; Kessler et al., 1994; Kessler, Crum, Warner, Nelson, et al., 1997; Skodol et al., 1999, 2002).

In regard to the financial costs, in 1990 in the United States, Greenberg, Stiglin, Finkelstein, and Berndt (1993) estimated that depression cost about $43.7 billion, and Greenberg et al. (1999) estimated that anxiety disorders cost about $42.3 billion. The cost of treating comorbid disorders may be higher. For example, the cost of treatment for patients with substance-related disorder and major depression or dysthymia is almost 5 times that of patients with substance abuse only (Westermeyer, Eames, & Nugent, 1998). Although some studies show that health service utilization is increased for individuals with mental health symptoms (Sansone, Wiederman, & Sansone, 1998), other studies have reported individuals with mental health problems report having trouble with access to care, especially care consistent with their needs (Young, Klap, Sherbourne, & Wells, 2001). Furthermore, there is an overlap between mental health problems, physical health problems, and substance use problems (Kessler, Crum, Warner, Nelson, et al., 1997; Musselman, Evans, & Nemeroff, 1998; Penninx et al., 2001; Weisberg et al., 2002).

Substance Abuse, Victimization, and Mental Health

The term *substance use* that we use throughout the book generally refers to substance use, misuse, abuse, and dependence. For specific research findings and when the original work specified the type of substance-related problem, the review follows the researcher's definition. In much victimization literature, the formal diagnostic nosology of substance abuse or dependence is not used because substance use measures include frequency or amounts but only rarely a diagnosis.

In general, both substance use and abuse are more prevalent in men than women in the United States (Substance Abuse and Mental Health Services Administration [SAMHAS], 2000). However, victimization experiences have been associated with substance use and abuse for women in a number of research studies (Brewer, Fleming, Haggerty, & Catalano, 1998; Covington, 1997; G. Dunn, Ryan, & Dunn, 1994; Gil-Rivas, Fiorentine, & Anglin, 1996; Kilpatrick, Acierno, Resnick, Saunders, & Best, 1997; B. Miller, Downs, & Testa, 1993). For example, research has found that women who have alcohol or drug problems are more likely to have a history of being sexually abused and physically assaulted than women without such problems (Covington, 1997; Kilpatrick et al., 1997; B. Miller et al., 1993). High rates of sexual and physical abuse among women in drug abuse treatment programs have also been found, with some studies reporting as many as two of three women entering treatment having a history of sexual abuse, physical abuse, or both (Covington, 1997; Dunn et al., 1994; Gil-Rivas et al., 1996; B. Miller et al., 1993).

Likewise, a number of research studies have found high rates of substance use among victims. For example, Kilpatrick et al. (1997) found in a longitudinal prospective study that both lifetime and recent assaults were associated with increased substance use and that victimization uniquely contributed to increased odds of substance abuse even after controlling for baseline substance use. Kilpatrick, Acierno, Saunders, Resnick, and Best (2000) reported results of a national household probability sample of adolescents between the ages of 12 and 17, and found that overall, a substantial proportion of adolescents met criteria for current substance abuse and dependence and that the experience of either physical or sexual abuse uniquely increased the risk of past-year substance abuse or dependence by a factor of two. In a sample of adolescents ages 14 to 18 who met *DSM–III–R* alcohol dependence criteria, Clark, Lesnick, and Hegedus (1997) found that 66% had experienced victimization (43% sexual victimization, 19% physical victimization, 8% severe victimization). Furthermore, 44% of those who met criteria for alcohol abuse had experienced victimization

(28% sexual victimization, 32% physical victimization, 8% severe victimization), whereas only 8% of those not meeting criteria for alcohol abuse or dependence had experienced victimization (3% sexual victimization, 5% physical victimization, 0% severe victimization). Perez (2000) found that adolescents who reported physical or sexual abuse (or both) reported significantly more drug use than adolescents who did not report abuse, even after controlling for academic achievement and family structure. Another study, which examined pregnant adolescents, found that adolescents who were physically abused were 2.54 times more likely to use alcohol and 4.25 times more likely to use drugs, adolescents who were sexually abused were 2.39 times more likely to use alcohol and 3.11 times more likely to use drugs, and adolescents who were both physically and sexually abused were 5.9 times more likely to use alcohol and 6.4 times more likely to use drugs (S. Martin, Clark, Lynch, & Lawrence, 1999). In other words, victimization appears to have a stepwise association with substance misuse, with higher rates of sexual and physical abuse being associated with greater severity of substance misuse or abuse.

Prescription drug abuse has recently become recognized as a problem, and data trends show that it is on the rise. Data from the 1999 National Household Survey indicate that 3.5% of 18- to 25-year-olds reported past-month nonmedical use of psychotropic medication, which is over twice the percentage reported in 1994 (SAMHAS, 2000). In addition, the data indicate a significant increase in the initiation of prescription pain relievers from 1980 to 1998 for youths and young adults (ages 12–25). Some research has indicated that women are significantly more likely to use abusable prescription drugs than men (Graham & Vidal-Zeballos, 1997; Simoni-Wastila, 2000). Women may be more susceptible to abusing prescription drugs because women are more likely to be diagnosed with depression and then be treated with prescription drugs (National Institute on Drug Abuse, 2001); however, women may also be more likely to seek medical care or to express emotional discomfort than men (Cafferata & Meyers, 1990; Simoni-Wastila, 1998; Svarstad, Cleary, Mechanic, & Robers, 1987). The potential for prescription drug abuse may be especially salient for victims because of the mental health and health problems that can result from a victimization experience. Antianxiety agents (including anxiolytics, sedatives, and hypnotics), such as the benzodiazepines, are commonly used in treating physical health conditions that are believed to have a psychological origin or component.

Alcohol abuse was estimated to cost society about $184.6 billion and drug abuse about $143.4 billion in 1998 (Harwood, 2000; Office of National Drug Control Policy, 2001). Alcohol use has been reported to have a greater impact on women's physical and mental health than men's (J. Johnson et al., 1995; Kessler, Crum, & Warner, 1997; Stein & Cyr, 1997). For example, women are more likely to develop liver-related problems over a shorter period of time and after consuming less alcohol than men (Gavaler & Arria, 1995; S. Greenfield, 2002; P. Hall, 1995). Drug use also involves risks to the health and mental health of women (W. Lynch, Roth, & Carroll, 2002). In addition, studies have indicated that drug and alcohol use is associated with increased risk of injury compared with nonuse and that injury risks are elevated for female compared with male substance abusers (S. Greenfield, 2002; T. Miller, Lestina, & Smith, 2001; Zador, 1991). Despite the high economic and personal costs associated with substance abuse, studies have shown that many individuals who need substance abuse treatment do not enter treatment (Schober & Annis, 1996); thus, many individuals in need of help do not obtain it.

The overlap of victimization, mental health, and substance abuse are all especially salient for women. Recognition and acknowledgment of these interrelationships is critical for effective treatment and better understanding of the specific factors and mechanisms that contribute to these problems for women.

Organization of the Book

We have found a conceptual model to be useful in both understanding and organizing the review of the vast literature on interpersonal victimization, mental health, and substance abuse among adult women. The model used here is based on an earlier version (Logan, Walker, et al., 2002) but has been modified for the purposes of this book. Figure 1.1 displays the basic elements of the model. Each chapter focuses on one of the four domains of this model in greater detail. In chapter 8, the complete model is presented and discussed along with implications for practice and research.

The first major domain in Figure 1.1, victimization manifestations and vulnerabilities, is discussed in chapter 2. More specifically, chapter 2 includes a review of research on the mental health and health manifestations of victimization and the genetic, stress, and biological vulnerabilities that may contribute to these manifestations. Chapter 3 focuses on lifestyle factors that may increase vulnerability to victimization and substance use, such as associations, expectancies, and impaired judgment. Chapter 4 expands on the various social factors that contribute to the increased risk of victimization, mental health, and substance use. Specifically, socioeconomic status and social environmental factors are discussed. Internal contextual factors, such as situation and response appraisals, are examined in chapter 5. At the end of each of these chapters, the review concludes not with the traditional implications but with a description of general gaps in research that seriously impede a clear and complete understanding of victimization and its antecedents and consequences. In this way, the review not only can summarize much of the past research but also contribute to clearer agendas for future study. Specific implications for interventions are noted throughout the chapters but are summarized in the conclusion section of each chapter.

After an extensive overview of the literature in each of the four main domains, chapter 6 reviews the outcome research for interventions targeting women with partner violence and sexual assault victimization experiences. Chapter 7 reviews justice system options and responses for women who have experienced victimization. Chapter 8 concludes the book by describing consistent themes identified across all of the chapters as well as implications for future research and interventions.

The literature reviewed in each chapter is organized by the conceptual model displayed in Figure 1.1, which grows in complexity and detail with each corresponding chapter. This conceptual model is only used heuristically to organize the literature. Obviously, the boundaries between concepts are not sharply divided or distinct. In some sense, the topical organization of the literature is

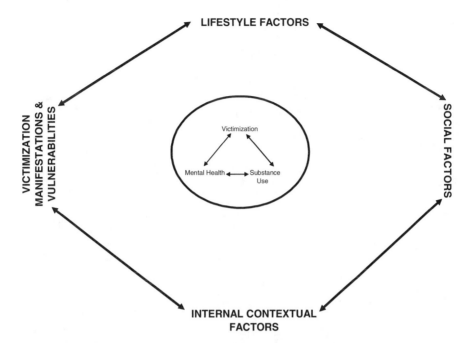

Figure 1.1. Basic outline of the conceptual model of factors contributing to victimization, mental health, and substance use.

arbitrary because these concepts and their categorizations are interrelated. In fact, it is likely that a different organizational construct could have served a similar purpose. Perhaps the best dynamic image to keep in mind in contemplating Figure 1.1 and its later permutations is a bidirectional hurricane with the swirling arms moving simultaneously toward and away from the center. Such is the relationship of many of these domains and the factors that are discussed in each of them. As will be seen, antecedent risk factors become their own outcomes, which then become antecedents to future related outcomes. For example, depression may be a risk factor for substance use and victimization, but at the same time, it is one of many outcomes of substance abuse and victimization. As the model grows in depth, the reader will come to better understand the interrelated quality of factors that result in the complex phenomenon of victimization.

Conclusion

This chapter has provided an overview of victimization and some of the prominent mental health and substance abuse problems that have been associated with it. In the next chapter, we begin our review of the literature with the first of the four domains depicted in Figure 1.1, victimization manifestations and vulnerabilities. With this and each succeeding chapter, we believe that readers will better understand the complex, interactive impact of adult victimization experiences and discover ways to further understand, extend, and use this knowledge productively.

2

Victimization Manifestations and Vulnerability Factors

The Case of Natalie L.

Natalie began seeing a counselor about ending her relationship with her husband. She presented with feelings of depression and problems sleeping that she attributed to the failure of her marriage. The counselor initially suggested Natalie try a regimen of antidepressants. Within a few weeks, however, Natalie reported she was not feeling any better and stopped taking the medication.

As therapy progressed, Natalie divulged that her husband had been physically, sexually, and emotionally abusive. Since they had been separated, her husband had been persistently stalking her and checking up on her at work and when she visited her family. Natalie was thinking about no longer visiting her family and friends because of her fear that he might harm others. Her husband also caused her to have an auto accident 2 years ago by punching her while she was driving. She had back pain after that time and began having severe stomach pains that came and went.

She also reported that her mother had suffered from severe depression for most of her life. Natalie dreaded the possibility that she, too, was embarking on a lifetime of depressive illness. In addition, she had begun having episodes of feeling detached from herself and reported being hypervigilant at home and at work. She was fearful and watchful, as if some dangerous event was about to happen. Most recently, she began to have nightmares and her sleep problems had become more severe. She described having panic attacks over "minor" irritations, such as being stuck in traffic. She had also lost her appetite and had begun losing weight.

To help her with these symptoms, the therapist urged Natalie to try a different antidepressant, one with anxiety-reducing effects. In addition, she used cognitive–behavioral techniques to help Natalie cope with her panic attacks and relaxation techniques to help her with her sleep problems. However, Natalie refused to try antidepressants again and told her therapist that she had begun using tranquilizers as well as occasional painkillers without a prescription, getting them from a friend at work. She said they were the only things that really helped, but her therapist shared with her concern about the addictive potential of these drugs.

In preparation for a consultation with her supervisor, the counselor reviewed Natalie's initial diagnosis of depression, noting that over time Natalie manifested symptoms of posttraumatic stress disorder (PTSD) as well as increasing anxiety and depression. To this mix, she noted her concern about substance abuse. The counselor was struggling to determine the primary disorder to treat and which interventions would be most helpful. She felt as if she were peeling an onion, with one disorder arising after another as therapy unfolded.

* * *

The complexity associated with studying, treating, and understanding disorders co-occurring with victimization is highlighted with this case study. It is precisely these multiple and co-occurring disorders, symptoms, and reactions to victimization experiences that are the focus of this chapter. At the most basic level, victimization is viewed as a stressful event that has antecedent vulnerability factors as well as acute and chronic consequences to overall health and mental health. More specifically, after a general overview of victimization stress and adaptation, health problems are reviewed. Health problems are classified into three main categories: acute health problems, chronic health problems, and stress-related health problems. The discussion of stress-related health problems also includes how physical health and mental health overlap as highlighted with such problems as nonmalignant pain, sleep problems, and eating disorders. Next, the most common mental health problems associated with victimization are discussed, including depression, anxiety, PTSD, and the somewhat controversial borderline personality disorder (BPD). This chapter covers genetic vulnerabilities to these disorders as well as to substance abuse that may exacerbate victimization responses. The biological substrates of stress related to victimization are the final key focus in this chapter.

Readers should note that although not all women experience major health or mental health problems with victimization, those who do may experience a wide range of problems that interact in complex ways. Furthermore, although this chapter presents concepts serially, in reality they do not occur in a linear fashion. Rather, chaos theory may be especially salient as a way of understanding the complexity and interrelationships among concepts reviewed in this chapter. As Poincaré (1905/1952) observed, "the aim of science is not things in themselves, as the dogmatists in their simplicity imagine, but the relations between things; outside those relations there is no reality knowable" (p. xxiv); that is, it is the interrelationships between multiple factors that are most important. This will become clearer as the chapter unfolds.

Victimization Stress and Adaptation

In general, humans have a remarkable ability to reorganize and adapt to adverse conditions (Bonanno, 2004); however, there are times when a person's equilibrium is thrown into disorder. At times, specific events that push people "over the edge" may appear to be somewhat insignificant, but consistent with the notion of chaos theory, the seemingly insignificant event is in fact the proverbial straw that breaks the camel's back (Kelso, 1995). Stressors or stressful events create distress in unique ways for each individual. Stress is a complex phenomenon because environmental, psychological, and physiological factors all contribute to how individuals interpret and respond to stressors (Selye, 1974, 1991). In other words, stress levels can be influenced by the event itself, other situational characteristics (e.g., number of different stressors), individual characteristics, genetic vulnerabilities, and biological vulnerabilities (e.g., physiological consequences of prior stressors). Furthermore, individuals' equilibrium can become persistently destabilized when stress endures too long or becomes too intense for the available coping capacities and strategies (Wheaton, 1997, 1999). Thus, stress can be an important factor in understanding how stable physical and mental health conditions can become unstable and move into clinical disorders.

There are two main kinds of stressors: acute stressors, or life events that are discrete in origin (Pearlin, 1999b), and chronic stressors, which are persistent, recurring, and long-term problems, threats, or conflicts (Aneshensel, 1992; Wheaton, 1997). Interpersonal victimization stress can be chronic for three primary reasons. First, the impact of interpersonal victimization can have long-lasting psychological effects in the form of reexperiencing the traumatic event as well as through other psychological consequences (Dickinson, deGruy, Dickinson, & Candib, 1999; Golding, 1999; Holtzworth-Munroe, Smultzler, & Sandin, 1997; Kilpatrick, Resnick, Saunders, & Best, 1998a, 1998b; Ozer, Best, Lipsey, & Weiss, 2003). Second, women experiencing an initial victimization often experience subsequent victimization (Elliott, Mok, & Briere, 2004; Gold, Sinclair, & Balge, 1999; H. Irwin, 1999; Mayall & Gold, 1995; Sappington, Pharr, Tunstall, & Rickert, 1997; Tjaden & Thoennes, 2000a). For example, childhood abuse experiences have been significantly associated with subsequent victimization in adolescence and adulthood (O'Keefe, 1998; Plichta, 1996; Whitmire, Harlow, Quina, & Morokoff, 1999). Third, as stated in chapter 1, for many women, victimization perpetrated by intimate partners is a repeated experience, and thus it is literally chronic (Tjaden & Thoennes, 2000a). All of these stressors can interact, and women with more frequent, severe, and multiple victimization histories are at greater risk for multiple physical and mental health problems (J. Campbell, 2002; J. Campbell et al., 2002; Leserman et al., 1997; McNutt, Carlson, Persaud, & Postmus, 2002). For example, one study surveyed 1,931 female patients from four primary care sites in the Baltimore area and found that women with both childhood and adult victimization reported more physical and mental health problems than women who reported either childhood or adult victimization alone, whereas women with either type of victimization reported more health and mental health problems than women without victimization histories (McCauley et al., 1997). The next section outlines more clearly the health manifestations that have been associated with interpersonal victimization experiences for women.

Physical and Mental Health Manifestations of Victimization

Physical Health Manifestations of Victimization

One consequence of physical or sexual assaults is a wide range of health problems that can be broken into three main categories: acute health problems, chronic health problems, and stress-related health problems.

ACUTE HEALTH PROBLEMS. Acute health problems such as bruises, cuts, broken bones, vaginal trauma, and head injuries have been identified among women who have sustained physical and sexual assault (J. Campbell, 2002; McCauley et al., 1995; Plichta, 1992, 1996; Plichta & Weisman, 1995; H. Resnick, Acierno, & Kilpatrick, 1997). One study of women from eight university hospital emergency rooms examined the acute injuries of women victimized by their partners and found that of 256 women, there were 434 contusions and abrasions, 89 lacerations, and 41 fractures and dislocations; a weapon was used to inflict injury in 27% of the cases (Kyriacou et al., 1999). Coben, Forjuoh, and Gondolf (1999) found in a sample of women with partners ordered to batterer treatment that women with violent partners sustained superficial injuries (33.7%), open wounds (16.9%), fractures (15.3%), head injuries (10.6%), and sprains and strains (9%) as well as other minor injuries. Women with sexual assault experiences also reported a number of acute injuries, including vaginal bleeding, anal trauma, genital irritation, STDs, various infections (including urinary tract), and various physical injuries (Letourneau, Holmes, & Chasendunn-Roark, 1999; Sommers, Schafer, Zink, Hutson, & Hillard, 2001).

CHRONIC HEALTH PROBLEMS. Health effects from victimization go beyond immediate injuries (Plichta, 1992). For example, women with sexual assault and partner violence victimization experiences have higher rates of disabilities and persistent health problems (Golding, 1994; Lown & Vega, 2001; Plichta, 1996; Plichta & Falik, 2001; Scott Collins et al., 1999). Ongoing health problems for victims can include headaches, gastrointestinal problems, stomach ulcers, genital irritation, painful intercourse, chronic pelvic pain, and other gynecological problems (J. Campbell, Woods, Chouaf, & Parker, 2000; Coker, Smith, Bethea, King, & McKeown, 2000; Letourneau et al., 1999; Leserman, Drossman, & Hu, 1998; McCauley et al., 1995). Also, women who experienced intimate partner violence reported cognitive difficulties, chronic headaches, and dizziness as well as undiagnosed hearing, vision, and concentration problems, which may point to possible neurological problems from head injuries (Diaz-Olavarrieta, Campbell, Garcia de la Cadena, Paz, & Villa, 1999; Jackson, Philp, Nuttall, & Diller, 2002; Monahan & O'Leary, 1999; Valera & Bernbaum, 2003). Other studies have shown that existing health problems such as arthritis, diabetes, epilepsy, high blood pressure, and migraine headaches are exacerbated by victimization experiences (J. Campbell, 2002; J. Campbell et al., 2002; Coker et al., 2000; McCauley et al., 1995; Stein & Barrett-Connor, 2000).

STRESS-RELATED HEALTH PROBLEMS. In general, women with both sexual assault and intimate partner victimization histories perceive themselves as having worse health than women without victimization histories (Cloutier, Martin, & Poole, 2002; Plichta, 1996; Plichta & Falik, 2001; Scott Collins et al., 1999). Stress-related health problems such as undiagnosed chest pain, choking sensations, diarrhea, constipation, shortness of breath, fatigue, disturbed sleep, disturbed eating patterns, vaginal burning, and painful menstruation are also common among women with victimization experiences (J. Campbell, 2002; Golding, 1994; Lown & Vega, 2001; McCauley et al., 1995, 1997). For example, in one study (Eby, Campbell, Sullivan, & Davidson, 1995), a sample of women from a shelter reported that their abuse had resulted in sleep problems (73%), pains in the heart or chest (72%), heart pounding or racing (72%), headaches (71%), nightmares (66%), constant fatigue (65%), poor appetite (69%), and weight change (65%). J. Campbell et al. (2002) examined women from a health maintenance organization sample and found that women with partner victimization histories reported a 50% to 70% increase in gynecological, central nervous system, and other stress-related health problems. They also had higher rates of headaches, back pain, appetite loss, and abdominal pain compared with women without partner abuse histories. Rape victims also have reported high levels of stress-related health problems such as gastrointestinal disorders, headaches, and abdominal pain compared with clinical population control participants without rape victimization experiences (Kimerling & Calhoun, 1994; Koss, Woodruff, & Koss, 1990). To better ground the research, one study found that about 10% of women without victimization histories reported nonspecific physical symptoms compared with 25.8% to 78.4% of women with interpersonal victimization histories (McNutt et al., 2002).

One extreme example of a victimization stress-related outcome is what happens to women experiencing victimization during pregnancy. Although victimization experiences during pregnancy are not necessarily more frequent than during nonpregnant times (J. Campbell, Oliver, & Bullock, 1993; Jasinski, 2001b; S. Martin, Mackie, Kupper, Buescher, & Moracco, 2001), there are obvious direct effects of victimization during pregnancy that can result in harm to the fetus, including miscarriage and other physical trauma (Huth-Bocks, Levendosky, & Bogat, 2002; Jasinski, 2004). For women who experience extreme stress (such as victimization) during pregnancy, there is also increasing evidence of serious effects on fetal development, including negative impacts on the length of gestation, infant birth weight, neonatal complications, and a variety of infant neurodevelopmental problems (Rini, Dunkel-Schetter, Wadhwa, & Sandman, 1999; Wadhwa et al., 2002). The effects of stress on premature birth are particularly well documented, with maternal stress activating the hypothalamic–pituitary–adrenal (HPA) axis and thus increasing the release of corticotrophin-releasing hormone (CHR). CHR levels typically increase just before birth because this hormone contributes to maternal and fetal placental separation (Sandman et al., 1999; Wadhwa et al., 2002). In fact, stress and CHR account for as much as 20% of gestational length variation (Ruiz, Fullerton, Brown, & Dudley, 2002). In contrast, however, a study of 230 pregnant women experiencing stress found that positive self-esteem, higher feelings of mastery, and greater optimism buffered stress effects on gestation length and birth weight (Rini et al., 1999). The significance of these findings for pregnant women with victimization experiences during pregnancy is that these internal protective factors of self-esteem and optimism may be compromised by stress from victimization experiences.

Another example of a common stress-related physical health problem for women with victimization histories is chronic irritable bowel syndrome (IBS; C. Irwin et al., 1996; Talley & Jones, 1998; Toner & Akman, 2000). IBS, characterized by abdominal pain and symptoms such as constipation or diarrhea (or both intermittently), lacks a clear biological marker but affects twice as many women as men (Brandt et al., 2002). Although research on the specific relationship of stress to IBS has been mixed, the literature strongly suggests that stress is at least a major contributing factor to the expression of the illness and can greatly exacerbate the symptoms (Drossman, 1997; Lynn & Friedman, 1998; Talley & Koloski, 2000; Toner, Segal, Emmott, & Myran, 2000). One hypothesis is that "the experience of symptoms derives from dysregulation of the bidirectional communication system between the gastrointestinal tract and the brain, mediated by neurendocrine and immunological factors and modulated by psychosocial factors" (Ringel, Sperber, & Drossman, 2001, p. 319). Thus, in considering health effects such as disturbance of the gastrointestinal tract, the stress effects from victimization experiences may outlive the relationship that started the disorder (J. Campbell, 2002). In other words, the brain–gut axes are highly sensitive to emotional disturbances in general and to fear in particular; thus gastroenterological problems are strongly associated with victimization and mental health (Toner et al., 2000).

Overlap of Physical and Mental Health Problems

The co-occurrence of physical and mental health problems shows that they can overlap, but one condition may contribute to the other as well—that is, physical health problems can contribute to mental health problems and vice versa (Dew, 1998). For example, a syndrome has been identified based on a study of male Gulf war veterans called *chronic multisymptom illnesses*, which is characterized by chronic pain, fatigue, and other neuropsychological complaints, often precipitated by physical and emotional stress (Fukuda et al., 1998). This classification, at least conceptually, may have application to women with victimization experiences as well. In addition, health problems such as anemia, arthritis, asthma, back pain, diabetes, eczema, kidney disease, lung disease, and ulcers have also been associated with PTSD (Weisberg et al., 2002). In fact, Zoellner, Goodwin, and Foa (2000) found that the severity of PTSD, controlling for anger, depression, and negative life events, predicted self-reported physical health problems among sexual assault victims. Depression has been associated with cardiovascular disease and increased cardiac mortality (Musselman, Evans, & Nemeroff, 1998; Penninx et al., 2001).

The presence of certain mental health problems such as PTSD and depression predicts adverse health outcomes, increased health care utilization, and greater sensitivity to physical pain for both men and women through a variety of mechanisms (Amir et al., 1997; Friedman & Schnurr, 1995; Linton, 1997; Walker et al., 2003). Thus, both specific diseases and physical symptoms that are difficult to diagnose have been associated with mental health symptoms (R. Taylor, Mann, White, & Goldberg, 2000; Weisberg et al., 2002).

Reasons for the overlap of health and mental health are still a mystery, although we are learning more about these pathways, as noted in the earlier discussions on stress and pregnancy and stress and IBS. For example, some research has indicated that stress affects the HPA axis, the system that manages the physiological response to stress. Hyperactivation of the HPA axis has effects not only on the central nervous system but also on the peripheral system, including the gastrointestinal track and cardiovascular system (Heninger,

1995; Kamarck et al., 1998). Furthermore, increased activation of the HPA axis can result in heightened sensitivity to pain (Melzack, 1999). The discussion that follows highlights research on three conditions that exemplify overlapping physical and mental health problems: pain, sleep disturbance, and eating disorders.

PAIN. Pain may be one of the most common examples of a condition that shows overlapping physical and mental health problems among victims. J. Campbell's (2002) review of five major studies of health among women with victimization experiences found significantly higher levels of reported headache pain in all five of the studies, back pain in four, pelvic pain in four, and abdominal pain in two. Women with histories of victimization have reported more physical pain, including more chronic painful conditions, more painful body areas, more diffuse pain, and more pain conditions such as fibromyalgia than women without victimization (Alexander et al., 1998; L. Campbell, Riley, Kashikar-Zuck, Gremillion, & Robinson, 2000; Dienemann et al., 2000; Letourneau et al., 1999; Li, Ford, & Moore, 2000; McCauley et al., 1995; Van Houdenhove et al., 2001; Walker et al., 1997).

Although child abuse has long been associated with greater susceptibility to chronic pain (Finestone et al., 2000; Goldberg, 1994; Green, Flowe-Valencia, Rosenblum, & Tait, 2001; Linton, 1997), specific examination of the association of adult victimization and chronic pain has received less research attention. In a study of 140 women presenting at a pain clinic for chronic pain, Green et al. (2001) found that 54% of the women reported combined childhood and adult abuse, and those women were most likely to experience chronic pain and a variety of somatic complaints. However, another study found that women with either child or partner violence victimization experiences were more likely to report pain symptoms than women without either of those experiences, yet, among the women with either childhood or adult victimization experiences, there were no differences in pain symptoms (Kendall-Tackett, Marshall, & Ness, 2003).

Chronic nonmalignant (i.e., noncancer) pain is a complex phenomenon with multiple causes and course progressions. Given the high rates of depression and anxiety disorders among victims, the relationships of these mental health problems to pain are important, but complex. For example, although there is evidence that individuals with depression are more likely to experience severe pain (Amir et al., 1997; L. Campbell, Clauw, & Keefe, 2003; Friedrich, 1999; Linton, 1997; Vines, Gupta, Whiteside, Dostal-Johnson, & Hummler-Davis, 2003; Von Korff & Lin, 2002; Willoughby, Hailey, Mulkana, & Rowe, 2002), there is also evidence that chronic pain leads to depression (J. Campbell et al., 2003; Poulos, Gertz, Pankratz, & Post-White, 2001; Von Korff & Lin, 2002). Other studies have implied that depression exacerbates pain (Pincus & Williams, 1999; Slesinger, Archer, & Duane, 2002). Still other studies point to a reciprocal relationship between pain and depression (Vines et al., 2003; Willoughby et al., 2002). Lair (1996) pointed out that this relationship becomes circular when "pain creates depression and, in turn, depression worsens the pain" (p. 92). From a survey of more than 18,000 people, Ohayon and Schatzberg (2003) found that individuals with major depressive disorder were 4 times more likely to report chronic pain than those without depression. Also, individuals who reported chronic pain experienced a much longer course of depression than those who experienced depression without chronic pain. Bair, Robinson, Katon, and Kroenke (2003) reviewed 56 articles on either depression among pain patients or pain among depressed subjects, and they estimated that between 38% and 56% of pain patients from orthopedic or rheumatology clinics have co-occurring depression (Bair et al., 2003). In nonclinical populations, 27% of pain patients are estimated to have co-occurring depression (Bair et al., 2003). In addition, depression is associated with worse pain treatment outcomes (Kems & Haythomthwaite, 1988).

It is interesting that the neurochemicals that mediate physical pain also mediate the psychological pain of social loss (Panksepp, 2003). The same brain regions that are involved in the experience of social loss or separation are involved in experiencing pain, thus suggesting that physical pain and social distress are mediated by common brain regions (Eisenberger, Lieberman, & Williams, 2003; Panksepp, 2003). Areas of the brain that "anticipate" pain exist in close proximity to the areas that actually mediate pain, and the anticipation of pain exacerbates an individual's actual manifestation of pain (Ploghaus et al., 1999). Migraines, for example, have been linked to victimization and depression, and studies have found a reciprocal relationship between depression and migraines (Breslau, Davis, Schultz, & Peterson, 1994; Breslau, Merikangas, & Bowden, 1994). It may be that migraines are associated with reductions in levels of the neurotransmitter serotonin as well as an insufficient supply of enkephalins, the brain's pain-relieving chemicals.

Beliefs about gender differences in pain perception, although widely discussed, have varying empirical support, largely because of the complexities of pain stimuli, contexts of pain experiences, the enormous variation in subjective accounts of pain, and the great variation in physiology (Berkley, 1997). However, certain pain disorders are more common among women, such as migraine with aura, fibromyalgia, IBS, and both chronic tension and *cervicogenic* (neck muscle–related) headaches (Berkley, 1997). In addition, women experience greater exposure to certain types of visceral insults such as injury to the bladder, uterus, and other internal organs because the vagina and cervix provide ready access to these organs (Berkley, 1997). Continual invasion of the vaginal canal also increases vulnerability to numerous infections (Berkley, 1997). Rape and other forms of sexual assault can result in acute and chronic health problems in the genitourinary and anal area, including greater risk for sexually transmitted diseases (Laws, 1998). These injuries or infections resulting from sexual assault can result in chronic pain for women as well. Pain disorders are also often associated with stress and therefore may be related to victimization. Stress most likely contributes to pain sensitivity, although pain can be a stressor in itself. Furthermore, the persistence of depression, anxiety, or PTSD among victims may act to perpetuate and accentuate pain. Recent notable studies of placebo effects on brain area activation have shown that the emotional distress from victimization experiences may also affect cognitive evaluation of pain and thus increase the actual experience of pain (Wager et al., 2004).

SLEEP DISTURBANCE. As mentioned earlier and as presented in the case example of Natalie at the beginning of the chapter, another health consequence for women with victimization experiences is disruption in sleep patterns (J. Campbell, 2002). One study of more than 750 women with protective orders found that for the preceding 30 days, 48% reported an average of less than 5 hours of sleep a night, 37% reported an average of between 5 and 7.5 hours of sleep, and less than 15% reported an average of 8 or more hours of sleep a night (Walker, Logan, & Shannon, 2004). For comparative purposes, a large national study of more than 600,000 women from the general population found that approximately 5% reported 5 hours or fewer, approximately 50% reported 5 to 7.5 hours, and 46% reported 8 or more hours of sleep a night, on average, in the preceding 30 days (Kripke, Garfinkel, Wingard, Klauber, & Marler, 2002). The contrast of these two studies underscores the association of sleep disturbance and victimization experiences.

Other studies also document sleep disturbances among women with victimization experiences. For example, D. Saunders's (1994) study of 192 battered women reported that approximately 78% reported trouble sleeping, and 75% reported dreams or nightmares that featured their abuse experiences. Another study examined sleep disorder and fatigue among 50 women in a shelter and found that 82% reported disturbed sleep patterns with frequent awakening during the night. When the sleep patterns of these women were compared with those of control subjects and with a clinical sample with diagnosed sleep disorders, the shelter sample had sleep disorder profiles similar to the clinical sleep-disordered sample (J. Humphreys, Lee, Neylan, & Marmar, 1999). Sleep disruption may occur because of the direct effects of the victimization experience, such as having a violent partner who deliberately keeps a woman awake to cause sleep deprivation or, more commonly, as a result of stress, fear, or other mental health disorders that victims may experience. Sleep problems among rape survivors are also common and have been found to be associated with health problems and to exacerbate mental health problems (Clum, Nishith, & Resick, 2001; Krakow et al., 2000).

Research has indicated that sleep-related problems are associated with physical and mental health problems (Breslau, Roth, Rosenthal, & Andreski, 1996; Eaton, Badawi, & Melton, 1995; McEwen & Lasley, 2002; Van Cauter & Spiegel, 1999; Weissman, Greenwald, Nino-Murcia, & Dement, 1997). For example, sleeping less than 4.5 hours per night or more than 8 hours per night has been shown to be associated with higher mortality rates, thus highlighting the overall health importance of a balanced and moderate amount of sleep (Kripke et al., 2002). Individuals with sleep problems are also more sensitive to pain (Jason et al., 2000). There is also some evidence that the severity of sleep problems may influence mental health problems (R. Taylor, Jason, & Jahn, 2003). In the Epidemiologic Catchment Area study of 7,954 individuals, 40% to 47% of those reporting either insomnia or hypersomnia also met criteria for a mental disorder, whereas only 16% of the people reporting no sleep complaints met criteria for a mental disorder (Ford & Kamerow, 1989). Sleep disturbances due to worry or dysphoria have been shown to increase risk for alcohol-related problems, because alcohol has pronounced sedative properties and may be used to induce sleep (Crum, Storr, Chan, & Ford, 2004).

More specifically, there is evidence of associations between PTSD and sleep disorders and, specifically, rapid eye movement (REM) sleep disturbance for some individuals with PTSD (Harvey, Jones, & Schmidt, 2003; Mellman, Bustamante, Fins, Pigeon, & Nolan, 2002; Singareddy & Balon, 2002). Sleep patterns can be dramatically altered by stress reactions, and sleep pattern disruption can alter hormone secretions associated with the stress response (McEwen, 2003). In fact, stress is the most cited reason for sleep problems (Dement & Vaughn, 1999), although the specific contributions of stress to sleep disorders have not been extensively researched (Germain, Buysse, Ombao, Kupfer, & Hall, 2003). Although the research on psychophysiological stress and sleep disturbances among women does not always indicate a significant relationship (Shaver, Johnston, Lentz, & Landis, 2002), studies that carefully assess not only the number of stressors but also perceived lack of control over their lives show greater association of stress with sleep disturbances (Morin, Rodrigue, & Ivers, 2003).

One of the other important factors relating to sleep is that the aminergic neurons that produce and transmit the excitatory neurotransmitters norepinephrine (which activates the HPA axis) and serotonin (involved in mood regulation and dampening of impulsivity) are allowed to "turn off" during sleep and during REM sleep in particular (Hobson, 1995). These two neurotransmitters have much to do with mediating clear and responsive thinking, and depletion of either or both is associated with depression and other mental health problems. Disturbed sleep, and disturbed REM sleep specifically, may play a role in diminishing the availability of these neurotransmitters, thus contributing to mental health problems and cognitive impairment (Jason et al., 2000; Van Cauter & Spiegel, 1999). Furthermore, Wagner, Gais, Haider, Verleger, and Born (2004) found that sleep was associated with restructuring memoral representations, which enables insight into problem formulation and resolution. Thus, sleep problems and disorders have many implications for mental health and cognitive functioning that can impact decision making.

EATING DISORDERS. Eating disorders are typically characterized as mental disorders; however, they are presented here as an example of the overlap between health and mental health problems. More specifically, eating disorders have been linked with mental health problems such as depression and anxiety (American Psychiatric Association Work Group on Eating Disorders, 2000; McCauley et al., 1995) and have major consequences for physical health, including cardiovascular, gastrointestinal, and endocrinal health, and mortality (Patrick, 2002). For example, the mortality rate for anorexia is high, with 10% of patients with anorexia dying within 10 years of the diagnosis. It is associated with elevations in the central nervous system arousal pathway, the HPA axis, amenorrhea, liver dysfunction, and disturbances in making red blood cells (abnormal hemapoiesis; Halmi, 2000; Patrick, 2002). About half of those with anorexia will develop bulimia as well (Halmi, 2000). Eating disorders have also been associated with substance use and abuse. For example, bulimia has been shown to have a high rate of comorbidity with alcohol abuse and dependence, but this relation appears to be mediated by borderline personality disorder (BPD; Bulik, Sullivan, Carter, & Joyce, 1997).

More limited evidence exists for the association of victimization and eating disorders. For example, one national telephone survey found that 26.6% of women with bulimia reported having been raped, compared with 11.5% of nonbulimic women; further, victimization contributed to the development of or continued problems with bulimia nervosa (Dansky, Brewerton, Kilpatrick, & O'Neill, 1997). In the Dunedin birth cohort study (a nonclinical sample), only 1.2% of nonvictims of any lifetime partner violence reported an eating disorder, compared with 6.1% of those with any lifetime partner violence and 7.4% of victims with severe partner violence victimization, thus showing a relation between victimization and rates of eating disorder (Danielson, Moffitt, Caspi, & Silva, 1998). Another study of 236 students reported that childhood experiences of emotional abuse, rather than physical or sexual abuse, was predictive of adult eating disorders (Kent, Waller, & Dagnan, 1999). In addition, a small number of studies with limited samples showed a relationship between obesity and childhood sexual abuse victimization (Wiederman, Sansone, & Sansone, 1999). Obesity has also been associated with depression and anxiety (Epel et al., 2000). It remains unclear, however, whether associations exist among overeating, obesity, and adult victimization.

Although some studies show support for the association of victimization and eating disorders, other literature does not. For example, one community-based study found that although the severity of physical abuse was robustly associated with bulimia, other factors may be more important contributors to eating disorders because the majority of participants with bulimia did not have physical or sexual abuse histories (Welch & Fairburn, 1996). Fairburn et al. (1998) reported that overall adverse childhood events, along with negative self-evaluation and exposure to negative comments about body shape, weight, or eating, all contributed to a binge eating disorder. Continuing this line of inquiry, a study of college students found little support for the idea that sexual abuse incidents alone resulted in eating disorders but rather that overall family–child interactions were more likely to explain the development of these disorders (Kinzl, Traweger, Guenther, & Biebl, 1994). A large-scale prospective study of eating disorders did not examine sexual or physical abuse but reported that body image preoccupation and social pressure were the primary contributors to development of eating disorders (McKnight Investigators, 2003).

Lifetime prevalence rates vary from 25% to 35% among women for eating disorders such as anorexia nervosa, bulimia nervosa, and binge disorder and for serious atypical eating patterns such as regularly using self-induced vomiting or laxatives to lose weight (Patrick, 2002). For example, approximately 2% of adult women have been found to have bulimia nervosa, whereas as many as 35% of adult women have been found to have a binge eating disorder (Brewerton & Dansky, 1995; Kendler et al., 1991; Patrick, 2002). Even with these prevalence rates, one factor that makes research associating victimization and eating disorders difficult to interpret is that most studies have been conducted with clinical samples from eating disorder treatment programs. Hence, findings may be biased because of sample characteristics. Even so, it is important to consider eating disorders in the context of health problems that may be associated with victimization experiences, given the significant overlap of eating disorders and mental health problems as well as the potential devastating health consequences of eating disorders. Another reason eating disorders may be an important area of consideration in victimization manifestation is the significant overlap of victimization experiences and anxiety disorders and the overlap of eating disorders and anxiety disorders. About two thirds of those with anorexia nervosa or bulimia nervosa reported phobias, generalized anxiety disorder, PTSD, panic, or agoraphobia (Kaye, Bulik, Thornton, Barbarich, & Masters, 2004). Thus, the link of eating disorders and victimization may be the presence of anxiety disorder, which for this sample had an onset prior to the eating disorder (Kaye et al., 2004).

Mental Health Manifestations of Victimization

Women with victimization histories have higher rates of several mental health problems. One prospective birth cohort study found that 55.7% of female victims of any lifetime partner violence met *Diagnostic and Statistical Manual of Mental Disorders* (3rd ed., rev. [*DSM–III–R*]; American Psychiatric Association, 1987) criteria for any mental disorder; 64.8% of women who experienced severe partner violence victimization had a mental disorder (Danielson et al., 1998). Golding (1999) conducted a meta-analysis of intimate-partner violence and mental disorders and found that the weighted mean prevalence of mental health problems among women with partner violence histories was 47.6% for depression, 63.8% for PTSD, 18.5% for alcohol abuse, and 8.9% for drug abuse. These rates are higher than rates in samples of women from the general population that include women with and without victimization experiences. In general population estimates of lifetime experience, about 21.3% of women experience lifetime depression, about 10.4% of women experience PTSD, about 6.3% experience alcohol abuse, and about 3.5% experience drug abuse (Kessler et al., 1994; Kessler, Sonnega, Bromet, Hughes, & Nelson, 1995). Rape victimization is also associated with high rates of mental health problems (Dickinson et al., 1999; Kilpatrick et al., 1998a; Resick, 1993). In fact, a recent study compared women who had no childhood sexual abuse but who had been raped as adults and had successfully prosecuted their offenders (90% of whom were raped by strangers) with women who had experienced life-threatening but nonsexual stressful events such as physical attacks and robberies (Faravelli, Giugni, Salvatori, & Ricca, 2004). Compared with nonraped women, raped women had significantly more depression (75% vs. 44%), eating disorders (53% vs. 6%), and anxiety disorders excluding PTSD (38% vs. 16%; Faravelli et al., 2004).

Although mental health problems are typically more severe during or immediately after victimization experiences (J. Campbell & Soeken, 1999a; Resick, 1993; Valentiner, Foa, Riggs, & Gershuny, 1996), there is some evidence that women with victimization histories have higher rates of mental health symptoms, even long after the victimization has ended, than do women with no victimization histories (Foa & Street, 2001; Kernic, Holt, Stoner, Wolf, & Rivara, 2003; Mertin & Mohr, 2001; Riggs, Kilpatrick, & Resnick, 1992; Riggs, Rothbaum, & Foa, 1995; Rollstin & Kern, 1998; Rothbaum, Foa, Riggs, Murdock, & Walsh, 1992). In addition, women with multiple victimization experiences may face an increased risk for mental health problems, more severe mental health manifestations, and longer term symptoms than women with single victimization experiences (J. Campbell & Soeken, 1999a; Green et al., 2000; Jones, Hughes, &

Unterstaller, 2001; Kilpatrick et al., 1998a, 1998b; McCauley et al., 1997). Another study found that women are more likely to develop PTSD after exposure to a traumatic event than men, even after controlling for type of event (Breslau, Chilcoat, Kessler, & Davis, 1999). In addition, these authors found that multiple traumas were related to an increased risk of developing PTSD, that the symptoms were persistent over time, and that prior exposure to assaultive violence was especially related to the risk of developing PTSD after experiencing a subsequent trauma (Breslau et al., 1999).

The true trajectories and vulnerabilities to mental health problems such as mood and affective disorders, which are most involved with victimization, are not fully understood at this time. However, certain vulnerabilities are likely to increase the risk of mental health problems and the risk of longer term mental health problems. A review of mental health problems most associated with victimization experiences for women indicates a high degree of congruence, if not overlap, of key disorders and symptoms among the disorders (Jones et al., 2001; Mertin & Mohr, 2001; O'Donnell, Creamer, & Pattison, 2004). For example, many women with PTSD also have at least one other co-occurring disorder (Friedman & Yehuda, 1995). More specifically, the mental heath symptoms often associated with victimization histories share common characteristics, such as negative appraisals about a stressful event, affect dysregulation, an excess of negative emotions, and mood disturbance (Gore-Felton, Gill, Koopman, & Spiegel, 1999; O'Donnell et al., 2004; van der Kolk, 1996a, 1996b).

DEPRESSION. Depression is one of the most often mentioned mental health problems for women with victimization experiences. Although not all are affected, women with intimate partner victimization consistently report more symptoms of depression than do other women (Arias, Lyons, & Street, 1997; J. Campbell, Kub, & Rose, 1996; Danielson et al., 1998; McCauley et al., 1995; Ratner, 1993). Rates of depression can vary depending on the specific samples used to estimate prevalence. For example, in community samples of women with intimate-partner violence experiences, 39% to 55% reported current depression or depression symptoms (J. Campbell, Kub, Belknap, & Templin, 1997; Scott Collins et al., 1999) compared with 68% to 69% of shelter samples reporting current depression (R. Campbell, Sullivan, & Davidson, 1995; Gleason, 1993). Depression rates have also been found to be higher for women with sexual assault experiences (B. Miller, Monson, & Norton, 1995; Muehlenhard, Goggins, Jones, & Satterfield, 1991; Resick, 1993; Siegel, Golding, Stein, Burnam, & Sorenson, 1990; Zweig, Barber, & Eccles, 1997; Zweig, Crockett, Sayer, & Vicary, 1999).

Findings from the Epidemiologic Catchment Area study show major gender differences in depression, with women being about twice as likely to experience depression as men (Robins & Regier, 1991). These gender differences are greatest for unipolar disorders, seasonal affective disorder, and dysthymia (Goodwin & Blehar, 1993; Parry, 2000; Weissman et al., 1993). The National Comorbidity Study found that girls are more likely to experience a major depressive episode than boys, whereas adult lifetime gender differences in depression may be a function of increased susceptibility to subsequent depressive episodes (Blazer, 2000; Kessler, McGonagle, Swartz, Blazer, & Nelson, 1993).

Although women and men in general share similar genetic risks for major depression, important differences in the prevalence of externalizing or internalizing traits may impact risk and pathways into depression (Kendler & Prescott, 1999). These differences may be attributable to physiological and hormonal factors (Parry, 2000) as well as cultural, social, and psychological factors, including interpersonal victimization experiences (Blazer, 2000; Gavranidou & Rosner, 2003). For example, an extensive review of 44 studies conducted between 1975 and 1989 of self-evaluative processes showed significant gender differences (Ruble, Greulich, Pomerantz, & Gochberg, 1993). Women and girls were more likely than men and boys to exhibit self-evaluative patterns that included less self-confidence, more sensitivity to negative feedback, and less willingness to attribute their successes to internal traits, all of which may have contributed to an increased vulnerability to depression through internalizing distress (Ruble et al., 1993). A ruminative style of responding to distress, which is more prevalent in women than men, is also associated with mental health problems, including depression and PTSD (Ehlers, Mayou, & Bryant, 1998; Nolen-Hoeksema, 1995).

There are gender differences in life events associated with depression. For women, the stressful events most associated with depression are loss of housing, loss of a confidant, or problems with someone close to them, whereas men tend to experience job or legal problems and serious accidents as more significant stressors (Gavranidou & Rosner, 2003; Kendler, Thornton, & Prescott, 2001). As stated in the victimization overview, women are also more likely to experience child sexual abuse, adult rape, and partner violence than men, and the combination of childhood and adult victimization stressors may have more implications for mental health problems than the kind of stressors men are more likely to experience (Gavranidou & Rosner, 2003; A. Silverman, Reinherz, & Giaconia, 1996).

Prevalence rates of mild depression do not greatly differ for men and women, but major differences emerge when depression and functional impairment (including difficulty maintaining work, household, or schooling functions) are considered, with lifetime rates for men at 29% and women at 37% (Foley, Neale, Gardner, Pickles, & Kendler, 2003). Furthermore, women who experience stressful events have an even greater likelihood of experiencing depression (Blazer, Kessler, McGonagle, & Swartz, 1994; Kendler, Kessler, Neale, Heath, & Eaves, 1993). For example, Maciejewski, Prigerson, and Mazure (2001) found from a community-based sample of almost 3,000 men and women that women were 3 times more likely to experience depression in response to a stressful life event than men. These authors concluded that in general, stressful life events pose a greater risk of depression for women than men.

Overactivation of the HPA axis due to stress may be the primary neurochemical mechanism for depression rather than low levels of serotonin or norepinephrine (C. Holden, 2003). In fact, Weiss, Longhurst, and Mazure (1999) concluded from a review of the literature that "childhood sexual abuse is an important early stressor that may predispose individuals to adult-onset depression by means of dysregulation of the HPA axis" (p. 816). HPA axis dysregulation may be involved in anxiety disorders such as PTSD as well. Childhood sexual abuse may contribute to earlier onset of depression among women and, more important, to co-occurrence of anxiety disorder (70% for those with victimization, 44% for those without; Gladstone, Parker, Mitchell, Wilhelm, & Austin, 2004).

ANXIETY AND POSTTRAUMATIC STRESS DISORDER. Anxiety has also been associated with intimate partner violence (J. Campbell, Pliska, Taylor, & Sheridan, 1994; Kovac, Klapow, Kroenke, Spitzer, & Williams, 2003; C. Lerner & Kennedy, 2000; S. Martin, Kilgallen, Dee, Dawson, & Campbell, 1998; McCauley et al., 1995; Mertin & Mohr, 2000) and sexual assault victimization among women (Dickinson et al., 1999; Resick, 1993). Anxiety disorders include phobias such as social phobias (social anxiety disorder), panic, agoraphobia, obsessive–compulsive disorder, and PTSD (American Psychiatric Association, 2000). Anxiety disorders in general are more prevalent among women than men, with women having a 1.5 to 2 times greater likelihood of experiencing one of these disorders (Horwath & Weissman, 1997, 2000). More specifically, about 6.6% of women and 3.6% of men report lifetime generalized anxiety disorder (Kendler, 1996; Robins & Regier, 1991). Prevalence rates vary for each specific anxiety disorder, including the phobias, panic, generalized anxiety disorder, and PTSD (Horwath & Weissman, 1997, 2000).

The anxiety disorder most associated with victimization experiences is PTSD. Physical, sexual, and even psychological abuse (particularly threats) can result in symptoms that are often understood within a PTSD framework (Creamer, 2000; Foa & Street, 2001; Jones et al., 2001). PTSD, like other anxiety states, is characterized by fear and increased somatic arousal (Chua & Dolan, 2000). When shelter and community samples of women with partner violence histories were examined, 58% to 77% reported PTSD symptoms (Astin, Ogland-Hand, Coleman, & Foy, 1995; Kemp, Green, Hovanitz, & Rawlings, 1995; Perrin, Van Hasselt, Basilio, & Hersen, 1996; Street & Arias, 2001; Vogel & Marshall, 2001). To better discriminate among stressors, Astin et al. (1995) found that women with intimate partner violence were significantly more likely to have PTSD than women who were experiencing marital distress. In other words, marital distress, although a potential cause of emotional distress, was found to be qualitatively different from the stress of partner violence, and partner violence was more likely to be accompanied by PTSD. Sexual assault victims also experience PTSD at high rates (Creamer, Burgess, & McFarlane, 2001; Foa & Riggs, 1994; Rothbaum et al., 1992).

The lifetime prevalence estimates of PTSD have changed, in part because of changes in the criteria for the disorder from the *Diagnostic and Statistical Manual of Mental Disorders* (3rd ed. [*DSM–III*]; American Psychiatric Association, 1980) to the *DSM–III–R* and the *Diagnostic and Statistical Manual of Mental Disorders* (4th ed., text rev. [*DSM–IV–TR*]; American Psychiatric Association, 2000; Breslau & Kessler, 2001). Nonetheless, the female-to-male ratio remains approximately 2:1, with women outnumbering men in overall lifetime prevalence estimates using either set of criteria (Horwath & Weissman, 1997, 2000; Wong & Yehuda, 2002). The National Comorbidity Survey indicated that women outnumber men in lifetime prevalence of PTSD, although the percentage of men with trauma exposures outnumbered women (Kessler et al., 1995). Most studies using *DSM–III–R* criteria have reported women at 10.4% to 12.3%

and men at 5.0% to 6.0% of the total population (Breslau, Davis, Andreski, & Peterson, 1991; Horwath & Weissman, 1997, 2000; Kessler et al., 1995). Some studies have put the range for lifetime PTSD at 19.4% for women and 7.6% for men (Bromet, Sonnega, & Kessler, 1998). Estimates of the prevalence of PTSD vary, in part because of differences in how the index event is defined and measured as an anchor for the disorder. In other words, the affective and cognitive symptoms of PTSD, absent an identifiable event, require a different diagnosis (Freedman & Shalev, 2000).

Because mood and anxiety disorders often co-occur, the clinical assessment and treatment for women with both disorders is more complicated (Breslau, Davis, Peterson, & Schultz, 1997; T. Brown & Barlow, 1992; Creamer et al., 2001; Horwath & Weissman, 2000; Kendler, 1996). In the most recent results from the National Comorbidity Study, 59.2% of the sample with major depressive disorders also met criteria for one of the anxiety disorders (panic disorder, generalized anxiety disorder, phobias, agoraphobia, PTSD, and obsessive–compulsive disorder; Kessler et al., 2003). More specifically, the lifetime rate for comorbid mental disorder is extremely high for those with PTSD. The National Comorbidity Survey also found that about 79% of women with lifetime PTSD experienced one other mental disorder and about 44% of women with a lifetime incidence of PTSD experienced at least three other mental health disorders (Kessler et al., 1995). In fact, women are twice as likely as men to have co-occurring depression with PTSD (Wong & Yehuda, 2002). Co-occurrence of PTSD and depression is also often noted among women with interpersonal victimization histories, and risk for co-occurring disorders is related to victimization severity and chronicity (Holtzworth-Munroe et al., 1997; Jones et al., 2001; Mertin & Mohr, 2001).

BORDERLINE PERSONALITY DISORDER. BPD is characterized by "a pervasive pattern of instability of interpersonal relationships, self-image, and affects, as well as marked impulsivity that begins in early adulthood and is present in a variety of contexts" (American Psychiatric Association, 2000, p. 706). A discussion of BPD in connection with victimization raises concerns because the disorder has a long and controversial history that includes the accusations of being associated with manipulative behaviors including self-injurious acts that are now referred to as *parasuicidal* (Linehan, 1993). Until usage of this term was established, words such as *manipulative* or *gesture* were widely used in a pejorative sense and suggested less than enthusiastic treatment and, in some cases, led to a "blaming the victim" stance toward individuals with BPD.

In addition, persons with BPD often "find it extremely hard to let go of relationships" and "may engage in intense and frantic efforts to keep significant individuals from leaving them" (Linehan, 1993, p. 11). In addition, BPD is found predominantly among women (American Psychiatric Association, 2000). In fact, women are more likely to be diagnosed with BPD than men (75% of those with BPD are women; Skodol & Bender, 2003).The traits associated with BPD are such that relationship problems of women with the disorder could be related to personality problems rather than to the violence of their partners. Likewise, the idea of "the intolerance of being abandoned" that has been used to characterize this disorder (Millon, 1981, p. 352) also can cloud understanding of victims' ambivalence in leaving violent partners for fear of retribution rather than their clinging to avoid separation. These mistaken attributions make a discussion of BPD in the context of victimization particularly sensitive. Nonetheless, a review of the literature on clinical conditions experienced by women with victimization cannot omit BPD.

Many symptoms and traits overlap between PTSD and BPD (van der Kolk, van der Hart, & Marmar, 1996). This is evidenced by the high degree of comorbidity of BPD and PTSD (Golier et al., 2003; Shea, Zlotnick, & Weisberg, 1999; Swartz, Blazer, George, & Winfield, 1990). For example, one study of 366 female inpatients with personality disorders found that 61% of women with BPD also had PTSD compared with 30% of women who had BPD but no PTSD (Zanarini et al., 1998). There are two hypotheses currently in the literature about the reasons for this overlap. One premise is that BPD is an extension of PTSD. In other words, many characteristic features of BPD may be attributable to abuse and neglect and may reflect long-term affective and behavioral accommodations to abuse experiences (van der Kolk & Fisler, 1994; van der Kolk, Perry, & Herman, 1991). However, considerable conflicting research exists about the association of victimization and BPD, and much of the literature has focused on child abuse as the traumatic event associated with BPD with little literature examining adult victimization and BPD (Paris, 1997; Sabo, 1997; Trull, 2001; Zanarini et al., 1997). Regardless of the etiology of BPD, chronic PTSD symptoms overlap with BPD symptoms, including characteristics such as affective instability, anger, dissociative symptoms, and impulsivity (Herman & van der Kolk, 1987; Zlotnick, Franklin, & Zimmerman, 2002). Using structural equation modeling with 421 college students (197 with BPD, 224 without BPD), Trull (2001) found support for the independent contributions of childhood abuse to disinhibition and to negative affectivity—two constructs associated with BPD.

The other main premise is that individuals with BPD are at an increased risk of PTSD as a response to trauma (Gunderson & Sabo, 1993). Given the prevalence of mood and affective disorders among women with victimization, it is likely that many victims might also present with characteristics such as affective instability or *neuroticism* as it is defined in the five-factor model of personality (John & Srivastava, 1999), a term that also characterizes BPD. The finding that has great importance to the understanding of victimization and revictimization is that personality traits such as neuroticism or trait emotional instability seem to increase vulnerability to traumatic events or to responding to trauma with more mental health manifestations (Breslau, Davis, & Andreski, 1995). In a 3-year prospective study, Breslau et al. (1995) followed a sample of 1,007 adults in a health maintenance organization, almost 40% of whom reported previous exposure to childhood or adult traumatic events. Although previous victimization was associated with subsequent victimization, neuroticism (which has been associated with BPD) and extraversion also influenced the likelihood of revictimization even when the previous trauma exposure was controlled (Breslau et al., 1995). Thus, certain personality characteristics, such as those identified with BPD, may account in part for the widely reported findings about the correlation between initial and subsequent victimization experiences. Van der Kolk et al. (1996) suggested that there is an enduring negative impact of childhood traumatic events on affect regulation and somatization. Affect dysregulation and somatization are also related to the personality construct of neuroticism, which has been shown to be associated with revictimization risk, BPD, and Axis I disorders, including anxiety disorders (Breslau et al., 1995; Trull, Widiger, & Burr, 2001), implying complex associations of personality traits with Axis I disorders and with revictimization. BPD, with its characteristic emotional instability, figures into these associations as well. BPD may represent an important vulnerability to victimization, and victimization may influence subsequent expression of BPD. In addition, serotonin dysregulation, which is involved in depression, also has been found in individuals with BPD, thus suggesting yet another vulnerability (Hollander at al., 1994).

Summary of Physical and Mental Health Manifestations of Victimization

Several physical health problems may be related to both the direct effects of victimization experiences and the indirect effects of stress associated with victimization experiences. Physical health problems can have an impact on mental health, and mental health can influence the expression of a variety of physical health problems. In addition, women with victimization experiences are particularly vulnerable to mental health problems such as depression, anxiety, PTSD, and BPD. It is also critically important to understand that physical and mental health problems overlap and may be especially salient among women with victimization histories. Pain, sleep disturbances, and eating disorders are examples of the overlap between physical and mental health and may be salient issues for women with victimization experiences.

Genetic Vulnerabilities

Genetic Vulnerability for Physical Health Problems

The likelihood of developing or having worse physical and mental health problems may be related to genetic vulnerability or risks. For example, even apart from various cancers, genetics influence certain diseases, including some autoimmune diseases, osteoporosis, osteoarthritis, and coronary artery diseases (Massart, Reginster, & Brandi, 2001; D. Smith & Germolec, 1999). In addition, certain health problems show significant gender differences in biological vulnerabilities (apart from specific anatomical variation), such as higher likelihood of women having IBS (related to slower gastrointestinal processing time among women than men; Lynn & Freidman, 1998; Whitehead, 1999) and osteoporosis (Krane & Holick, 1998). Bartels, Van den Berg, Sluyter, Boomsma, and de Geus (2003) reviewed the literature and found evidence for the heritability of cortisol levels. This has implications for both physical and mental health because of the important dispositional differences in HPA axis activity. There has also been some preliminary research examining genetic influences on eating disorders (Strober, Freeman, Lampert, Diamond, & Kaye, 2000).

Genetic Vulnerability for Mental Health Problems

Several mental health disorders have been examined in twin, adoption, genetic marker linkage, and family studies to determine whether they are heritable and, if so, how much risk is increased by heritability (Costello et al., 2002; Kuehner, 2003; Merikangas et al., 2002). For example, anxiety disorders have evidence of intergenerational transmission, although specific mechanisms have not been identified (Fyer, 2000). In addition, specific anxiety disorders have been found to have a varying heritability risk (Fyer), even though some disorder groups (such as anxiety disorders and depression) may share common genetic factors (Kendler, Heath, Martin, & Eaves, 1987; Kendler, Neale, Kessler, Heath, & Eaves, 1993; Weissman et al., 1993).

Apart from genetic vulnerability of specific disorders, one recent study of mono- and dizygotic twins found evidence that all components of fear conditioning demonstrated moderate heritability (Hettema, Annas, Neale, Kendler, & Fredrickson, 2003). Thus, specific anxiety disorders might be phenotypical expressions of a fundamental genotype of fear sensitivity. In addition, fear sensitivity among women may be greater than among men, and this difference may account for gender differences in risk-taking behavior (Byrnes, Miller, & Schafer, 1999). Innate sensitivities to fear stimuli may be an exacerbating factor when interpersonal victimization threats are present. However, the fear that plays the most important role in victimization is fear of injury, not a mild anxiety such as stage fright or embarrassment (A. Campbell, 2002). Genetic factors may underlie some aspects of victimization fear responses; however, it would appear that the combination of threatening circumstances and genetic vulnerability may pose the greatest likelihood for expression of an anxiety disorder.

The genetic factors associated with depressive disorders have also received extensive research (P. Sullivan, Neale, & Kendler, 2000; Tsuaung & Faraone, 1990). One study found that in families with parental depression, the offspring were 3 times more likely to also develop depression compared with offspring without depressed parents (Weissman, Warner, Wickramaratne, Moreau, & Olfson, 1997). Kendler, Gardner, and Prescott (2002) used structural equation modeling on data from 1,942 adult women to generate a comprehensive model of depression in women. This multifactorial developmental model included lifetime experiences and previous 12-month stressors as well as genetic factors. Although this model stresses the complexity of interactions between environmental and situational factors in the incidence of a depressive episode or course of depression, genetic factors were strongly predictive of severity of depression and comorbidity with other disorders such as substance abuse (Kendler et al., 2002). Kendler et al. (1995) concluded from a large twin study that "genetic factors influence the risk of onset of major depression in part by altering the sensitivity of individuals to the depression-inducing effect of stressful life events" (p. 833). In comparison, a recent population-based sample of more than 7,500 individuals found that stressful events nearly always precede depressive episodes and that gender differences for depression decrease with greater chronicity of adversity in the environment (Kendler, Kuhn, & Prescott, 2004). Although the personality trait of neuroticism (which has genetic load) predicted depression, its robustness decreased as chronicity and severity of adversity increased (Kendler et al., 2004), thus reiterating the potency of environmental stressors, including acute episodes, on depression.

Genetic Vulnerability for Substance Abuse

There is evidence of a genetic susceptibility for alcohol abuse or dependence (Anthenelli & Schuckit, 1997) and substance abuse or dependence in general (Hopfer, Crowley, & Hewitt, 2003; Karkowski, Prescott, & Kendler, 2000; Kendler, Jacobson, Prescott, & Neale, 2003). Alcohol alone has direct or indirect effects on gamma-amino-butyric acid (GABA), N-methyl-D-aspartate, serotonin, dopamine, glutamate, norepinephrine, and the opiate peptides (Hunt, 1998). In addition, most psychoactive drugs of abuse are associated with multiple transmitter systems in the brain, and genetic contributions to dysregulation of any of these neurotransmitter systems may increase liability for becoming substance dependent or substance abusing (Crabbe, 1999; Hunt, 1998). LaForge and Kreek (1999) presented evidence of genetic factors related to opioid receptors and the contribution of these factors to addictive disease. Other evidence indicates that specific genetic factors influence addictive sensitivity to specific substances such that opiate addiction may involve somewhat different alleles (Kreek, 2001). Certain personality characteristics or temperament and even prefrontal lobe function, which is associated with cognitive ability, may be influenced by genetic factors (Bouchard, McGue, Hur, & Horn, 1998; Swendsen, Conway, Rounsaville, & Merikangas, 2003; Winterer & Goldman, 2003). This may be relevant in that certain characteristics, such as impulsivity, could be genetically influenced, which then may lead to certain behaviors such as substance use (Hopfer et al., 2003; Iacono, Carlson, Taylor, Elkins, & McGue, 1999).

Summary of Genetic Vulnerabilities

Heritability must be considered in understanding the development of health problems, mental health problems, and substance abuse among women with victimization. Individual variations in experience and environment are nonetheless significant, and the genetic component is but one among many complex factors. Another challenge in studying the heritability of mental health problems is that often various mental health problems co-occur. The co-occurrence rates of disorders such as PTSD, depression, and substance abuse can confound findings about the specific genetic liability of mental disorders. For example, polydrug users who have depression and PTSD may have inherited multiple biogenetic susceptibilities that can be triggered by stressful events such as victimization. Even so, the awareness of heritability liability for mental disorders is important in the understanding of overall vulnerability of victims to mental disorders and substance abuse. If victimization can be understood as a robust vulnerability factor for mental disorder, heritability should be seen as yet one other vulnerability substrate. Appreciating the significance of heritability can decrease the stigma associated with mental disorders by reducing the belief about intentional contributions to symptoms (Kelso, 2000).

Stress, Biological Vulnerabilities, and Substance Abuse

Stress and Victimization

As noted in the introduction to this chapter, the subjective experience of stress is a complex phenomenon. The two main components of a stressor include the objective or quasi-objective portion of the stressor (e.g., the actual stressful event) and the individual experience of the stressor, which is related to the level of distress in response to the event (Agnew, 1992; Pearlin, 1989; Turner & Wheaton, 1997). Generally, individuals have a remarkable capacity to adapt to stressful events (Aspenwall & Staudinger, 2003; Bonanno, 2004; Selye, 1956). However, severe and chronic stressors have important implications for the understanding of victimization. In Wheaton's (1997) definition of chronic stress, a stressor poses a threat that demands resolution; it cannot be allowed to continue indefinitely without serious damage to the person. Likewise, Selye's (1982) description of the phases of the general adaptation syndrome includes a stage of exhaustion at which individuals deplete their coping reserves if stress cannot be relieved or if the stressor is repeated.

Stressful life events are significant contributors to mental health problems, even when other factors such as genetic risk are controlled (Kendler, Karkowski, & Prescott, 1999). Furthermore, the more severe the stressful life event, the greater the likelihood of mental health problems; thus, what matters for mental health may not be the number of independent stressful life events that occur but rather their severity or the dependent number of stressors (Kendler et al., 1999). For example, a study examining the impact of recent stressful life events on the likelihood of developing stress disorder symptoms among adult women with childhood sexual victimization found that their sensitivity to recent stressors was high compared with women without childhood victimization (Classen et al., 2002). Another study examining the psychological and other effects of partner violence on 205 pregnant women who had recently been abused found that the effects were far greater for those who had extensive histories of abuse, suggesting that negative acute stress responses may be intensified by chronic victimization stress (Bogat, Levendosky, Theran, von Eye, & Davidson, 2003).

In addition to the sheer chronicity of stress, another key to understanding victimization as a stressful event is that when victimization includes a threat to the fundamental integrity of the person—what Wheaton (1997) called a threat to key elements of personal identity, including one's sense of self-worth, power, and control over one's life (S. Taylor & Brown, 1991)—it will most likely have a negative impact on an individual. This idea is clearly acknowledged by the requirement of an anchor criterion for diagnosis of PTSD that involves the experience of, witness to, or confrontation with an "event or events that involved actual or threatened death or serious injury, or a threat to the physical integrity of self or others" (American Psychiatric Association, 2000, p. 467; Yehuda, McFarlane, & Shalev, 1998). Kendall-Tackett (2000) summarized the stress phenomenon by concluding that

> the stress response becomes a problem when the stressor is an extreme one-time occurrence that floods the system with stress hormones, or a chronic

stressor in which the response that is supposed to be an acute emergency becomes a frequent occurrence. (p. 800)

Chronic stress deserves careful attention in examining the mental health and substance abuse coping strategies used by victims with repeated victimization experiences, for several reasons. First, the exhaustion or fatigue from chronic stress may be indistinguishable from depression and may include high levels of anxiety. In fact, stress may be the gateway condition from which various mental health and substance abuse problems are expressed (Kessler, 1997). Second, chronic stress can induce individuals to try to take actions to "correct" or to facilitate the adaptation to their stress, which may be problematic. Van der Kolk (1996b) stated that

> traumatized people employ a variety of methods to regain control over their problems with affect regulation. Often these efforts are self-destructive and bizarre; they range from self-mutilation to unusual sexual practices, and from bingeing and purging to drug and alcohol abuse. (p. 188)

Briere (1996), in a clinical text, described these efforts as "tension-reduction" behaviors and gave similar examples, including risky sexual behaviors, bingeing and purging, self-mutilation, and substance abuse. Third, some behavioral stress responses can create increased stress. Drug use, for example, may be used as a coping mechanism but also may create legal problems that increase stress levels. Fourth, certain stress responses can result in *epiphenomenal stress*—further stress that results from stress responses and reactions (Gottlieb, 1997). For example, certain stress responses, such as hypervigilance and stimulus avoidance in the aftermath of rape or assault, may induce biological changes that disregulate certain physiological systems, which may induce more stress.

Stress and Biological Vulnerabilities

Stress has been difficult to define in psychological and physiological literatures, but at neuroanatomical and neurochemical levels, it generally refers to alterations in homeostasis or equilibrium (Cullinan, Herman, Helmreich, & Watson, 1995). As noted earlier, although not all victims experience PTSD or trauma-related mental disorders, the likelihood of these disorders increases with repeated interpersonal victimization experiences. Furthermore, evidence from a fast-growing literature on the neurobiology of trauma points to an increased likelihood of victimization-related changes in brain and hormonal systems. In other words, the risk for biological disequilibrium increases with the severity and persistence of victimization experiences, just as the risk for developing mental health problems is likely to be related to the type of victimization and the persistence or severity of exposure. Evidence for the association of abuse severity and the severity of mental health consequences may be found in the identifiable neurobiological correlates of trauma and severe life-threatening stress (Bremner et al., 1999; Bremner, Southwick, & Charney, 1997; Bremner,

Southwick, Johnson, Yehuda, & Charney, 1993; Charney & Bremner, 1999). For example, individuals who are more likely to have PTSD following stressful events may have lower levels of GABA, a neurotransmitter that modulates the HPA axis and that is associated with dampening excitatory activity (Vaiva et al., 2003). In fact, Charney (2004) identified 11 possible neurochemical, neuropeptide, and neurohormonal mediators of psychobiological responses to stress that may relate to vulnerability or resilience (or both).

Overall, this literature suggests that traumatic stress may result in changes to brain structures, neurochemistry, and stress hormone function (Charney & Bremner, 1999; Sapolsky, 1996; Sapolsky, Alberts, & Altman, 1997). Normal responses to stress involve the activation of the HPA axis. This is an important component of the brain–body system for detecting and responding to emergencies and threats. Normally, the HPA axis reacts to threats by signaling the brain and body to react physically and emotionally to protect the organism. With severe stressors such as ongoing partner victimization, this complex chemical (neurotransmitter and hormonal) process may become dysregulated, with important consequences to thinking, feeling, and behaving. This more or less permanent dysregulation may be part of resetting the basic biological homeostasis involved in chronic stress that McEwen (2000) termed *allostatic load*, in which hormones that normally play a protective role in the short run have damaging effects if sustained over time. In other words, adaptive stress reactions cause changes in the activity of the HPA axis, a situation that Sterling and Eyer (1988) called *allostasis*. A failed process for turning off this stress reaction is called *allostatic state*, and the sustained wear and tear on the brain and body resulting from this state is *allostatic load* (McEwen, 2003). Thus, the body's normal physiological response to stress can become fixed, like a household thermostat that gets stuck at 85 degrees, and this reset "hot" state can result in altered brain structures and chemical equilibrium.

There are several indicators of sustained biological abnormalities in response to trauma, including adrenocorticotropic hormone (ACTH) and cortisol levels. For example, Heim et al. (2000) found women with both childhood abuse histories and current depression had a 6 times greater ACTH response to stress compared with women who had no abuse history and no depression and compared with women who had only one condition—childhood abuse history or depression. Weiss et al.'s (1999) review of the literature indicated that childhood sexual abuse is associated with adult-onset depression and that childhood sexual abuse may predispose individuals to adult-onset depression by means of dysregulation of the HPA axis, which mediates cortisol levels. Resnick, Yehuda, Pitman, and Foy (1995) found that cortisol levels, within several hours of a rape, were lower in women with histories of rape or assault compared with women who did not have previous victimization histories. Cortisol is a stress-related hormone that is generally found at higher levels during stressful periods. Thus, Resnick et al.'s (1995) study comparing rape victims who had prior trauma with those without chronic abuse demonstrated preliminary evidence of sustained biological changes due to cumulative life trauma. There is some evidence that individuals with PTSD have abnormally low levels of cortisol and abnormally high levels of norepinephrine, the neurotransmitter that is associated with arousal (Yehuda, 1999; Yehuda et al., 1996). In addition, acute biological responses to trauma exposure such as heart rate and cortisol levels may actually mediate the onset of PTSD (Yehuda, 1999; Yehuda et al., 1998). Although individuals usually experience increased heart rates on exposure to threatening events, those with much higher heart rates immediately following the exposure as well as those with lower cortisol levels may be at greater risk for PTSD and more sustained biological variance from normal values (Yehuda et al., 1998). Furthermore, women with chronic pelvic pain have been shown to have higher rates of severe abuse and lower levels of cortisol (Heim, Ehlert, Hanker, & Hellhammer, 1998).

In contrast, individuals with depression are more likely to have abnormally high levels of cortisol and low levels of norepinephrine (DeSouza, 1995; Owens & Nemeroff, 1993; Shively, 1998; Shuchter, Downs, & Zisook, 1996; Thase et al., 1996). Some trauma victims have PTSD, depression, and anxiety disorders, and the association of the three disorders may be affected by disturbance of the HPA axis as well as other neurochemical systems (Friedman & Yehuda, 1995; Holden, 2003). One study compared individuals with PTSD and depression with those who had PTSD only (Yehuda et al., 1998). This study found that lower levels of norepinephrine were associated with more severe depression, whereas elevated norepinephrine levels were found in those who were not depressed. Abnormal levels of cortisol and norepinephrine can contribute to and prolong PTSD, depression, and anxiety (Yehuda et al., 1998). Because these neurochemicals are constituents of affects and moods, their chronic dysregulation, either as an overabundance or a shortage, can affect the expression of clinical disorders. Abnormal levels of these neurotransmitters and neurohormones not only can lead to increased vulnerability to PTSD, depression, or anxiety, but can also impair responses to danger cues such as magnifying a shock-induced freezing response in the presence of danger (Heim et al., 2000).

Other neuroanatomical and neurochemical changes in response to trauma have been identified in addition to increased vulnerability to mental health symptoms and impaired stress responses. One of the more important aspects of the neurobiology of trauma has to do with the understanding of memory and the reported memoral difficulties that trauma victims may have for parts of their experience. Research has reported problems with the recovery of memories among physical and sexual abuse survivors (Chu, Frey, Ganzel, & Mathews, 1999; Herman, 1992; Koss, Figueredo, Bell, Tharan, & Tromp, 1996; Krikorian & Layton, 1998; van der Kolk, 1997; van der Kolk, Pelcovitz, et al., 1996; van der Kolk, van der Hart, et al., 1996b). For example, one study reported that 38% of individuals who had experienced abuse severe enough to require an emergency room visit had no recall of the event 20 years later (Bremner, Krystal, Southwick, & Charney, 1995). In a survey of 3,000 women, Koss et al. (1996) reported that rape survivors (30% of the sample) had poorer recall of their rape experiences than other subjects had of other emotionally intense events. Bremner, Scott, et al. (1993) found that individuals with PTSD scored lower in measures of total recall, short-term memory, and long-term memory. However, McNally (2003b) questioned these studies with respect to the accuracy of findings about recall disorders among trauma victims and questioned whether cognitive impairments such as memory problems might precede PTSD or even whether cognitive impairments may be risk factors for the clinical disorder. In fact, cognitive ability is rarely assessed among trauma subjects in studies of memoral difficulties associated with trauma and traumatic events (McNally, 2003b). In addition, other mental health problems such as depression can affect memory—potentially even at subclinical thresholds—and PTSD studies do not always control for preexistent or concurrent symptoms of other disorders. Much of the literature on memoral problems associated with abuse has focused on childhood sexual abuse. However, in recent research using linear regression to control for factors traditionally associated with memoral difficulties, such as relationship to the offender, gender, and number of traumatic events, the severity of PTSD symptoms actually predicted greater recall and detail of abuse incidents, even among this population (Alexander et al., 2005).

The memory problems of women with victimization experiences also may be related to reduced cell volume in the hippocampus, the primary area of the brain responsible for "placing" long-term life event memories (Bremner, 1999; Bremner et al., 1999; Bremner, Scott, et al., 1993; Squire, 1987; Squire & Knowlton, 1995). Cortisol abnormalities, which may occur in response to stress, can affect hippocampal function by shutting down cell metabolism of glucose, causing neuronal cell loss (Sapolsky, 1990, 2000; Sapolsky, Romero, & Munck, 2000). Decreases in hippocampus cell volume may impair storage of new information as well as the directed retrieval of memories about life events, because the hippocampus is involved both in memory encoding and retrieving as well as putting memories in place and time sequence (Eichenbaum, Otto, & Cohen, 1994; Squire & Knowlton, 1995). The biological contributions to memory impairment may have consequences for the interpretation of victim behavior as well as treatment for victims, although the research on the exact nature of memoral problems for victims is unclear (McNally, 2003b). One study on hippocampal cell volume found that cell volume loss was greatest among women with childhood abuse experiences plus PTSD and was least among women with neither childhood abuse nor PTSD (Bremner et al., 2003). This study also found, however, that women with PTSD had more severe child abuse experiences than women with child abuse experiences but no PTSD. On the other hand, not all research has confirmed an association of hippocampal cell volume loss with either PTSD or victimization. For example, a recent study found that among younger women, there were no memoral or hippocampal cell volume differences among those with childhood abuse with PTSD, childhood abuse without PTSD, and control subjects with neither PTSD nor abuse histories (Pederson et al., 2004).

It is also possible that the hippocampal cell loss observed in trauma victims may be worse among victims who also are long-term heavy alcohol users or who are severely depressed, because heavy alcohol use and depression may contribute to the dysregulation of the HPA axis and excess cortisol release (E. Brown, Rush, & McEwen, 1999; Ehrenreich et al., 1997). Specifically, long-term alcohol ingestion is associated with activation of the HPA axis, and both acute and longer term abstinence is associated with dampened HPA responses (Wand, 2000). Heavy alcohol use also complicates effects on the arousal response hormonal system, as evidenced by heightened cortisol levels among active alcoholics and decreased adrenal function after abstinence (Wand, 2000). Heavy alcohol use can also contribute to damage in immune systems (Rivier, 1993, 2000).

Combined with its effects on HPA axis functioning, alcohol use can lead to increased susceptibility to illness and more complicated treatment outcomes (Wand, 2000). Heavy alcohol use and depression have also been shown to be associated with *hypercortisolemia*, the condition of excessive release of cortisol, and related cortisol mediated damage to the hippocampus (E. Brown et al., 1999; Vakili et al., 2000; Wand, 2000).

In addition to reduced hippocampal volume associated with PTSD and alcohol abuse, there is evidence of similar phenomena with depression. Although not all studies have found an association of depression and lower hippocampal volume, a recent meta-analysis of 20 studies found that specificity of imaging accounted for more robust findings of hippocampal volume decreases among depressed persons (S. Campbell, Marriott, Nahmias, & MacQueen, 2004). In other words, studies that failed to find differences in hippocampal volume by depression status more often used overall volumes of the hippocampus and the amygdala combined, which yielded nonsignificant differences compared with studies that discriminated between the two (S. Campbell et al., 2004). More specifically, one study compared first-episode depressives with nondepressed control subjects; the depressed subjects had significantly smaller hippocampal cell volumes than those who were not depressed (Frodl et al., 2002). This finding was challenged because it did not control for victimization among the depressed subjects, which might account for hippocampal volume differences (Vythilingam et al., 2002). However, a recent study using participants who reported no adult or childhood victimization experiences found reduced blood flow in the hippocampus and anterior cingulate among depressed subjects compared with nondepressed subjects (Bremner, Vythilingam, Vermetten, Vaccarino, & Charney, 2004). In addition, other studies have shown hippocampal volume reductions are related to the duration of depressive symptoms (Flores et al., 2004).

With mood disorders, research has focused less on structural damage and more on neurohormonal and neurotransmitter dysregulation. Research has investigated numerous biological substrates to depression, including the hyperactivity of the HPA axis and altered cortisol levels; the hypothalamic–pituitary–thyroid axis; the hypothalamic-growth hormone axis; the hypothalamic–pituitary–gonadal axis; pineal gland functions regulating circadian cycles, norepinephrine and adrenergic receptors, dopamine and monoamine oxidase, acetylcholine, low GABA levels, serotonin dysregulation, and other messenger systems (Flores et al., 2004). The relation of lower hippocampal volume to trauma and related disorders is also complicated by the fact that lower hippocampal volume has been reported for other disorders such as schizophrenia without evidence of trauma (Szeszko et al., 2003). Changes in the amygdala have also been associated with extreme stress. These changes may also have serious consequences for processing emotion and for mediating reward, as well as fear conditioning and extinction (Charney, 2004). If there is compromise of the amygdala's ability to experience rewards, then the reward value of social experiences as well as socioemotional reasoning may become blunted, thus affecting social functioning (Charney, 2004).

Victimization, mental health problems, and substance use all contribute in complex ways to neurobiological phenomena, which in turn affect health, mental health, substance use, and, potentially, vulnerability for revictimization. Neuroanatomical anomalies and neurochemical dysregulation may be both effects of and contributors to mental disorder and victimization.

Stress and Substance Abuse

Coping with continuous threats is qualitatively different from coping with isolated events. In particular, coping with an unpredictable threat can lead to hypervigilance and a need to reduce the continual stress (Gottlieb, 1997). Coupled with this stress, there may be periods of "giving up" the struggle with stressors or of exhausting emotional reserves and resorting to substance use as a coping strategy (Carver & Scheier, 1999). However, substance abuse as a coping response to victimization may greatly complicate problems. Substance abuse by women with victimization issues has received attention in the research literature, although some are cautious about this topic because of its risk of victim blaming.

The idea of substance use as a response to physical or emotional pain seems to have some credibility given the literature reviewed earlier regarding the significant physical and mental health manifestations of victimization (Harrison, Fulkerson, & Beebe, 1997; Khantzian, 1990, 1997; McCormick & Smith, 1995; Wills & Filer, 1996; Wills & Hirky, 1996). For example, chronic pain is a risk factor for substance abuse (Passik & Portenoy, 1998). Emotional or physical discomfort and pain may motivate an individual to engage in behaviors to try to diminish the pain (Beckham et al., 1995; Kilpatrick, Saunders, Veronen, Best, & Von, 1987). Negative emotions such as hopelessness, depression, and other forms of emotional distress have been associated with greater alcohol use (Burch, 1994; Hesselbrock & Hesselbrock, 1992; Newcomb & Bentler, 1986; Newcomb, Vargas-Carmona, & Galaif, 1999; Regier et al., 1990; Roy, DeJong, Lamparski, George, & Linnoila, 1991; Weiss, Griffin, & Mirin, 1992). The coping hypothesis to explain substance abuse is supported by research showing that alcohol can and does reduce stress and negative affect for certain people under certain circumstances (Carpenter & Hasin, 1999; Cooper, Russell, Skinner, Frone, & Mudar, 1992; Sayette, 1999). The direct pharmacological and psychological effects of alcohol and some drugs decrease the perception and awareness of negative affect (Brady & Lydiard, 1992; B. Cox, Norton, Sinson, & Endler, 1990; Kushner, Sher, & Beitman, 1990).

Women with substance use disorders are likely to experience co-occurring mood or affective disorders, and this synergy of negative affect and substance use appears significant. In fact, women with alcohol abuse or dependence are 2 to 3 times more likely to have anxiety and depression than are alcohol-abusing men (Kessler, Crum, & Warner, 1997). Epidemiological research showing relationships between negative affect and substance use does not answer the question about which is precedent. In other words, women with negative affects are more likely to initiate substance use, and women with substance abuse are more likely to experience negative affects that may, in part, be a result of substance use. Other research indicates that women who hold stronger beliefs about the tension-reducing qualities of alcohol drink more frequently, yet women who drink to reduce stress are more likely to experience negative consequences of alcohol use (Hittner, 1995; Perkins, 1999).

In addition to the many neuroanatomical and neurochemical alterations associated with trauma and victimization, substance abuse has numerous other complexities. Victims who begin using substances as a coping response to the abuse may encounter changes in brain function and structure that make recovery and adaptation more difficult. Alcohol and other drugs affect many of the same brain structures that PTSD and depression affect, including the amygdala, where intense emotion is recognized and mediated to higher cortical areas; the extended amygdala, including the basal ganglia, where intentional motor functions are mediated; the orbitofrontal lobes, where emotion is further processed; and the cingulate cortex (Heimer, 2003; Kilts, 2004). In fact, the amygdala is the brain region most involved in conditioned learning and is a primary mediator of fear (Halgren, 1992; LeDoux, 2000). Impairment or disturbance of emotion-processing areas of the brain may have implications for how clinicians view women with victimization experiences. In other words, these women may have difficulty with emotion regulation, leading mental health professionals to view them as having mental or personality disorders rather than unusual or extreme neuropsychological system responses to severe stress.

Substance use may also affect or complicate health problems. For example, gastroenterological disorders may be exacerbated by unhealthy behaviors such as alcohol and opiate drug use (Tsigos & Chrousos, 1996), indicating complex physiological sequelae to such behaviors in addition to the victimization experience. In another example, alcohol, because of its sedative effects, may be used to speed up sleep onset; however, this accelerated onset is offset by disruption of later sleep cycles (National Institute on Alcohol Abuse and Alcoholism, 1998). Alcohol suppresses REM sleep, thus reducing the "restorative" factor for aminergic neurons (Hobson, 1995). Alcohol is not alone in causing sleep disorder. In fact, alcohol, amphetamines, cocaine, and sedative–hypnotics (benzodiazepines) intoxication and withdrawal can disturb sleep (American Psychiatric Association, 1994). In sum, substance use as a coping strategy for stress may actually decrease the body's ability to respond to stress.

Summary of Stress, Biological Vulnerabilities, and Substance Abuse

A more complete understanding of victimization should include appreciation for recent research findings on differences in brain structure and functioning. It would now be old-fashioned or quaint to use the term *chemical imbalance in the brain* to capture the clinical manifestations of victimization on brain functioning and structures. However, knowledge about the neuroanatomy and neurochemistry of trauma is in its infancy. The evidence about differences in brain structures for those with PTSD, however, suggests that neuroanatomical and neurochemical factors cannot be ignored in understanding the potential impact of victimization. The data show that victimization in adulthood carries with it a probability of accumulated and accumulating burdens to an individual's physiological systems that may be manifest in any of a number of mental health and substance abuse problems. The cycle is one of stress producing mental health problems, which diminish appropriate responses to stress, which increases stress levels, which then contributes to increased severity of mental health problems.

Because of recent advances in neuroanatomical studies, the understanding of victimization and related mental health and substance abuse among women is in the process of major revision. The purely psychological or sociological dimensions of interpersonal victimization must now include the role of biological manifestations such as changes to brain structure and function. However, the observed differences in brain structure among abuse victims and among those with PTSD cannot be shown to be purely an effect of victimization (Bremner et al., 2003). In fact, the hippocampal volume differences may have existed before victimization experiences and may have contributed to the susceptibility to PTSD, depression, or other disorders (Bremner et al., 2003, 2004). Charney's (2004) review of the many possible neurochemical, neuropeptide, and hormonal mediators of psychobiological responses to extreme stress merely opens the door to a complex area for future research. These mechanisms, including hormones such as estrogen and progesterone, have both beneficial and detrimental effects on psychobiological functioning. In addition, the neural mechanisms of reward and motivation (hedonia, optimism, and learned helpfulness), fear responsiveness (effective behaviors despite fear), and adaptive social behavior (altruism, bonding, and teamwork) were found to be "relevant to the characteristics associated with resilience" (Charney, 2004, p. 195). Whether neuroanatomical and neurochemical differences serve as risk factors or are a result of trauma exposure, it is important to appreciate the potential impact of these differences for victimized women who need maximal internal and external resources to achieve safety and health (Hobfall, Freedy, Green, & Solomon, 1996).

Summary

As mentioned at the beginning of this chapter, humans are incredibly resilient in coping with major life events and stressors. Although some women may not experience negative health or mental health problems associated with trauma experiences, other women may experience a wide variety or combination of physical and mental health problems. The response to specific traumas such as victimization is likely associated with situational factors as well as numerous genetic, biological, and other strengths and vulnerabilities. Women with victimization experiences may experience acute and chronic health problems as well as stress-related health problems. Depression, PTSD, other anxiety disorders, and BPD are among the primary mental health problems common among women with victimization experiences, in part because each of these disorders can be triggered or exacerbated by severe stressful life events. In addition, PTSD, depression, certain types of substance use and abuse, and severe stress can result in changes to neuroanatomy and neurochemistry that have profound effects for victims' memoral systems and emotion processing—both of which are vital to coping with and surviving violence. These disorders also tend to co-occur with each other. Mental health problems, along with stress, intersect with physical health and can cause chronic effects that may also help explain why some victims may have memory problems and decreased coping capacities.

Furthermore, the combination of disorders can increase the risk of negative outcomes for women with mental health problems. For example, having PTSD in addition to depression may increase the risk of suicide attempts (Oquendo et al., 2003). The accretion of comorbidities among women with victimization may mean declining levels of functioning and increased risk for more disorders such as substance abuse. Thus, this research review delineates a complex web of interacting and interconnected relationships among victimization, mental health, and substance use.

Strengths and Weaknesses in the Literature

This chapter has concentrated on some of the most obvious areas of study that overlap with victimization—specifically, physical and mental health manifestations. It also has examined aspects of these factors that are often overlooked. For example, the close connection of physical–mental health and genetic–neurobiological vulnerabilities are important for understanding victimization but are not often integrated into victimization studies. Although the early research has been promising in helping to explain associations between physical health problems and victimization, the specific contributions remain unclear. In effect, the research on victimization has suffered from silo processes that leave large domains unexplored while pursuing narrow and often discipline-specific examinations. Holistic theories and research designs incorporating these complexities have been lacking. For example, the literature has only begun to explore the many connections between repeated victimization experiences and physical health. Studies of physical pain, gastroenterology, gynecology, immunology, and other systems are starting to open the door to understanding the multiple contributions of childhood and adulthood victimization.

In addition, research into mental health problems among victims cannot ignore the role of substance use in both victimization and mental disorder. The established psychiatric literature affirms this pattern of co-occurrence to the point that a study that ignores one or the other is likely to be faulty. Likewise, research into the development of mental disorders cannot ignore the profound contributions of both childhood and adult victimization to the etiology, if not the course of, disorders. Much attention has been given to men with combat-related PTSD and the temporal associations between combat exposure, PTSD, and substance abuse, but insufficient research has been committed to these same issues among women with victimization histories (S. Stewart & Conrod, 2003). Carefully examining the differences between combat-related trauma effects and the effects of sustained, periodic abuse from a partner would greatly increase the understanding of PTSD and substance abuse among women.

Furthermore, although the literature has grown exponentially on factors related to abuse and mental and physical health problems, it has not rigorously differentiated childhood from adult experiences. "Abuse" is not a singular phenomenon but a general category of human experiences that may have very different developmental consequences and trajectories in an individual's life. Given the current knowledge base on the co-occurrence of health and mental health problems for women with victimization experiences, the burden of research should be on understanding the unique contribution of separate victimization experiences to health and mental health outcomes rather than reiterating earlier findings of simple associations.

Estimates of mental health problems among women with victimization histories may be underreported because the epidemiology of disorders is inevitably distorted by inaccurate recall of previous mental states and symptoms— particularly if an individual is affected by a current mental disorder (Blazer, 2000). Although the prevalence of mental disorders appears to be higher among women with victimization, it is likely that current estimates understate the numbers because of the potential for underreporting lifetime symptoms (Blazer, 2000). This factor is particularly important in estimating the prevalence of disorders among women with victimization, because there is extensive, although not definitive, research on the relationship of trauma to both short- and long-term memory alterations (Golier, Yehuda, & Southwick, 1997). Longitudinal prospective studies are thus critical in examining victimization, physical health, mental health, and substance use to better understand mechanisms and pathways. Furthermore, the development of new technologies to measure or gain more accurate recall may be important.

Finally, the wealth of new research on the neurobiology of mental disorders has revised purely psychological or sociological explanations of mental disorders and victimization. Yet this research raises as many questions as it answers. For example, the literature on lower than expected hippocampal cell volume among those with depression, PTSD, or serious substance abuse does not clarify whether the cell volume was a result of disorder or a contributing cause. It may well be that lower cell volume in the hippocampus is indicative of an impaired ability to code and process information, and this difficulty may be associated with the development of mental disorders.

Conclusion

The research reviewed in this chapter underscores the complexity of the interacting and interconnected relationships among victimization, health, mental health, and substance abuse. Thus, the conceptual model initially presented in chapter 1 becomes more complex. Specifically, we can add to our conceptual model boxes and arrows that represent the interrelationships between physical and mental health manifestations; genetic vulnerabilities; and stress, biological vulnerabilities, and substance abuse (Figure 2.1).

The physical health manifestations of victimization include acute, chronic, and stress-related health problems; the mental health manifestations of victimization include depression, anxiety, PTSD, and BPD. There is a significant overlap of physical and mental health problems that are sometimes manifest in complaints of pain, sleep disturbance, and eating disorders. Genetic vulnerabilities of health problems, mental health problems, and substance abuse also contribute to the physical and mental health manifestations of victimization as well as to stress, biological vulnerabilities, and substance abuse. Meanwhile, increased stress contributes to biological vulnerabilities and substance abuse, which in turn can affect physical and mental health.

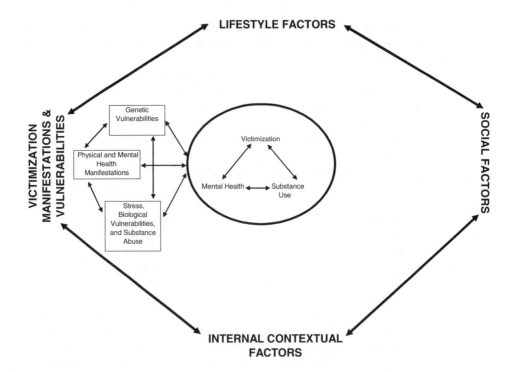

Figure 2.1. Conceptual model of factors contributing to victimization, mental health, and substance use: victimization manifestations and vulnerabilities.

Poincaré's quote at the beginning of this chapter points out that science should be concerned more about the relations between things than the things themselves. This chapter has focused on the relations between victimization and the plethora of phenomena associated with it. Repeated victimization encompasses numerous mental health and physical health manifestations—some of which are consequences, some of which are vulnerability factors for victimization responses. In tracing the various disorders back to commonalities, severe stressful life events emerge as the powerful engine behind this wide array of problem manifestations. As noted in the case at the beginning of the chapter, Natalie had symptoms of PTSD, depression, anxiety, and possibly substance abuse. Natalie's therapist was having trouble determining the primary disorder to account for all the symptoms that were emerging and felt like she was peeling an onion, with one disorder after another arising on assessment.

Practitioners may be wondering what relevance the information in this chapter has for them. The first step in helping women with victimization histories is to understand that a level of complexity exists that is not necessarily linear or clearly explainable. What can create serious problems for one person may have little effect on another. Thus, there is a clear need for a client-centered approach to assessment and treatment with women who have experienced repeated and chronic victimization. Responses to trauma depend on a variety of factors, including both strengths and vulnerabilities, which are all interconnected: genetic risk; the synergy among the individual's specific stress levels, health issues, and mental health problems; and the resultant social and biological consequences. More specifically, it is critically important to understand that because of the complex nature of responses to chronic stress and trauma, women with chronic and repeated victimization experiences should not be treated with a simple diagnosis or simple solutions. Each chapter in this book suggests the need for comprehensive and ongoing assessments for a variety of problems. Practitioners should consider each woman within the larger context of her life, with an understanding that big and small things that happen do matter and that these complexities and interrelationships are important.

In the next chapter, we expand this context by reviewing research on lifestyle factors related to victimization. These factors influence and are influenced by some of the vulnerabilities as well as consequences of victimization described in this chapter.

3

Lifestyle Factors

The Case of Sara M.

Sara was being interviewed by a counselor at the local rape crisis center. She confided in the counselor about her recent sexual assault and her life over the past several years.

Sara was dating one of the young attorneys in the law firm where she worked as a paralegal. She was not happy with her job and for several months had been looking for other employment without much luck. She and her boyfriend began going to bars until nearly midnight two or three times each week. They also started going to raves, where she had her first exposure to the drug "ecstasy."

One evening they went to a rave after being at the bar for several hours. Her boyfriend got angry with her and left. She was upset but determined to have a good time because it was "her night out." She began drinking one beer after another and danced with another man, who offered her some ecstasy, which she took. Hours later, the man she had been dancing with asked her to go to the "back room." She refused but was too substance impaired to stop him from taking her there. She was physically assaulted and raped. She was taken to the emergency room, where she was then referred to a rape crisis counselor. In counseling, she reported that she had been raped once before when she was in college and at a fraternity party while she was "really, really wasted."

* * *

This chapter explores lifestyle factors and how they may contribute to increased risk of victimization, as highlighted in Sara's case. The term *lifestyle* implies free volition, making the discussion of lifestyle factors troubling because it may seem to imply that victims "chose" to be victimized. In other words, the inference about "choice" in lifestyle assumes an undistorted and fully informed understanding of the consequences of risky situations. On the contrary, inadvertent and incautious actions can have unintended effects. Furthermore, certain behaviors are typically the culmination of many factors, including prior experiences, the perception of reality, and mental states, all of which are unknown to anyone but the individual. In a letter to his sister, Ludwig Wittgenstein, the 20th-century philosopher, described the discrepancy between an individual's efforts at survival and other people's interpretation of the behavior:

> You remind me of someone who is looking through a closed window and cannot explain to himself the strange movements of a passer-by. He doesn't know what kind of storm is raging outside and that this person is perhaps only with great effort keeping himself on his feet. (quoted in Edmonds & Eidinow, 2001, p. 187)

Like Wittgenstein, there may be forces at work that influence personal choices and make a person's behavior seem elective when it is actually mere survival or an automatic response. A better understanding of lifestyle risk factors does not mean that victims should be blamed for their victimization, even though lifestyles are generally thought of as "chosen." Lifestyle and victimization has sometimes been understood and dismissed by this inference of choice. In fact, *intention* is generally defined as having an idea of what one is going to do in conscious process before one does it (Wegner, 2002). In other words, to make an inference about willful contribution to victimization, women would have to form a conscious idea of violent events and take a course of action that anticipates or even intends these outcomes. There is no evidence for this in any research literature, no matter how unconstructive some lifestyle choices might appear. Consistent with the absence of findings to the contrary, nothing in this chapter suggests that responsibility for violence lies with anyone other than the offender. Nonetheless, evidence does indicate that certain lifestyles can contribute to heightened risk for victimization and revictimization.

This chapter provides a broader context within which to understand how lifestyles, especially lifestyle activities that involve substance use, might contribute to the risk of victimization. Three main lifestyle factors are discussed in this chapter: (a) associations with others, (b) others' perceptions of women's vulnerability, and (c) women's own risk perceptions. Associations or exposure to potential offenders in the environment and vulnerability or the perceived vulnerability of a target by an offender were primarily derived from what has been termed *lifestyle or routine activities theory* (L. Cohen & Felson, 1979; M. Felson, 1998; Hindelang, Gottfredson, & Garofalo, 1978). In general, this theory states that when individuals associate or come in contact with criminal offenders, they may be more likely to experience victimization (M. Felson, 1998). In other words, the presence of offenders—in a crack house, at a party, or in a high-crime area—is an important element to consider in understanding risk of victimization. In addition, the more offenders there are in an area (i.e., the greater the density of offenders), the greater the likelihood of perpetration of crimes and violence. In addition, according to lifestyle or routine activities theory, the degree to which offenders perceive a victim as a vulnerable target is important in understanding increased vulnerability to victimization (M. Felson, 1998). Target vulnerability can be influenced by several factors, such as an individual's level of intoxication or how intoxicated a person is perceived to be and whether there are credible witnesses to crimes. Although a discussion of neighborhood or community violence may seem appropriate in this chapter because exposure to potential offenders is increased in some neighborhoods, neighborhood violence is discussed in chapter 4 within the social factors context. The focus in this chapter is on lifestyles or activities that may place women in closer associations with offenders and potential offenders rather than, for example, exposure due to socioeconomic status.

The last section of this chapter includes a discussion of how risk perceptions are compromised by lifestyle factors, especially substance use and expectancies or expectations for behavior. Expectations are derived from personal experiences, observations of others' experiences, and norms. Expectancies for behavior while using substances as well as expectations about others, especially "known" others, can influence risk perceptions. The literature reviewed in this section overlaps information presented in chapter 5 regarding cognitive appraisals of risk.

Substance use is especially salient in the discussion of lifestyle factors because substance use can facilitate associations with others who are either involved in criminal behavior or predisposed to it. In addition, intoxication is an important factor in creating perceived vulnerability of potential victims. Substance use also impairs cognitive processes and influences the expectations of situations, and both of these can influence risk perceptions. Traditionally, substance use has been associated with the *perpetration* of violence (A. Klein, 1996; Maiden, 1997; Roizen, 1997). As highlighted in Sara's case at the beginning of this chapter, however, a victim's drug and alcohol use can be an important factor to consider (Kessler et al., 1995; Mustaine & Tewksbury, 1998, 1999; Windle, 1994). For example, Kilpatrick, Acierno, Resnick, Saunders, and Best (1997) reported in a prospective longitudinal study that drug use alone or in conjunction with alcohol use at baseline increased the odds of a subsequent assault, even after controlling for prior assault experiences and demographic variables. Falck, Wang, Carlson, and Siegal (2001) found that 62% of the women in their sample who reported heavy drug use reported being the victim of physical attack, and 32% reported being raped since they had initiated the use of crack. Testa and Livingston (2000), after controlling for prior sexual aggression experiences, also found that self-reported alcohol-related problems at baseline increased the odds of sexual aggression victimization experiences 12 months later. Similarly, Greene and Navarro (1998) found that a composite measure of excessive alcohol use and alcohol-related problems predicted subsequent sexual aggression victimization experiences among college students. Other research indicates that a substantial proportion of victims were using substances at the time of sexual assault (Abbey, 2002). However, as Testa (2004) noted in a recent review of the literature on substance use and violence against women, although research clearly has indicated an association between substance use and victimization, it is important to understand the mechanisms underlying these associations.

Lifestyle Factors

Associations

Although there may be some controversy regarding the degree to which lifestyle or routine activity theory actually predicts behavior (Finkelhor & Asdigian, 1996; Miethe & Meier, 1990), proximity to, or association with, offenders at least plays a role in the risk of victimization for both males and females. Thus, if a person hangs out with a rough crowd, he or she might be more likely to engage in riskier behavior compared with how he or she might behave, for example, with a study group. Furthermore, adolescents involved in delinquent activities are at increased risk of both interpersonal and property victimization (Lauritsen, Sampson, & Laub, 1991; Zhang, Welte, & Wieczorek, 2001). Woodward and Fergusson (2000) found from a prospective longitudinal study that male and female adolescents most at risk for physical assault victimization were those who engaged in risk-taking behavior such as drug and alcohol use and violent, property, and other juvenile status offenses and were those involved with the most delinquent peers. The risk of victimization has been related to drug use and criminal offending among adult males and females as well (Lauritsen, Laub, & Sampson, 1992; Placios, Urmann, Newel, & Hamilton, 1999; Woodward & Fergusson, 2000).

High-risk environments, such as bars, parties, and fraternity houses, also contribute to increased risk of victimization (Fagan, 1993; R. Felson, 1997; Harford, Wechsler, & Seibring, 2002; H. Johnson, 1996). Consistent with the scenario presented at the beginning of the chapter, contact with aggressive people is more likely in certain types of environments, such as bars or raves, especially when the particular environment attracts a high number of younger individuals or where competitive or illegal activities are commonplace (Buddie & Parks, 2003). In fact, almost a quarter of victims who experienced violence reported that the incident occurred while they were taking part in a leisure activity away from home (e.g., restaurant, bar) as opposed to participating in other kinds of activities (e.g., at work or school, traveling to or from work or school, running errands; Bureau of Justice Statistics, 2000). For example, Parks and Zetes-Zanatta (1999), in a sample of women who reported drinking in bars, found that about two thirds (63%) of the women in the study reported that moderate physical or sexual assault or severe violence occurred after drinking in a bar and that there was a significant correlation of frequency of bar drinking and severity of bar-related victimization. Schwartz and Pitts (1995) also found that women who went out drinking more often were more likely to report sexual victimization. Fraternities and sororities also have been associated with problem behavior. Larimer, Anderson, Baer, and Marlatt (2000) found that men belonging to fraternities and women belonging to sororities reported more alcohol use, more alcohol-related problems, and greater alcohol-related aggressive behavior than students not involved in the Greek system.

Environmental factors have implications for intimate-partner violence risk as well. When women spend time in certain environments, the likelihood of partnering with an individual from that same environment increases. Thus, if a woman is spending a lot of time in bars drinking or in other high-risk environments, she may be more likely to partner with someone from those environments (Krueger, Moffitt, Caspi, Bleske, & Silva, 1998). There is an overlap of illegal behavior, general violence, and partner violence perpetration (Holtzworth-Munroe & Stuart, 1994; Monson & Langhinrichsen-Rohling, 2002). For example, Moffitt and Caspi (1999) reported that more than half of the men convicted of a violent crime in their sample also perpetrated intimate-partner violence. Thus, spending time in risky environments where other crime may be committed may also increase a woman's vulnerability to stranger, acquaintance, and intimate partner violence victimization.

Exposure to offenders can be increased in ways other than simply being around illegal activities. For example, substance use as well as some mental health problems have been associated with higher risk sexual behavior (J. Anderson, Wilson, Barker, et al., 1999; J. Anderson, Wilson, Doll, Jones, & Barker, 1999; Combs-Lane & Smith, 2002; Morrill, Kasten, Urato, & Larson, 2001). Several other studies have associated high-risk sexual behavior (greater number of partners, more casual "hook-ups") with the increased likelihood of sexual victimization (Arata, 2000; Testa & Dermen, 1999; Tyler, Hoyt, Whitbeck, & Cauce, 2001; Whitbeck, Hoyt, & Yoder, 1999). Tyler et al. (2001) found that young women engaging in *sex exchange*—having sex in exchange for drugs, money, or other necessities, such as a place to stay—were more likely to be victimized than women not engaging in sex exchange. Other research studies have found that the number of partners a woman has had is significantly associated with victimization (Halpern, Oslak, Young, Martin, & Kupper, 2001). High-risk sexual behavior may be associated with increased risk of victimization primarily because of frequency of exposure to potential offenders—the greater the number of sex partners, the increased likelihood of crossing paths with an offender.

Perceived Vulnerability

Potential offenders may perceive women who use or are dependent on a substance to be more vulnerable targets. This perception can result in offenders' making deliberate efforts to get women intoxicated or to take drugs in order to take advantage of them. In other words, it is not simply that an individual is surrounded by others immersed in illegal behavior that necessarily increases risk but that a selection process on the part of the perpetrator may also influence risk of victimization (M. Felson, 1998). Target vulnerability includes offenders' perception of the intoxication of potential victims, social stigma, and lack of credible witnesses. Several factors influence perceived and actual intoxication status. First, certain environments may promote drug or alcohol use. In a national probability sample of adults, H. Klein and Pittman (1989) found that the average amount of beer consumed in a bar was twice that consumed at home. Other research has also found that alcohol consumption at bars or parties is higher than in other contexts (I. Chang, Lapham, & Barton, 1996; Clapp & Shillington, 2001; Jones-Webb et al., 1997; Leeman & Wapner, 2001). As mentioned earlier, fraternity or sorority residence is associated with more frequent and heavier alcohol use for both male and female students than among students not associated with such organizations (Larimer et al., 2000; Sher, Bartholow, & Nanda, 2001). In general, alcohol consumption is thought to be most influenced by the social behavior and the drinking of an individual's primary social group (Marlatt, Baer, & Larimer, 1995).

Alcohol consumption patterns are important, especially within a social context, because individuals who are more intoxicated than a potential assailant may be more likely to be targeted for a crime (Homel, Tomsen, & Thommeny, 1992). In fact, Parks (2000) found that women who experienced bar-related aggression in a 12-week period of time reported that before a bar-related aggressive event, they had drunk more alcohol compared with nights of drinking in a bar when aggression did not occur. Research also indicates that men may view women who are drinking as more sexually available (George, Cue, Lopez, Crowe, & Norris, 1995; George, Gournic, & McAfee, 1988; Seto & Barbaree, 1995). In addition, intoxicated men may be more likely to persist with sexual advances, more likely to ignore cues that indicate women are unwilling, more likely to interpret ambiguous cues as signs of sexual interest, and less able to inhibit aggressive responses (Abbey, Ross, & McDuffie, 1994; Fillmore & Weafer, 2004; Testa & Parks, 1996).

Lifestyle factors also can carry social stigma, which may contribute to increased vulnerability to victimization in that women who engage in risky activities like drug use may be more attractive and less risky targets. For example, women who are heavy drug users may be less willing to call the police than "nonoffender" victims (Sparks, 1982). Even in the general population, the literature documents that women are not likely to report their victimization experiences to the police (Rennison, 2002; Tjaden & Thoennes, 2000b). For example, in a National Violence Against Women survey, only a small proportion of female victims reported intimate partner violence incidents to the police (17.2% of rapes, 26.7% of physical assaults, and 51.9% of stalking were reported; Tjaden & Thoennes, 2000b). The most commonly cited reasons for not reporting interpersonal crime victimization experiences included victims thinking the police would not believe them (7.1% of rape victims, 61.3% of physical assault victims, and 98.2% of stalking victims) or not believing that the police could do anything about the crime (13.2% of rape victims, 99.7% of physical assault victims, and 100% of stalking victims; Tjaden & Thoennes, 2000b). There are similar trends of nonreporting for sexual assault victims as well. One study found only 32% of women who experienced sexual assault had reported the crime to the police (Rennison, 2002).

In addition to the barriers of not reporting interpersonal crimes for women in general, women involved in risky or illicit activities may be even less inclined to report interpersonal victimization out of fear of implicating themselves in criminal behavior. Substance-using victims may also be concerned that the police will not believe their story or will discount their victimization experience, given their risky activities, lifestyle, or drug use (Staton, Leukefeld, & Logan, 2001). Women's perceived stigma of victimization, particularly when lifestyle factors are considered, may increase vulnerability to crimes because they may be less credible complainants or witnesses to their victimization. In fact, substance users who experience interpersonal assaults are stigmatized more for their victimization (Hammock & Richardson, 1997; Ruback, Menard, Outlaw, & Shaffer, 1999). For example, Whatley (1996) conducted a meta-analysis of studies examining characteristics related to victim blaming in rape and found that rape victims with negative characteristics (e.g., high-risk sexual behavior, level of intoxication) were blamed more for the rape than victims without these socially negative characteristics. Abbey (2002) reviewed the literature and concluded that sexual assault victims were more likely to be blamed for their attack if they were intoxicated. Another study found that when college students rated vignettes, more blame was attributed to women experiencing intimate partner violence who had been drinking alcohol than nondrinking victims, and the victims who were drinking were rated as less truthful than victims who had not (Harrison & Esqueda, 2000). Thus, women with riskier lifestyle activities may be at increased risk for victimization because offenders may estimate that their crime is less likely to be reported. Furthermore, women who engage in riskier lifestyle activities may be afraid to report crimes that they have experienced because they fear being blamed for their victimization.

In fact, the fear of social stigma and blame for victimization among women engaged in risky behaviors may be an accurate assessment according to some research.

Perceived vulnerability may also be influenced by the lack of credible witnesses to the crime. For example, walking alone at night in certain environments (e.g., on college campuses, downtown in some cities, or in some neighborhoods) may be termed an unsafe activity (Furby, Fischhoff, & Morgan, 1990). Going to bars or parties alone or with others who are highly intoxicated may also contribute to increased vulnerability because there may be few credible witnesses if a crime were to occur. Substance abusers may be especially vulnerable for this reason. Living in secure surroundings or in settings with environmental protections can reduce the risk of certain types of victimization. In the case of intimate-partner violence, however, being at home could increase risk, given that most intimate partner violence takes place at or near the home (75% of the time) rather than in public places where others can witness the violence, call the police, or in some other way stop the violence (Greenfeld et al., 1998).

Summary of Associations and Perceived Vulnerability

Lifestyle or routine activities theory posits that individuals' lifestyles and daily activities are associated with differential exposure to dangerous people and places, creating the potential for crime opportunities and therefore increasing the likelihood of victimization. Those individuals most involved in illegal drug use, other crime behavior, and violence perpetration are also more likely to be victimized, according to some literature. In addition to proximity, increased exposure (e.g., the greater number of sexual partners) and increased density of offenders can contribute to the likelihood of victimization. Perceived vulnerability (e.g., intoxication level of the victim), social stigma, and lack of credible witnesses may also interact with offender exposure to increase risk.

It is likely that the combination of offender exposure and an individual's perceived vulnerability contribute to the risk of victimization rather than one of these factors alone. One extreme example in which these factors are highlighted is within the homeless population. In general, studies have indicated that homelessness is associated with victimization (Hoyt, Ryan, & Cauce, 1999; Link et al., 1995; Padgett, Struening, Andrews, & Pittman, 1995; Terrell, 1997; Tyler, Hoyt, & Whitbeck, 2000). Homelessness creates an environmental situation that substantially increases the risk of victimization because of four primary factors: (a) homeless individuals may congregate in areas with high densities of low socioeconomic status people who are struggling to meet daily survival needs (close associations with potential offenders), (b) homeless individuals do not have privacy or the protection of private space with locks (target vulnerability), (c) many homeless people need to engage in strategies for survival purposes (e.g., sex exchange) that increase their risk of victimization, and (d) many homeless women use and abuse alcohol and illegal drugs (Bassuk et al., 1997; Fitzpatrick, LaGory, & Ritchey, 1999; Geissler, Bormann, Kwiatkowski, Braucht, & Reichardt, 1995; Nyamathi, Leake, & Gelberg, 2000).

Risk Perceptions

Women who are intoxicated may be more vulnerable targets for offenders, in part because alcohol and drug use may impair cognitive processing that may reduce risk or threat perceptions (Fillmore & Vogel-Sprott, 1999). Risk perceptions may also be compromised because of expectations, which can impair judgment alone or interact with substance use to influence behavior.

Cognitive Impairment

In general, females appear to become more impaired than males after drinking equal amounts of alcohol, because of higher blood alcohol concentrations and a greater sensitivity to alcohol neurotoxicity (Hommer, Momenan, Kaiser, & Rawlings, 2001; Mumenthaler, Taylor, O'Hara, & Yesavage, 1999). It has been demonstrated that alcohol disrupts performance on tasks that require attending to multiple stimuli at the same time as well as performance on tasks requiring prolonged attention to changing stimuli (Fillmore, Dixon, & Schweizer, 2000; Holloway, 1995; Koelega, 1995). In one study, researchers found that although participants who received an alcohol placebo drink and participants who received an alcoholic drink did not differ in response on attention-based tasks before consuming their assigned drink, but they did differ on responses after ingesting their beverages, showing that alcohol was associated with an impaired performance on the task that required the ability to divide attention (Fillmore et al., 2000). In addition, alcohol has been found to impair decision-making processes at fairly low blood alcohol levels (Fillmore et al., 2000; Naranjo & Bremner, 1993; Walls & Brownlie, 1985).

Alcohol has also been shown to have deleterious effects on judgment (Norris, Nurius, & Dimeff, 1996; Peterson, Rothfleisch, Zelazo, & Pihl, 1990; Testa & Parks, 1996). For example, one study found that the recognition of angry facial expressions was reduced at both high and low blood alcohol level conditions compared with a placebo-alcohol condition (Borrill, Rosen, & Summerfield, 1987). Alcohol intoxication may also contribute to sexual risk taking by reducing perceptions of personal risk (Frintner & Rubinson, 1993; Fromme, Katz, & D'Amico, 1997; MacDonald, Zanna, & Fong, 1995). For example, Fromme, D'Amico, and Katz (1999) conducted several experiments to examine the impact of alcohol on sexual risk taking. In one study, participants were assigned to one of three conditions—alcoholic drink, alcohol placebo drink, or a no-alcohol drink. They were asked to complete surveys and then ingested their assigned drinks. After a 20-minute absorption period, participants answered additional questions. Participants who had had the alcoholic beverage reported lower risks associated with unsafe sexual practices compared with participants who had had the placebo and no-alcohol drinks. A second experiment by these same researchers asked participants to list positive and negative consequences of having sex without a condom (Fromme et al., 1999). Although participants listed the same number of positive consequences regardless of which drink they received, participants who drank alcohol listed fewer negative consequences, indicating selective attention to the positive aspects of risky sexual behavior. Other research has indicated that drug and alcohol use impairs impulse inhibition or increases impulsive behavior (Fillmore et al., 2000; Fillmore & Vogel-Sprott, 2000). Another study found that women who had drunk alcohol perceived the behavior of a sexually aggressive man in a story as less forceful and more acceptable than women who had not drunk alcohol (Norris & Kerr, 1993). Thus, intoxicated women may downplay the risks in a specific situation or be more likely to make impulsive decisions that increase their vulnerability to victimization.

Although alcohol has received the most attention with regard to cognitive impairment using experimental conditions, other research has found evidence that drug use, including marijuana, cocaine, and ecstasy, can also impair cognitive processes (McCann, Mertle, Eligulashvili, & Ricaurte, 1999; Pope, Gruber, Hudson, Huestis, & Yurgelun-Todd, 2001; Strickland et al., 1993). For example, researchers found that marijuana users had impaired skills while high from marijuana use as well as from residual effects on attention, memory, and learning between 12 hours and 7 days after last use (Pope et al., 2001; Pope, Gruber, & Yurgelun-Todd, 1995). Cocaine has been associated with paranoid delusions, depression, and compulsive behaviors (M. Gold & Miller, 1997). In addition, Rogers et al. (1999) found that chronic amphetamine or opiate users had difficulty making decisions, especially decisions that involved competing choices. Ecstasy has also been associated with impairment in visual and verbal memory, and the effects appear to be dose related (i.e., the more use, the more impairment; McCann et al., 1999).

Expectancies

Studies have shown that the expectations of the effects of substance use can greatly affect judgment (Fillmore & Vogel-Sprott, 1998). In other words, substance use expectancies—the expectations of what impact alcohol or other drugs will have on behavior or future outcomes—may impact actual behavior. Substance use expectancies are developed from a collection of experiences (prior personal experiences), observations (vicarious learning through parents, peers, television, and movies), and norms (substance-use norms of primary peer groups or specific organizations with which the individual affiliates; Annis & Davis, 1988; M. Goldman, Del Boca, & Darkes, 1999; S. Greenfield et al., 2000). For example, Dermen, Cooper, and Agocha (1998) found from telephone surveys of adolescents that alcohol use was associated with more sexual risk behavior among those who expected alcohol to increase risky sexual behavior, regardless of gender. Similarly, Leigh (1990) reported that individuals with sex-related alcohol expectancies were more likely to initiate sexual activity when drinking than were those without such expectancies. In fact, alcohol may serve as a rationalization or an excuse for sexual behavior that is incongruent with traditional stereotypes about women's sexual behavior (Dermen et al., 1998). One study found that individuals with high sexual expectancies (i.e., individuals who believe that alcohol has a disinhibiting effect on their sexual behavior) reported stronger benefits to engaging in unsafe sex regardless of whether they drank alcohol—suggesting that it may not be the alcohol per se that is influencing behavior but the expectation of what will happen while drinking alcohol

(Fromme et al., 1999). Other research has found that intoxication increases risk-taking behavior and diminishes the perception of threats (Parks & Miller, 1997; Testa & Livingston, 2000). In laboratory studies, alcohol use has impaired social judgment, reaction times, and the ability to integrate multiple sources of information, and these impairments have interacted with alcohol expectancies (Gordon, Carey, & Carey, 1997; Maisto, Galizio, & Connors, 1995).

Alcohol expectancies also interact with the environment. In other words, drinking in an environment such as a bar or party can increase alcohol expectancies for pleasure while decreasing attention to risks in the environment (Wall, McKee, & Hinson, 2000; Wall, McKee, Hinson, & Goldstein, 2001). In general, drinking in social settings typically promotes expectations of pleasure and fun. Women are more likely to report tension-reducing and social outcome expectations than men (Larimer et al., 2000). Thus, women drinking in bars may be more likely to attend to the environmental cues involving socializing and pleasure rather than the incongruent cognitions involving danger and assault (Norris et al., 1996; Nurius & Norris, 1996).

Expectancies for how individuals will or should behave may also affect risk perception. More specifically, Nurius (2000) made the point that women generally report low levels of perceived risk from men they know. Other studies have found that risk factors for sexual assault include being in a casual relationship with the perpetrator (Abbey, 2002; Abbey, McAuslan, Zawacki, Clinton, & Buck, 2001). This perception of low risk may decrease defensive comportment against sexual aggression, especially if substance use is involved. Women not only perceive a low risk of danger from acquaintances, but also, even if faced with sexual aggression from an acquaintance, are unlikely to use extreme physical or verbal resistance to the aggression (Hickman & Muehlenhard, 1997; Norris et al., 1996). These authors also speculated that part of the reason women have low risk perceptions with acquaintances is that women are expected to have dual cognitions in social situations. That is, in social situations with traditional sex-role stereotypes, women dress and act in a sexy manner to attract men. At the same time, they must protect themselves from exploitation by the very men whom they may be trying to attract. When substances are used, it may be even more difficult to divide one's attention between these competing goals. A recent study by K. Davis, George, and Norris (2004) tested this premise. Intoxicated women in their study, compared with women who were not intoxicated, were more likely to report that they would consent or respond passively to a dating partner's sexual advances if they wanted to have a relationship with that partner, even if they did not wish to engage in sexual activities. This dual cognitive focus may also contribute to situational ambiguity in that offenders under the influence may understand the flirting but miss the "not so fast" cues.

Expectancies on the part of men must also be considered. For example, intoxicated men may be more focused on their immediate sexual arousal than on cues such as a woman's discomfort or the negative consequences of their actions (Abbey, Zawacki, Buck, Clinton, & McAuslan, 2001). In general, research has indicated that men report greater expectations of sexual and aggressive outcomes from drinking (Larimer et al., 2000). W. George et al. (1995) found that men with higher alcohol expectancies for social behavior attributed more sexual responding to women drinking alcohol than to women drinking soda;

however, men who reported low alcohol expectancies rated the sexual responses of the women similarly, regardless of what the women were drinking. It is interesting to note that women in this particular study did not make any differential attributions about sexual responses on the basis of what the target woman was drinking. Wilson, Calhoun, and McNair (2002) found that men who reported a history of sexual coercion also reported more alcohol consumption and alcohol expectancies about sexual behavior. There was, however, an interactive effect, in that men with the highest alcohol consumption and highest alcohol expectancies were more likely to self-report sexually coercive behavior toward women. Bouffard (2002) noted that "self-reported sexual arousal was found to increase the likelihood of engaging in sexual coercion and also increased subjects' perceptions of sexual pleasure as a currently important benefit" (p. 121). This researcher concluded that offender mood or arousal may influence decision making. It may be that alcohol increases the likelihood that friendliness will be misinterpreted, consequently encouraging men to become more sexually aroused and aggressive, whereas women are not necessarily aware of these cues (Abbey, 2002; Abbey et al., 1994; Abbey, Ross, McDuffie, & McAuslan, 1996).

Another factor to consider is that men and women tend to have stereotypic gender beliefs about the effects of alcohol on behavior (Abbey, McAuslan, Ross, & Zawacki, 1999). Abbey et al. (1999) found that men and women rated men as being more aggressive and having an increased sexual drive while drinking, whereas women were rated as having increased sexual feelings and increased vulnerability to sexual coercion when drinking. Gender-role expectations may lead to misinterpretations of cues because "these beliefs reinforce stereotypes of men having uncontrollable sexual urges and women being more appropriate targets for sexual aggression" (Abbey et al., 1999, p. 181). In fact, Abbey et al. (1996) found evidence that the frequency of self-reported past friendly behavior being misinterpreted as sexual was positively related to experiencing sexual assault for women in their study. Both men and women have reported that sexual aggression is likely in certain situations, such as when a woman "leads a man on" or when the use of drugs or alcohol is involved (S. Cook, 1995). Male and female expectations of sexual aggression in certain situations may reduce the likelihood of assertive refusals, as well as correctly perceived refusals, and thus may increase the risk of assault.

Summary of Risk Perceptions

Substance use and expectancies seem to exert a strong influence on judgment and behavior. The interaction of expectations with reduced cognitive ability likely works to reduce one's ability to recognize danger cues while drinking or using drugs.

Summary

Sara, whose case we described at the beginning of the chapter, was clearly in a risky situation. She was alone, intoxicated, and in an environment where a number of individuals were likely engaging in criminal behavior (e.g., distribution of illicit drugs). She also may have been particularly vulnerable to the impact of ecstasy and alcohol on her cognitive functioning as well as her expectations. She clearly had positive expectancies of drug and alcohol use. Partying helped to offset the negative feelings she had about her job. She wanted "her night out," and these very expectancies may have been a part of her risk for victimization. Her judgment clouded by stimulants, her mind focused on "having a good time," and the presence of predatory men combined to increase her situational risk.

This chapter has reviewed research on three selected lifestyle factors: associations, perceived vulnerability, and risk perception. Substance use is a particularly important factor in lifestyle risk because of the high overlap of substance use with each of the selected lifestyle factors reviewed. Substance abuse increases vulnerability to victimization in multiple ways. Heavy substance use often leads to lifestyles that place women with people who are more likely to be criminals or high-risk sex partners, and substance use decreases a woman's judgment about high-risk situations and impairs decision making. Furthermore, heavy substance use can be perceived by potential offenders as an invitation to sexual activity and the perception of being "willing" (i.e., open to sexual advances). Some researchers have expressed concern that examination of how lifestyle factors contribute to victimization blames the victim. The findings reviewed in this chapter and elsewhere in this book do not support this simplistic understanding of risk factors among women. Instead, a complex pattern of interactions is associated with increased risk for certain women.

Strengths and Weaknesses in the Literature

This chapter has focused on selected lifestyle factors that can contribute to increased risk for victimization or revictimization. The literature on lifestyle factors provides important findings for clinicians, researchers, and educators in understanding the complexities of victimization among women. Although much has been learned over the past decade about the contribution of lifestyles to victimization and revictimization, several gaps exist in the literature. First, some have criticized lifestyle or routine activities theory, and research seeking to support it has had mixed findings (Moriarty & Williams, 1996; Mustaine, 1997; Rodgers & Roberts, 1995). The most significant criticism of this theory has involved the idea that many individuals who are victimized (e.g., children) do not have the lifestyle or routine activities that would put them at risk (Finkelhor & Asdigian, 1996). This criticism is moderated, however, if lifestyle is understood to be a contributing factor, rather than a causal factor, of victimization. It is critical to distinguish between proximate causes, which in Sara's case included attending a rave and being alone in the presence of sexually predatory men, and intentional causes, which focus on what Sara was seeking through her activities. Lifestyles can increase risk, but they are not, of themselves, causes of victimization. Theories integrating the various lifestyle factors that contribute to risk of victimization need to be developed.

On a smaller scale, research examining the associations of mental health functioning with lifestyle factors is almost nonexistent. This represents an obstacle to understanding lifestyle factors for women with victimization experiences. Women who are depressed or have posttraumatic stress symptoms and use drugs or alcohol may have different levels of cognitive impairment and different expectancies—and different interactions between these two factors—compared with women who do not have these mental health problems. Understanding the mental health manifestations of victimization and the impact they have on cognition and lifestyle is critical to understanding the factors that contribute to women's risk of further victimization, substance use, and mental health problems. Many studies have examined these factors independently, but research must begin to assimilate these factors to identify the lifestyle context of victimization. Also, it may be important to examine the impact of alcohol and other drugs on decision making in social contexts more generally, as well as to examine the impact of social environment on alcohol or drug-taking behavior for women with and without victimization histories.

Research on victimization experiences often has lacked important details. Specifically, there are gaps in the research regarding the timing of victimization, victimization type, multiple experiences, frequency and severity of experiences, perpetrator type, and specific pathways between lifestyle factors or victimization. For example, examining child, adolescent, and adult victimization separately, examining type of victimization (e.g., psychological, sexual, or physical), and examining perpetrator characteristics (e.g., stranger, acquaintance, or intimate partner) may yield different results compared with studies that treat victimization as a simple dichotomy (i.e., victimization–no victimization or victim–perpetrator). In addition, there may be an important difference between women with multiple abuse and trauma histories and women with single-incident victimization in regard to impaired decision making and expectancies.

Conclusion

The research review in this chapter builds on the model presented in chapters 1 and 2, allowing the reader to appreciate the complexity of the precursors to and sequelae of victimization. Specifically, this chapter reviewed the literature on the ways that associations, perceptions of vulnerability, and risk perceptions can contribute to an increased risk for victimization (see Figure 3.1).

The case of Sara at the beginning of the chapter illustrates the potential for these factors to contribute to the increased risk of victimization. However, Sara's internal world consisted of complex issues, thoughts, perceptions, and difficulties that may not be apparent to others (as the quotation from Wittgenstein suggests). This "internal storm" may have affected her judgment and behavior. There is no evidence that victims enter into a given lifestyle with an understanding or awareness of how "choices" are contributing to increased risk. In fact, the opposite is probably the case. Certain factors such as prior victimization—particularly early childhood victimization—and mental health problems and substance abuse appear to diminish the appreciation of risk in social circumstances, thus contributing to the risk for revictimization. Sara's case study

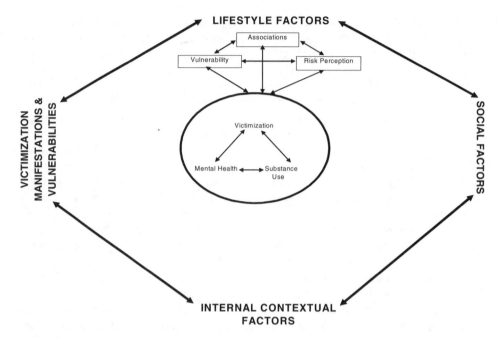

Figure 3.1. Conceptual model of factors contributing to victimization, mental health, and substance use: lifestyle factors.

exemplifies how substance use and its attendant social patterns put persons in situations where victimization is more likely.

Although an association between risky environments and victimization has been established, this remains an area needing further study. Even with the gaps we have identified, there are important implications for clinical and social service professionals who provide services to victims. For example, Sara should be assessed for substance abuse as well as for other lifestyle factors that may increase her risk. A clinician worried about blaming the victim might avoid exploring Sara's lifestyle factors for fear of making her feel guilty for her own rape. Yet as we have seen in this chapter, to ignore factors that could influence Sara's risk for revictimization would be a mistake. Her safety may depend on direct attention to her substance-use patterns and the lifestyle factors associated with her drug use.

The next chapter expands our conceptual model. We will examine social factors that may interact with victimization manifestations, vulnerabilities, and lifestyle factors to contribute to victimization, mental health, and substance abuse among women.

4 _____

Social Factors

The Case of Maria G.

Roberto and Maria have been married for 6 years. They lived with Roberto's parents when they were first married. During that time, Maria witnessed several acts of violence between Roberto's parents, and Roberto disclosed to Maria that his father had abused his mother throughout his childhood.

Soon after they moved out of his parents' home, Roberto began to be emotionally abusive to Maria. After this had gone on for a while, he became physically abusive. Maria left Roberto and, being unemployed with a young child, she went on welfare. Soon after, she began working with her caseworker on finding a job so she could get off welfare. She was living in subsidized housing, and her apartment was upstairs from her mother and four of Maria's siblings who still lived at home.

Maria was struggling to live independently from Roberto and from her mother, but she had not finished high school and was having difficulty locating employment and day care for her 5-year-old daughter. Maria turned to her mother for support when she separated from Roberto, but her mother told her that she had also suffered violence from two husbands and that Maria should expect no better.

Maria began wavering in her resolve to stay separated. She was feeling particularly vulnerable after witnessing the murder of a homeless woman on the streets of her neighborhood. She had also witnessed several incidents of violence against women by their boyfriends.

At her last appointment, Maria broke down and disclosed to her caseworker that Roberto was stalking her and that she was afraid he would try to kill her. She also disclosed that most of her friends were smoking marijuana heavily and admitted that she had been using marijuana and alcohol to help her "get through the day." She was feeling particularly distressed because she believed there was no avenue of escape from her circumstances.

*   *   *

In classical sociological theory, individual behaviors are understood in the context of the relationships of individuals to their social environments (Ritzer, 1999). Weisstein's (1971) comment highlights the need for integrating individual and social perspectives: "The . . . reason for psychology's failure to understand what people are and how they act is that psychology has looked for inner traits when it should have been looking for social context" (p. 2). In the same vein, Milgram (1974) stated that "the social psychology of this century reveals a major lesson: often it is not so much the kind of person a man is as the kind of situation in which he finds himself that determines how he will act" (p. 205).

An understanding of victimization experiences and responses requires examination of both internal psychological factors and a multitude of social factors that affect individuals and groups in similar ways. Parsons (1951) suggested that individuals and their social environments are interactive and that it is the interaction that forms the essential structure of the social system. Parsons hypothesized that the cultural system mediates the values and norms within which individual actions are conceived, whereas the social system consists of a group of individuals interacting within environments. More contemporary philosophy also emphasizes the importance of sociocultural factors and their role in shaping behavior as well as the complex interactions of the individual personalities within specific cultures or social environments (Modell, 1996). Although social factors such as socioeconomic status and social environment can serve as protective factors against the risk of victimization as well as in coping with victimization experiences (Diener, Oishi, & Lucas, 2003; Hobfall, Freedy, Green, & Solomon, 1996; Tiet et al., 1998), they can also contribute to increased risk of victimization, mental health problems, and substance use.

Social factors, particularly socioeconomic status, social environment, and perceived options, may contribute to women's risk of victimization beyond psychological, biological, and lifestyle factors. Socioeconomic status is associated with victimization, physical health, mental health, and substance use. Researchers have suggested several possible pathways for the association of socioeconomic status and social outcomes that are discussed here. These hypothesized pathways will provide readers with a better foundation for understanding the effect of socioeconomic status on physical health, mental health, substance use, and risk for victimization. Social environment factors are discussed next, including family of origin, neighborhoods, and social norms. Finally, the link between social factors and limited resources, taxed reserve capacity, and future expectations are examined along with their importance to increased vulnerability of mental health, victimization, and substance use. Consistent with the premise that has been articulated throughout the book, the social factors described here interact with all the other factors in complex ways, and although this chapter shows how social factors contribute to increased risk of mental health, victimization, and substance use, they are not entirely independent of the individual-level factors discussed in earlier chapters.

Socioeconomic Status

Low socioeconomic status has been associated with a number of adverse social outcomes for women. Findings relevant here are associations with victimization, physical and mental health problems, substance abuse, and limited access to treatment or services for these problems (Scott Collins et al., 1999; Substance Abuse and Mental Health Services Administration [SAMHSA], 1997, 2000; U.S. Department of Justice, 1997). The association of low socioeconomic status with negative outcomes, such as physical and mental health problems, is generally linear. In other words, lower socioeconomic status is related to decreased physical and mental health functioning (E. Goodman, 1999; Marmot et al., 1998; Marmot, Ryff, Bumpass, Shipley, & Marks, 1997). This chapter uses the term *socioeconomic status* with the recognition that research results are generally consistent across three typical socioeconomic indicators: education, income, and occupation (Gallo & Matthews, 2003; Marmot et al., 1998).

Socioeconomic Status and Victimization

In early literature on violence against women, an association was established between partner violence and poverty; revisionist feminist perspectives reminded policy makers that middle- and upper class women were affected as well. This led to a widely held belief among some advocates that partner violence victimization was equally prevalent among all women regardless of socioeconomic status. However, more recent research has shown that women with the lowest household incomes are far more likely to be victims of all kinds of violence, including sexual assault and intimate partner violence (U.S. Department of Justice, 1997), and that women on welfare have reported high rates of victimization in the past (50% and 60%) as well as recently (20%–30%; Bassuk, Browne, & Buckner, 1996; Brookes & Buckner, 1996; Browne & Bassuk, 1997; Lyon, 1997; Tolman & Raphael, 2000). By comparison, in the general and clinical populations, between 22% and 41% of women have reported a lifetime history of physical or sexual assault by an intimate partner, and between 1% and 17% have reported past-year rates of physical or sexual assault by an intimate partner (Richardson et al., 2002; Tjaden & Thoennes, 2000b; Wilt & Olson, 1996). Another study found that women with the lowest incomes were almost 7 times more likely to be victims of intimate violence than women in households with the highest annual incomes (U.S. Department of Justice, 2000). Byrne, Resnick, Kilpatrick, Best, and Saunders (1999) analyzed data from a large household telephone survey (N = 2,863) conducted with 1-year follow-ups and found that socioeconomic levels were significantly associated with risk of new victimization.

Socioeconomic Status and Physical Health, Mental Health, and Substance Use

Lower socioeconomic status has been associated with higher rates of physical and mental health problems (Dohrenwend et al., 1992; E. Goodman, 1999; Kessler et al., 1994; Mulatu & Schooler, 2002). Individuals in higher socioeconomic groups tend to have fewer physical health problems and live longer than individuals in lower socioeconomic status groups (Adler & Snibbe, 2003; Buka, 2002; Gallo & Mathews, 2003). Similar trends exist for mental health as well. For example, Gallo and Mathews (2003) reviewed the literature and found strong support for the association of lower socioeconomic status and depression. More specifically, one survey study found that low-income women were at greater risk for depressive symptoms and a diagnosis of depression or anxiety than higher income women (Scott Collins et al., 1999).

Although there is not overwhelming evidence that lower socioeconomic status groups use more drugs or alcohol than others, some research has indicated that socioeconomic status is associated with negative health behaviors such as smoking and other substance use (D'Onofrio, 1997; E. Goodman & Huang, 2002). For example, the National Household Survey on Drug Abuse found a positive correlation between lower education and employment status with greater illicit drug use (SAMHSA, 2001a). Other studies have reported that drug use is more common among welfare recipients than nonrecipients (Delva, Neumark, Furr, & Anthony, 2000; Pollack, Danziger, Seefeldt, & Jayakody, 2002; L. Schmidt & McCarty, 2000). Also, employment problems have been associated with drug use (J. Bachman, Wadsworth, O'Malley, Johnson, & Schulenbarg, 1997; Bray, Zarkin, Dennis, & French, 2000; R. Bryant, Samaranyake, & Wilhite, 2000; Montoya, Bell, Atkinson, Nagy, & Whitsett, 2002), whereas stable employment has been associated with decreased relapse episodes and increased substance abuse treatment retention (Wolkstein & Spiller, 1998). Although it is not clear exactly why socioeconomic status is associated with outcomes related to physical health, mental health, and victimization, the next section reviews some hypothesized reasons.

Several theories have been developed to explain the association between socioeconomic status and physical and mental health, including selection or drift theory, social causation, and indirect selection theory. Many chapters in this book do not include theories to explain the relationship between various factors; however, the concepts of socioeconomic status and physical and mental health are broad and conceptual, and they include many mediating factors. Conceptual and theoretical backgrounds are essential as a framework for understanding the various associations.

Hollingshead and Redlich (1964) pioneered the idea of social drift theory to explain the higher prevalence of mental disorders among lower socioeconomic groups. Their theory included the notion that severe mental disorder leads to decreased employment, reduced economic status, and thus a "drift" into lower socioeconomic areas of a community (Hollingshead & Redlich, 1964, 1993). In other words, according to the selection or drift hypothesis, individuals select into or drift into certain environments because of their physical or mental health status (Dohrenwend et al., 1998). For example, a woman who becomes severely depressed may not be able to hold a job and may be forced to live in lower income housing and impoverished conditions. Persons with disabilities might cluster in areas where there are halfway houses, clinics, and public transportation. In addition, certain disorders such as depression can have both direct and indirect impacts on work productivity (W. Stewart, Ricci, Chee, Hahn, & Morganstein, 2003). For example, the American Productivity Audit found that workers with depression had an average of 5.6 hours per week of lost productivity, with 48% of the lost time directly because of depression, thus showing an interaction of mental health factors, employment, and potential earnings loss (W. Stewart et al., 2003).

The social causation hypothesis posits that poverty includes adverse environmental circumstances that are stressful, and stress levels are associated with physical and mental health problems (Dohrenwend et al., 1998; Evans & Kantrowitz, 2002). For example, a single mother may have difficulty affording housing and basic necessities for herself and her children. Thus, she may need to live in a disadvantaged neighborhood and use public transportation, and she may have difficulty finding gainful employment and day care. Such problems are likely to increase her levels of stress, which, as described in chapter 2, may then contribute to a host of physical and mental health problems. In addition, her stress and poverty levels may interfere with a healthy diet, sleeping adequately, and being able to obtain medical care for herself and her children. In general, poverty has been related to chronic stress because of the amount of time and effort needed to meet the basic demands of living in addition to the stress of living with higher crime rates, greater perceived threat of crime, poor transportation, limited recreational facilities, overcrowding, lower standards of housing, and greater exposure to physical hazards such as noise and air and water pollutants (Evans & Kantrowitz, 2002; S. Taylor, Repetti, & Seeman, 1997).

Marmot et al. (1997) discussed another explanation, the indirect selection hypothesis, for the association of socioeconomic status with physical and mental health problems. According to this hypothesis, family background, including socioeconomic status, affects the social circumstances of adults, which impacts health. For example, individuals born into poverty who develop depression may have difficulty escaping that environment if their mental health problems keep them from obtaining or maintaining employment. This conclusion is related to "cycle of poverty" perceptions that often prevail in society. In fact, family-of-origin factors can affect the physical and mental health of offspring (Maccoby, 2000; McLoyd, 1998). In support of the indirect selection hypothesis, Leventhal and Brooks-Gunn (2000) reviewed the literature and found that children and adolescents living in low-income neighborhoods had more adverse mental health, criminal and delinquent behavior, lower achievement and educational attainment, and higher risk sexual behavior compared with counterparts in higher income neighborhoods. Gilman, Kawachi, Fitzmaurice, and Buka (2002) prospectively followed a birth cohort for 29 years and found that children who lived in poverty during the first 7 years of life had a greater risk of depression in adulthood, even after controlling for maternal age and single-parent status at birth, gender, race and ethnicity, family history of mental illness, age at adult interview, and adult socioeconomic status. It is likely that early family environment factors such as socioeconomic status have a lifelong impact on health or mental health problems.

Summary of Socioeconomic Status

Low socioeconomic status appears to be related to higher risk of victimization and physical and mental health problems. Various theories hypothesize that (a) individuals select or drift into lower socioeconomic status because of physical or mental health problems, (b) socioeconomic environments increase the risk for physical or mental health problems, and (c) early childhood experiences of low socioeconomic status affect later adult socioeconomic status as well as physical and mental health status. It may be that individuals living in lower socioeconomic conditions have higher stress levels and reduced access to resources—both of which affect physical and mental health status. These individuals may also be more likely to engage in risk behaviors such as substance use to cope with physical or mental health problems or as an escape from their daily stress-ful lives.

Social Environment

As the case at the beginning of this chapter exemplifies, social environments have a significant impact on people's lives. Violence was present in Maria's family of origin, and she witnessed violence as a daily part of life in her neighborhood. In addition, it is likely that both her lack of employment opportunities and her social environment contributed to her feelings of being trapped. The next section examines research on how the social environment may increase vulnerability to victimization and substance use through family-of-origin experiences, neighborhood environment, and social norms.

Family-of-Origin Environment

Repetti, Taylor, and Seeman (2002) concluded from a review of the literature that "childhood family environments represent vital links for understanding mental and physical health across the lifespan" (p. 330). One of these important links is that the social learning that takes place in the family-of-origin environment can influence risk for victimization, substance abuse, and other risk behaviors. Family-of-origin factors can create conditions that contribute to problem behavior in adulthood through several pathways, including socialization, family management styles (e.g., family supervision, family communication patterns, and parent–child relations), and adverse environmental circumstances (Chilcoat & Anthony, 1996; R. Johnson, Hoffman, & Gerstein, 1996; McLoyd, 1998; Wills & Yaeger, 2003).

SOCIALIZATION. Socialization includes social learning from family and parental modeling of behaviors such as partner relations. For example, parental divorce and offspring divorce rates have been positively correlated (Amato, 1996; Amato & Booth, 1991; Wolfinger, 1999, 2000, 2001). In addition, research has found associations among family-of-origin characteristics and entry into parenthood, attitudes toward marriage, conflict resolution styles, and other relationship dynamic outcomes (Amato & DeBoer, 2001; Barber, 2000; Conger, Cui, Bryant, & Elder, 2000; Furstenberg & Weiss, 2000; Levy, Wamboldt, & Fiese, 1997). One recent study found, from husband and wife self-reports of family-of-origin experiences and marital adjustment, that compared with husbands, the wives' family-of-origin experiences were more strongly related to both their own reported marital adjustment and their husbands' reported marital adjustment (Sabatelli & Bartle-Haring, 2003).

In a review of the literature, Carlson (2000) estimated that approximately 10% to 20% of children each year witness intimate partner violence and that as many as 33% may be exposed to parental violence at some point in their childhood. In fact, as many as two thirds of children in violent families actually witness (either see or hear) violence between their parents (G. Holden, Geffner,

& Jouriles, 1998; Hotton, 2001; Hutchison & Hirschel, 2001). Witnessing parental violence is associated with negative outcomes in adulthood (Edleson, 1999; G. Holden et al., 1998; H. Hughes, 1988). McNeal and Amato (1998) found that parents' self-reports of partner violence occurring when their children were between 11 and 19 years old predicted offspring reports of negative psychological and relationship status in early adulthood (23 years old on average). These negative outcomes included poorer parent–child relationships, lower psychological well-being, and more violence within their own relationships, independent of factors such as nonviolent parental conflict, divorce, child abuse, and substance abuse (McNeal & Amato, 1998).

Substance use by family members, parents, or siblings significantly increases the chance that other family members will also use substances (Biederman, Faraone, Monuteaux, & Feighener, 2000; Denton & Kampfe, 1994; Schuckit, 1992; Windle, 2000). Parental behavior and attitudes toward substance use have been significantly associated with substance-use attitudes and expectancies of their children (Brody, Ge, Katz, & Arias, 2000; C. Jackson, Henriksen, & Dickinson, 1999). In addition, White, Johnson, and Buyske (2000) found that parental modeling of alcohol use made a larger contribution to their children's alcohol use than parenting style. Biederman et al. (2000) found that although exposure to parental substance use at an early age did not have a significant impact on later substance use by children, parental substance use during adolescence was associated with a threefold risk of substance use by these children when they became adults. In addition to modeling substance use, parents may also influence their children by modeling antisocial attitudes, such as failure to disapprove of drug use, and by neglecting to teach children critical social and academic skills (Finn et al., 1997; Rutter, 1987, 1990; SAMHSA, 2001b; Zucker, Ellis, Fitzgerald, Bingham, & Sanford, 1996). Furthermore, access to alcohol and drugs is increased when it is present in the home, thus potentially increasing children's use of substances (C. Jackson et al., 1999).

FAMILY MANAGEMENT. Family management styles socialize behavior more by negligence than by overt modeling of negative behavior or through abuse. Family risk factors can be grouped into three main areas: family supervision, family communication patterns, and parent–child relations. Family supervision includes not only actual supervision practices, but also family composition, which affects supervision because of the number of parents available to relate to children. In other words, family composition—most notably the single-parent family structure—may contribute to adolescent drug use in several ways, including less available supervision and even neglect, which have both been associated with increased risk of problem behaviors (Chassin, Curran, Hussong, & Colder, 1996; Chilcoat & Anthony, 1996; Garis, 1998; Jenkins & Zunguze, 1998; R. Johnson et al., 1996). Single parents often have limited incomes, time, and resources to assist with child care and support (Amato, 1999; McLanahan & Booth, 1989). Limited parental supervision may also mean that children have more unstructured time to engage in delinquent activities, whereas more supervision can increase school performance and commitment to educational outcomes (Heymann, 2000). For example, studies have found that girls in single-parent families have an increased risk of delinquent behavior, including substance use (S. Duncan, Duncan, Strycker, & Chaumeton, 2002; Griffin, Botvin, Scheier, Diaz, & Miller, 2000; McKnight & Loper, 2002) and teen pregnancy (B. Miller, 2002; B. Miller, Benson, & Galbraith, 2001).

Other family-of-origin patterns that are associated with adolescent drug abuse include negative communication patterns, inconsistent and unclear behavior limits, unrealistic parental expectations, and ineffective discipline patterns (Denton & Kampfe, 1994; Kosterman, Hawkins, Guo, Catalano, & Abbott, 2000). For example, research has found that lax, inconsistent, or harsh discipline; high levels of negative reinforcement; failure to set clear rules with consequences; and excessive unrealistic expectations of or demands on a child have been associated with drug use (G. Barnes, 1990; D. Jones & Houts, 1990; M. Marshall & Chassin, 2000; S. Stewart, 1996). Other studies have reported that the lack of family cohesion, parent–child conflict, and the lack of maternal involvement are related to drug initiation and use (Bray, Adams, Getz, & Baer, 2001; Brook, Cohen, Whiteman, & Gordon, 1992; T. Duncan, Duncan, & Hops, 1994; Pillow, Barrera, & Chassin, 1998; Wills & Yaeger, 2003). Also, negative parent–child conflict and communication have been associated with risk behavior such as associating with delinquent peers and running away from home, which may increase the risk of victimization (Agnew, 1991; Hays & Revetto, 1990; Ringwalt, Greene, & Robertson, 1998).

ADVERSE ENVIRONMENTAL CIRCUMSTANCES. Another hypothesized pathway through which family-of-origin factors are thought to influence adult functioning is adverse childhood circumstances. Children who live in extreme poverty or who are abused may be more vulnerable to negative adult outcomes. Familial patterns play a major role in socializing children into patterns similar to those learned or modeled in the family of origin.

Family-of-origin poverty levels have been associated with adolescent and adult outcomes such as educational attainment, delinquency in adolescence, and mental health (G. Duncan, Yeung, Brooks-Gunn, & Smith, 1998; Jarjoura, Triplett, & Brinker, 2002; Schoon, Sacker, & Bartley, 2003). G. Duncan et al. (1998) found support for the notion that poverty in the family of origin during early childhood was associated with a lower likelihood of school completion. In this study, poverty levels in middle childhood and adolescence were found to negatively influence college attendance, which can affect later adult socioeconomic status and, in turn, health and mental health status. Schoon et al. (2003) hypothesized that parental socioeconomic status at birth influences the child's behavioral adjustment, which has detrimental, cumulative, and persistent effects on later adjustment. In addition, poverty levels of single-parent families can impact parental stress and coping, thus affecting parenting behavior and increasing the likelihood of maladjustment in children (McLoyd, 1990; McLoyd, Jayaratne, Ceballo, & Borquez, 1994).

Adverse childhood circumstances, in addition to poverty levels, can also influence adult outcomes. Parental violence overlaps child abuse in 30% to 60% of cases, and child abuse has been associated with negative outcomes in adulthood, including mental health problems, substance abuse, and increased risk for revictimization (McCloskey, Figueredo, & Koss, 1995; National Research Council, 1993; S. Ross, 1996). Women with child victimization histories have more symptoms of posttraumatic stress disorder (PTSD), depression, and other mental health problems, and these mental health problems tend to have early onset (Arata, 1999a, 1999b; Briere, 1988; Briere & Runtz, 1987, 1988; S. Gold, Sinclair, & Balge, 1999). Putnam's (2003) literature review found that child sexual abuse was a significant risk factor for adult depression and substance abuse. Wilsnack, Vogeltanz, Klassen, and Harris (1997), using a large, nationally representative sample of women, found that women with childhood sexual abuse histories were significantly more likely to report recent alcohol use, recent alcohol intoxication, alcohol-related problems, alcohol dependence symptoms, and illicit drug use than women who did not report child sexual abuse. R. Duncan, Saunders, Kilpatrick, Hanson, and Resnick (1996) found in their nationally representative sample that women who reported serious childhood physical assault were significantly more likely to report abusing prescription drugs, illegal drugs, and alcohol as adults than women who did not report such assaults. Polusny and Follett (1995) conducted a review of the literature and found that in general, female victims of childhood sexual abuse were more likely to become alcohol abusers and alcoholics at some point in their lives (27%–37%) compared with women who were not victims of child sexual abuse (4%–20%); 14% of women sexually abused as children developed drug-related problems compared with 3% to 12% of women who were not abused. In addition, research has indicated that women who reported early victimization are also more likely to report initiating drug and alcohol use at an earlier age (R. Duncan et al., 1996; Kilpatrick et al., 2000). Initiating substance use at an early age has been identified as a major risk factor for the later development of substance abuse and dependence disorders (Hawkins, Catalano, & Miller, 1992; Hawkins et al., 1997; Rutter, 1990; Werner & Smith, 1992). Studies also have indicated that women with child abuse experiences are more likely to report sexual assault and intimate partner violence in adulthood than are women without such experiences (DiLillo, Giuffre, Tremblay, & Peterson, 2001; Elliott, Mok, & Briere, 2004; Gilbert, El-Bassel, Schilling, & Friedman, 1997; Tjaden & Thoennes, 2000a). Hence, childhood exposure to abusive family-of-origin environments may result in increased risk of adult victimization, mental health, and substance abuse.

In addition, it is probably rare to find children with child abuse experiences who did not also experience other adverse family-of-origin problems. For example, as noted earlier, interparental violence and child abuse overlap, and growing up in a violent home with either or both of these problems may be associated with adult-partner-violence victimization among women (Stith et al., 2000). One study of children 18 years old or younger found no significant differences in psychosocial outcomes (e.g., mental health, social competence, aggression, and academic) among children witnessing interparental violence, children who were physically abused, and children who experienced both witnessing parental violence and child abuse (Kitzmann, Gaylord, Holt, & Kenny, 2003). On the other hand, Ehrensaft et al. (2003) followed a sample of more than 500 children for 20 years and found that exposure to interparental violence posed the greatest independent risk for experiencing partner violence themselves, controlling for child abuse, punishment style of parents, conduct disorder, and demographic factors.

Other research has found that experiencing both interparental violence and child abuse may be more associated with adjustment problems than experiencing only one condition. For example, Pelcovitz, Kaplan, DeRosa, Mandel, and Salzinger (2000) found that adolescents who experienced both child abuse and interparental violence were at greater risk for depression, anxiety, and PTSD than adolescents who experienced child abuse without interparental violence or adolescents who experienced neither. Finally, different outcomes may be linked to different childhood adversities. For example, Maker and Kemmelmeier (1998) found that young women who reported witnessing parental violence reported more violence in dating relationships; more antisocial behaviors; and more mental health problems, including depression. When sexual abuse was examined in conjunction with witnessing parental violence, however, the authors concluded that although mental health problems in adulthood were more strongly associated with childhood sexual abuse, witnessing parental violence was also related to adult partner victimization.

Additionally, violence in the family of origin is associated with substance use and abuse in the family of origin—that is, according to some limited research, the more alcohol and drug abuse in the family, the higher the likelihood of child abuse and family violence (Bays, 1990; Feig, 1990). Furthermore, the more family risk factors, the more negative outcomes there will be for children (Bagley & Mallick, 2000; Evans & English, 2002). For example, Yama, Fogas, Teegarden, and Hastings (1993) found that women who experienced childhood sexual abuse in addition to parental alcoholism had more mental health problems than women who experienced either child sexual abuse or parental alcoholism alone.

Neighborhoods

Research indicates that individuals in low-income neighborhoods have lower mental health functioning (Boardman, Finch, Ellison, Williams, & Jackson, 2001; Hendryx & Ahern, 1997) and more stress as well as health problems (D. Cohen et al., 2000; Malmstrom, Sundquist, & Johansson, 1999). In fact, a few studies examined the impact of neighborhoods on families by randomly assigning families to move to a similar neighborhood, to a neighborhood with higher income indices, or to stay in the same neighborhood and then comparing health, mental health, and other outcome indices (L. Katz, Kling, & Liebman, 2001; Ludwig, Duncan, & Hirschfield, 2001; Rosenbaum, Reynolds, & Deluca, 2002). Preliminary results indicated that households moving to higher income neighborhoods experienced increased feelings of safety, less distress, better health among household heads, fewer behavior problems among boys, and reduced criminal behavior by adolescents in those families (Katz et al., 2001; Leventhal & Brooks-Gunn, 2003a, 2003b; Ludwig et al., 2001). Another study found that when families moved to higher income neighborhoods, they had more perceived control over their lives and felt safer than families who moved to lower income neighborhoods (Rosenbaum et al., 2002). Leventhal and Brooks-Gunn (2003a) summarized the importance of the neighborhood context: "Evidence from randomized experiments, studies employing advanced statistical models, and longitudinal studies controlling for family characteristics indicates that neighborhoods, and particularly their socioeconomic compositions, do matter" (p. 30). Although these authors were specifically referring to child and adolescent outcomes, neighborhood characteristics have also been linked to adult outcomes (Ross & Mirowsky, 2001).

Neighborhoods may influence adult health and mental health outcomes for several reasons. In general, neighborhood context has been associated with increased risk of victimization by both partners and nonpartners (Lauritsen & White, 2001). For example, a study of emergency room visits found that neighborhood characteristics were associated with the risk of violent injuries from both partner and nonpartner perpetrators (Grisso et al., 1999). Other studies have found that economically deprived areas of a community have higher rates of intimate partner violence than wealthier areas (Benson, Fox, DeMaris, & Van Wyk, 2000; Cunradi, Caetano, Clark, & Schafer, 2000; Mears, Carlson, Holden, & Harris, 2001; Miles-Doan, 1998). Also, many women living in high-risk neighborhoods have higher levels of fear for personal safety (Alvi, Schwartz, DeKeseredy, & Maume, 2001; Ross & Mirowsky, 2001), and women in lower income areas may endure more sexual harassment (DeKeseredy, Alvi, Schwartz, & Perry, 1999).

High-risk neighborhoods may also influence physical health, mental health, and victimization risk because of drug and alcohol use. More specifically, higher and more severe rates of alcohol and drug use have been shown to cluster in disadvantaged, impoverished neighborhoods (Currie, 1994; Finch, Vega, & Kolody, 2001; Kadushin, Reber, Saxe, & Livert, 1998), and perceptions of drug use and actual drug use both cluster by neighborhood (Petronis & Anthony, 2000; SAMHSA, 2002). Other research has found that drug arrests cluster by neighborhood (Rosenfeld & Decker, 1999; Warner & Coomer, 2003), and drug-related emergencies are more frequent in inner-city hospitals compared with suburban hospitals (Bertram, Blachman, Sharpe, & Andreas, 1996). One explanation for drug-related arrests clustering by neighborhood is that drug crimes are more visible in certain neighborhoods, thus attracting the attention of law enforcement (Saxe et al., 2001; Warner & Coomer, 2003). The visibility of drug use may increase access to drugs and decrease perceptions of the negative aspects of drug use while simultaneously decreasing neighborhood cohesion, increasing fear and stress levels of residents, and increasing social isolation through stigma associated with visible drug-related crime (S. Lambert, Brown, Phillips, & Ialongo, 2004; Ross, Mirowsky, & Pribesh, 2001; Saxe et al., 2001; Warner & Coomer, 2003). Thus, the impact of substance use in neighborhoods on individual well-being may be direct, through increased use given increased access, and indirect, because of decreased negative attitudes toward substance use, and increased fear, stress, crime, and violence.

Certain neighborhoods may have higher rates of crime because of social and physical deterioration (D. Cohen et al., 2000; Kornhauser, 1978; Warner & Coomer, 2003):

> In other words, community members are less likely to feel attached, to think highly of the area, to neighbor, or to get involved in any form of problem-solving when they view the community as a place where the people cannot be trusted, are conflict-oriented, are neglectful of property, or are disinclined to watch out for one another. (Woldoff, 2002, p. 107)

The social disorder view postulates that collective poverty weakens community bonds or attachments and diminishes social control mechanisms, leading to more crime behavior. Community bonds are weakened, in general, because of high residential instability and, thus, increased anonymity and social isolation (Merton, 1968; Sampson, 1991). In other words, neighborhoods where individuals are more knowledgeable and friendly with each other tend to be more cohesive and have lower crime rates (M. Lee, 2000; Sampson & Raudenbush, 1999). A recent study of adolescent drug use found that adolescents who perceived greater neighborhood disorganization as defined by levels of safety, violence, and drug activity were more likely to use substances at a 2-year follow-up compared with adolescents who did not have those kinds of neighborhood perceptions (S. Lambert et al., 2004).

Certain socioeconomic status indicators may characterize neighborhoods, but factors such as more tolerant attitudes toward crime may also be salient in understanding violence or substance use rates in neighborhoods (Browning, 2002). In a nationally representative telephone survey, T. Simon et al. (2001) found that participants with lower incomes had higher acceptance ratings for "hitting to keep one's partner in line" than participants with higher incomes. It may also be the case that individuals are less willing to get involved or to call the police in certain neighborhoods, leading to an environment that becomes more susceptible to violence and substance use (Sampson, 1997). Also, certain neighborhoods may receive less attention from police, which could encourage higher rates of violence and substance use (R. Stark, 1987).

Social and Cultural Norms

Social or cultural norms may define and influence the behavior of men and women in relationships and shape substance use patterns as well (Ehrhardt & Wasserheit, 1991). *Culture* refers to shared beliefs, values, and attitudes among members of a group, and cultural norms are often transferred from generation to generation and maintained over time through social ties (Hammond, 1978; Kasturirangan, Krishnan, & Riger, 2004). Social norms may promote the initiation and maintenance of certain behaviors as well as deter behavior changes. Norms can come from a variety of sources, including racial and ethnic groups, peers, and partners. These three sources are interrelated, as seen throughout the following discussion.

RACIAL AND ETHNIC GROUP NORMS. Three important caveats must be noted before discussing the influence of race and ethnic group norms on victimization, mental health, and substance use. First, there is a significant overlap of race–ethnicity and socioeconomic status. Ethnic minority groups are disproportionately poor, with 49% of African American families and 61% of Hispanic families below 200% of the federal poverty level compared with 26% of White families (Staveteig & Wigton, 2000). In addition, African American families (55%) and Hispanic families (33%) are more likely to be characterized as single-parent families than White families (19%), and single-parent households in which the mother is the head of the household are more likely to live in poverty (Morgan,

1991). Second, certain racial and ethnic groups may be better defined by neighborhood cultures that have norms regarding violence and substance use that are largely independent of race or ethnicity. In other words, what may seem to be an ethnic factor may actually be a neighborhood effect that is shaped more by socioeconomic and other neighborhood characteristics than by race or ethnicity. Much of the research that examines racial and ethnic differences does not control for socioeconomic status or neighborhood effects, making the interpretation of findings difficult. Third, many studies still use broad generalizations to characterize ethnicities and races. For example, the research findings may focus on "Hispanics" with little discrimination among subgroups with important differences. The term *Hispanic* can include upper middle class Cubans, lower socioeconomic level Mexicans who are also Native Americans, Puerto Ricans, Guatemalans, and others. It is ill-advised to assume that "Hispanic" is a uniform group any more than "English speaking" is a uniform group. Even so, a discussion of cultural norms must include consideration of racial and ethnic differences and similarities.

Some studies find few differences in victimization rates among racial and ethnic groups. For example, the National Violence Against Women survey found that approximately 18% of both White and African American women reported rape, about 50% reported physical assault, and about 7% reported stalking victimization by any perpetrator in their lifetimes (Tjaden & Thoennes, 2000a). Hispanic and non-Hispanic women's rates of victimization were close as well (14.6% of Hispanic and 18.4% of non-Hispanic women reported rape, 53.2% of Hispanic and 51.8% of non-Hispanic women reported physical assault, and 7.6% of Hispanic and 8.2% of non-Hispanic women reported stalking victimization in their lifetimes by any perpetrator). There were also minimal differences among White, African American, and Hispanic women for intimate partner violence victimization (Tjaden & Thoennes, 2000b). On the other hand, some studies reported higher rates of intimate partner violence among African American and Hispanic women compared with White women (Field & Caetano, 2003; Jasinski, 2001a), whereas in other studies, after controlling for socioeconomic status, most racial and ethnic differences disappeared (Krivo & Peterson, 1996; Rennison & Planty, 2003).

Although clear differences in rates of victimization by racial and ethnic groups has not been firmly established, considerable literature indicates that responses to violence may vary by racial and ethnic groups (Field & Caetano, 2004; Locke & Richman, 1999; Logan, Cole, Shannon, & Walker, in press; Tjaden & Thoennes, 2000d; West, Kaufman Kantor, & Jasinski, 1998). For example, Joseph (1997) compared African American and White battered women and found similar rates of abuse. However, African American women reported tolerating the violence longer, were less likely to report they had called the police or to report using other services to cope with the abuse (e.g., protective order, shelter), and were more likely to leave and then return to the relationship than White women, even though the African American women were also more likely to have been hospitalized with abuse-related injuries. African American women may lack options to stop violence because of social and financial limitations (Mays & Cochran, 1988), and again, neighborhood effects may be operating in ways that are poorly addressed by extant research.

Several theories or hypotheses are discussed in the literature about why the context of partner violence may be different for African American women. One hypothesis is that African American women may be reluctant to report violence to the police because they fear discrimination or potential unfair treatment of their assailant because of his race (Hampton, Oliver, & Magarian, 2003; Joseph, 1997; Lefley, Scott, Llabre, & Hicks, 1993). In fact, Bent-Goodley (2001) concluded from a review of the literature that African American women often do not report interpersonal crimes out of "racial loyalty." That is, African American women feel that if they report a crime perpetrated by an African American man, they will be "traitors" to their community, and they might believe that they should sacrifice to protect their community. Another hypothesis for why the context of victimization differs for African American women is one based on the gender ratio imbalance. That is, among African Americans, there are fewer men than women because of a birth gender ratio imbalance and higher rates of mortality and incarceration for African American men compared with their female counterparts (Fullilove, Fullilove, Haynes, & Gross, 1990; Guttentag & Secord, 1983; E. Johnson, 1993; Mays & Cochran, 1988; L. Miller et al., 1995; T. Smith, 1994). When one gender outnumbers the other, members of the scarcer gender may have a bargaining advantage in male–female relationships because more alternative relationships are open to them (Albrecht, Fossett, Cready, & Kiecolt, 1997; Guttentag & Secord, 1983; Heer & Grossbard-Shechtman, 1981). Such an imbalance among African Americans may lessen the perceived value of women by men and lead to increased violence (Airhihenbuwa, DiClemente, Wingood, & Lowe, 1992; Cochran, 1990; L. Miller, Burns, & Rothspan, 1995). In addition, if eligible male partners are perceived as scarce, women may be more reluctant to leave relationships or take actions that could threaten the relationship, such as calling the police (Adimora et al., 2001; Hetherington, Harris, Bausell, Kavanaugh, & Scott, 1996; Sobo, 1993, 1995; Sterk-Elifson, 1994). These race and ethnicity factors, combined with neighborhood, family-of-origin, and cultural norms may not necessarily stop women from addressing victimization but can contribute to barriers to seeking safety and a different context within which victimization occurs.

In another example of ethnic differences in partner violence, researchers have found that Hispanic women experiencing partner violence are younger and more economically dependent than battered White women (O'Keefe, 1994; Straus & Smith, 1990; West et al., 1998). Numerous other complexities surround not only research on partner violence among Hispanics but also, as noted earlier, major problems in defining "Hispanic." In addition, violence experiences among acculturated Hispanics may be in some measure attributable to non-Hispanic values (Kaufman Kantor, Jasinski, & Aldarondo, 1994). In their 1994 study, Kaufman Kantor et al. found that Hispanics born in the United States had a greater likelihood of experiencing partner violence than those born in a Hispanic country. In addition, according to some studies, Hispanic women have higher thresholds for defining partner violence and are less likely to describe behaviors such as being pushed, shoved, grabbed, or having things thrown at them as abusive; they are also less likely to report emotional aggression as abusive (Lefley et al., 1993; Torres, 1991). Furthermore, Hispanic women are less likely to use health, mental health, or justice system services than White women in response to partner violence. For example, Krishnan, Hilbert, VanLeeuwen, and Kolia (1997) reported that although Hispanic women experienced more physical violence in their intimate relationships and more violence during pregnancy, they were less likely to report the violence to law enforcement or to seek medical attention than White women. Other research has indicated that Hispanic women experiencing partner violence were less likely to seek both formal and informal resources than White women (O'Keefe, 1994; West et al., 1998). Hispanic women reported that issues of fear and mistrust, lack of knowledge about where to seek help, language and transportation barriers, and deeply ingrained social and cultural norms were impediments to seeking help (Krishnan et al., 1997). Hispanic women also have displayed strong gender-role stereotypes about how men and women should behave as well as strong religious beliefs about the sanctity of marriage that may influence their experiences and responses to violence (Marin, 1996, 2003; Sorenson, 1996).

The experience of victimization also may differ for women depending on race and ethnicity because their ability to seek help through agencies is limited by stereotyping and discrimination by the agencies (Bent-Goodley, 2005). For example, Hispanic women might fear that excessive focus on immigration status may impede access to agencies. It is likely that these influences combined with the social constraints of poverty and family-of-origin, peer, and partner norms contribute to the sociocultural context of violence among different racial and ethnic groups. Much work remains to be done to understand specific cultural and ethnic factors associated with partner violence victimization.

As with victimization, overall prevalence rates of mental health problems appear similar across racial and ethnic groups; however, responses to mental health problems may differ (Robins & Regier, 1991; SAMHSA, 2001c; Scott Collins et al., 1999). Minorities tend to have different patterns of service utilization, a greater mistrust of treatment providers, an increased level of stigma about mental health problems, and perceptions of racism and discrimination that affect the experience of mental health problems (Alegria et al., 2002; SAMHSA, 2001c). For example, African Americans are less likely to utilize formal services and may rely more on the "norm" of handling their mental health problems on their own or turning to their spirituality (Broman, 1996; Cooper-Patrick et al., 1997; Neighbors, Musick, & Williams, 1998; Sussman, Robins, & Earls, 1987), whereas Hispanics have reported experiencing language barriers in trying to access health and mental health care (SAMHSA, 2001c). Also, according to some research, minorities have reported the perception that doctors or health providers treated them unfairly compared with Whites (E. Brown, Ojeda, Wyn, & Levan, 2000; LaVeist, 2000). Thus, it appears that perceptions and experiences of discrimination contribute to health and mental health problems (M. Hughes & Thomas, 1998; Krieger, Sidney, & Coakley, 1999; Ren, Amick, & Williams, 1999; Williams, 2000; Williams, Yu, Jackson, & Anderson, 1997).

Research also has shown racial and ethnic differences in substance use and substance-related problems (Hoffman, Barnes, Welte, & Dintcheff, 2000; Kandel, 1995; Reardon & Buka, 2002; Wallace, Bachman, O'Malley, & Johnston, 1995). Table 4.1 displays the estimated proportion of White, African American, and Hispanic women who reported alcohol use and illegal drug use in the prior month. Although there are differences in substance use among these groups,

Table 4.1. Drug and Alcohol Use of Women by Race and Ethnicity

Drug and alcohol use (%)	White	Black	Hispanic
Alcohol use			
Past month any use	49.7	32.3	33.6
Past month heavy use	2.5	1.8	2.0
Past month illegal drug use	4.5	5.2	4.5

Note. Data are from National Institute on Drug Abuse (2003).

the differences are subtle. However, contexts and consequences of substance use differ among ethnic and racial groups. More specifically, Wallace (1999) stated that

> although racial/ethnic differences in the epidemiology of alcohol and other drug use are not large, there are significant racial and ethnic differences in the experience of negative mental, physical, and social health consequences associated with the use and abuse of drugs. Because substance-related problems impact black and Hispanic adults disproportionately, black and Hispanic young people, particularly those who are children of substance abusers are at elevated risk for myriad problems. (p. 1126)

Certain ethnic and racial groups may have increased exposure to important risk factors for substance use and abuse (Gil, Vega, & Turner, 2002; Wallace & Muroff, 2002), and long-term consequences of substance use and abuse are more negative for minority groups (Wallace & Muroff, 2002). For example, Wallace (1999) reported in a review of the literature that African Americans suffered greater alcohol-related mortality and morbidity, and substance-related problems and more negative social consequences such as racial profiling or the targeting of certain neighborhoods by law enforcement for drug crimes (Wallace & Muroff, 2002). Wallace (1999) and Wallace and Muroff (2002) also noted that a factor in substance use and abuse patterns is the disparity in access, marketing, and availability of substances across various neighborhoods. In other words, low-income neighborhoods are targeted by tobacco and alcoholic beverage companies and retailers with increased advertising, more alcohol retail outlets, more potent substances often sold at lower cost, and less monitoring of sales to minors.

PEER NORMS. Cultural norms are likely to be influenced by peer norms, and peer norms are often passed on and maintained through a system of socialization. An individual's social support network often provides benchmarks for what is and is not acceptable. Reasons for using substances, when it is appropriate to use them, and how much and the type of substance to use are all potentially determined by social norms (T. Greenfield & Room, 1997). In some cases, peer norms or peer pressure may facilitate behavior that might otherwise not have occurred (Kandel, 1996; Labouvie, 1996; Wills & Cleary, 1999). Probably the most familiar example of the influence of peer norms is associated with adolescent substance use. Peer behavior is an important risk factor for adolescent substance use and delinquency (Curran, White, & Hansell, 2000; Wills & Cleary,

1999). For example, one study found that 48% of adolescents who reported their friends would not be upset about their drug use also reported using marijuana in the past year, compared with only 2% of adolescents who reported their friends would be very upset about their drug use (SAMHSA, 2001b). Peer networks may also be defined by drug use patterns. Leonard, Kearns, and Mudar (2000) found that the social networks of heavy drinkers were different from those of regular or infrequent drinkers, although the levels of emotional, financial, and practical support among these drinking groups did not differ. Another study found that peer drug use and time spent with friends were predictive of movement from nonuse or light use of alcohol to moderate use, and from nonuse or light use of marijuana to moderate use (Brook et al., 1992). In other studies, peer group interactions were significantly associated with both current and later drug use (Curran et al., 2000; Latimer, Winters, Stinchfield, & Traver, 2000). Adult social networks have also been found to influence substance-use behavior (Bullers, Cooper, & Russell, 2001; Leonard & Mudar, 2000).

Peers may influence each other directly by pressure to use drugs or indirectly by seeking approval through drug use or not wanting to be ostracized for refusing drugs (Suls & Green, 2003; Susman et al., 1994). For example, in several surveys of college students, Suls and Green (2003) found that there was a perception that men have more peer pressure to drink and would experience more embarrassment and negative social consequences if they expressed concerns about drinking. Other research has found that perceived norms may influence behavior, regardless of whether those perceived norms are accurate. Wild (2002) noted that

> compared with lighter drinkers, frequent heavy drinkers (1) believed that heavy alcohol use is more normative in social reference groups, (2) overestimated the amount of alcohol that social and problem drinkers consume in different contexts, (3) rated several criteria (e.g., frequency of intoxication) as less definitive of problem drinking, and (4) did not exhibit pluralistic ignorance (i.e., they shifted private approval of the drinking habits of others to match [mistaken] social norms of reference groups). (p. 469)

There is also some evidence of male peer support for violence against women. For example, DeKeseredy and Kelly (1995) found that male peer support was an important predictor of sexual violence in university college dating relationships, and Schwartz and DeKeseredy (1997, 2000) found that male peer support for violence against women was strongly associated with the perpetration of physical and sexual violence. One study found that men who drank alcohol two or more times a week and had male peers that supported violence against women were almost 10 times more likely to admit to being sexual aggressors compared with men without these characteristics (Schwartz, DeKeseredy, Tait, & Alvi, 2001). In other words, men who believe that their friends approve of sexual or physical violence against women are more likely to engage in such violence (Schwartz & DeKeseredy, 2000; Schwartz & Nogrady, 1996; J. Silverman & Williamson, 1997), and substance use may exacerbate these behaviors. Norms about violence toward women may be directly or indirectly communicated in peer support networks (A. Cox & Cox, 1998). For example, men may get direct information or advice on how to "handle" women in certain situations that may include violent behaviors. Their behavior may also be influenced less directly through jokes about violence against women, by the objectification of women, or by tolerance among their peers of these kinds of jokes or communications (Capaldi, Dishion, Stoolmiller, & Yoerger, 2001; DeKeseredy & Schwartz, 1993; Reitzel-Jaffe & Wolfe, 2001; Schwartz & DeKeseredy, 1997, 2000; J. Silverman & Williamson, 1997). Other indirect cues may come from peer modeling through which men take cues about how to relate to women from watching others' behavior (Mitchell, Angelone, Hirschman, Lilly, & Hall, 2002).

Although much less research supports the notion that women may also be influenced by their peer and family support networks in defining and validating beliefs about violence, it may be an important consideration in understanding their experiences and responses to interpersonal victimization. Many women who experience partner violence do turn to friends and family for support and guidance (Krishnan, Hilbert, & VanLeeuwen, 2001; Tan, Basta, Sullivan, & Davidson, 1995; Thompson et al., 2000). For example, in a domestic violence shelter sample, 91% of respondents indicated talking to either a friend or a family member about violence they had experienced (Goodkind, Gullum, Bybee, & Sullivan, 2003). Arriaga and Foshee (2004) found some support for the hypothesis that women may be influenced by peers with results of their study, in which female adolescents' dating-violence experiences were associated with their reports of friends' dating-violence experiences. Although there has been limited research on peer influence of partner victimization on women (Goodkind et al., 2003; Kocot & Goodman, 2003), qualitative and anecdotal research has indicated that some women may experience peer and family pressure to preserve the family at all costs or not to cause trouble for the perpetrator (Kearney, 2001; Logan, Stevenson, Evans, & Leukefeld, 2004). For example, in focus groups of women from rural and urban communities, one study found a perception among rural participants that reporting partner violence to authorities would incite community backlash, especially if the perpetrator were well known within the community (Logan, Stevenson, et al., 2004). Nurius and Norris (1996) hypothesized that

> a woman's perceptions of what constitutes appropriate male sexual behavior, how to respond to men's advances in general, and unwanted advances in particular, are likely to be affected to some extent by the types and degree of interaction a woman has had about these topics with friends. (p. 125)

PARTNER NORMS. Partners may influence the perception of norms as well as behavior. Partners may influence each other's behaviors in several ways. (a) Individuals may select partners on the basis of characteristics that are socialized as "normal" by the family-of-origin experiences or who share certain attributes, thus perpetuating specific behavior norms such as substance use. (b) Individuals may select partners who are different from themselves, but one partner's behavior may influence the other's behavior over time (i.e., reciprocal socialization or interpersonal influence). (c) Partners may react similarly to certain social or stressful experiences, which influence and maintain behavior patterns or norms.

ASSORTATIVE MATING. Assortative mating is a theory about why individuals from very similar backgrounds, interests, and experiences tend to partner with each other. *Primary assortative mating* occurs when people initially partner on the basis of similar characteristics, whereas *secondary assortative mating* describes selection of a partner from particular social groups (Kalmijin, 1991a, 1991b; Mare, 1991). The term *selection* is used more in a Darwinian than intentional sense, in that choices may be narrowly defined by cultural, social, and family backgrounds. More to the point, the choice of partners may be influenced by the limited opportunities one has for meeting and interacting with others that may be confined to specific social opportunities such as schools, work, neighborhoods, or other social gathering places, like a gym (Kalmijn & Flap, 2001; Laumann, Ellingson, Mahay, Paik, & Youm, 2004). Spending a lot of time in bars or clubs where drugs are used increases the likelihood of relationships with substance users as described in chapter 3. Women who use drugs and spend time in places where drugs are used and bought may be more likely to meet partners who are also drug users, even though they are not specifically seeking such partners. The "selection" is an artifact of limited opportunity. Selection of partners can be influenced by opportunities, and opportunities can be influenced by interests or characteristics (e.g., drug use). Similarly, partner selection is likely to be mutually influenced by opportunity and similar characteristics. For example, women who are problem drinkers, compared with those who are not, are more likely to marry men who are also problem drinkers (McLeod, 1993; Windle, 1997). Krueger, Moffitt, Caspi, Bleske, and Silva (1998) found that assortative mating occurs in relation to self-reported and peer antisocial behaviors.

Research has provided support for the idea that intimate partners influence each other's substance use behavior. For example, in several studies, husbands' drinking before marriage was found to be a risk factor for wives' drinking, but the reverse was not true, at least for the 1st year of marriage (Leonard & Das Eiden, 1999; Leonard & Mudar, 2003). However, in a more recent study, husband-to-wife drinking influence changed in the 2nd year of marriage, with wives' drinking patterns in the 1st year of marriages predicting husbands' drinking in the 2nd year of marriage (Leonard & Mudar, 2004). L. Roberts and Leonard (1998) found support for what they termed *drinking partnerships* and found that alcohol can have both positive and negative effects on a couple's relationship. For example, in some cases, dissimilar substance use patterns among couples can cause marital problems, whereas similar substance use patterns are less likely to do so, at least regarding that specific issue (Leadley, Clark, & Caetano, 2000; Mudar, Leonard, & Soltysinski, 2001). Stressful life events within the family are also experienced jointly by husbands and wives, which could result in similar drinking patterns as coping mechanisms; partners may also be influenced by joint socializing patterns (Leonard & Das Eiden, 1999). For example, couples that experience traumatic events or serious losses may both use substances to relieve their pain.

Although limited attention has been given to the impact of mating patterns on interpersonal violence patterns, conflict resolution perceptions and behaviors have been shown to be influenced by family history (Levy et al., 1997). Women who grow up in families with violence and substance abuse may be more likely to mate with partners who are violent and abuse substances or may be more tolerant of those behaviors in their relationships than women without such a family history (Hampton & Gelles, 1994; G. Holden et al., 1998; Holtzworth-Munroe, Smultzler, & Sandin, 1997; Malik, Sorenson, & Aneshensel, 1997; Mihalic & Elliott, 1997). Furthermore, both assortative mating and partner influence on substance use could contribute to violence in the relationship because of the substantial co-occurrence of substance use and violence in relationships (T. Brown, Werk, Caplan, Shields, & Seraganian, 1998; Leonard, 1999; Moore & Stuart, 2004). Cunradi, Caetano, and Schafer (2002) found that alcohol problems among men and women and drug use among women were significantly correlated with partner violence.

Summary of Social Environment

Social environments may influence mental health, physical health, substance use, and relationship and partnering behaviors. Family-of-origin factors, cultural norms, peer and partner influences, and assortative mating can all shape expectations and perceptions about what is "normal" and acceptable. These social factors can also support and maintain perceptions and behaviors.

Perceived Options

We have discussed here how both socioeconomic status and the social environment directly and indirectly contribute to a woman's risk for victimization, mental health problems, and substance use. Socioeconomic status may reduce access to resources, and social environment may facilitate and perpetuate behaviors that increase risk through definitions of what is "normal," tolerated, and not tolerated. These factors may also contribute indirectly to women's risk of victimization, mental health, and substance-related problems by influencing a woman's perceived options. Buka (2002) noted that

> disadvantage is relative to one's social position. Across socioeconomic levels, for almost all populations and all societies, people of higher social position live longer and remain healthier than people of lower position. This concept of relative inequities across the socioeconomic spectrum should be incorporated into conceptual models. (p. 121)

Buka went on to speculate that the reason disparities exist in health and mental health across socioeconomic status gradients is the lack of resources such as money, knowledge, prestige, power, social connections, and other opportunities or resources. McPherson, Smith-Lovin, and Cook (2001) stated that social network similarity "limits people's social worlds in a way that has powerful implications for the information they receive, the attitudes they form, and the interactions they experience" (p. 415). It may be that poverty and particular social environments reduce an individual's perceived opportunities, choices, or alternatives, creating situations that affect an individual's risk for victimization, mental health problems, and substance use.

Limited Resources

Resources such as access to the justice system, counseling, and treatment programs are important for coping with partner violence, sexual assault, mental health concerns, and substance abuse problems. Also, having no alterative living conditions can affect women's exposure to partner violence; if they have nowhere to go, leaving the relationship becomes a diminished alternative (Logan, Walker, Jordan, & Campbell, 2004; Menard, 2001). It is not just the availability of alternative housing but women's perception of it that can be critical (Logan, Stevenson, et al., 2004). In other words, shelters or other housing may be available, but if women are unaware of them, the option to leave abusers is closed. Furthermore, limited neighborhood resources can include limited access to positive leisure or social activities that many individuals and families utilize to reduce stress and to increase healthier behavior (D. Cohen et al., 2003; Wilton, 2003). Having a social network that is knowledgeable and supportive of alternative options is also important in terms of expanding perceived options. For example, one study found that individuals living in poor neighborhoods had fewer friends who were stably employed or college educated and more friends who were on welfare (Rankin & Quane, 2000). Having a social network that includes employed individuals may potentially be important in learning about jobs, obtaining jobs, and maintaining jobs (W. Wilson, 1987, 1996). Similarly, having social contacts with people who know about resources to prevent or cope with violence against women may be critical in helping women.

Taxed Reserve Capacity

Just as social networks contribute information, support, and ideas about how to cope or respond to environmental circumstances such as violence, internal resources can also be important. Gallo and Matthews (2003) postulated that socioeconomic status affects health because "(a) low-[socioeconomic status] individuals are exposed to more situations in which they must use their resources and (b) their environments prevent the development and replenishment of resources to be kept in reserve" (p. 34). The idea of taxed reserve capacity, which suggests that people have a limited amount of emotional energy to expend on day-to-day functions (Gallo & Mathews, 2003; Link & Phelan, 1995), may be an important factor in understanding the availability of internal resources to cope with violence, mental health, and substance abuse problems. For example, low-income mothers have been found to expend considerable energy just meeting daily transportation and child-care needs. Merely attending to daily functions may use considerable energy that might be needed either to protect their families from danger or to seek a safer environment for them (Bostock, 2001). A "reserve" simply does not exist, and a reserve is essential to one's ability to exercise options for change. Leaving a relationship takes an inordinate amount of energy for all individuals regardless of whether abuse and fear are involved (Logan, Walker, et al., 2004), but for women dealing with survival issues, it may be too overwhelming. Leaving a relationship also involves a drawn-out set of stressful events, and the lack of an energy reserve may mean that women simply take the fastest and easiest solution rather than trying to resolve the bigger issue. Similarly, reporting a sexual assault to the police may require more energy or resource utilization than a woman may have available. This notion of taxed reserve capacity or limited internal resources will be discussed further in chapter 5.

Future Expectations

How women view the world is influenced by social surroundings, and those views in turn influence women's behavior. For example, Adler, Epel, Castellazzo, and Ickovics (2000) found that perceived social status was significantly associated with psychological and health-related problems even after controlling for more objective measures of socioeconomic status, and that both poverty and relative social position, which is associated with perceived options, have a strong association with health and mental health problems. Hill, Ross, and Low (1997) found in a survey that individuals who had a higher perception of future unpredictability and who predicted a shorter life span for themselves reported more risk-taking behavior than individuals who believed their future was more predictable and long term. These authors concluded that individuals consider survival expectations as well as expectations about future conditions, such as whether they will be better or worse in the future, in deciding whether to take behavioral risks. These social comparisons can affect the expression of mental health problems such as depression, which includes a bleak view of the future.

Summary of Perceived Options

As the case of Maria highlights, escaping poverty and one's social and cultural environment is complicated and difficult. Perceived and actual options are diminished by low socioeconomic status, with its concomitant limited partnering opportunities and limited social, economic, and personal mobility to change (S. Taylor et al., 1997). Internal and external resources are important for coping with stress as well as for thinking and acting on alternative living arrangements. Women who perceive that they have few options in their environment or a dismal future may be less vigilant about their safety or less able to leave risky environmental situations. It is precisely this dynamic that may be important in recognizing what may look like a "cycle of violence" for individuals within certain socioeconomic strata.

Summary

The vast research literature on psychological and biological factors associated with victimization has added greatly to the understanding of the effects of victimization. However, the growing literature on social and cultural contexts demonstrates that factors external to the person also play a major role in victimization and its effects on victims. In the broadest context, social factors such as socioeconomic status, family characteristics, and culture can contain areas of vulnerability for women. Many of these factors can also have protective value, however (Diener et al., 2003; Hobfall et al., 1996; Tiet et al., 1998). If, as noted in the Weisstein quote at the beginning of this book, interventions target only individual behavior without consideration of social context, they are likely to fail. Link and Phelan (1995) summarized the issues as follows:

> Those who craft policy for populations can be led astray if their purview is narrowly limited to a focus on individually-based risk factors . . . . [There are] two reasons why this is so. First, without understanding the social conditions that expose people to individually-based risk factors, interventions will fail more often than they should. This will occur because interventions will be targeted to behaviors that are resistant to change for unrecognized reasons . . . . Second, some social conditions are fundamental causes of disease and as such cannot be effectively addressed by readjusting the individually-based mechanisms that appear to link them to disease in a given context. If we wish to alter the effects of these potent determinants of disease, we must do so by directly intervening in ways that change the social conditions themselves. (p. 89)

Socioeconomic status is associated with victimization rates, physical and mental health problems, and substance use. The most commonly cited pathways for the association between these factors are (a) selection, (b) stress, and (c) indirect selection. The selection and stress hypotheses have both received research support, but study results differ depending on the specific outcome of interest (Dohrenwend et al., 1992; Miech, Caspi, Moffitt, Wright, & Silva, 1999). In reality, selection and stress are most likely reciprocal (Gallo & Matthews, 2003). Regardless of whether a person "self-selects" into poverty, it is likely that lower socioeconomic status environments increase risk of health and mental health problems because of the high stress levels of being poor. Several studies have found an almost linear relationship between degree of low socioeconomic status (e.g., lowered income) and severity or prevalence of health, mental health, and cognitive functioning problems (G. Duncan, 1996; J. Lynch, Kaplan, & Shema, 1997). Higher levels of stress that ensue from low socioeconomic status may also increase negative health behaviors such as substance use.

In addition, social environments consist of various social layers, including family-of origin experiences, neighborhood environment, cultural norms, and partner norms. Family of origin likely plays an important role in shaping social environment and has multiple interacting pathways. Family socialization includes modeling as well as the adaptations of positive or negative coping strategies in adverse familial circumstances that may carry into adulthood. Neighborhoods may significantly affect victimization, mental health, and substance use and may contribute to stress and distress through fear and social isolation. Another way neighborhoods can affect a person is through cultural norms. Unfortunately, as mentioned earlier, it is difficult to make conclusions about race and ethnicity differences in interpersonal victimization and substance use because they are confounded with other sociological factors, including poverty and living conditions. Race and ethnicity are not the primary cultural factors to consider in understanding differences, and other social norms or cultural norms must be evaluated (Beauvais & Oetting, 2002). In other words, there are certain cultures, such as an "adolescent culture," that promote the use of substances and that cut across all racial and ethnic groups. On the other hand, race or ethnic identity may serve as a protective factor if a culture promotes negative views of substance use (Beauvais & Oetting, 2002; Furst, Johnson, Dunlap, & Curtis, 1999). Peer and partner norms also may have significant impacts on risk of victimization, mental health, and substance abuse among women. Close social networks help to define reality in terms of what is "normal" and acceptable behavior and reactions to things that happen.

Finally, poverty and particular social environments reduce women's perceived opportunities, choices, or alternatives, which creates situations that impact their experience of and response to victimization, mental health problems, and substance use. Women who perceive few alternatives to their life circumstances and a dismal future for themselves may be less vigilant about their safety or less able to leave risky environmental situations, such as an abusive relationship. In addition, women who live in poverty expend a considerable amount of energy on daily survival, which taxes their internal resources. Whether women have reserve capacity to go beyond daily survival and what motivates women with limited reserve energy to seek help in preventing or coping with increased risk of victimization, mental health, and substance use are topics in need of more research.

Strengths and Weaknesses in the Literature

The literature identifies many important ways in which social factors affect vulnerability to victimization, health and mental health problems, and substance use. Unfortunately, the specific pathways by which social factors affect individual behavior are less clear. There are four main weaknesses in the extant research literature that will be discussed. The first is the need for social scientists to integrate the study of social factors with the study of individual behavior and risk. Few theories specifically focus on women's risk of victimization, physical and mental health problems, and substance use, and even fewer address the reciprocal effects of individual and social factors on these concerns. Future theories should consider the context within which risks occur in order to facilitate the development of more effective interventions, or to put it another way, "interventions seeking to change individual risk profiles [should] contain an analysis of factors that put people at risk of risks" (Link & Phelan, 1995, p. 89).

The second major weakness in the literature is the limited understanding of the impact, interactions, and distinct contributions of socioeconomic factors, race and ethnicity, neighborhoods, and other social environmental factors on outcomes (Kasturirangan et al., 2004; Murry, Smith, & Hill, 2001). For example, the literature often does not account for specific types of neighborhood or cultural stressors and does not differentiate among stressors such as intimate-partner violence and worry about financial status (Israel, Farquhar, Schulz, James, & Parker, 2002). These two types of stressors, intimate partner violence and financial worry, are quite different and may have different effects on mental health. Furthermore, examination of the specific interaction of the two may be the key to understanding mental health rather than simply examining "stress" more globally.

Despite the popularity of the cultural diversity theme in the current literature, there are still major problems in defining exactly what is meant by the many terms and concepts used in these studies. Different measures for socioeconomic status and neighborhoods as well as race, ethnicity, and culture can produce different outcomes. Kaplan and Bennett (2003) stated that

> racial/ethnic categories are at best approximations of socially defined groupings to which individuals are based largely on skin color, country of origin or ancestry, and language or dialect spoken. The racial/ethnic categories commonly used in biomedical sciences and epidemiology are broad and overlapping. Individuals do not fit neatly into these categories, and these broad groups can obscure significant within-group heterogeneity. (Kaplan & Bennett, 2003, pp. 2709–2710)

Beiser (2003) also suggested that it is extremely important to examine culture, rather than simply race and ethnicity, because it plays an important role in expectations and attitudes in defining health and mental health problems. Simplistic interpretations or sweeping generalizations do not further the understanding of these issues. Complicating the matter even more is that the social environment at the neighborhood level is related to outcomes, yet it is unclear how race and ethnicity, socioeconomic status, and culture may all interact within specific neighborhoods (Sampson, Morenoff, & Gannon-Rowley, 2002; Small & Newman, 2001). Research on neighborhoods should also differentiate census tracts from neighborhoods. For example, although census tract data have been used to generate information about localities with higher partner violence rates, these studies do not necessarily describe neighborhood-level factors. These issues need basic research conducted along with complex studies to tease apart various relationships and to understand the impact of social factors on individual outcomes.

The third major weakness of this literature is that much is lacking in the knowledge base regarding family-of-origin factors and their influences on adult outcomes (Carlson, 2000; Jouriles, Norwood, McDonald, & Peters, 2001; Mohr, Lutz, Fantuzzo, & Perry, 2000; Stith, Rosen, & McCollum, 2000). There is limited understanding about the mechanisms of early violence experiences or of witnessing violence on adult outcomes (Adamson & Thompson, 1998; Henning & Leitenberg, 1996; Hines & Saudino, 2002; Levendosky & Graham-Bermann, 2001; Margolin & Gordis, 2000; Margolin, Oliver, & Medina, 2001). Future research must include not only the examination of specific victimization experiences but also the social contexts that surround them (Gilfus, 1999). For example, several studies of child abuse found that family environment factors (e.g., having an alcoholic father, being socially isolated, and mother's mental health problems) contributed to problems in adulthood along with the severity of child abuse experiences (Fleming, Mullen, Sibthorpe, & Bammer, 1999; Molnar, Buka, & Kessler, 2001; Ryan, Kilmer, Cauce, Watanabe, & Hoyt, 2000; Stermac, Reist, Addison, & Millar, 2002). Perhaps child abuse alone does not

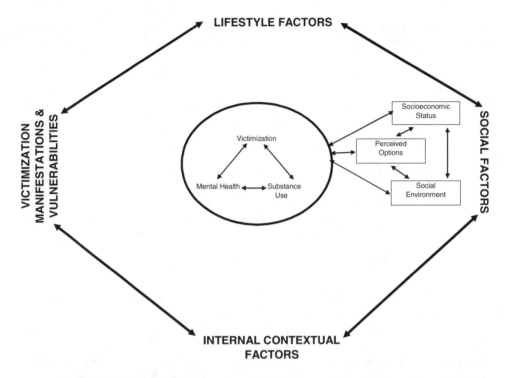

Figure 4.1. Conceptual model of factors contributing to victimization, mental health, and substance use: social factors.

predict revictimization and other adverse outcomes, but in the context of other life stressors and social factors, it may create vulnerability to increased mental health and substance abuse problems, which then increase vulnerability to revictimization (Banyard, Williams, & Siegel, 2001; Horwitz, Widom, McLaughlin, & White, 2001; Siegel & Williams, 2003). Research in this area needs to separate various types of adverse childhood events and examine the overlap of such events (Jouriles et al., 2001). Types of adult outcomes also need to be examined with longitudinal studies that can better examine mediating and moderating factors (Carlson, 2000; Mohr et al., 2000).

Future research should examine more closely the distinctions between victimization and perpetration when examining "abuse." It remains an empirical question whether perpetration and victimization represent two sides of the same coin of an abuse construct. However, on the basis of the literature to date, it would appear that victimization and perpetration represent very different phenomena and that the social construction around the two should be examined carefully and separately.

Finally, there is a great need for more research on norms influencing both men's and women's labeling of violence and the emotional valence surrounding it. Research should also consider peer and family support and norms for experiencing violence. The influence of cultural, neighborhood, peer, and partner norms on mental health and substance use is also an area for continued research. Even in the face of clear, objective standards, group norms strongly influence behavior; normative social influence rather than informational influence is a primary force in behavior (Zimbardo & Leippe, 1991). Consequently, the role of the environment, including norms, in promoting and maintaining risk behaviors is an important factor that is often ignored in research on victimization.

Conclusion

Socioeconomic status, social environment, and perceived options are interrelated social factors that influence the risk of victimization, mental health problems, and substance use. Figure 4.1 adds to the conceptual framework first described in chapter 1 of this book. Social factors are conceptualized as contributing to the risk of victimization, mental health, and substance use as well as interacting with victimization manifestations and vulnerabilities (chap. 2) and lifestyle factors (chap. 3).

More specifically, poverty may increase individuals' risk of victimization or revictimization by limiting living options and access to treatment and other kinds of services that might relieve the burden of victimization, mental health problems, and substance abuse. In addition, family, cultural, peer, and partner norms may play important roles in partner selection, influencing behavior and tolerance of certain behaviors. If victimization and substance abuse are and have always been part of an individual's "normal" reality, alternatives to their current lifestyle may not be available or considered. Clinicians and researchers must recognize the impact and the interaction of the social environment and individual factors that contribute to increased vulnerability for victimization, mental health problems, and substance use. Social factors must also be recognized as potential sources of strengths or protective factors to build into interventions as well.

5

Internal Contextual Factors

The Case of Susannah P.

Susannah is a 26-year-old woman who lives in a medium-sized city, where she was born and raised. During her childhood years, she dreamed of marrying and having a family. Susannah married Tommy when she was 20 years old.

From the beginning of their marriage, Tommy drank heavily. Susannah entered her marriage believing that "being a good wife" meant she was to spend time with her husband and develop an interest in his activities. Other than his job, however, Tommy's main activity was drinking. So she began drinking with him at home, at parties, and when they went out to eat. Although she had always worried a little about Tommy's drinking, in the past year, her own drinking had begun to worry her as well. Even when Tommy was not there, she often felt the need for a drink.

Recently, after a particularly bad fight, Susannah confided in her mother about the violence. Her mother told Susannah that fighting is a normal part of marriage and that she should focus on being a "better wife" so Tommy wouldn't get so angry. This seemed to confirm what Tommy had been telling her. Additionally, in the last 6 months, she and Tommy have begun arguing more because he accuses her of flirting with other men when they go out. More than once, these verbal arguments have ended with Tommy becoming violent toward her. Tommy always apologizes and treats her nicely for a few days afterward, but he always tells her that the arguments would not start at all if she would simply "do her job" around the house and quit "playing with fire" around other men.

Often Susannah believes that their relationship problems are her fault. She is not sure whether she might sometimes unintentionally flirt with other men. Since she's been drinking during the day, she wonders whether her housekeeping has slipped as well. Other times, she believes Tommy's complaints are unjustified. But she generally feels so worthless that she doesn't stand up for herself and then feels even less motivated to change the behavior he complains about.

She also feels depressed and knows that she needs help. Susannah called the helpline recently when she was sober after she realized that Tommy's violence toward her was becoming worse. He used to hit her with an open hand, and now he has begun using his fists. He hits her in the stomach, where no one can tell. She told the crisis counselor that she felt trapped in her relationship with Tommy. She has lost most of her friends, some because of her own drinking and some because Tommy doesn't like them. She feels hopeless and helpless and drinks to keep these feelings at bay. Other than calling the helpline, though, she is afraid to reach out for help. She believes that others will see her as a failure and at fault for the deterioration of her relationship. She is also embarrassed about her alcohol use. She looked in the mirror one day and found she couldn't even tell who she was anymore. All she knew was that she was in trouble and needed to find help—if only she knew where to turn.

*   *   *

This case highlights another set of factors that contribute to the risk for victimization—internal contextual factors. *Internal contextual factors*, as used in this book, include the views of self and the ways in which the world and events are understood. It is the psychological lens through which the world is perceived. In other words, internal contextual factors influence how individuals perceive and respond to both positive and negative situations. One of the distinguishing features of internal contextual factors, when compared with factors highlighted in previous chapters, is that they are a part of personal and introspective processes that may never be apparent to others. Bonaro Overstreet (1902–1985) noted the importance of considering internal contextual factors in understanding individual reactions, thoughts, emotions, and behaviors:

> No emotional crisis is wholly the product of outward circumstances. These may precipitate it. But what turns an objective situation into a subjectively critical one is the interpretation the individual puts upon it—the meaning it has in his emotional economy; the way it affects his self-image. (quoted in Cook, 1997, p. 536)

This quote highlights the notion that individuals react differently to seemingly objective stimuli or experiences (Charney, 2004; Shalev, 2002). Thus, at least part of the explanation for different responses to similar experiences, such as victimization, may be found in the internal context that influences emotional and behavioral responses. This chapter highlights the importance of understanding internal contextual factors and reviews the literature on factors that may influence how individuals interpret and respond to threatening, negative, or stressful events and conditions. These internal contextual factors are deeply interwoven with all the other factors that have been covered in earlier chapters, but their domain lies somewhat outside the typical victimization literature. Internal contextual factors point to research on the many cognitive and emotional components of stress, threat appraisal, and coping responses. Although some may use the term *schemas* to describe these cognitive phenomena, we use the term *internal contextual factors* to emphasize the context that they provide when victimization events occur. In other words, these factors include the domain within which stressful events are appraised as threatening and within which women respond and develop individualized adaptations and coping styles to threats.

The first section of this chapter provides background information on the notion of internal contextual factors, including a more general discussion of the appraisal process or how individuals perceive and interpret events. This foundation is critical to understanding the relevance of internal contextual factors for victimization, mental health, and substance use as well as for interpreting the research in this area. After providing background information, internal contextual factors will be discussed. Internal contextual factors consist of three major elements: (a) *situation* or *primary appraisals*, which make up how events are perceived and interpreted; (b) *response* or *secondary appraisals*, which include how events and situations are responded to; and (c) *cognitive constraints*, which impose limitations on situation appraisals and reponse appraisals.

Specifically, situation appraisals are influenced by knowledge and understanding, memory, cognitive biases, personal goals, agency (i.e., the belief that one's behavior can influence both desired and undesired effects), and mood and personality. Response appraisals are often influenced by blame, anticipated outcomes, and self-efficacy/self-esteem. Three cognitive constraints are discussed in this chapter: cumulative stress, multiple victimizations, and psychological abuse. This chapter emphasizes the internal context within which individuals perceive and respond to events; however, these perceptions are influenced and interact with many factors outlined in earlier chapters of this book, including mental health, substance use, norms, socialization, lifestyles, and socioeconomic status. This is the final chapter in our discussion of the contributing factors outlined in the conceptual model (see Figure 5.1).

Overview of Appraisal Processes

In general, *appraisals*, defined as interpretations or perceptions of events, are thought to elicit emotions, which are, in turn, essential for adaptation and well-being (Lazarus & Folkman, 1984; C. Smith & Kirby, 2001). Emotions such as fear, anger, sadness, and happiness all motivate individuals toward behavior that may be necessary for adaptation and even survival. Readers are probably familiar with the physiological response of "fight or flight," in which the emotion of fear is thought to induce behaviors of either running away or attacking the threat stimulus to ensure safety. Many theorists suggest that appraisals precede emotions; thus, the key mechanism to understanding emotions is appraisal (Lazarus & Folkman, 1984; C. Smith & Kirby, 2001). This premise does not exclude the possibility that emotions can be elicited without cognitive appraisals. In fact, in certain circumstances, hormones or neurotransmitters may activate or alter emotions without cognitive mediation (Izard, 1993; Roseman & Smith, 2001). Providing evidence to support the notion that emotions can be elicited independent of appraisal, Izard (1993) used the example of medications for depression or anxiety that alter neurochemicals, which in turn modify emotions. Roseman and Smith (2001, p. 16), however, argued that "in the majority of cases, emotions are not arbitrary responses that are unrelated to the situations in which they occur; rather, most emotions are reactions to events, and reactions that are dependent on the way the situation is perceived and evaluated by a particular person." Even when an individual is physiologically aroused without a prior cognition, appraisals are often made to "explain" the arousal. Schacter and Singer (1962) conducted several classic experiments to examine this premise by administering adrenaline to participants and then manipulating their social experiences. They concluded that when people are physiologically aroused, the interpretation of the arousal (i.e., the emotion attribution) depends on the social context in which the arousal takes place. Thus, emotions are dependent on the situation appraisal.

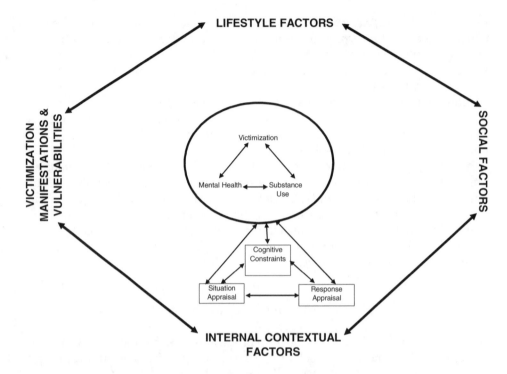

Figure 5.1. Conceptual model of factors contributing to victimization, mental health, and substance use: internal contextual factors.

One important assumption of the appraisal process is that it does not operate through objective information processing; rather, appraisals are inherently subjective and personally unique because they are meaning based and evaluative. In other words, the appraisal is a reflection of whether the event or stimulus is thought to be beneficial or harmful to the person and whether the situation is congruent or incongruent with personal motives, goals, or concerns (Planalp & Fitness, 1999; Roseman & Smith, 2001; C. Smith & Kirby, 2001; Tomaka, Blascovich, Kibler, & Ernst, 1997). According to appraisal theorists, it is this dynamic that explains why individuals respond so differently to the same situation and why people may change their response to the same stimulus at different times (Roseman & Smith, 2001). Thus, "according to appraisal theories, it is the interpretations of events, rather than events themselves, that cause emotions" (Roseman & Smith, 2001, p. 6). Emotions are then hypothesized to shape decisions about possible as well as actual behavioral responses (Ellsworth & Scherer, 2003; Lazarus, 1999; Roseman & Smith, 2001).

So how does the appraisal process work? This question has not been definitively answered (C. Smith & Kirby, 2001; Roseman & Smith, 2001). In general terms, Lazarus and Folkman (1984) hypothesized that people make two kinds of appraisals: primary and secondary. The *primary appraisal process* is when individuals assess whether the situation is threatening, negative, or stressful. Scherer (2001) expanded the description of this process by proposing that people assess situations by appraising whether a situation is congruent with their goals, motives, or concerns on the basis of their self-perception and social norms as well as on how serious the implications or consequences of the situation would be. Roseman (2001) also suggested that the unexpectedness of a situation or event affects whether the appraisals are positive or negative. Secondary appraisals, called *response appraisals*, occur once a situation has been perceived as harmful or incongruent with goals. Individuals then assess what they can do about the situation to reduce harm or align the situation with their goals (Lazarus & Folkman, 1984). In other words, individuals assess how well they believe they can cope with or adjust to the consequences of the stimulus or event (Scherer, 2001). Roseman suggested that individuals also assess whether the situations are caused by circumstance, self, or another person and how controllable the situations appear to be. Emotions are hypothesized to result from these two types of appraisals.

Although emotions, behaviors, goal pursuits, and situation evaluations are commonly thought to be a result of conscious choice and volitional guidance, they are more likely to be arrived at by a mixture of conscious and automatic processing (Bargh, 1994; Bargh & Chartrand, 1999). Many of the appraisals that people make are accomplished on "automatic pilot." Once goals or motivations are activated, regardless of whether they are activated through automatic or conscious processes, they influence appraisals, affect, and behavior (Bargh & Chartrand, 1999). This premise makes sense because it seems impossible to appraise, continually and consciously, every stimulus presented; a person would simply be overloaded if this were true. In fact,

> a great deal of human behavior can dispense with consciousness because it flows smoothly along automatic pathways, guided by habits, past experiences, established goals and motivations, and situational cues. Consciousness does, however, intervene occasionally to take behavior out of those rutted pathways. It can break a link in the causal chain that normally leads straight from motivations and activating cues to behavioral responses. (Baumeister & Sommer, 1997a, p. 77)

The automatic processing of certain behaviors (e.g., driving a car) and social perceptions (e.g., stereotypes) has both positive and negative consequences. On the positive side, automatic processing allows individuals to survive a daily barrage of information (Bargh & Chartrand, 1999). On the negative side, it may influence moods without the individual necessarily understanding the factors contributing to specific moods (Beck & Clark, 1997). Negative moods often impel individuals to look for information or reasons why they feel bad, which may or may not result in accurate interpretations of the cause of the negative mood. Misattributing causes for negative moods can affect behavior such as making decisions based on erroneous information (Bargh & Chartrand, 1999). The phrase *misplaced anger* comes to mind as an example of this particular phenomenon.

Another example of automatic processing is that individuals can be motivated toward behavior that may or may not be appropriate. Thus, people may be drawn to more immediately rewarding or distracting tasks when on "automatic pilot" as opposed to making themselves focus on issues, decisions, or tasks that need attention for better health and well-being (Bargh & Chartrand, 1999).

An example of this may be when an unemployed individual spends more time on wishful thinking or cleaning the house than the task of looking for a job. Bargh (1994) summarized this process as follows:

> The automatization of routine thought processes frees one's limited attentional resources for nonroutine matters, and enables a reduction of the massive amount of stimulation and information bombarding one at any given moment into a more manageable subset of important objects, events, and appraisals. But with the increased efficiency of thought also comes a lack of awareness of engaging in that process, leading to a likelihood of misattributing the causes of one's feelings and loosening of one's intentional grip over decisions and judgments. (p. 31)

Complicating the understanding of the appraisal–emotion process further is that it seems to be an ongoing, reiterative process rather than a linear and sequential one. Some appraisal theories hypothesize that self-organizing cognitive–emotion interactions have continuous, recursive, and reiterative functions (Lewis & Granic, 1999). In contrast, other theories describe the process in more serial terms, with the sequence following a pattern of appraisal, emotion, action (based on the emotion), and then secondary cognition, sometimes termed *reappraisal* (Lazarus & Folkman, 1984). Regardless of how the process is described, it is likely that appraisals do not necessarily move smoothly from one stage to another but may involve numerous reiterative processes that are based on feedback from internal and external factors such as self-concept schemas (i.e., individuals' evaluation or framework about themselves) and the environment.

Adding to the complexity is that individuals cannot always control appraisals and emotions (Roseman & Smith, 2001). Roseman and Smith offered several reasons for this. First, as mentioned earlier, appraisals can occur automatically, intuitively, and outside of focal awareness and through deliberate, directed processes as well, such as when an individual deliberately searches for information to alter emotions (e.g., when people try to "look on the bright side"; Roseman & Smith, 2001; C. Smith & Kirby, 2001). The fact that appraisals can occur at multiple levels of awareness suggests that there can be conflicts between automatic, nonconscious appraisals and more consciously deliberated appraisals. This can result in emotions that are difficult to control or that appear unreasonable or irrational (Bargh, Gollwitzer, Lee-Chai, Barndollar, & Trotschel, 2001; Roseman & Smith, 2001). This has important implications for women with victimization experiences. Just like someone looking out of a window of a tall building who feels fear in spite of knowing that falling is unlikely, victims can experience automatic pilot fear that can motivate unconstructive responses. Second, the motivational and perceptual bases of appraisals are not always controllable. Appraisals involve the evaluation of whether events are relevant or congruent with a person's goals, needs, or concerns, yet these are not always under an individual's volitional control. For example, hunger or the need for affiliation are strong physiological and psychogenic motives that are not necessarily produced volitionally and thus may make appraisals and emotions difficult to ignore or control (Roseman & Smith, 2001). Third, multiple and conflicting emotions can be experienced simultaneously; for example, individuals can feel happy and sad, pleasure and displeasure at the same time (G. Sullivan & Strongman, 2003). Simultaneous emotions may increase difficulty in controlling emotions and appraisals. Fourth, emotions can affect physiological functioning, which can then affect emotions (Charney, 2004; McEwen & Lasley, 2002; Shalev, 2002). When physiological functions are affected, emotions and appraisals may be more difficult to control.

Furthermore, because appraisals are subjective perceptions, appraisal errors can occur, which can cause what is sometimes viewed as irrational, inappropriate, or inconsistent emotions (Roseman & Smith, 2001). Lazarus (1999) contended that individuals make appraisal errors that lead to "foolish assumptions about the world, which program us to experience unrealistic emotions in our daily lives" (p. 88). Erroneous appraisals can also facilitate emotions that increase negative affects, which can influence future appraisals (Frijda, 1993; Lazarus, 1991; Siemer, 2001). For example, erroneous appraisals might initiate, increase, and maintain high levels of anxiety (Beck & Clark, 1997) or may lead an individual to believe a certain situation is safe when it is not. Lazarus (1999) described five main causes of erroneous judgments: mental health problems or brain disorders, lack of knowledge about the situation, selective attention (i.e., toward or away from specific threat cues), denial, and ambiguous cues.

In summary, appraisals are important in understanding how emotions arise and how they serve critical adaptive functions. Appraisals are ongoing and are likely to include a reiterative process that fluctuates in unpredictable ways rather than moving smoothly from one stage to another. These complications make appraisals difficult to examine scientifically. In addition, appraisals are subjective rather than objective information processes, suggesting great opportunity for error. Yet these appraisals, regardless of whether they are accurate, lead to emotions and behavior. Appraisals and generated emotions may be difficult to control because they occur both consciously and automatically. They are not always determined volitionally, and conflicting emotions and appraisals can be experienced simultaneously. Appraisal errors can result in emotions that cause suffering rather than adaptation.

In a more concrete example of how the appraisal process influences behavior, Martin, Rothrock, Leventhal, and Leventhal (2003) discussed how our appraisals of health symptoms influence whether we seek formal health care. In other words, if we experience a novel pain feeling one day, our appraisals of that pain will determine how we respond to the symptom. If we have just spent all day moving furniture and boxes, we might expect to feel pain and decide it is not necessary to see a doctor. If we do not perceive any reason that we should be feeling pain and begin to feel anxious about the meaning of the pain, we are more likely to seek help from a doctor. Also, although initially we may attribute the pain to moving heavy objects, if the pain lasts for a longer period of time than we would expect, our appraisal of the pain experience will likely change from one of lesser to greater concern. If we add in a variety of other symptoms, we may continually appraise the situation, making evaluations and attributions about the pain and other symptoms (e.g., "Is this normal given my activities? Is this normal compared with how others feel after these experiences? Do these symptoms seem indicative of a serious illness? What do my friends and family members say about this?"). We may also experience other emotions (e.g., increased anxiety about the symptoms), behavior (e.g., taking a pain reliever), and reappraisal of the situation (e.g., initially, the pain seemed normal, but increased anxiety and lack of pain medication effect increases concern). These steps may or may not occur in a serial, linear fashion. Through this example, it is easy to see how different interpretations of an experience affect not only our emotions but also our behavior. Furthermore, the process is continuous, sometimes with loops and double-backs in its path. This appraisal process is experienced by everyone in many personal and social contexts. However, appraisal processes take on special characteristics in the context of partner and sexual assault victimization experiences.

Lazarus and Folkman (1984), as mentioned earlier, discussed two kinds of appraisals, termed *situation appraisals* and *response appraisals*. We discuss these in the context of extant research and in its application to victimization studies. However, this chapter only provides a cursory overview of the appraisal literature because it is complex, and much remains unknown or controversial (Roseman & Smith, 2001). This leaves no simple way to examine components of the appraisal process. There are, however, key components that may provide insight into the appraisal process for women with victimization histories.

Situation Appraisal

An example of how appraisals of an event or a behavior can be perceived differently depending on circumstance is highlighted in a partner-violence study by Hamby and Gray-Little (2000), who found that although their entire sample of women had experienced something at least as violent as being grabbed by their partner, only 62% labeled their personal experiences as violent. Yet when these same women read short statements about a woman being grabbed, slapped, or punched, 100% labeled at least one of these acts as abusive. Thus, even if women perceive certain behaviors as threatening in general, they may appraise their personal experiences differently. The following section focuses on factors that may influence situation or primary appraisals, which include knowledge and understanding, memory, cognitive biases, personal goals, agency (i.e., the belief that one's behavior can influence both desired and undesired effects), and mood and personality.

Knowledge and Understanding

One factor that may influence appraisals is the perception of whether the situation is harmful, fair, or normal (Agnew, 2001; Dewe, 1991; Ellsworth & Scherer, 2003; Lazarus, 1999). Scherer (2001) described appraisals as including two reference checks: internal standards checks and external standards checks.

An *internal standards check* is made against a personal, internal standard of what is fair, normal, or congruent with personal goals, motives, or concerns (Ellsworth & Scherer, 2003; Leary, 2003). Guilt, for example, may be elicited in response to behavior that is perceived as inconsistent with one's internal standards for certain behavior. Alternatively, individuals may expect to be treated in certain ways, and if they perceive the interaction contrary to their expectations, they may be upset. Events or behaviors are checked against an internal road map of expectations or what is thought to be "right," and if the event or behavior is not "right," negative emotion may be elicited. Each person's road map is different and may be based on knowledge or beliefs that are not immediately apparent to others. Evidence of the importance of knowing and understanding in the appraisal process can be found in the research showing variations in how women label or define violence and threat. Several studies of rape have reported that only 49% to 62% of women who were raped according to a legal definition actually defined their experience as rape or as a crime when asked directly (Fisher, Cullen, & Turner, 2000; Koss, Dinero, Seibel, & Cox, 1988). Perhaps these women's rape experiences did not meet their internal definitions of rape, and thus they did not define the experience as rape. This likely influenced responses such as whether to report the event to authorities. In fact, Fisher et al. (2000) found that many of the women in their study who reported being raped indicated they did not report the crime because they were not sure it was a crime or that harm was intended (44%); others did not think it was serious enough to report (65%).

The second way individuals appraise situations or events is by comparing them with external or social references: "This check evaluates to what extent an action is compatible with the perceived norms or demands of a salient reference group in terms of both desirable and obligatory conduct" (Scherer, 2001, p. 98). If an experience seems "normal" according the perception or understanding of how others experience it in similar situations, individuals are less likely to perceive it as negative or harmful and will respond accordingly. If individuals perceive an event as unfair because they know or understand that this situation is not "normal" for others, a variety of emotions are likely to be elicited in response to that perception (Ellsworth & Scherer, 2003). This process is similar to the social comparison theory made popular by Festinger (1954). Consistent with more recent studies, Festinger theorized that social comparisons are used to gain self-knowledge, to evaluate self-concepts, to regulate feelings (on the basis of upward or downward social comparisons), and to evaluate situations or circumstances (Buunk, Gibbons, & Visser, 2002; Suls, Martin, & Wheeler, 2002; Wood, 1989).

Cultural norms, or perceived cultural norms, may also play an important role in external reference checks, as discussed in chapter 4. More specifically, there are likely to be cultural differences in the definitions and acceptance of victimization experiences that may influence appraisals (Barnett, 2001; Kearney, 2001). Cultural factors, when they have become internalized, can influence even basic perceptual functions (e.g., how hot pepper is) and have even greater influence in situations that involve appraisal of complex interpersonal situations (Rozin, 2003). Partner or acquaintance violence, especially rape, clearly involves complex sociocultural norms that affect individual perception and appraisal processes. For example, as discussed in chapter 4, studies have found that Hispanic women were less likely to appraise such behaviors as being pushed, shoved, grabbed, or having things thrown at them as abusive or threatening. They were also less likely to report emotional incidents as abuse compared with White, non-Hispanic women (Lefley, Scott, Llabre, & Hicks, 1993; Torres, 1991). Norms or social references may also be influenced by various group affiliations such as religious beliefs, but it is unclear how religious views affect women's appraisals about violence within relationships. In essence, definitions of violence are deeply embedded in culture and thus provide the template against which women will evaluate their experiences.

In summary, before women can cope with stressful situations or threats, they must recognize them as threatening, stressful, or incongruent with their goals (Lazarus, 1999; Livingston & Testa, 2000). A woman who has never seen or heard of a man slapping his wife or girlfriend may react differently than a woman who routinely saw her mother being slapped by her father or who has been slapped by previous boyfriends. The latter may expect slapping as a normal part of fighting between couples, or at least is not surprised when it happens.

Memory

Memories can facilitate or hinder situation appraisals in terms of understanding and knowledge, especially appraisals at the automatic level (LaBar & LeDoux, 2001). Memories of past experiences may influence how women perceive themselves or how they define their goals, motives, or concerns (Higgins, 1996). According to Reyna (2004), however, individuals often rely on "gist" representations for understanding situations and risk, which are present in memory but may be encoded with less detail than verbatim representations. Gist representations are less precise and thus can cause errors in judgment and decision making:

> Once the gist of presented information has been mentally represented, reasoners must make contact with information stored in memory (such as values and preferences) in order to derive judgments and decisions . . . errors in risk estimation spring from distinct sources, including knowledge deficits, failure to encode appropriate mental representations of risk categories, failure to retrieve known information in context, and processing interference arising from difficulties in processing nesting or overlapping categories of risks. (Reyna & Adam, 2003, p. 326)

More specifically, when people encounter new situations that have familiar cues at either conscious or automatic levels but that were not previously understood as negative or threatening, they may be less likely to perceive these situations as threats (Scherer, 2001). On the other hand, it is possible that certain environmental cues remind individuals of past negative, harmful, or stressful events that influence future appraisals (McNally, 2003a, 2003b; A. Wilson, Calhoun, & Bernat, 1999). For example, women with victimization histories may process threat cues or information differently, and this could depend on how the victimization experience memories were encoded or on how the women respond to victimization experience memories (e.g., denial). A. Wilson et al. (1999) found that women with multiple victimization histories and posttraumatic stress disorder (PTSD)–related symptoms were almost hypervigilant to threatening cues. A. Wilson et al. (1999) speculated that hypervigilance could reduce the risk of future victimization. Overactivation or hypervigilance to threat cues may increase stress levels, however, which may then affect information processing because increased stress responses have been associated with poorer judgment and decision making (McEwen & Lasley, 2002).

A. Wilson et al. (1999) also found that women with multiple victimization histories without current PTSD-related symptoms attended to threat cues less than the women with PTSD-related symptoms. The hypothesis was that these women may have had impairment in information processing of threat cues, which could increase their risk of future victimization. Specifically, A. Wilson et al. hypothesized that women with multiple victimization histories without current PTSD-related symptoms "might not have attached the meaning of threat or danger to the assault experiences in their histories and thus have not developed a fear structure that would evoke anxiety and the perception of danger in this sexual situation" (p. 709).

This hypothesis may be consistent with research that has found, for example, that denial or attempts to suppress unwanted emotions, thoughts, or memories may result in increased mental health problems and substance abuse (Boeschen, Koss, Figueredo, & Coan, 2001; Krause, Robins, & Lynch, 2000; T. Lynch, Robins, Morse, & Krause, 2001; Marx & Sloan, 2002; Polusny, Rosenthal, Aban, & Follette, 2004; S. Stewart, Zvolensky, & Eifert, 2002), both of which could be associated with impaired information processing. There is some thought that avoidance or suppression of traumatic events can be harmful to individuals because traumatic experiences need to be processed; when they are fully processed and integrated, individuals will better adapt to their past and current circumstances (E. Solomon & Heide, 2005). In addition, even when individuals try to avoid thinking about traumatic events, they can often reexperience them:

> Traumatic memories can be triggered by stimuli that are in some way associated with the traumatic event. Terrifying memories, including the affect associated with them, may be reexperienced with their original intensity. Survivors feel the terror and may lose their sense of time and place. (Solomon & Heide, 2005, p. 54)

Thus, suppressing or failing to process traumatic memories may affect appraisals and responses. Although this hypothesized relationship between unprocessed traumatic memories and subsequent problems makes intuitive sense, it has not yet received empirical confirmation (McNally, 2003a, 2003b).

In summary, it may be that individuals with victimization histories either ignore threat cues or overattend to them such that when there is real threat, they may not recognize it (McEwen, 2000; Panksepp, 1998; A. Wilson et al., 1999). Although memory of traumatic events plays an important role in appraisals, responses, and adjustment, gaps in the literature prevent an understanding of the specific underlying mechanisms. According to Friedman, Charney, and Deutch (1995),

> in many respects, PTSD is a disorder of memory. Research into the neural mechanisms subserving the acquisition and retrieval of traumatic events

will enhance our understanding of many of the clinical features of PTSD, and may facilitate the development of novel treatment approaches. (p. 531)

There is not yet a consensus in the research literature about the PTSD effects on memory process or the degree to which processing traumatic events is associated with memory for all people who experience traumatic events and for people who develop PTSD (McNally, 2003a, 2003b). Thus, much work remains to be done in understanding the effects of traumatic memory among those with and without PTSD or other mental disorder and the interaction of memory and biological mechanisms in appraisals (McNally, 2003a, 2003b).

Cognitive Biases

Another phenomenon that can reduce women's perception of personal risk is grouped here under the label *cognitive biases*. Two of these are described here: *optimistic* bias, or the illusion of control (C. Klein & Helweg-Larsen, 2002; McKenna, 1993), and the *belief in a just world* bias (M. Lerner, 1980). An optimistic bias may predispose individuals to turn their attention away from any negative or threatening information or cues because of a bias toward believing that nothing bad will happen. This phenomenon can be observed daily. Individuals might believe they are at less risk than other people, for example, of getting cancer, becoming addicted to drugs or alcohol, experiencing the negative effects of smoking, divorcing, being injured in a car accident, or being the victim of interpersonal violence (C. Klein & Helweg-Larsen, 2002; McKenna, 1993). Although women are more likely to recognize risk of interpersonal violence for other women, they are less able to see their own vulnerability when faced with the same risk factors, even if the situation involves a high risk of harm (Cue, George, & Norris, 1996; Norris, Nurius, & Dimeff, 1996; Parks, Miller, Collins, & Zetes-Zanatta, 1998). This phenomenon may be more common when women are familiar with the individuals who pose a potential risk. As described in earlier chapters, interpersonal violence from strangers is far less common than violence from intimate partners, relatives, and acquaintances (Tjaden & Thoennes, 1998, 2000a). The optimistic bias or illusion of control may be especially relevant in situations where acquaintances or loved ones are those who pose the risk. In other words, it may be especially difficult for people to imagine that someone they know, or even someone they do not know well, would intentionally harm them (Norris et al., 1996; Nurius & Gaylord, 1998; Nurius, Norris, Dimeff, & Graham, 1996).

In addition, M. Lerner (1980) hypothesized that people have a bias toward a "just world"—that is, many believe the world is a fair and just place where good or bad things happen to the people who deserve them (Crome & McCabe, 2001). People construe events to fit this belief by blaming individuals who suffer negative situations and by justifying why they themselves were not afflicted. Some women might blame a rape victim for the incident because she dressed provocatively, for example, and reason that because they themselves do not dress provocatively, they will not be raped. According to M. Lerner, people also use tactics to eliminate threats to their just world beliefs; these include denying that suffering exists or reinterpreting negative events as positives. For example, individuals with jobs may deny that the unemployment rates are rising or may justify that a friend who has recently lost her job is better off because she didn't like the job anyway. These cognitive biases may influence an individual's appraisal of situations and threats (Crome & McCabe, 2001).

Personal Goals

Appraisals are also influenced by personal goals or goals that are congruent with self-concepts (Leary, 2003). In fact, self-concept goals may be one of the more important constituents in the appraisal process. Self-concepts are developed through individuals' internal representations of themselves, what is important to them (*self-relevancy*), and what they want out of life (Rosenberg, 1979; Shavelson, Hubner, & Stanton, 1976). They define goals that are important to each person. "Much, if not most, of our responses to the environment in the form of judgments, decisions, and behavior are determined not solely by the information available in that environment but rather by how it relates to whatever goal we are currently pursing" (Bargh & Chartrand, 1999, p. 468). Appraisals include questions about whether a stimulus or event is congruent or incongruent with one's goals, motives, or concerns. Situations that are incompatible with goals relevant to self-concepts require appraisals or actions to somehow align the situation more closely with self-concept goals (Lazarus, 1999). Self-concepts are developed and maintained through appraisals, memories, emotions, and behaviors. They are also maintained because people can imagine scenarios and the emotional responses to them (Higgins, 1996). Worry, for example, is mediated by picturing threats to one's goals and sense of self (Leary, 2003).

Although people may have countless self-concept goals, they tend to have basic goal hierarchies, including affiliation, power achievement, personal growth, altruism, stress avoidance, and sensation seeking (Novacek & Lazarus, 1990). Baumeister and Leary (1995) concluded from a literature review that both men and women have a basic fundamental and pervasive motivation to form and maintain strong, stable interpersonal relationships. Fitzsimons and Bargh (2003) concluded from their study that "relationship partners are among the most important and fundamental aspects of a person's life, having the power to strongly influence thoughts, feelings, and motivations, even when they are not physically present" (p. 160). Recent research has even found that biological factors such as endogenous opiates, the amine system, oxytocin, and vasopressin play a role in regulating mechanisms for affiliation and attachment among mammals in general and primates in particular (Carter, Lederhendler, & Kirkpatrick, 1999; Kraemer, 1992). Attachment theory suggests that affiliation is important for well-being in adulthood (Bartholomew & Horowitz, 1991) and that attachment bonds and patterns are developed early through the mother–infant connection (Bowlby, 1982; Kraemer, 1992). Thus, affiliation has both physiological and psychological importance for adaptation and well-being.

Affiliation goals may be especially salient in understanding women's appraisals and victimization experiences. One of the strongest and most consistent differences between men and women is the degree to which women have self-concepts characterized by the importance of relationships and possess characteristics or skills associated with strengthening those relationships (Cross & Madson, 1997a; Kiecolt-Glaser & Newton, 2001; R. Lee & Robbins, 2000; Sanathara, Gardner, Prescott, & Kendler, 2003; Tamres, Janicki, & Helgeson, 2002). It is not that relationships are unimportant to men; rather, there is evidence that men and women differ in how they go about meeting their needs for affiliation and in the meaning of relationships for their respective self-concepts. More specifically, for men, status, power, and uniqueness are important for securing connections to others on a broader social level; in contrast, women tend to value interdependence with others and to be more concerned with dyadic close relationships (Baumeister & Sommer, 1997b; Cross & Madson, 1997a, 1997b).

Women are more likely to describe themselves in terms of their relationships (Cross & Madson, 1997a; Cross, Bacon, & Morris, 2000; Pratt, Prancer, Hunsberger, & Manchester, 1990). They are also more concerned with establishing close relationships than men (Cross & Madson, 1997a; Cross et al., 2000; Josephs, Markus, & Tafarodi, 1992). More often than men, women provide social support to others, such as caring for aging parents, providing nurturance to children, helping and sacrificing for others who are close to them, and emphasizing sensitivity and caring for others (Finlay & Trafimow, 1998; D. George, Carroll, Kersnick, & Calderon, 1998; Killen & Turiel, 1998; S. Taylor et al., 2000). Cross and Madson (1997a) summarized interdependent self-concepts (which they refer to as *interdependent self-construals*) as follows:

> For the person with an interdependent self-construal, relationships are viewed as integral parts of the person's very being. Indeed, one's thoughts, feelings, and wishes may be interpreted and understood in light of the thoughts, feelings, and behaviors of close others. . . . Consequently their goals, activities, plans, interactions, values, and self-systems are continually shaped by these contexts. (pp. 7–8)

Starting early in life, girls show a concern for preserving social relationships even when attempting to further their goals (Maccoby, 1990). Maccoby contended that girls develop skills to facilitate social relationships through communication to minimize coercion and dominance while maximizing agreement and group cohesion. Research supports this notion with studies indicating that women's feelings about themselves are responsive to feedback from others (Hodgins, Liebeskind, & Schwartz, 1996; Moran & Eckenrode, 1991; T. Roberts & Nolen-Hoeksema, 1989, 1994; Schwalbe & Staples, 1991). For example, relationship stress has a greater association with feelings of guilt and subsequent lower self-esteem for girls and women than for their male counterparts (Baumeister, Reis, & Delespaul, 1995; Baumeister, Stillwell, & Heatherton, 1995; Hodgins et al., 1996; Moran & Eckenrode, 1991; Zuckerman, 1989). In fact, women are more likely than men to perceive negative interpersonal consequences as the worst outcome of conflict (M. Harris, 1992). Women also experience greater psychological distress than men as a result of negative changes in their lives, conflict in their relationships, and negative life events that occur within their social networks (R. Barnett, Raudenbush, Brennan, Pleck, & Marshall, 1995; Birditt & Fingerman, 2003; Hammen et al., 1995; Kessler & McLeod, 1984). Sanathara et al. (2003) found that interpersonal dependence, which was more characteristic for women than men, was also strongly associated with lifetime depression. The reason for this may be found in Allen and Badcock's (2003) conclusion from their literature review that "depression often centers around the loss of relationships, lack of close relationships, and especially, issues of feeling valued or devalued by significant others" (p. 907). Kiecolt-Glaser and Newton (2001) conducted a meta-analysis examining the consequences of marital functioning on health and concluded that

> the physiological studies of marital interaction from the past decade provide evidence that gender is an important moderator of the pathway from negative marital conflict behaviors to physiological functioning; this pathway is stronger for women than for men, and women's physiological changes following marital conflict show greater persistence than men's. (pp. 493–494)

Some might argue that the importance of relationships for women's self-concepts is outdated and that gender ideals and roles have changed. However, a recent national telephone survey of more than 3,000 women found that 75% of the sample said being married or in a committed relationship was important to their self-concept; 91% reported that being a mother was important to their self-concept (Center for the Advancement of Women, 2003). In fact, more than 50% of White, African American, and Hispanic women believe relationships with a partner, relatives, and children are very important and rank those relationships higher in importance than money (see Table 5.1). When these women were asked why a relationship with an intimate partner was important to them, the vast majority emphasized emotional aspects (75% or more), such as companionship, love, affection, and family, rather than practical aspects, such as physical protection, financial well-being, or having someone to do demanding work around the house.

Consistent with this notion, women in committed relationships often place relationship maintenance and enhancement as a priority (Misovich, Fisher, & Fisher, 1997; Surrey, 1991). Beadnell, Baker, Morrison, and Knox (2000) found that higher relationship satisfaction among women was associated with being more motivated to do what a woman's steady partner wanted. Women may be more likely to accommodate a relational partner to create or maintain a harmonious relationship (Arriaga & Rusbult, 1998; Cross et al., 2000; Cross, Morris, & Gore, 2002) and thus may be more likely to change their behavior, to accept certain behaviors from partners, and to minimize conflict in close relationships (Aron, Paris, & Aron, 1995; Cross et al., 2002).

Girls and women have expressed a willingness to comply with a partner's requests even when they do not necessarily want to or feel uncomfortable complying (Impett & Peplau, 2003; Peplau, 2003; Purdie & Downey, 2000). For example, women, more so than men, initiate drug use in the context of an intimate relationship (Amaro & Hardy-Fanta, 1995; Amaro, Zukerman, & Cabral, 1989; Anglin, Ryan, Booth, & Hyser, 1988), and the overwhelming majority of female drug users initiate drug use in the context of close relationships more

Table 5.1. Percentage of Women Reporting on the Dimensions That Are Very Important to Their Self-Concepts

Dimension	White	African American	Hispanic	Total
Being a mother	81	87	89	86
Connection with relatives	73	82	85	80
Religious beliefs	64	87	72	74
Education	57	81	71	70
Work	51	61	63	58
Being married or involved	53	52	66	57
Racial or ethnic background	24	74	58	52
Physical appearance	38	66	53	52
Female friendships	55	41	56	51
Political beliefs	32	57	34	41
Money	21	49	43	38
Being a feminist	16	39	35	30

Note. Data are from Center for the Advancement of Women (2003).

generally (e.g., partners, siblings, and friends; Maher, 1995; Nyamathi, Bayley, Anderson, Keenan, & Leake, 1999). Substance use within the context of a close relationship may serve as a bonding mechanism (Covington & Surrey, 1997). This characteristic was evident in the case scenario presented at the beginning of this chapter. Furthermore, as noted in an chapter 4, the drug and alcohol use of a woman's partner most likely affects her substance use patterns (L. Roberts & Leonard, 1997, 1998; Salomon, Bassuk, & Huntington, 2002). Using substances with partners may increase violence because of the overlap of substance use and violence (Amaro & Hardy-Fanta, 1995; El-Bassel, Gilbert, & Rajah, 2003; Leonard & Quigley, 1999; Scott, Schafer, & Greenfield, 1999). Substance use may serve as a bonding mechanism and also moderate a woman's perception of risk (see chaps. 3 and 4).

Women may provide excuses or rationalizations in situations with multiple and conflicting cues (Hock, Krohne, & Kaiser, 1996) or because they are attending to cues that are more congruent to their relational self-concept goals (Norris et al., 1996; Truman-Schram, Cann, Calhoun, & Vanwallendael, 2000). For example, Livingston and Testa (2000) found that although women recognized the potential danger of sexual aggression from acquaintances, they frequently discounted concerns in favor of facilitating a relationship or by believing they could manage any risk posed. These appraisals prevailed regardless of whether they had consumed alcohol. In another example, Truman-Schram et al. (2000) found that women experiencing partner violence who were still involved with those partners reported higher relationship satisfaction and more positive feelings toward that partner compared with women who had left violent relationships. This may suggest that even when women stay with violent partners, they recognize some level of threat; however, they may focus on the satisfactory aspects of the relationship and positive regard for their partner rather than threat cues or other self-concept goals (Herbert, Silver, & Ellard, 1991; Pape & Arias, 2000).

Agency

Agency is defined here very generally as the belief that one's behavior can influence both desired and undesired effects. Agency is an important construct in understanding how individuals make appraisals.

> To be an agent is to intentionally make things happen by one's actions. Agency embodies the endowments, belief systems, self-regulatory capabilities and distributed structures and functions though which personal influence is exercised. . . . The core features of agency enable people to play a part in their self-development, adaptation, and self-renewal with changing times. (Bandura, 2001, p. 2)

Stated differently, "Many crucial functions of the self involve volition: making choices and decisions, taking responsibility, initiating and inhibiting behavior, and making plans of action and carrying out those plans. The self exerts control over itself and over the external world" (Baumeister, Bratslavsky, Muraven, & Tice, 1998, p. 1252). The following discussion of agency includes two main features: influence and self-regulation.

The first aspect of agency, influence, includes the degree to which an individual believes oneself to be capable of shaping his or her own motives, behavior, and future possibilities (Bandura, 2001):

> Among the mechanisms of personal agency, none is more central or pervasive than people's beliefs in their capability to exercise some measure of control over their own functioning and over environmental events. . . . Unless people believe they can produce desired results and forestall detrimental ones by their actions, they have little incentive to act or to persevere in the face of difficulties. (Bandura, 2001, p. 10)

If people believe they have no control over what happens to them or that they deserve bad things, they may be less likely to take self-protective steps in various situations (Mirowsky & Ross, 1989, 2003; Ross & Mirowsky, 1989). As Ross and Mirowsky (1989) concluded,

> if a person thinks that the outcome is contingent on his or her own behavior and abilities (an internal locus of control), he or she learns quickly, and actively seeks rewards and avoids punishments. If a person believes that the outcome is determined by luck, fate, chance, powerful others, or complex, uncontrollable, and unpredictable forces (an external locus of control), he or she learns slowly (if at all), and passively accepts the reports and punishments that come along. . . . an internal locus of control encourages a person to think about problems, to try to solve them, to limit their undesirable consequences and to avoid them in the future. In the long run a personal history of meeting and solving problems improves one's conditions, skills, and self assurance. (p. 207)

Agency has been associated with psychological well-being across the life span (G. Smith et al., 2000). Hobfall, Schroder, Wells, and Malek (2002) found that higher agency was associated with assertiveness, less worry about social relationships, and more social involvement. Individuals who perceive situations as not in their control or who perceive that they will have little control over their futures have higher symptoms of distress than individuals with higher levels of perceived control or agency (E. Carlson & Dalenberg, 2000; Dalenberg & Jacobs, 1994; Turner, Lloyd, & Roszell, 1999). One study found that women with low agency beliefs who had experienced completed or attempted raped were more likely to be depressed (Regehr, Regehr, & Bradford, 1998). Similarly, another study found that women with low agency beliefs who experienced partner violence had worse mental health outcomes (O'Neill & Kerig, 2000).

The influence component of agency is often encompassed in more familiar terms such as *locus of control* (Rotter, 1966), *personal autonomy* (Seeman, 1983), *instrumentalism* (Mirowsky, Ross, & Van Willigen, 1996), *power and control* (Mirowsky & Ross, 2003), and *mastery* (Pearlin, Lieberman, Menaghan, & Mullen, 1981) or can be conceptualized as the opposite of fatalism (Wheaton, 1980) and helplessness (Seligman, 1975). These constructs are not necessarily conceptualized as the same thing, however; researchers use different measures for them, and how they are measured could greatly affect the results. In addition, agency is defined here as encompassing more than just an external versus an internal locus of control. It is conceptualized as including perceived control over past events, current events, and future events as well as perceived control over internal processes. It is the degree to which one is the driver of a car rather than a rider on a bus; this applies to mental processes as well as actions. The person with a high degree of agency takes ownership of his or her experiences and sees them in the context of personal decisions and interpretations.

The second component of agency, termed *self-regulation* here, is critical to environmental adaptation and achieving personal goals. Self-regulation consists of three primary components (Baumeister, Heatherton, & Tice, 1994). First, there must be some kind of standard or abstract concept of how one should act, which may be derived from social norms, personal goals, and expectations of others. Second, there must be self-awareness or some way to monitor current circumstances to determine progress toward reaching goals and make decisions accordingly. Third, there must be some way to self-regulate emotions and responses to bring about desired changes or responses consistent with goals. Bandura (2001) suggested that self-regulation requires self-awareness and corrective self-reactions. Muraven, Tice, and Baumeister (1998, p. 774) noted that "the failure of self-control has immense personal and societal repercussions . . . breakdowns in self-control are linked with depression . . . obsessive or ruminative thoughts . . . and aggression." Baumeister et al. (1994) stated that many of the problems individuals face in their lives, such as substance abuse, are associated with regulatory failure. Self-regulation and self-awareness have important implications for appraisals. Self-awareness is associated with how individuals see themselves in the world and how they perceive the world responds to them. Self-regulation is associated with controlling certain emotional and behavioral reactions to ensure appropriate responses are displayed. Appraisal errors, for example, can be corrected and controlled through self-awareness and self-regulation.

A prime example of self-awareness and self-regulation processes and how these affect appraisals is called *self-talk*: What individuals tell themselves about situations affects their emotions (Leary, 2003). If individuals engage in positive self-talk, they may be able to calm anxiety; if they engage in negative self-talk, they may make themselves feel worse. Self-talk also may allow individuals to interpret negative information or threat cues accurately, or it may distract them from doing so. Individuals may also seek to distract themselves from continual internal dialogue and negative emotions by using substances or through other methods (Leary, 2003). Self-regulation can protect individuals from acting on impulses that may be motivated by negative emotions. Impulsivity and negative emotions can interact to facilitate behavior that may serve to alleviate negative emotions in the short term, even though it may be more harmful to an individual in the long term. Tice, Bratslavsky, and Baumeister (2001) concluded from their research that

> emotionally distraught people indulge their impulses because they hope that indulgence will bring pleasure that may repair their mood and dispel their distress. Impulse control is sometimes at odds with affect regulation and acute bad moods seem to shift the balance in favor of the short-term pursuit of pleasure instead of the self-denial required to pursue long-term goals. (p. 64)

Tice et al. (2001) found that emotional distress interfered with self-regulation when individuals perceived that an impulsive behavior would reduce their immediate distress and when they only considered the short-term benefits of the behavior. Others have concluded that when emotional reactions to threat cues diverge from cognitive assessments of the threat, emotion will have a greater impact on behavior (Loewenstein, Weber, Hsee, & Welch, 2001). This may be related to a lack of self-awareness or limited self-regulation abilities. In other words, emotional reactions may drive behavior even when cognitive assessments of a situation suggest that these behaviors are not beneficial. For a concrete example, Susannah, the woman in the case presented at the beginning of this chapter, may feel so depressed and emotionally overwhelmed that the desire to feel better by using alcohol may be more influential on her behavior, even though she likely recognizes that seeking mental health treatment or going to a shelter would probably be better in the long run. Thus, self-regulation failure may play a key role in substance use and other risk behavior (Baumeister, 2003; Tice et al., 2001) as well as in appraisals of risk or threat and responses to threats.

In summary, agency plays a critical role in the appraisal process. Individuals who do not believe they can influence their world will appraise events differently than people who believe their actions can and do make a difference in what happens to them. In addition, individuals who do not understand, do not accurately interpret, or cannot control their emotions will appraise situations and outcomes differently than those with higher levels of self-awareness and self-regulation abilities. A person's sense of agency, including self-regulation, can be affected by moods and personality characteristics as well.

Mood and Personality

Moods and specific personality characteristics can influence appraisals through two primary mechanisms. First, as mentioned earlier, automatic information

processing as well as physiological factors can affect emotions and moods. Physiological arousal then elicits cognitions to help "explain" the emotion or mood.
Bargh (1994) hypothesized that automatic information processing and subsequent arousal may lead to the misattribution of the cause of a feeling, leading a
person to make erroneous judgments and decisions. For example, a driver involved in a car accident may exit the car and have difficulty controlling an angry verbal response toward the other driver. It may be that the driver is angry
with the other driver, but it may also be that the driver is simply physiologically aroused from the accident because he feared injury. The driver might have
misidentified the arousal as anger at the other driver. As another example, a
woman who has just been physically assaulted by her partner may yell and
scream at a telemarketer who happens to call at the wrong time. Her arousal
and feelings of anger present from the assault may be directed at the
telemarketer.

Second, moods and specific personality traits can influence which situational
cues or information people focus on for appraisals. Both emotions and cognitions use information from the environment to develop responses and to guide
behavior. "Essentially . . . the cognitive system orients us to what makes sense
whereas the emotional system orients us to what matters" (Planalp & Fitness,
1999, p. 734). In other words, what people choose to focus on, whether remembering things that have happened in the past or cues from the current situation, may be influenced by moods (Forgas, 2003; Hemenover & Zhang, 2004;
Mineka, Rafaeli, & Yovel, 2003). The old question, "Is the cup half full or is it
half empty?" comes to mind—that is, how do people frame experiences or information from the environment? For example, anxious individuals tend to focus
on information that may be threatening, whereas depressed individuals tend to
focus on negative events from the past and on negative more than positive information in the present (Mineka et al., 2003; Oliver & Brough, 2002). People
with PTSD give heightened attention to trauma-relevant words and memories
(McNally, 1998; McNally, Clancy, Schacter, & Pitman, 2000).

Thus, emotions affect self-perceptions, self-efficacy, self-regulation, and
attention to environmental cues (Leary, 2003). Furthermore, this cycle is continually reiterative so that the resulting emotions influence other emergent
self-perceptions, attention to the environment, and appraisals. Consequently,
more sustained emotions (moods and affective states) can influence information processing and appraisals (E. Chang & Strunk, 1999; Forgas, 2003; Mineka
et al., 2003). Emotions or moods may prime emotion-specific content in memory
as well as in attention or focal awareness.

Certain personality traits also affect individuals' appraisal of stress and
distress (Gunthert, Cohen, & Armeli, 1999; O'Brien & DeLongis, 1996; Tomaka
et al., 1999). For example, individuals who scored high on neuroticism (characterized by anxiety, depression, and sensitivity) appraised more events as stressful
and had higher levels of distress than individuals scoring lower on neuroticism
(Gunthert et al., 1999). Trait optimism (the tendency to see the positive or best
aspects of situations) and pessimism (the tendency to see the negative or worst
aspects of situations) have also been associated with differential appraisals,
coping, and adjustment to stressful events (E. Chang, 1998).

Certain individuals are more susceptible to involuntary and automatic responses to stressful circumstances or threats, such as worry or repetitive negative thoughts (Ayduk, Downey, & Kim, 2001; Compas, Connor, Osowiecki, & Welch, 1997). This kind of response (which has no intentionality or agency) is associated with exacerbated depression and other mental health problems (Compas et al., 1997; Hartlage, Alloy, Vazquez, & Dykman, 1993). Thus, moods and personality characteristics can influence situation appraisals by directing attention toward or away from environmental cues that are used to inform appraisals. In addition, negative emotions and moods may compel individuals toward behaviors to relieve discomfort, even when they know it may not be the best thing to do in the long run (Loewenstein et al., 2001; Tice et al., 2001). For example, Saladin et al. (2003) found that PTSD symptoms were significantly predictive of drug cravings after participants thought about a trauma they had experienced, which is consistent with more general research suggesting that negative emotions are associated with craving drugs or alcohol (Rees & Heather, 1995).

Summary of Situation Appraisal

Situation appraisals are unique to each individual because they are meaning based and evaluative. Situation appraisals are also complex in that they are constantly interacting with emotions and environmental feedback. Several factors are thought to influence appraisals, including knowledge and understanding of the situation, memory, and cognitive biases. In addition, personal goals are thought to influence appraisals, especially whether the situation is congruent or incongruent with personal goals. If a situation is incongruent with a person's goals, then stress and emotional distress are more likely to occur (Agnew, 1992, 2001). One especially salient self-concept goal is affiliation. As mentioned earlier, women are more likely to have self-concepts that are defined by relational contexts, which may influence appraisals regarding risk of violence as well as influence mental health problems when important relationships are characterized by conflict and violence. Agency is also important, especially the influence of beliefs and self-regulatory process components on agency. Moods and certain personality characteristics can influence appraisals by directing attention toward or away from important information. For example, negative moods can influence people to direct their attention toward more negative interpretations of events, which probably creates a cycle of continued stress, worry, and continued negative appraisals.

Examining the situation of a woman in a violent intimate relationship may help to highlight how these factors contribute to and interact with situation appraisals. Women in violent relationships often experience repeated abuse over a period of years (Tjaden & Thoennes, 1998, 2000b), suggesting that women in abusive relationships may not recognize or respond to the violence initially. However, many women in abusive relationships do eventually leave their partners (Logan, Walker, Jordan, & Campbell, 2004); thus, at some point women apparently do perceive the situation as negative, stressful, or threatening. Women in partner-violence situations may be more likely to appraise threat when the violence is frequent, severe, or increasing in intensity or frequency, or when a woman realizes her children are threatened in some way (Hamby & Gray-Little, 2000; Holtzworth-Munroe, Smutzler, & Sandin, 1997; Kearney, 2001; Pape & Arias, 2000; P. Smith, White, & Holland, 2003). These women initially may not understand their experience as violence for a number of reasons. For example, there may be ambiguous cues or cognitive biases at work. Perhaps the situation does not meet a woman's internal or external reference as definition of violence. Finally, some women may believe they deserve this kind of treatment or are depressed or too anxious to focus on threat cues.

Some research has begun to examine this process of change with the transtheoretical stages of change model (Prochaska, DiClemente, & Norcross, 1992). According to this theory, the process of change incorporates several stages: the *precontemplation stage*, in which individuals do not perceive the possibility of change or even perceive a problem; the *contemplation stage*, in which individuals begin to perceive that change is needed in their lives and perhaps begin to weigh the pros and cons of potential changes; the *preparation stage*, in which individuals prepare to make a change; the *action stage*, in which individuals actually make the change; and the *maintenance stage*, in which individuals work to maintain the change (Haggerty & Goodman, 2002). This theory has primarily been applied to health-related and addiction problems, but some recent research has begun to use it to understand women's perceptions of their situations and for interventions with women in violent relationships (Burke, Denison, Gielen, McDonnell, & O'Campo, 2004; Burke, Gielen, McDonnell, O'Campo, & Maman, 2001; Dienemann, Campbell, Landenburger, & Curry, 2002; Frasier, Slatt, Kowlowitz, & Glowa, 2001; Haggerty & Goodman, 2002).

Response Appraisal

Response appraisals have been referred to as *secondary appraisals* by Lazarus and Folkman (1984) and are important in understanding the overall appraisal process. The review of factors influencing response appraisal discussed here consists of three components: blame, anticipated outcomes, and self-efficacy. Again, situation and response appraisals are not necessarily linear. Rather, they are ongoing, reiterative processes in which an individual goes back and forth between situation appraisal, response appraisal, and reappraisal. Thus, the concepts described in this section often refer to a "process" rather than just "responses."

Blame

Blame for a negative, threatening, or incongruent situation or event influences appraisals because different blame attributions result in different emotions and response appraisals (Lazarus, 1999). More specifically, an individual who blames someone else for an event might become angry, whereas an individual who perceives an event as his or her own fault might feel sadness; the two people thus cope with the same event in very different ways (Lowe et al., 2003). For example, women in violent relationships who assume responsibility for their partner's violence, attribute it to relationship problems, excuse it because of temporary stressful situations (e.g., work-related problems or substance abuse), or assume responsibility for helping their partner overcome problems or a past injustice (e.g., abuse during childhood) may be less likely to leave their partner than women who hold their partner accountable for his violence (Barnett, Martinez, & Keyson, 1996; Cantos, Neidig, & O'Leary, 1993; Ferraro, 1993; Holtzworth-Munroe, Jacobson, Fehrenbach, & Fruzzetti, 1992; Katz, Arias, Beach, Brody, & Roman, 1995; E. Klein, Campbell, Soler, & Ghez, 1997). Studies have reported that women in abusive relationships had higher levels of self-blame than women who were no longer with their violent partners and that women with higher levels of self-blame had more mental health symptoms (Andrews & Brewin, 1990; O'Neill & Kerig, 2000; Truman-Schram et al., 2000). Attributions of responsibility for violence typically change over time from self-blame to perpetrator blame and that blaming the perpetrator is associated with a woman's intentions to leave (Pape & Arias, 2000).

Women who blame themselves for a rape have more health problems and mental distress than women who do not blame themselves (Arata & Burkhart, 1995, 1998; Frazier, 2003; Koss, Figueredo, & Prince, 2002). Furthermore, self-blame was associated with lower confidence in taking assertive resistance actions against sexual assault by an acquaintance (Nurius, Norris, Young, Graham, & Gaylord, 2000). One study found that women who labeled forced sexual experiences as rape were more likely to blame the perpetrator for the event compared with women who did not label the experience as rape (Kahn, Jackson, Kully, Badger, & Halvorsen, 2003).

Some research has highlighted two kinds of self-blame attributions: *behavioral self-blame*, which is associated with behavior and is thus assumed to be controllable or modifiable, and *characterological self-blame*, which is related to an aspect of the self (e.g., character or personality) and is assumed to be less controllable (Janoff-Bulman, 1992). Studies with physical and sexual assault victims that have examined the associations of these two kinds of attributions show mixed results; some found higher associations of characterological self-blame and psychological distress (Boeschen et al., 2001; Koss et al., 2002), and others found that both contribute to distress (Frazier, 1990; Frazier & Schauben, 1994; O'Neill & Kerig, 2000). Several studies have also found high correlations between behavioral and characterological self-blame (Boeschen et al., 2001; Frazier, 1990; Frazier & Schauben, 1994).

Women who experienced multiple victimizations have reported more self-blame (Koss et al., 2002; Neville, Heppner, Oh, Spanierman, & Clark, 2004). Furthermore, when women are unsure about where to assign blame, they may be slower to react to negative situations and threats (Hock et al., 1996; Norris, Nurius, & Graham, 1999). In other words, in a situation in which there are multiple but conflicting cues, women may be less likely to appraise the situation as harmful. For example, a woman with a psychologically abusive partner who tells her he loves her and cannot live without her yet threatens to beat her up and kill her may create ambiguity about where to place blame for the violence. In fact, causal uncertainty has been associated with low agency beliefs as well as depression (Edwards & Weary, 1998; Jacobson, Weary, & Edwards, 1999).

Anticipated Outcomes

Response appraisals are also shaped by the anticipation of outcomes that might result from actions taken to reduce a threat (Lazarus, 1999). Women's response appraisals may resemble a cost–benefit analysis (Lazarus, 2001), but such assessments are not necessarily based on realistic outcomes. What is important is women's perception of their outcomes, because perceptions ultimately influence responses.

Anticipated outcomes are influenced by immediate visceral reactions (feelings of fear, anxiety, or dread in thinking about the risk and uncertainty of decisions or behaviors), anticipated emotions (emotions expected to occur with certain decisions or behaviors), and subjective probabilities of what will actually occur after a decision or behavior (Loewenstein et al., 2001). Women may perceive, on the basis of several factors, that taking certain actions will require great personal risk. For example, a woman experiencing partner violence may think about calling the police, which elicits an immediate visceral fear reaction because she is afraid of retaliation. She may perceive, too, that if she calls the police, her neighbors will find out about her embarrassing situation. She might perceive that calling the police could result in her own arrest and in her children being taken away from her; in the perpetrator going to jail, which could have financial implications for her and her children; or that the police will take no action (Logan, Stevenson, Evans, & Leukefeld, 2004; Logan, Walker, Cole, & Leukefeld, 2002; Logan, Walker, et al., 2004). Thus, a woman who believes that calling the police will incite violence or other negative consequences may be influenced by immediate feelings of fear, future anticipated fear and anxiety, and the probability that the action will not be helpful (Loewenstein et al., 2001). Thus, one simple act (i.e., picking up the phone to call the police) could result in perceptions of great costs and few benefits.

Women do consider these factors in deciding whether to turn to the criminal justice system. Studies of rape and partner-assault victims have indicated that women do not report the crimes to the police because they anticipate negative outcomes, including negative and blaming reactions, embarrassment, fear of perpetrator retaliation, or services' lack of efficacy (Logan, Evans, et al., 2004; Logan, Stevenson, et al., 2004; Rennison, 2002; Sudderth, 1998; Tjaden & Thoennes, 2000b). Immigrant women face numerous barriers to seeking help (Bui, 2003; M. Goldman, 1999; Menjivar & Salcido, 2002; Raj & Silverman, 2002). They may have concerns related to deportation, language barriers, financial survival, social isolation, and a lack of culturally tailored services. Prior negative experiences with the criminal justice system can also affect future use (Byrne, Kilpatrick, Howley, & Beatty, 1999; Erez & Belknap, 1998b). For example, women who use drugs may fear that if they report abuse, they will be blamed, not believed, or even implicated for illegal drug behavior (Ruback, Menard, Outlaw, & Schaffer, 1999; Staton, Leukefeld, & Logan, 2001).

A woman who considers leaving a violent partner must also consider the financial impact of separation, the impact on the well-being of her children, and the impact on her social support networks (Logan, Walker, et al., 2004). In other words, she may ask herself whether her perceived standard of living after separation will stay the same or worsen compared with her current situation (Choice

& Lamke, 1997; I. Johnson, 1992; Knoester & Booth, 2000; Logan, Walker, et al., 2004; Rusbult & Martz, 1995). Women with fewer financial resources, including lower employment, education, and limited transportation resources, are less likely to leave a relationship (Esterberg, Moen, & Dempster-McCain, 1994; Rusbult & Martz, 1995; South, 2001). In fact, some research has shown that women's incomes decline after separating from a partner, and single mothers experience an inordinate amount of initial stress (possibly because of potential changes in living arrangements, child care, and jobs) as well as ongoing stress (possibly because of role strain, financial difficulties, and legal issues; Logan, Walker, et al., 2004).

Furthermore, women considering separation may be concerned about perpetrator retaliation and ongoing violence. Those perceptions are likely to be accurate in that violence is likely to continue even after separation, as are persistent threats of violence (J. Campbell, 1995; Hall Smith, Moracco, & Butts, 1998; McFarlane et al., 1999), stalking (McFarlane et al., 1999); forced sex (J. Campbell, 1995); and threats and violence toward others (McFarlane et al., 1999; Riger, Raja, & Camacho, 2002; Websdale, 1999). One study found that 95% of women who separated from violent relationships experienced ongoing psychological abuse after separating from their partner; 39% experienced continued physical violence after separating (Hotton, 2001). Gondolf, Heckert, and Kimmel (2002) reported that almost 75% of the men from a sample of batterer program participants verbally abused their partners at least once during the 15-month follow-up, and about half (44%) of the participants verbally abused their partner during the last 3 months of the 15-month follow-up. Furthermore, separation has been identified as an important risk factor for lethal violence (J. Campbell et al., 2003; Dawson & Gartner, 1998; Kurz, 1996; Saltzman & Mercy, 1993; Sev'er, 1997; M. Wilson & Daly, 1993; M. Wilson, Johnson, & Daly, 1995). About one third of female murder victims are killed by an intimate partner, and intimate-partner homicide is the largest category of femicides (R. Bachman & Saltzman, 1995; Bailey et al., 1997; National Institute of Justice, 1997). According to police and medical examiner records, between 21% and 70% of female homicide victims were separated from their partner at the time of the murder (Hall Smith et al., 1998; McFarlane, Campbell, & Watson, 2002; McFarlane et al., 1999; Morton, Runyan, Moracco, & Butts, 1998; Websdale, 1999). Thus, women's perceptions of future violence are likely to be accurate and must be considered in safety planning, interventions, and research with women in violent relationships.

The perceived threat of losing custody of children as well as concern for children's safety are both important considerations in weighing response options and outcomes (Jouriles, Norwood, McDonald, Vincent, & Mahony, 1996; Knoester & Booth, 2000; Laumakis, Margolin, & John, 1998). Threats from violent partners directed toward children are common, especially during separation (McCloskey, 2001; Mechanic, Weaver, & Resick, 2000). Partner violence and child abuse often overlap (McCloskey et al., 1995; National Research Council, 1993; S. Ross, 1996). Women also may be concerned about their children's safety during paternal visits. In addition, they may fear that child protective service agencies will remove their children if they disclose victimization (Barnett, 2001; Busch & Wolfer, 2002; Echlin & Marshall, 1995; Edleson, 1999).

Women may also be concerned that the court system will overlook or dismiss their safety concerns (Newmark, Harrell, & Salem, 1995). Violent ex-partners have used the court system to maintain control, intimidate, and harass their victims (Jaffe, Lemon, & Poisson, 2003). From a sample of women in custody disputes, Newmark et al. (1995) found that abused, compared with nonabused, women were more likely to fear future harm and to avoid disagreeing openly with their ex-partner because of potential repercussions. Also, certain custody and visitation arrangements (e.g., joint custody) may actually provide opportunities for a violent ex-partner to continue to harass his victim (Henderson, 1990; Hilton, 1992; Shalansky, Ericksen, & Henderson, 1999). For example, Arendell (1995) found from a study of fathers that the majority of the separation violence occurred during child exchanges.

Women's response appraisals may also be influenced by their perception of social responses to their situation. For example, social support levels are often negatively affected by separation (Kitson, 1992; Marks, 1996; O'Connor, Hawkins, Dunn, Thorpe, & Golding, 1998; C. Ross, 1995). Women may also be concerned about finding another partner (Ferraro, 1993; South & Lloyd, 1995; South, Trent, & Shen, 2001; L. White & Booth, 1991), and this expectation can contribute to negative anticipated outcomes. Furthermore, if a woman's partner is supplying her with drugs, she may be even more isolated and more dependent on him (Amaro, 1988; Amaro & Hardy-Fanta, 1995; Galaif, Nyamathi, & Stein, 1999).

Self-Efficacy

Self-efficacy, which is related to but not synonymous with agency, is an assessment of the specific skills, abilities, or resources needed to carry out a specific decision (Bandura, 1999; Eccles & Wigfield, 2002). More generally, self-efficacy has been associated with positive health behaviors (Bagozzi & Edwards, 2000; Bandura, 1997; Shaw, 1999) and with confidence in coping with a serious illness (Gallagher, Parle, & Cairns, 2002). Individuals must believe they have the available personal and environmental resources to take specific actions (Bandura, 1997; Hobfall, Freedy, Green, & Solomon, 1996; Lazarus, 1999). For example, a woman living in an abusive relationship must consider her perceived ability to talk with a police officer, to negotiate the criminal justice system, and to maintain independent living and caring for children before taking any of these actions.

Self-efficacy and self-esteem are highly interrelated, according to some researchers (Judge, Erez, Bono, & Thoresen, 2002). Victimization is associated with lower self-esteem (Campbell & Soeken, 1999a; S. Lynch & Graham-Bermann, 2000; Petersen, Gazmararian, & Clark, 2001; Resick, 1993; Tuel & Russell, 1998), and low self-esteem is associated with mental health and substance use problems (Baumeister, Campbell, Krueger, & Vohs, 2003; Leary, 1999; Scheier, Botvin, Griffin, & Diaz, 2000). For example, Petersen et al. (2001) interviewed 392 women from a managed care organization and found that 70.9% who reported a history of partner violence had negative self-esteem compared with 44.3% not reporting a history of partner violence. H. Smith and Betz (2002) reported that the combination of self-efficacy and self-esteem predicted depressive symptoms (accounting for 48% of the variance in women). C. Brown, Reedy, Fountain, Johnson, and Dischiser (2000) found that high self-esteem was related to higher self-efficacy toward work among women with histories of partner violence.

Self-efficacy is derived from past experiences, vicarious experiences, and the encouragement of others (Bandura, 1997) and thus is not defined exclusively by personal experiences but depends on social experiences to validate and support it. In general, social support is important for both health and mental health (Brewin, Andrews, & Valentine, 2000; Uchino, Cacioppo, & Kiecolt-Glaser, 1996); it also buffers the effects of stress (S. Cohen, Gottlieb, & Underwood, 2000; Israel, Farquhar, Schulz, James, & Parker, 2002; Turner, 1999). Nonetheless, social support systems can have both positive and negative impacts on women who have been victimized (Kawachi & Berkman, 2001; Lewis & Rook, 1999; Rose, Campbell, & Kub, 2000; Uchino, Uno, & Holt-Lunstad, 1999).

The majority of women with victimization histories disclose their abuse to friends or family members (Krishnan, Hilbert, & VanLeeuwen, 2001; Rose et al., 2000; Tan, Basta, Sullivan, & Davidson, 1995; Thompson et al., 2000), and certain types of support are more helpful for coping with victimization (Goodkind, Gillum, Bybee, & Sullivan, 2003). For example, one study found that although positive emotional support was not related to well-being for women in abusive relationships, tangible support was critical (Goodkind et al., 2003). On the other hand, if a woman's social support network is negative or blaming toward her, or if her friends and family insist that abuse is "normal," the effect can be further damage to her mental health and increased isolation (El-Bassel, Gilbert, Rajah, Foleno, & Frye, 2001; Goodkind et al., 2003; Rose et al., 2000; Ullman, 1999). According to Nurius et al. (2003), "negative social interactions affect well-being through a variety of mechanisms such as eroding feelings of worth, personal control, hopefulness, or motivation as well as stimulating negative cognitive, emotional, and physiological stress responses" (p. 1425). Negative feedback from support network members can diminish self-efficacy and may affect response appraisals.

Summary of Response Appraisal

Like situation appraisals, response appraisals are reiterative, continuing processes that involve multiple and interrelated factors. Response appraisals are central to understanding how individuals interpret and actually respond to various situations. Response appraisals are influenced by blame, the anticipated outcome of specific responses, and self-efficacy beliefs in whether a potential action can be carried out. D. Anderson and Saunders (2003) concluded from a review of the literature that women in violent relationships undergo a process: First, they may struggle to cope with the violence by denying or directing attention away from negative or threat cues; next, they may acknowledge the stress or threat and evaluate how serious it is; finally, they may leave the situation. When women leave such a relationship, they often must ask themselves two questions that encompass the response appraisal discussion in this chapter: First, will they be better off if they leave their partner (i.e., is the situation negative because of the partner's behavior, and what are the anticipated outcomes)? Second, can they survive without their partner (i.e., does she have efficacy in her ability to leave and live independently; Choice & Lamke, 1997)?

Cognitive Constraints

This section reviews literature on selected factors that may have relevance for appraisals, including cumulative stress, multiple victimization experiences, and psychological abuse. These specific experiences have been selected because they are hypothesized to influence the appraisal components process in ways that are especially salient to women with victimization histories.

Cumulative Stress

Situation appraisal often takes place in the context of many stressors inherent in daily living (Pearlin, 1999a, 1999b); that is, individuals rarely face only one stressor or negative situation at a time. Women may be coping with poverty, marital discord, stressful work, and difficulties raising children in addition to victimization or risk of victimization. Women in an abusive situation may recognize that the relationship has problems, but compared with the other issues they confront, it may not seem as threatening as it would under different circumstances. In addition to daily stress, there are other significant life events, both positive and negative, that may influence stress levels (e.g., family illness, employment problems, child problems, health problems, stranger victimization, and property crime). Furthermore, one life stressor often creates a domino effect, with other stressors following (Logan, Walker, et al., 2004; Pearlin, 1999a, 1999b). Thus, it is critical to understand the negative impact of cumulative stress on an individual's appraisals (Tafet & Bernardini, 2003) as well as on mental health functioning and risk behavior such as substance use (Kendler, Kuhn, & Prescott, 2004; Pearlin, 1999a, 1999b; Turner, Sorenson, & Turner, 2000; Turner, Wheaton, & Lloyd, 1995).

Cumulative stress may affect appraisals for three reasons. First, individuals may be too overwhelmed by day-to-day stress to attend to negative situations or threat cues (Gallo & Matthews, 2003; G. Link & Phelan, 1995). Hobfall et al. (1996) pointed out that "following stressful circumstances people tend to have an increasingly depleted resource pool to combat future stressful circumstances" (p. 326). Those who lack resources (both internal and external), such as women with low financial or social resources or who have mental health problems, are more vulnerable to stress and to the domino effect (one stressor creating other stressors; Hobfall & Lilly, 1993; Logan, Walker, et al., 2004; Pearlin, 1999a, 1999b).

More specifically, Baumeister (2003) argued that internal resources for dealing with stress are limited. A number of experiments have shown that individuals who were required to make specific decisions, control positive or nega-

tive emotions volitionally, actively resist temptations, or actively suppress specific thoughts performed worse on a variety of subsequent tasks than participants who were not required to utilize such internal resources (Baumeister,
2003; Baumeister et al., 1998; Muraven, Baumeister, & Tice, 1999; Muraven,
Collins, & Nienhaus, 2002; Muraven et al., 1998; Vohs & Heatherton, 2000).
Baumeister (2003) concluded that

> these studies suggest that the self has a single resource, akin to energy or
> strength. The same resource is used for a broad variety of activities: all forms
> of self-regulation (including regulating emotions, thoughts, impulses, and
> task performance), choice, and decision-making; active instead of passive
> responding; and mental tasks requiring the active manipulation of informa-
> tion (such as in reasoning). The resource appears to be quite limited, insofar
> as a brief exercise of self-regulation is sufficient to cause significant impair-
> ments in subsequent performance. (p. 283)

When internal resources are limited, individuals have less strength to focus on decisions or problems that need attention. For example, women living in
poverty who have violent partners may have more difficulty seeking help. Their
internal resources may be depleted because of the constant focus on daily and
life stressors, because they must try to control feelings of anger or depression
associated with abuse, or because they are trying to manage a partner's violent
outbreaks. Similarly, women living in poverty who are sexually assaulted may
not have the internal resources to report the crime. It may be that calling the
police (assuming easy access to a phone), talking with them, and having the
energy to follow through with pressing charges against her attacker may be
more than she can imagine taking on.

Limited internal resources due to stress can affect risk in other ways as
well. For example, individuals with depleted internal resources may have less
energy to control impulsive or other risky behaviors such as substance use
(Baumeister, 2003). As an example of how the depletion of internal resources
can affect substance use, Muraven et al. (2002) randomly assigned male participants to one of two conditions—thought suppression or doing mental arithmetic.
The participants were then offered an opportunity to sample beer but were told
that they were going to be given a driving test after drinking. Participants who
were asked to suppress a specific thought for a period of time consumed more
alcohol and had higher blood alcohol content than participants assigned to the
arithmetic condition, even though all participants had motivation (a subsequent
driving test) to limit their alcohol intake. Measures on mood, arousal, and frustration did not differ between the groups.

A second reason cumulative stress is important in the appraisals process is
that stress is connected to both physiological and psychological systems. Once
stress overload is initiated, reactions can create greater stress in both systems
(Charney, 2004; McEwen & Lasley, 2002; Shalev, 2002). Stress can activate the
sympathetic nervous system, and when these systems are activated too often or
for too long, these systems can actually be damaged, causing difficulty in regulating the stress system as well as physical and mental health problems (McEwen
& Lasley, 2002). A third reason cumulative stress may be associated with mental health symptoms and distress is that together, stress and mental health

problems may have significant deleterious impacts on judgment, attention, cognitions, and risk behavior (Clements & Sawhney, 2000; Dutton, Burghardt, Perrin, Chrestman, & Halle, 1994; Kendler et al., 2004; McCabe, Gotlib, & Martin, 2000; McEwen & Sapolsky, 1995; Nurius, Furrey, & Berliner, 1992). Furthermore, a cyclical affect of stress may increase vulnerability to health and mental health problems, which then further increase stress (McEwen & Lasley, 2002).

Multiple Victimizations

In general, it has been found that once a woman has been victimized, she is at increased risk for subsequent victimization (Desai, Arias, Thompson, & Basile, 2002; Feerick, Haugaard, & Hien, 2002; Humphrey & White, 2000; P. Smith et al., 2003). The most robust example of this is the number of studies connecting abuse as a child with adult victimization experiences. For example, child abuse has been associated with both stranger and acquaintance victimization in adolescence and adulthood as well as with intimate partner violence in adulthood (Gilbert, El-Bassel, Schilling, & Friedman, 1997; Messman-Moore & Long, 2000, 2002; Ornduff, Kelsey, & O'Leary, 2001). Roodman and Clum (2001) conducted a meta-analysis focused on child and adult sexual victimization. They found that for the 19 research studies included in the analysis, there was an effect size of .59, indicating a medium effect of child sexual abuse on later adult victimization. Consequently, these results provide relatively strong evidence of the link between child sexual abuse and later revictimization among women. Another study found that more women who were raped as minors reported adult rape than women without this childhood experience (Tjaden & Thoennes, 2000a). Likewise, more women who were physically abused as minors reported adult physical abuse, and more women who were stalked as minors reported being stalked as adults (Tjaden & Thoennes, 2000a).

There are large gaps in the knowledge about revictimization. Although it is generally accepted that initial victimization is associated with revictimization, the pathways and mechanisms for this risk are only speculative at this point. Furthermore, much of the research on revictimization has been conducted with women who were victimized in childhood and then revictimized in adulthood. Thus, there are many confounding factors such as developmental age, other adverse childhood factors, problems with retrospective recall, and measurement issues that can all affect research outcomes. In addition, even less is known about the risk of revictimization when the initial victimization experience is in adulthood. These caveats should be kept in mind when reading the literature reviewed here.

Victimization and, more important, multiple victimization experiences may affect information processing in several ways. First, victimization has been associated with mental health problems, which may increase vulnerability to revictimization. Nishith, Mechanic, and Resick (2000) found that it was the cumulative impact of multiple victimizations (child and adult) that was associated with current PTSD symptomology. Green et al. (2000) also concluded that exposure to multiple traumas was associated with more mental health symptoms compared with exposure to single or less traumatic stressful events. Some studies have found that women with victimization histories are more suscep-tible to negative outcomes from stressful life events, which may influence ap-praisals by affecting emotions, moods, judgments, and decisions (Classen et al., 2002; Thakkar & McCanne, 2000). Cloitre (1998) argued that early abuse expe-riences may interfere with self-regulation skills, which may in turn increase mental health problems. Other studies have shown that how women cope with the memories of victimization experiences affects mental health; for example, avoidance or suppression of unwanted thoughts is associated with more nega-tive mental health (Boeschen et al., 2001; Cloitre, 1998; Coffey, Leitenberg, Henning, Turner, & Bennett, 1996; Futa, Nash, Hansen, & Garbin, 2003; Krause et al., 2000; T. Lynch et al., 2001; Marx & Sloan, 2002; Polusny et al., 2004). It may be that women who deal with the aftermath of trauma using certain cop-ing styles (e.g., trying not to think about it; rumination) use up limited internal resources, thus limiting resources available for information processing or ap-praising future threat.

Second, it has been hypothesized that women with multiple victimization experiences may have inhibited or delayed appraisal of negative events or threat cues and responses (Kendall-Tackett, 2002; Kuyken & Brewin, 1995; Read, Agar, Argyle, & Aderhold, 2003). As an example, A. Wilson et al. (1999) examined the impact of multiple victimizations on risk assessment by using three groups of women: women with no victimization history, women with a single assault ex-perience, and women with multiple assault experiences. These researchers played a tape of a couple engaged in foreplay that moved toward coercion, with the male partner initially using verbal coercion and then moving to threats of harm while the female partner made it clear that she did not want to engage in sexual intercourse. The three groups of women were asked to decide when the male partner had gone too far. A significantly greater proportion of women with multiple victimization experiences indicated the interaction had gone too far only once actual verbal threats (or worse) were used. Women with child abuse experiences may have difficulty interpreting interpersonal events and making causal connections among other people's thoughts, feelings, and behav-iors (Ornduff et al., 2001). In other words, some women may have biased or selective attentional processes shaped by early or repeated victimization expe-riences (Field et al., 2001).

Third, there is an association of repeat victimization experiences with self-assertion, self-blame, or other problems with interpersonal relationships and boundaries that may influence appraisals of negative situations or threat cues (Arata, 1999b, 2000; Coolidge & Anderson, 2002; Dufour & Nadeau, 2001; Fleming, Mullen, Sibthorpe, & Bammer, 1999). For example, Classen, Field, Koopman, Nevill-Manning, and Spiegel (2001) found an association of victim-ization history and lower assertiveness. Another study found that nonvictimized women reported a higher likelihood of using verbally and physically assertive behavior in response to unwanted sexual advances than women with victimiza-tion histories (Nurius et al., 1996). Arata (1999b) found that women with child and adult victimization experiences were more likely to report self-blame for their victimization than women with adult victimization but no child victimiza-tion history. Other studies have noted that poor stress-trauma coping styles and attachment issues contribute to the risk of revictimization (Cloitre, 1998;

S. Gold et al., 1999; Irwin, 1999; Rumstein-McKean & Hunsley, 2001) by affect-ing cognitive dimensions of appraisal, which may alter women's ability to read danger cues and thus to respond assertively to threats.

Fourth, multiple victimizations have been associated with more substance use, greater frequency of high-risk sexual behavior, and increased mental health problems—all of which can affect risk appraisal (Gidycz, Hanson, & Layman, 1995; Lang et al., 2003; McCauley et al., 1997; Messman-Moore, Long, & Siegfried, 2000; Parillo, Freeman, Collier, & Young, 2001; Testa, Livingston, & Leonard, 2003). In addition, women with sexual assault victimization histories have reported more positive expectations of the effects of alcohol, and as a re-sult, drink more frequently and consume more alcohol than women with-out sexual assault histories (Corbin, Bernat, Calhoun, McNair, & Seals, 2001; Fleming, Mullen, Sibthorpe, Attewell, & Bammer, 1998; Marx, Nichols-Anderson, Messman-Moore, Miranda, & Porter, 2000). In addition, high-risk sexual behavior has been associated with both child and adult victimization (Davis, Combs-Lane, & Jackson, 2002; El-Bassel, Witte, Wada, Gilbert, & Wallace, 2001; Fergusson, Horwood, & Lynskey, 1997; Parillo et al., 2001; West, Williams, & Siegel, 2000). Consensual and high-risk sexual behavior has also been associated with victimization and revictimization (Arata, 2000; Mayall & Gold, 1995; Whitmire, Harlow, Quina, & Morokoff, 1999). Davis et al. (2002) found that college women who experienced multiple victimizations and mul-tiple types of victimization (both physical and sexual assault) reported greater risky sexual behavior than women not reporting those experiences. Bensley, Van Eenwyk, and Simmons (2000) found, from a population-based telephone survey, that early and chronic sexual abuse was associated with a sevenfold increase of risky sexual behavior for women. These risky practices can lead to increased exposure to potential offenders and high-risk environments, thus in-creasing the risk of revictimization.

Psychological Abuse

Invalidating social environments can affect individuals' sense of self, self-worth, and agency (Bandura, 1999). Negative social environments can result in a situ-ation in which the "core sense of personal value is removed or never allowed to develop" (Sullivan & Strongman, 2003, pp. 222–223). Attacks on an individual's self-worth through repeated psychological abuse or invalidation can result in distortions or biased appraisals (Marshall, 1999; Sullivan & Strongman, 2003). This process can occur during childhood as well as adulthood, as in the case of intimate-partner psychological abuse. Psychological abuse is perhaps the most pervasive aspect of partner violence, and it can affect internal contexts for all kinds of decisions and risk appraisals. Psychological abuse, which may have more effects on mental health than physical abuse (Arias & Pape, 1999; Sackett & Saunders, 1999), can distort women's perceptions of reality and undermine feelings of self-worth and efficacy (Marshall, 1999), thus distorting appraisals (Straight, Harper, & Arias, 2003). For example, psychologically abusive part-ners may blame women for their violent behavior and tell women they cannot survive without them. Violent partners may also tell victims that they are "crazy" to the point that women actually begin to question their own judgments. Consequently, the cumulative impact of degrading comments or threats can influence how women see themselves and others. In fact, in Marshall's (1999) findings, subtle psychological abuse (undermining, discounting, and isolating behavior) had the greatest impact on mental health and relationship perceptions compared with overt psychological abuse (verbal abuse and controlling behavior) as well as physical and sexual abuse.

Summary of Cognitive Constraints

Cumulative stress, multiple victimization experiences, and psychological abuse affect situation and response appraisals, with the greater number of victimizations and stressors creating not only greater stress but also vulnerability to revictimization. Psychological abuse appears to distort appraisals and responses by distorting beliefs about the self and about efficacy.

Summary

Internal contextual factors are important for understanding victimization, mental health, and substance use among women in that they interact with and underlie all of the other contributing factors described in this book. Although much literature has been developed on mental health and substance problems, socioeconomic factors, and relationship factors associated with victimization, little research has been done on the complexities of cognitive processes among women with victimization experiences. However, these internal appraisal and cognitive factors appear to be critical to the understanding of victimization, victimization risk, and the potential pathways to adaptation. Appraisal is the key concept to be understood when considering internal contextual factors. Appraisals are important in understanding emotions, and emotions serve critical adaptive functions, such as compelling an individual to run or fight as a behavioral response to the emotion of fear. Appraisals are not always based on objective information processing; rather, they are meaning-based and evaluative. Individuals attach personal meaning to appraisals through several mechanisms, including knowledge and understanding, memories, cognitive biases, personal goals, and agency. Once situations are appraised as threatening, negative, or incongruent with goals, motives, or concerns, people must consider what they can do about the situation. Response appraisals primarily involve three steps: (a) determining who or what caused the situation; (b) determining possible actions that might rectify the situation; and (c) once a viable action is determined, deciding whether one has the skills and resources to carry out the decision (efficacy).

The primary and secondary, or situational and response, process of appraisal, although seemingly simplistic, is not without several complications that must be noted if the process is to be fully understood.

1. Goals, motives, and concerns on which appraisals are evaluated are not always determined willfully.

2. Appraisals can occur at multiple levels, including automatically and consciously.
3. Emotions are not always under volitional control; they can be elicited automatically, and they may or may not be changeable by volition.
4. Conflicting emotions can be experienced simultaneously.
5. The appraisal–emotion process is not linear but ongoing and reiterative.

These factors may increase the likelihood of appraisal error, which may elicit and maintain negative emotions and make ignoring certain emotions or environmental stimuli more difficult.

Appraisals are also influenced by several external events, including cumulative stress, multiple victimization experiences, and psychological abuse. Cumulative stress affects both the psychological and physiological systems, which in turn affect attention, judgment, and decisions. Furthermore, there is some speculation that internal resources are limited, and using them in one area of life (e.g., regulating emotions, making decisions) limits the availability to use them in other areas of life, at least in the short term. The limitations of the internal resource system may affect appraisals by limiting attention, judgment, and decision-making abilities. Multiple victimizations are also thought to influence information processing. There are numerous hypotheses to explain the revictimization phenomenon, and most include increased mental health problems, reduced internal resources, inhibited threat-cue identification and processing, decreased assertiveness, increased self-blame, and increased risk behavior, all of which affect information processing. Finally, psychological abuse cuts to the core of self-concept and agency and increases the ambiguity of threat cues, and these have major implications for appraisals. Internal contextual factors are also influenced by, and interact with, external factors. The combined impact of mental health problems, substance use, social and family environments, and appraisals may work together to increase the constellation of victimization risk, mental health problems, and substance use.

Strengths and Weaknesses in the Literature

This literature review suggests that internal contextual factors are important to understanding victimization, mental health, and substance use among women. In addition, given that these factors are essentially cognitive, they are important to consider in clinical interventions. However, many complexities and gaps exist in the research regarding internal contextual factors. The four main issues discussed here are the following: (a) the limited application of appraisal-processes inquiry among samples of women with interpersonal victimization experiences; (b) the need for better understanding of how risk is defined and appraised within relationships for women; (c) the need to examine the intersections among the automatic and voluntary appraisal processes, emotions, and biological mechanisms, especially among women with victimization experiences;

and (d) the ways that appraisals and components of the appraisal process can be incorporated into interventions.

One problem in the literature that is cause for the most concern is that appraisal science has largely been developed around general populations rather than populations with special defining characteristics such as victimization, leaving important gaps in the current research knowledge. For example, we do not know how internal and external references affect appraisals with regard to victimization and help seeking. More specifically, the specific mechanisms for how social networks, social comparisons, or religious beliefs and norms contribute to situation and response appraisals are unclear.

Another gap relates to the context of how other chronic and cumulative stressors influence the appraisal process (A. Wilson et al., 1999). It may be important to assess more decisively how characteristics of specific types of victimization affect appraisals such as the age (or developmental age) of first abuse as well as the frequency, severity, type, and co-occurrence of other family problems. Research shows that women abused earlier in life, who experience more frequent and severe abuse, who are abused by someone close to them, and who experience multiple types of abuse experience more trauma symptoms and exhibit higher risk behavior than women without these specific abuse experiences (Arata, 1999a; J. Davis et al., 2002; Freeman, Collier, & Parillo, 2002; Kendler et al., 2000; Schaaf & McCanne, 1998; Thompson, Arias, Basile, & Desai, 2002). These findings do not address mechanisms or pathways of victimization experiences and later adjustment, however, especially with regard to the appraisal processes. Thus, a developmental cumulative life perspective that incorporates internal contextual factors in addition to external factors is especially needed to facilitate the understanding of this phenomenon.

In addition, more research is needed to understand how women define risk, especially within close relationships, and to understand the association between perceptions of risk and help-seeking behaviors (Gondolf & Heckert, 2003). The transtheoretical stages-of-change model (Burke et al., 2001, 2004; Dienemann et al., 2002; Frasier et al., 2001; Haggerty & Goodman, 2002; Prochaska et al., 1992) may provide some general guidance in examining the appraisal process and components more specifically over time for women in violent relationships or for understanding how women view sexual assaults. More research is needed on additional theories that can be used to understand internal contextual factors among women with single and multiple victimization experiences, their responses, and the context within which the experience and the response occurs that are consistent with the general appraisal literature.

Furthermore, a careful examination is needed of gender differences in affiliative goals and the influence of such goals on the appraisal process. Relationships for women have both negative and positive aspects. One negative aspect of the relational self-concept may be that women are often victimized by individuals whom they once trusted, which may have important implications for mental health and information processing. In addition, women who have high relational self-concepts may be sensitive to feedback from others, interpersonal conflicts, and others' feelings, which increases stress levels. On the other hand, women's connections and interest in others may be extremely important to self-concepts or personal goals as well as for nurturing both children and partners, and this may enhance family functioning. Consequently, women's attributes of compassion, cooperativeness, empathy, and interest in the welfare of others contribute to their commitment to an intimate relationship, regardless of how dysfunctional that relationship may be (Granello & Beamish, 1998; Wright & Wright, 1991).

A better understanding of how automatic appraisals occur in conjunction with voluntary appraisals is also needed (Compas et al., 1997). Expanding this literature will require innovative methods to measure and distinguish between voluntary and involuntary reactions to situations and the associated appraisal processes (Compas et al., 1997; Ellsworth & Scherer, 2003). According to Parkinson (1997), the knowledge base on appraisal processes is more conceptual than empirical, and it is critical to examine appraisals and emotion management in real time to better determine the emotion and cognitive appraisal process. Measuring how one thinks in a particular encounter may be the key to determining how that person copes (Dewe, 1991).

Furthermore, understanding how certain components of trauma interact with biological processes and how the influence of trauma experiences and the biological consequences interact with appraisals is important. More research on the mechanisms that underlie internal resource depletion is also needed (Vohs & Heatherton, 2000), especially for women who have experienced victimization and multiple victimizations. The notion that certain coping styles, whether conscious or automatic, may exhaust internal resources for adaptation and safety is one that may be important to pursue with further research (Baumeister et al., 1998).

Internal contextual factors have significant application for interventions. What makes internal contextual factors especially salient for interventions is the focus of interventions on cognitive and behavioral aspects of appraisals, emotion and mood regulation, and behavior. Three specific concepts that may have application for interventions but need more targeted and specific research include the importance of relationships, social comparison processes, and internal resource depletion and strength.

At the practice level, the importance of relationships and affiliation in women's lives has resulted in a call for new interventions that embrace this characteristic as a strength rather than a weakness (e.g., Amaro, 1995; Amaro & Hardy-Fanta, 1995; Chodorow, 1978; Erikson, 1968; Finkelstein, Kennedy, Thomas, & Kearns, 1997; Gilligan, 1982; J. Miller, 1986). In part, this call for new interventions responds to interpretations of women's affiliative goals as being negative because they hold women to a male standard of independence, implying that women are not "normal." It also responds to the fact that women who value relationships are sometimes blamed for their relationship problems. For example, the codependency literature has focused on the negative aspects of the importance of relationships for women and ignored the positive characteristics and developmental experiences that result from understanding self in the context of relationships (Haaken, 1990; Springer, Britt, & Schlenker, 1998). Although the codependency construct is popular, it has been poorly defined, lacks empirical research, is culturally determined, and pathologizes women's affiliative needs and goals (Granello & Beamish, 1998). The problem with pathologizing the tendency to value connectedness and to maintain relationships, even difficult relationships, is that affiliative goals are normal (Mayr & Price, 1993; Webster, 1990). Thus, interventions that validate women's affiliative goals are critical. Also, in violent relationships, isolation of victims is often part of the abuse dynamic (El-Bassel, Gilbert, et al., 2001; Goodkind et al., 2003; Rose et al., 2000). It may be important for interventions not only to validate the importance of relationships as a strength, but also to help women reconnect with others and with the community. In some cases, it may even be necessary to help women increase skills for reconnecting with others .

As another example of an area in which appraisals may play an important role in interventions is the social comparison process. Social comparisons are a normal part of everyday life for most individuals, and as mentioned earlier, social comparisons play an important role in appraisals. Some evidence indicates that social comparisons can be used to facilitate adjustment when coping with difficult health problems or threatening circumstances. For example, studies have investigated the use of social comparisons in coping with cancer, crime victimization, and chronic pain, which all suggest that social comparisons improved adaptation and increased mood (Affleck, Tennen, Urrows, Higgins, & Abeles, 2000; Bennenbroek, Buunk, van der Zee, & Grol, 2002; Winkel, Blaauw, & Wisman, 1999). Unfortunately, there has been limited research related to the social comparison process among women with victimization experiences. This is one area for future research, both at the basic level and for intervention development.

Finally, the research on internal resource depletion and strength has implications for interventions among women with interpersonal victimization experiences. In Baumeister's (2003) formulation, internal resources are limited, and when internal resources are depleted, there is an increased risk of impulsive and negative health behaviors as well as other difficulties in managing subsequent stress or threats. Baumeister suggested three ways to replenish or increase depleted internal resources: (a) rest and sleep, (b) increase positive emotional experiences, and (c) exercise self-regulation. The first two suggestions seem obvious; sleep and positive emotional experiences are important for health, mental health, and emotion regulation. The third suggestion is one area that should receive increased research attention in the future. In essence, the premise is that self-regulation involves altering cognitive processes, feelings, and behaviors, and this process depletes internal resources. Over time, however, it may be that repeated exercise in self-control decreases vulnerability to internal resource depletion, especially when coupled with rest and positive emotional experiences (Muraven et al., 1999). Baumeister et al. (1994) also recommended managing internal resources in terms of setting priorities and judiciously allocating resources to those priorities as needed. They also recommended setting challenging but achievable goals and that meditation may be useful in increasing self-regulation skills. Meditation has shown some positive associations with psychosomatic and mood regulation (Grossman, Niemann, Schmidt, & Walach, 2004; Monk-Turner, 2003). What is unknown at this time is how internal resources are depleted and replenished in the wake of victimization experiences and how this concept can be applied to interventions targeting this population.

Conclusion

This chapter has included a review of research on internal contextual factors, a domain that has received limited attention in victimization research. This domain was presented last as a way to highlight the critical role that individual psychological processes can play in mediating victimization experiences. It is one thing to examine social, cultural, and clinical factors related to victimization. Each of these can be discussed as risk factors based on studies of large groups of women who have experienced victimization. However, the study of internal contextual factors shifts the focus of study away from groups to individuals, because the degree of differences among individual cognitions is limitless. All of the factors discussed in chapters 2, 3, and 4 must at some level pass through the sieve of individual psychological processes to translate into actual effects. As antecedents, all three are key constituents, but as effects, there is a likely engagement of internal psychological process.

Appraisals of risk and of possible response to threats constitute the actions that materialize and activate all the other factors. The internal contexts provide the means by which social and cultural factors become active ingredients in safety seeking or revictimization. Appraisal factors help explain how women get drawn into violent relationships and how they find difficulty extricating themselves. As highlighted in the case study, Susannah said that she believed she needed to become more involved in her husband's way of life, and this led her to increased drinking, with all its resulting problems. In addition, Susannah interpreted her husband's violence as "normal" and their relational problems as her fault. She even found herself thinking as he compelled her to think—doubting her own motives and worrying that she might be flirting as he accused her of doing. These appraisals influenced her feelings about the situation and would likely influence her responses. Furthermore, her appraisals were continually shaped by psychological abuse and the effects of alcohol abuse. Figure 5.1 displays the internal contextual factor dimension in the conceptual model, including situation and response appraisal and cognitive constraints.

Appraisals are personal, and circumstances or events that may seem obviously risky to one person may not seem so to another. Several personal factors influence appraisal: knowledge and understanding, memories, cognitive biases, personal goals, agency, and mood and personality. Even once a risk is perceived or a situation is determined to be negative, a second level of appraisal is required to determine responses or possible alternatives. Response appraisals incorporate perceptions of who is "at fault" for the situation, the costs and benefits of various responses, and the perceived efficacy in taking various actions. Situation and response appraisals are all carried out in the context of fluctuating, simultaneous, and possibly conflicting emotions. Reappraisals continually arise on the basis of the environment and emotion feedback. Although a great deal is known about the appraisal process and the factors that influence it, much remains to be gained from research on women with victimization experiences. The complexity of individual cognitive processes must be considered along with all the other factors reviewed in this book. The limitations in research findings to date—especially with women who experience victimization—limit the degree to which these factors are known to predict future risk or safety-seeking behaviors. However, among all the factors presented in this book, the internal contextual factors extend far beyond pathology or the problem focus of much of the book. These factors also represent a potent resource for coping, and thus they open a door to future research about how women endure, survive, and surpass the harm that they have experienced.

In fact, each of the aspects of appraisal that we have discussed carries an equal chance of being either a risk or a protective factor. Although this book is focused primarily on risk factors, the protective possibilities of internal contextual factors should be kept in mind. The introduction of internal contextual factors, with their potential for risk or protection, provides a logical pathway to chapter 6, which examines the literature on interventions, and then to chapter 7, which reviews justice system responses to victimization.

6

Clinical Interventions

The Case of Janice P.

Janice called a local crisis line one afternoon. Her husband had been drinking earlier in the day, had raped her, physically assaulted her, and then left the home. She was tearful and anxious. She thought that she had injuries to her face, elbow, and "elsewhere," but she was uncertain whether it would be wise to go to an emergency room for treatment. She feared that the hospital staff would learn what caused her injuries and that her husband would be even angrier and more violent if she disclosed what had happened. She also told the crisis counselor that she was so upset that she could not focus on what else to do. She reported taking a couple of her "nerve pills" to calm down. After helping her to feel calmer, the crisis line counselor gave her information about the services available and the steps she could take to get help. The counselor strongly suggested that Janice go to the hospital to see if she had sustained serious injuries. She also gave her the phone number for the local shelter, saying that she would feel safe there while planning what to do next. Janice also decided to see a doctor for her physical symptoms.

After Janice was seen by a physician, she was referred to a counselor at the local rape crisis center. She was reluctant to follow up with the visit because her spouse had returned home, and he had not been violent for several days. Her friend encouraged her to keep the appointment. During the first visit, the counselor began exploring Janice's relationship history and the history of violence that she had experienced. Janice did not volunteer much information but continued to respond truthfully to questions. Janice began to feel validated about her feelings that something was terribly wrong in her marriage. She no longer felt that the violence was the result of something *she* was doing. She felt as if she saw a bit of light at the end of a very long tunnel. As she began disclosing her various symptoms to her counselor, it became clear that that she was experiencing a number of mental health problems. Symptoms of posttraumatic stress disorder (PTSD), depression, and substance use began to emerge during the counseling process.

*   *   *

Given the complexity and diversity of interpersonal victimization experiences and associated physical and mental health problems, clinical interventions may play an important role in helping women with victimization experiences. A major challenge in intervening with women who have experienced victimization, however, is the wide variety and diversity of co-occurring problems and situations that may accompany victimization experiences. In other words, a single diagnosis is not always adequate to help women with victimization experiences and multiple co-occurring problems, as highlighted in the following quote: "Several conclusions emerge, the most important being that psychiatry's current practices of diagnosing and explaining disorders are limited in scope, insufficient . . . and begging for revision" (McGuire & Troisi, 1998, pp. x–xi).

The purpose of this chapter is to review outcome research for interventions targeting women with victimization experiences and related problems. Several key points must be mentioned before discussing the clinical intervention outcomes. First, because this chapter is devoted to the review of research literature on clinical interventions for women with victimization experiences, the general clinical literature that does not incorporate victimization or closely associated mental health problems is largely outside its scope. Second, much of the clinical intervention literature is prescriptive and philosophical. Third, the clinical intervention outcome literature specifically for women with victimization experiences is limited. Fourth, although there is a growing body of research on clinical outcomes, there are vast differences in study methodologies, sample selection criteria, sample sizes, and measurement approaches (Kendall, Holmbeck, & Verdun, 2004). Comparability among studies—even of supposedly similar clinical populations—may be, on closer inspection, limited because of these differences. With these caveats in mind, this chapter focuses on interventions that address victimization or mental health and substance abuse problems that are closely associated with victimization and that have demonstrated outcomes.

In general, limited research is available on intervention effectiveness, and little consensus exists as to the best interventions or intervention components for women who have victimization histories (Howard, Riger, Campbell, & Wasco, 2003; Lundy & Grossman, 2001). There are several reasons for the limited number of interventions for victimization. (a) Victimization is not a discrete clinical, social, or legal phenomenon; rather, it is better characterized as a cluster of problems that may include psychiatric, physiological, social, and legal problem areas. (b) Victimization responses also include great diversity in problem severity and complexity, ranging from women with minimal symptoms of distress to women with severe physical and mental health problems and co-occurring substance abuse. (c) Research on interventions is not uniformly useful because some interventions have received extensive research and others have received virtually none. (d) Finally, there is not a clear consensus for what constitutes "good" outcomes. For example, is effectiveness defined as simply mental health or health symptom reduction? Or is intervention effectiveness better defined by eliminating revictimization? Or should a "good" outcome be inclusive of all of these other outcomes before an intervention can be pronounced "effective"? The lack of clarity about what constitutes "good" or "appropriate" intervention outcomes is problematic when trying to make comparisons across interventions. Also, studies that examine narrow outcome criteria may achieve "success" within these criteria but may ignore other troubling aspects of a clinical condition. The problems associated with focusing solely on narrowly defined outcomes may be especially salient for women with victimization histories. For example, a woman in a clinical trial on treatment for PTSD might experience a reduction in PTSD symptoms while still experiencing ongoing stalking and threats from her violent ex-partner. In addition, she could continue to misuse opiate analgesics to relieve physical pain and distress—conditions that may lie outside the scope of the study. Would her situation constitute a positive treatment outcome with this one area of improvement? If she were a participant in a study examining responses to a treatment for PTSD, her case could be exemplary of a positive outcome. Examined from a larger perspective, however, her quality of life might not have improved even though PTSD symptoms were diminished. Thus, there is a need for a wide range of outcomes to determine whether interventions are truly effective (Westen & Morrison, 2001).

This review of interventions is organized around three general categories of interventions: crisis interventions, brief interventions, and longer term interventions. Interventions for women during the crisis period are more likely to be focused on immediate safety. Brief interventions often focus on education, referrals, and advocacy. Longer term interventions have a greater focus on sustained mental health conditions such as PTSD, depression, substance-related problems, or other disorders.

Crisis Intervention

Crisis interventions for sexual assault and partner violence victimization are relatively time limited and are usually initiated through two pathways: the health care system and the social service system.

Crisis Intervention Within the Health Care System

Some women with victimization experiences may seek health care for acute physical injuries. For example, Tjaden and Thoennes (2000a) found that 31.5% of women who reported being raped also reported having a rape-related injury, but only 35.6% of women with rape-related injuries received medical care. They also found that 39% of women who reported physical assault were injured, and 30.2% of those women sought medical care for the injuries. In other studies on rape victims, between 16% and 32% of injured women sought medical care (R. Campbell, Wasco, Ahrens, Sefl, & Barnes, 2001; Coker, Derrick, Lumpkin, Aldrich, & Oldendick, 2000; L. George, Winfield, & Blazer, 1992; Rennison, 2002; Resnick, Holmes, et al., 2000), whereas in studies on partner assault victims, between 6% to 43% reported using the medical health care system in response to the assault (Brownridge & Halli, 2001; Coben, Forjuoh, & Gondolf, 1999; Keilitz, Hannaford, & Efkeman, 1997; Resnick, Holmes, et al., 2000). Of the women who seek health care, about half seek care through an emergency room, whereas the other half seek services through outpatient and inpatient clinics (Rennison, 2002; Tjaden & Thoennes, 2000a). Also, one study found that over a 5-year period, half of all the women who were victims of an intimate-partner homicide had been in the emergency room at least once in the 2 years before their deaths (Wadman & Muelleman, 1999).

Regardless of where health care is sought following victimization, physicians are often poorly equipped to help women with interpersonal victimization experiences, for several reasons (Loring & Smith, 1994). For example, physician identification of partner violence victimization is low. Studies using health care worker self-reports have shown that even when women present with injuries that would suggest partner violence, partner violence victimization is screened for between 37% and 79% of the time (Abbott, John, Loziol-McLain, & Lowenstein, 1995; Alpert, 1995; Hamberger, Ambuel, Marbella, & Donze, 1998; Rodriguez, Bauer, McLoughlin, & Grumbach, 1999; P. Smith, Danis, & Helmick, 1998). True rates of screening are difficult to detect because studies generally rely on health professionals' self-reports, and existing self-reported rates may be on the high end.

Furthermore, identification of women with victimization experiences in health care settings does not necessarily mean that health or safety will be improved (Ramsay, Richardson, Carter, Davidson, & Feder, 2002; Wathen & MacMillan, 2003). From a review of the literature, Ramsay et al. (2002) found few studies that examined the positive or negative outcomes that may result from screening women in the health care system, and the studies that have examined such interventions have shown limited effectiveness. The issue of whether health care professionals can intervene in an effective matter has to do, in part, with how they respond when victimization is disclosed. In contrast to the health care worker self-reports, a survey of female patients found that only one in five women who were abused reported that their doctor had raised the subject of abuse. Of those who had discussed their abuse with a doctor, less than half were referred to support services, and less than one quarter were referred to the police (Scott Collins et al., 1999). In fact, the initial encounters with services following victimization experiences may be difficult for women and may actually contribute to greater distress than to resolution of the crisis situation (R. Campbell, Ahrens, Sefl, Wasco, & Barnes, 2001; R. Campbell, Wasco, et al., 2001; Logan, Evans, Stevenson, & Jordan, 2004). As an example of how distress may be increased by seeking help from the health care system for sexual assault,

> the standard forensic rape examination . . . must take place soon after the rape, and requires the woman to both verbally review their assault in detail and submit to a pelvic-vaginal exam. Thus, many components of the forensic rape examination (e.g., pelvic exam) may serve as strong rape-related fear cues, and these related procedures, as routinely administered, may increase victims' acute post-rape distress. If initial level of distress does, in fact, predict future psychopathology, then anxiety produced by forensic exams may additionally increase risk. (Resnick, Acierno, Holmes, Kilpatrick, & Jager, 1999, p. 361)

Even though limited studies have examined the effectiveness of screening, the standard of care in medical settings to date includes screening and referrals to community resources (Rhodes & Levinson, 2003). As chapter 2 highlighted, there are many direct and indirect health manifestations associated with victimization, making the overlap of victimization, mental health, substance use, and health problems probable, complex, and important to address. Nonidentification of victimization experiences by health care providers may contribute to misdiagnosis or to an inappropriate clinical response. According to some studies, screening for partner violence in health care settings is acceptable to many women (Ramsay et al., 2002; Richardson et al., 2002). Women seeking help in these settings report that the health care professional should listen, withhold blame and judgment, validate their experiences, and ask directly and privately about the abuse (Hamberger et al., 1998; Lutenbacher, Cohen, & Mitzel, 2003; Rodriguez et al., 2001). Documentation of the abuse, education and referrals to community resources, advocacy services, and safety planning could be incorporated into health care settings and could be important to help women cope with victimization experiences (Eisenstat & Bancroft, 1999; Resnick, Acierno, Holmes, Dammeyer, & Kilpatrick, 2000; Richardson et al., 2002). Interdisciplinary health care settings may respond more effectively to women with victimization experiences than solo practice settings, because women could be screened by nurses or social workers who have better training and possibly more time to spend in screening, educating, and referring women to appropriate services (Shields, Baer, Leininger, Marlow, & DeKeyser, 1998).

Crisis Interventions With Social Services

There are two main social service crisis interventions for women with victimization experiences outside of the health care and justice systems: crisis lines and shelters. By using a crisis line, rather than only going to an emergency department, Janice may have received more ready identification and validation of her victimization experiences as well as appropriate referrals to address her needs. For example, crisis centers may have better links with other community organizations and the justice system, which may provide more support for women with victimization experiences (Martin, DiNitto, Byington, & Maxwell, 1998). Unfortunately, only a small percentage of women actually reported having used crisis lines (5%–25%), and there have been virtually no outcome studies to examine crisis line effectiveness (Brownridge & Halli, 2001; R. Campbell & Martin, 2001; R. Campbell, Wasco, et al., 2001; Coker et al., 2000; L. George et al., 1992; Hutchison & Hirschel, 1998; Ullman & Filipas, 2001; Wasco et al., 2004). In a statewide program evaluation of rape crisis centers, Wasco et al. (2004) found that rape victims using hotlines and brief advocacy received substantial support, information, and help in making decisions. As stated earlier, however, the effectiveness of crisis centers is difficult to evaluate, in part because of ill-defined criteria for success and in part because women in crisis may be too upset to answer questions for the purpose of an evaluation of services (Wasco et al., 2004).

Women's shelters may offer immediate help. However, only a small percentage (3%–21%) of women victimized by partners use shelter services (Brownridge & Halli, 2001; Gondolf, 1998; Hutchison & Hirschel, 1998; Logan, Cole, et al., 2004; West, Kaufman Kantor, & Jasinski, 1998). Women who live in shelters tend to represent the most extreme cases of partner victimization experiences (L. Jones, Hughes, & Unterstaller, 2001; Salazar & Cook, 2002). Shelters typically offer a variety of services, including emergency and temporary housing, counseling, advocacy, group counseling, crisis counseling, and others (Sullivan & Gillum, 2001; Tutty, 1999). Studies have not consistently clarified what "use a shelter" means. Some studies have combined staying at a shelter or calling a shelter for information, crisis help, or other reasons under "use," whereas others refer to women who stay at least one night. As an example of how these differences can affect use rates, one study found that only 9% of their sample reported staying at a shelter, but 25% called a shelter (Hutchison & Hirschel, 1998). In addition, there is limited evaluation information about shelters and shelter services (Abel, 2000; Tutty, 1999). However, in self-reported satisfaction studies, the majority of women found the shelter services "helpful" (Sullivan & Gillum, 2001; Tutty, 1999).

Another group of brief crisis interventions, often classified as critical stress debriefing or other simple debriefing strategies, has received limited support as a required or necessary professional response to trauma exposure (Hollon & Beck, 2004; Kamphuis & Emmelkamp, 2005). This may be in part because this intervention has been used in compulsory ways for trauma survivors; however, forcing individuals to go through debriefing programs may be counterproductive (Kamphuis & Emmelkamp, 2005). It has even been suggested that debriefing may interfere with natural processing of threatening events for certain individuals, and there is no evidence about who would be a good candidate for this form of crisis response (Hollon & Beck, 2004; Kamphuis & Emmelkamp, 2005). Furthermore, use of this specific intervention for women with sexual assault and partner violence victimization experiences has received limited research attention.

Brief Interventions

Initial crisis interventions may result in brief interventions in the form of education, referrals, and advocacy. Brief interventions shortly after victimization experiences may also be important strategies in helping women. For example, Resnick et al. (1999) examined the use of an educational video for sexual assault victims among 46 women (13 who watched a video and 33 who did not) who were victimized within the previous 72 hours, reported the crime to the police, and agreed to a forensic exam. The video provided information about the forensic exam as well as about self-directed exercises and strategies to control anxiety and improve mood. Results found that the intervention group had lower anxiety and stress scores immediately after the exam compared with the control group or the nonintervention exposure group (which in this case was treatment as usual, including meeting with a victim advocate). A later study using the same intervention with a sample of 124 women aged 15 or older who completed the 6-month follow-up (61 in the video condition and 63 in the nonvideo condition) found trends toward reduced substance use following exposure to the intervention (Acierno, Resnick, Flood, & Holmes, 2003).

Women may also be put in contact with advocacy services through crisis lines, shelters, and the police. Such services generally include education about violence, such as facts about sexual assault or partner violence, safety planning, education about various community resources, and facilitation of access to needed services (Mears, 2003). For example, one study of 278 women who were recruited from women's shelters provided either advocacy services or no advocacy services for about 10 weeks and found that the advocacy group had higher scores on quality-of-life measures, were more likely to have utilized community services, and were less likely to report revictimization at the 2-year follow-up (C. Sullivan & Bybee, 1999). Subsequent analysis of this study's results led the authors to conclude that lower revictimization rates for the advocacy group were associated with an increased quality of life, which was enhanced by obtaining community resources and increased social support (Bybee & Sullivan, 2002).

Another study examined the impact of safety planning with pregnant women who had violent partners by comparing a group who had had an intervention that included three counseling sessions consisting of education about violence and safety planning ($n = 132$) with a group who had received a wallet-sized card with information about community resources ($n = 67$). Results showed a reduction in violence among the intervention group in contrast to the comparison group (Parker, McFarlane, Soeken, Silva, & Reel, 1999). A similar intervention was used for 150 women with violent partners who were recruited from the justice system in seeking protective orders and assigned to the intervention ($n = 75$) or control ($n = 75$) group. The intervention group received six telephone calls focused on safety planning over the course of 8 weeks and were then surveyed at 3 and 6 months after the initial baseline interview. Results indicated that women in the intervention group reported practicing more safety behaviors at 3 and 6 months compared with the control group (with retention rates of both groups at greater than 98%; McFarlane, Malecha, et al., 2002).

McFarlane, Soeken, and Wiist (2000) compared pregnant women seeking health services who were randomly assigned to three interventions: a brief intervention that included a resource card and brochure about violence, a counseling intervention that included access to counseling services, and an outreach intervention that included access to counseling and pairing with a peer mentor. At the 2-month follow-up, these researchers found that the brief intervention group and the outreach plus the brief intervention group had experienced significantly less violence than the counseling-only group. However, violence was significantly reduced at the longer follow-up periods for all three groups regardless of intervention (McFarlane, Soeken, & Wiist, 2000).

Summary of Crisis and Brief Interventions

Crisis interventions can be initiated either through the health care system or through the social service system. As reported above, health care professionals tend to underidentify victimization, and even when victimization is identified, the quality of care and safety may not be improved. Few evaluative studies have been done, and the few that have been conducted have shown limited effectiveness of health care system intervention. Even so, many women do intersect with the health care system for a variety of problems, including immediate injury, thus suggesting a logical point for interventions that target women with victimization experiences. More research is needed to better understand what kind of intervention might be most helpful for women in health care settings as well as to study the outcomes of victimization-specific interventions in health care settings. Social service crisis interventions include crisis lines and shelters. Few women who have been victimized use crisis lines or shelters, and few outcome evaluations of these services have been conducted. Obviously, evaluation of these services presents some challenges because it may be difficult to ask women during these crisis periods to participate in research (Wasco et al., 2004). It is critical to find ways to improve and build on the potential value of these services. Brief interventions, such as education, referrals, and advocacy services, can be initiated through health care personnel, crisis lines, and shelters. Although education, referral resources, and safety planning for victims are highly recommended in prescriptive and clinical literature (Jordan, Nietzel, Walker, & Logan, 2004; Jordan & Walker, 1994), they have received less research attention under controlled conditions. The few studies that have examined these kinds of interventions have been promising, with the exception of critical stress debriefing, which has received limited and qualified support in the literature.

Longer Term Interventions

Women may engage in longer term interventions to cope with victimization experiences after using crisis or brief interventions, or they may skip crisis interventions and seek longer term interventions first. Between 12% and 50% of rape and physical assault victims have reported using counseling or mental health services to cope with their experience (Campbell, Wasco, et al., 2001; Coker, Derrick, et al., 2000; L. George et al., 1992; Gondolf, 1998; R. Harris et al., 2001; Henning & Klesges, 2002; Hutchison & Hirschel, 1998; Ullman & Filipas, 2001). However, the majority of these studies have reported the percentage of their samples that used these services in response to victimization but have not always separated victim services such as crisis lines and shelters from other forms of assistance, such as seeing a mental health counselor or psychiatrist. In addition, it is less clear what proportion of women with victimization histories seek counseling for mental health problems specifically because of their victimization versus other reasons that may even precede the victimization events.

Most of the literature on longer term interventions for victimization is specific to mental disorders. In fact, the victimization literature centers heavily on treatment of PTSD or mood disorders, and little work has been conducted on the outcomes of victimization counseling apart from psychiatric disorders. The discussion in this chapter of longer term interventions includes treatment for PTSD, depression, eating disorders, borderline personality disorder, and substance abuse. Before examining the longer term intervention outcomes for specific mental health disorders, however, victim-specific counseling services and couples therapy are discussed with regard to the limited outcomes and the different perspectives on the value of these approaches.

Victim-Specific Counseling Services

Longer term victim-specific interventions generally include counseling and group therapies. Although many counseling approaches for victimization experiences have been described in the clinical and practice literature, few have been examined for effectiveness or efficacy; the few that have attempted outcome studies had methodological problems, such as small or convenience samples, no comparison groups, or high dropout rates (Abel, 2000; Howard et al., 2003; Kubany, Hill, & Owens, 2003; Norton & Schauer, 1997; Tutty, Bidgood, & Rothery, 1996). An example of the limited pre- and posttest studies on treatment outcomes is a study of 20 women with victimization experience who were assigned to 8 weeks of feminist-oriented or grief-resolution counseling (Mancoske, Standifer, & Cauley, 1994). Results showed no differences between groups and no change in symptoms over time for the two groups (Mancoske et al., 1994). It is difficult to know whether both interventions were ineffective, whether the number of participants in the treatment conditions was too small to be able to detect a change even if there truly was a change, or if there was some other methodological problem with the study that contributed to the lack of findings (e.g., high dropout rates, lack of adherence to the intervention).

Another problem with evaluating the effectiveness of victim-specific counseling is that studies do not always include comparison groups. For example, Howard et al. (2003) conducted a large-scale evaluation of partner violence and rape crisis services for one state. They specifically examined pre- and posttest measures for 500 of 5,200 women who had sought partner violence counseling at any one of the 54 programs in the state. To be eligible for this study, women must have completed both the pre- and posttest measures, responded either yes or no to the question asking whether their partner had sexually assaulted them, and have been at least 18 years old. Well-being and coping improved over time for these women. These authors also examined differences in outcomes for women with both sexual assault and partner violence (29% of the sample) compared with partner violence victims without sexual assault experiences. Results indicated that although the group with sexual assault histories had lower scores on the well-being and coping measures both pre- and posttest, they had greater overall changes over time. Although this study seems to have positive results, it is difficult to tell whether the change in scores was due to the counseling or whether they had improved for some other reason. The sample was biased, given that only about 10% of the total number of women who had sought services were included in the analysis and no comparison group was used, which makes attributing the results to the services much more difficult. Women included in the study may have improved on their own for some reason, or other factors may have contributed to improvements (e.g., they were using other services or the offender may have been in jail during this time).

Couples Therapy

Another treatment that is sometimes recommended as an intervention for victimization within relationships is couples therapy. Some couples therapy focuses on the offender's violence in the relationship. Much controversy surrounds the effectiveness and safety of couples interventions in cases of intimate-partner violence, however, and limited research has been conducted to ascertain the reductions in violence that can result from marital interventions for less violent cases (Brown & O'Leary, 1997; Jordan et al., 2004; Stith, Rosen, & McCollum, 2003). Clinical guides typically have cautioned against the too-ready use of couples approaches in cases where there is violence (Jordan et al., 2004). There is some thought that couples therapy may be appropriate in less violent cases where alcoholism is seen as the primarily contributor to the violence (O'Farrell & Murphy, 1995) or when the level of aggression is low and the relationship is essentially intact (Brown & O'Leary, 1997). The latter situation is rare, however, when victimization has reached the point at which a woman seeks medical or other interventions. One literature review of conjoint therapy for couples with partner violence found six experimental studies that compared couples approaches with individual treatment, other interventions, or no intervention (Stith et al., 2003). These authors reported limited positive outcomes (e.g., some evidence of lower recidivism rates; some evidence that violence did not increase during the treatment and follow-up period), although there were a number of methodological problems with the studies (Stith et al., 2003). Stith et al. (2003) also concluded that the studies evidencing the most success incorporated careful screening and safety measures, such as (a) excluding clients who had seriously injured their partner; (b) ascertaining, in separate and private interviews, that both parties wanted to participate in couples therapy; (c) making the elimination of all forms of partner violence, not saving the relationship, the primary focus of treatment; and (d) placing emphasis on taking responsibility for violence and on anger management skills. Thus, couples therapies remain largely untested among couples with persistently violent offenders, and empirical support for using these approaches as a primary intervention for partner violence is limited.

Posttraumatic Stress Disorder

PTSD is one of the common psychiatric manifestations of victimization, and several therapies have been proposed for treating it. Janice, in the case illustration, might have begun to exhibit symptoms of PTSD. Most therapies for this disorder use some variant of cognitive or cognitive–behavioral therapy. Cognitive therapy focuses on changing the ideas, automatic thoughts and inferences, and beliefs that create negative emotions. Hembree and Foa (2003) suggested that "these ways of thinking are thought to influence the manner in which events are interpreted and it is the interpretation of events, rather than events themselves, which lead to particular emotional responses" (p. 190). Thus, cognitive therapy targets thought patterns and beliefs that may be negatively affecting an individual, including the automatic thoughts that can affect situation appraisals (see chap. 5). The term *cognitive therapy* is not always distinct from *cognitive–behavioral therapy* or *cognitive processing therapy*. For example, exposure therapy has been described as a cognitive therapy (Hembree & Foa, 2003) and as a behavioral intervention (Vonk, Bordnick, & Graap, 2004). Psychodynamic theorists have developed cognitive–behavioral therapies that emphasize cognition, whereas more behaviorally oriented approaches have conceptualized cognition more concretely, emphasizing the separateness of behavioral components (Hollon & Beck, 2004). Several variants of cognitive or cognitive–behavioral approaches are described in this section.

Exposure therapy, or prolonged exposure, is a cognitive approach that includes helping clients confront the objects, situations, memories, and images that are creating fear or anxiety (Hembree & Foa, 2003). Exposure therapy is an intervention that manipulates cues associated with the event to modify emotions and thoughts about the event (Vonk et al., 2004). This kind of therapeutic approach includes asking clients to imagine the stressful situation in progressively greater detail or in closer proximity to the threat within the context of the safety of the counseling environment and less toxic cognitions about the event (Foa, Olasov Rothbaum, & Molnar, 1995). Eventually, after having developed the ability to neutralize negative inferences regarding the stimulus, patients may actually visit the site of the traumatic event. On the basis of limited research findings, Meadows and Foa (1998) recommended prolonged exposure as the primary treatment for rape-related PTSD, but it is unclear whether this effectiveness is equally beneficial for women with intimate-partner violence experiences.

Stress inoculation training approaches anxiety and fear from the perspective that stress results from "the interaction of the person and the environment when the person appraises environmental events as straining his coping resources and threatening his well-being" (Hembree & Foa, 2003, p. 190). This approach helps clients develop or enhance stress management skills and may include breathing and relaxation exercises, cognitive restructuring, guided self-dialogue, assertiveness training, role-playing, covert modeling, and thought-stopping as therapeutic techniques (Hembree & Foa, 2003). The therapy teaches the use of relaxation devices to "inoculate" against negative affects when stress events are encountered or imagined.

Eye movement desensitization reprocessing (EMDR), a combination of body- and cognitive-focused treatments, involves patients recounting events and rehearsing positive cognitive responses and thought-stopping while keeping their eyes focused on the therapist's moving finger to elicit saccadic eye movement (Hembree & Foa, 2003; F. Shapiro, 1989, 1995). This therapy uses essentially cognitive approaches while instructing patients to move the eyes continuously from side to side, and thus it can be described as cognitive–behavioral.

As noted from the various descriptions of these intervention approaches, cognitive or cognitive–behavioral elements are included in many interventions for PTSD. In general, cognitive approaches have been used to help clients with a variety of symptoms, including PTSD, in response to a variety of trauma experiences (Blake & Sonnenberg, 1998; Ehlers et al., 2003; Foa & Meadows, 1997; Hembree & Foa, 2003). For example, one study of 97 motor vehicle accident survivors who needed emergency care and who exhibited symptoms of PTSD randomized subjects to three conditions—cognitive therapy, a self-help booklet, and repeated assessments (Ehlers et al., 2003). Improvements in PTSD symptoms, depression, anxiety, and disability were observed over the 9-month course of the study for all the intervention groups; however, greater improvements were observed for participants assigned to the cognitive therapy group.

Blake and Sonnenberg (1998) reviewed cognitive–behavioral approaches to PTSD treatment and found 29 outcome studies that offered "compelling evidence that PTSD symptoms can be ameliorated" (p. 38), particularly the arousal and anxiety-related symptoms, using cognitive–behavioral therapeutic approaches. Few of the studies focused on samples of women with intimate partner physical or sexual assault, however. For example, there were 11 studies with empirical evidence for EMDR, with a total of 377 participants, none of which were exclusively female; furthermore, none of the studies analyzed results by gender and none were focused on a single type of victimization exposure. In addition, the flooding and desensitization intervention studies focused mostly on male war veterans, whereas other studies included in the review used college students with more of a phobic reaction to a stimulus than global or complex PTSD resulting from major life events over a sustained period of time (Blake & Sonnenberg, 1998). Combat veterans or college students with phobic reactions may have very different treatment needs and outcomes than women in long-term intimate partner violence situations or women who have been raped.

Consistent with Blake and Sonnenberg's (1998) review, there are limited studies examining PTSD interventions specifically for women with intimate partner violence histories. Even the studies that focus on rape survivors often do not report outcomes by perpetrator relationship type (spouse, boyfriend, stranger), even though some literature suggests that rape by an intimate partner is accompanied by other forms of violence, is more often repeated, and may be associated with more distress (likely because of the contextual differences of repeated violence and rape) in comparison with rape by strangers (Bennice & Resick, 2003; Mahoney, 1999). One study of women with partner violence experiences in treatment for PTSD found that cognitive therapy did reduce PTSD and depression symptoms; however, the sample size was small ($N = 37$), and it was a convenience sample, which may have biased study results (Kubany et al., 2003).

A larger number of studies have examined cognitive therapies with rape victims, and outcomes of these studies are generally positive. For example, Foa, Hearst-Ikeda, and Perry (1995) studied 20 women with recent sexual and nonsexual assault in two equal groups. One group of 10 women received a brief cognitive–behavioral approach consisting of four sessions, whereas the comparison group received repeated assessments. Although both groups experienced decreased PTSD and depression symptoms over time, significantly more women in the brief treatment group were symptom free approximately 6 months postassault than women in the control group (Foa et al., 1995). Resick, Nishith, Weaver, Astin, and Feuer (2002) randomized 171 rape victims (only 121 of whom completed treatment and follow-up protocols), who had experienced rape 3 months to 33 years earlier, into three conditions: (a) wait-listing for 6 weeks (with therapists calling every 2 weeks to check on emergency needs), (b) prolonged exposure, and (c) cognitive-processing therapy. Prolonged exposure in this study consisted of four components: education–rationale, breathing exercises, behavioral exposures, and imaginational exposures. Cognitive-processing therapy included education, reexperiencing, thought questioning and challenging, examination of problematic cognitions, and changes in overgeneralized beliefs (Resick & Schnicke, 1993). Cognitive processing particularly targets maladaptive beliefs about safety and trust (Hollon & Beck, 2004; Resick & Schnicke, 1993). Outcome measures for the study included improvement of PTSD and depression symptoms and of trauma-related guilt, with both treatment groups having reduced symptoms and the wait-list group showing no improvement (Resick et al., 2002). Both treatments were effective in reducing PTSD and depression symptoms, especially in contrast to the comparison group. One difference that did emerge was that the cognitive-processing therapy produced reductions in guilt that were not evident with the prolonged exposure intervention (Resick et al., 2002). Most important, treatment outcomes were the same for those with long-standing versus recent disorders, and the effect sizes for cognitive-processing therapy were as large or larger than for other treatments that have been examined (Resick et al., 2002).

Another study (Foa, Dancu, et al., 1999) examined prolonged exposure therapy and stress inoculation among female assault victims in 96 women (69 rape and sexual assault victims and 27 victims of aggravated assault or assault with a weapon; it was not clear whether these were intimate-partner assault victims). The women were randomized into three treatment groups and a wait-list comparison group. The three treatment groups received nine biweekly sessions consisting of (a) prolonged exposure, (b) stress inoculation training, or (c) a combined intervention using techniques from both the prolonged exposure and stress inoculation approaches. The prolonged exposure intervention used techniques to recount the traumatic event and tape recorded the accounts for subjects to listen to on a daily basis as homework. It also used stress inoculation focused on relaxation skills, thought-stopping, cognitive restructuring, and role-play. Results indicated that women in all three intervention groups had symptom reductions 1 year postintervention, with 52% of the prolonged exposure group, 42% of the stress inoculation group, and 36% of the combined group having reductions in PTSD and depression symptoms (Foa, Dancu, et al., 1999). In fact, approximately 65% of treatment completers no longer met PTSD criteria 1 year after treatment (Foa, Dancu, et al., 1999). Zoellner, Feeny, Fitzgibbons, and Foa (1999) compared the results of this study for African American and Caucasian women. Results indicated that there were no differences in the responses to treatment between the two groups, thus suggesting that cognitive–behavioral therapy holds promise across racial groups, at least for White and African American women.

In another small study focused on behavioral treatments for PTSD, 45 female rape victims with PTSD were randomized into four groups: (a) stress inoculation, (b) prolonged exposure, (c) supportive counseling, and (d) a wait-list comparison (Foa, Rothbaum, Riggs, & Murdock, 1991). Nine biweekly sessions delivered the interventions to the women, whose rape experiences had occurred between 3 months and 12 years before the study. Results indicated that both prolonged exposure and stress inoculation were associated with significantly reduced PTSD symptoms following treatment (about half of participants still met PTSD criteria; Foa et al., 1991). Ninety percent of the clients receiving supportive counseling and all of the wait-list participants still met PTSD criteria at posttesting, with some reduction of arousal symptoms but not of intrusion and avoidance symptoms (Foa et al., 1991). The other interesting finding was that at the 3-month follow-up, there were no differences in the percentage of clients meeting PTSD criteria among the three treatment groups, although there were still differences in symptoms by group, with prolonged exposure having a greater impact on symptoms than the other two treatments.

Another study used a randomized controlled trial of a three-session imagery rehearsal therapy (using an imagery and cognitive restructuring framework) compared with a wait-list control (Krakow et al., 2001). The study included 168 women, 95% of whom had PTSD (eligibility criteria included age of 18 years or older, self-reported nightmares, insomnia, and posttraumatic stress symptoms). The majority of participants were receiving some other form of treatment (79%) consisting of counseling, medication, or both. Only 114 participants (60 wait-listed and 54 intervention) completed the protocol and were followed up 6 months postintervention, but this brief therapy reduced chronic nightmares, improved sleep quality, and reduced PTSD symptoms (Krakow et al., 2001).

EMDR, as described earlier, is a relatively new approach to treating PTSD that builds on systematic desensitization and cognitive reprocessing (Rothbaum, 1997; F. Shapiro, 1989). This intervention has received much attention, but there are conflicting assessments of its effectiveness, and there are problems with extant outcomes methodology (Blake & Sonnenberg, 1998; Cahill, Carrigan, & Frueh, 1999; Devilly & Spence, 1999; Hembree & Foa, 2003; Lee, Gavriel, Drummond, Richards, & Greenwald, 2002). Furthermore, some research suggests that the saccadic eye movement component is not essential in the treatment response (Cahill et al., 1999; Hembree & Foa, 2003).

Some studies have found EMDR to be more effective than no treatment or other treatment interventions. For example, Rothbaum (1997) randomly assigned 18 rape survivors with PTSD to four sessions of EMDR or a wait list and found 90% of the treatment group (compared with 12% of the comparison group) no longer met criteria for PTSD at posttest, and improvements were sustained at the 3-month follow-up. Another study reported the efficacy of EMDR by examining 60 young women with PTSD who were randomly assigned to EMDR or active listening (Scheck, Schaeffer, & Gillette, 1998). Although there was a large dropout rate (29%) for the two-session intervention and one follow-up 90 days after the intervention, both groups had significant improvements in symptoms. However, the EMDR group had almost double the effect size for change variables (e.g., PTSD symptoms, Beck Depression Inventory ratings, avoidance symptoms) compared with an active listening control group. S. Wilson, Becker, and Tinker (1995) found that of the 80 participants experiencing traumatic memories (50% female), those who had received EMDR treatment showed decreases in symptoms of anxiety and increases in positive cognitions compared with the delayed treatment group.

On the other hand, several studies have found EMDR to be less effective than comparison treatments. For example, Devilly and Spence (1999) found that a cognitive–behavioral approach was statistically and clinically more effective than EMDR at posttreatment, with 58% of the cognitive–behavioral therapy group no longer meeting all of the *Diagnostic and Statistical Manual of Mental Disorders* (4th ed., text rev. [*DSM–IV–TR*]; American Psychiatric Association, 2000) criteria for PTSD, compared with only 18% of the EMDR group. This study included only 23 participants, however, and 34% were men. R. Taylor et al. (2003) compared prolonged exposure therapy, relaxation training, and EMDR among clients (75% were women) referred from physicians and media advertisements (*n* = 45 completers, with 60 intent-to-treat participants). Almost all of the participants (97%) in this study had chronic PTSD, and almost half of the 60 patients were on medication. Results indicated that the exposure therapy group had the greatest reduction in reexperiencing and avoidance symptoms and the largest number of patients no longer meeting *DSM–IV–TR* criteria for PTSD (Taylor et al., 2003).

There is evidence that medications may reduce PTSD symptoms among women, but pharmacotherapy is most likely to be used adjunctively with other cognitive or behavioral approaches (Solomon, Gerrity, & Muff, 1992). A limited number of clinical trial studies have examined tricyclic antidepressants (desipramine), adrenergic inhibitors (clonidine), anticonvulsants (valproate), antimanic agents (lithium), monoamine oxidase inhibitors, serotonergic drugs (paroxetine), and benzodiazepines to treat PTSD (Friedman & Southwick, 1995; Hembree & Foa, 2003; Solomon et al., 1992). The selective serotonin reuptake inhibitors (SSRIs) have been shown to be particularly effective (Foa, Davidson, & Frances, 1999). The fact that PTSD involves many neurochemical and neurohormonal pathways (see chap. 2) means that the medical interventions are likely to be equally complex and potentially different for individual patients (Friedman & Southwick, 1995). Among the studies conducted on medications for PTSD, however, none specifically examined differences in women versus men or considered differences in clinical responses among those with and without victimization experiences. One recent study examined administrative data on prescribing practices for a state's Medicaid population, which was mostly female (88%) and in whom 38.6% had co-occurring depression (Mellman, Clark, & Peacock, 2003). Almost one fourth (23%) of those with PTSD were prescribed an SSRI, and 17% received antipsychotic medications (Mellman et al., 2003). Furthermore, 41% of the Medicaid patients with PTSD were prescribed benzodiazepines, and 54% of those with co-occurring depression received the same prescription (Mellman et al., 2003). These findings may be of concern, especially if the patients are not closely screened for substance use disorders or monitored for side effects, because of the abuse potential of benzodiazepines.

In summary, in examining the literature on treatment of PTSD, clinicians may consider using a combination of cognitive and medical approaches; both have demonstrated effectiveness in reducing major symptoms. Distinctions in effectiveness among cognitive therapies are less clear because of the limited number of studies using comparison groups and the very small sample sizes and methodological constraints. Although overall outcomes suggest that cognitive therapy is promising for reducing mental health symptoms in general clinical populations and for women with sexual assault experiences in specific, little information in the literature focuses on the effectiveness of cognitive–behavioral therapy for women with partner violence experiences. Furthermore, there are limited studies examining cognitive therapies for women with PTSD and co-occurring disorders such as substance use, and the few studies that have reported outcomes have mixed findings (Foa & Meadows, 1997). In fact, many PTSD studies of cognitive–behavioral therapy excluded women from study if they had substance use disorders (Olasov Rothbaum et al., 2000). However, recent research suggests that combined cognitive–behavioral therapy for PTSD and substance abuse can be effective compared with traditional supportive approaches (Hien, Cohen, Miele, Litt, & Capstick, 2004).

Depression

As described in chapter 2, it is likely that victims experience depression following victimization experiences. Some studies have suggested that both medical and counseling therapies for depression are effective. In fact, the combination of counseling and medical treatment for depression has long-standing empirical support (Hollon, Thase, & Markowitz, 2002). More specifically, studies have shown that cognitive therapy is beneficial to adults, adolescents, and children with depression (Chambless & Ollendick, 2001; Hollon et al., 2002; Hollon, Shelton, & Davis, 1993; Reinecke, Ryan, & DuBois, 1998). Many of the studies of cognitive therapy described earlier have shown reductions in depression symptoms as well as anxiety and PTSD, as noted in several other reviews (Hembree & Foa, 2003; Olasov Rothbaum et al., 2000).

Some evidence indicates that the use of a longer term application of cognitive therapy reduces relapse and recurrence in patients with the highest risk for recurrent depression (Jarrett et al., 2001). Jarrett et al. (2001) compared a group of individuals with recurrent unipolar depression assigned to two variations of cognitive therapy. One group received cognitive therapy that included a continuation phase to teach clients skills to prevent relapse, and the other group received cognitive therapy but without the continuation phase. This study with 84 patients (73% women) randomized into control or continuation therapy found that those exposed to the cognitive–behavioral continuation therapy, even after the 8-month intervention was over, had significantly lower rates of recurrent depression (Jarrett et al., 2001). Merrill, Tolbert, and Wade (2003) also found that improvement in depression ratings was greater for those receiving more treatment but that the rate of improvement slowed as the number of sessions increased. It is not clear, however, whether changes made in later therapy sessions are qualitatively different from changes made in earlier sessions, whether there is an optimal number of sessions, or whether certain clients may benefit from more sessions (e.g., clients with more severe depression; Merrill et al., 2003; D. Shapiro et al., 1994).

There is also research suggesting that treatment can benefit patients with varying degrees of depression, including minor depression, which may be present with or without a history of major depressive disorder (Rapaport et al., 2002). In fact, among 162 patients meeting *DSM–IV–TR* criteria for minor depression, only about half (52%) had a history of serious depressive illness (Rapaport et al., 2002). Given the low rate of onset of major depressive disorder within the 4 weeks of the study (only 2.2% developed major depressive disorder), the authors concluded that minor depression, although existing on a continuum, may also be a discrete and stable disorder needing treatment (Rapaport et al., 2002).

Although antidepressant medications have long been used to treat major depressive episodes and major depressive disorder, there are important differences in how women respond to these medications compared with men (Kornstein, 1997). In some studies, premenopausal women responded better to sertraline (an SSRI), had less favorable responses to a tricylic antidepressant (imipramine), and had a slower treatment response to tricyclics than men, although postmenopausal women had responses similar to men's to tricyclics (Kornstein, 1997; Kornstein et al., 2000). A recent double-blind study of gender differences in tricyclics (clomipramine) and SSRIs (citolopram) did not support these findings (Hildebrandt, Steyerberg, Stage, Passchier, & Kragh-Soerensen, 2003). A meta-analysis of depression treatment for patients with alcohol or other drug dependence examined 14 studies out of 44 that had placebo controls (Nunes & Levin, 2004). Of the 14 studies, 8 included alcohol-dependent patients, 4 included patients who were taking methadone, and 2 included cocaine-dependent patients; the studies had a combined sample size of 848 (Nunes & Levin, 2004). These authors found that antidepressant medication was effective in reducing depressive symptoms among substance-dependent patients and that the medication also had a significant, although modest, effect in reducing the amount of substance used.

Benzodiazepines are frequently prescribed in outpatient clinics for a variety of emotional complaints (Simon, Vonkorff, Barlow, Pabiniak, & Wagner, 1996). Women who seek treatment for depressed mood may be prescribed benzodiazepines either along with or instead of antidepressants because benzodiazepines have a more immediate effect (Valenstein et al, 2004). Benzodiazepines have been shown to reduce blood flow to the amygdala and to deactivate forebrain controls of wakefulness (Kajimura et al., 2004). However, because benzodiazepines reduce amygdaloid activation during sleep, they may have additional appeal to women with victimization because the amygdala is primarily involved in fear recognition. Benzodiazepines pose a risk for dependence, however (Nishino, Mishima, Mignot, & Dement, 2004).

In summary, cognitive therapies and antidepressant medications have demonstrated effectiveness in reducing symptoms of depression. However, few studies of depression treatment outcomes have specifically examined women with partner violence and sexual assault victimization histories. Furthermore, medications in combination with psychotherapies may be an effective treatment approach, but some medications raise concerns about unintended effects, such as the risk for dependence or abuse.

Eating Disorders

There is limited treatment-effectiveness literature on eating disorders in general. However, in a few studies, women with bulimia have had positive responses to cognitive therapy (Fairburn, 2002; Jacobi, Dahme, & Dittman, 2002; Ricca, Mannucci, Zucchi, Rotella, & Faravelli, 2000). For example, a study of 91 women with bulimia nervosa (but not anorexia nervosa) in a primary care clinic randomly assigned women to one of four conditions: (a) placebo alone, (b) fluoxetine alone, (c) placebo and guided self-help, or (d) fluoxetine and guided self-help. Results indicated that fluoxetine was associated with a greater reduction in bulimic episodes and decreased mental health symptoms (Walsh, Fairburn, Mickley, Sysko, & Parides, 2004). However, only 28 patients in any of the four conditions completed the protocol (Walsh et al., 2004). Despite high mortality for anorexia (Eckert, Halmi, Marchi, Grove, & Crosby, 1995; P. Sullivan, 1995), a review of the literature found no outcome research on interventions for the disorder (Pike, Walsh, Vitousek, Wilson, & Bauer, 2003). In their very small inpatient sample, however, Pike et al. (2003) compared cognitive therapy with nutritional counseling for posthospitalized women with anorexia nervosa and found that participants being treated with cognitive therapy stayed in treatment longer and had significantly longer periods before relapse than participants receiving only nutritional counseling. As with the other conditions examined earlier, the limited studies suggest that cognitive approaches for treatment of bulimia, and possibly anorexia, appear to have the greatest support from outcomes literature.

Borderline Personality Disorder

Borderline personality disorder (BPD) has been identified as one of the more difficult disorders to treat. As mentioned in chapter 2, discussion of BPD co-occurring with victimization raises concern because it can suggest active contribution to victimization, and the diagnosis carries stigma. The literature has shown, however, that BPD has associations with partner violence and sexual assault victimization. Treatment should address the condition if it is presented.

In a recent review of 1,803 articles on BPD published between 1990 and 2002, Paris (2002) found 938 on treatment but only 26 that specifically examined the links between outcome and treatment. Some of these used extremely long follow-up periods of 15 or 27 years. There is mounting evidence that BPD has a "waxing and waning course: when assessed every few months, patients may or may not meet criteria, depending on what is occurring in their lives" (Paris, 2002, p. 317). One of the key factors in the area of what is occurring in their lives is the personality or other characteristics of their intimate partners, including whether their partners are abusive (Paris & Braverman, 1995). In fact, according to Paris (2002), there may be three main mechanisms associated with BPD remission: maturation, strong and nurturing social support networks, and the avoidance of intimacy or choosing partners who exhibit less pathology.

In addition, a 6-year follow-up study of inpatients with BPD found that the symptoms of *DSM–IV–TR* Axis I disorders (depression, anxiety, dysthymia, obsessive–compulsive disorder, etc.) diminished over time with treatment but remained clinically significant (Zanarini, Frankenburg, Hennen, Reich, & Silk, 2004). Axis I symptoms also decreased more in patients whose BPD also decreased (Zanarini et al., 2004). The single factor most associated with remission from BPD was the absence of a substance use disorder (Zanarini et al., 2004).

One of the more promising treatments for BPD is dialectical behavior therapy (DBT; Linehan, 1993; Linehan, Armstrong, Suarez, Allmon, & Heard, 1991). DBT is an amalgam of skills training, exposure, cognitive modifications, contingency management, problem solving, and mindfulness, among other activities (Koerner & Linehan, 2000). Compared with treatment as usual (which included traditional psychotherapies), Linehan, Heard, and Armstrong (1993) found decreases in parasuicidal, self-injurious acts short of clear suicide attempts; fewer days of psychiatric hospitalization; lower depression scores; and greater treatment retention than controls for patients who had DBT (Linehan et al., 1993). This study included only 47 participants, however, with 24 receiving DBT. Other small-scale studies have found similar results using different mixes of patients with BPD (Koerner & Linehan, 2000). A German inpatient study reported similar findings regarding reduced depression, anxiety, social adjustment, and interpersonal functioning (Bohus et al., 2004). Furthermore, DBT has demonstrated effectiveness in a controlled trial with opiate-dependent women on levomethadyl for their addiction problem who also met BPD criteria (Linehan et al., 2002). In this study ($N = 23$), DBT was examined next to a client-validating, nondirective approach that did not use cognitive–behavioral techniques and made extensive use of 12-step meetings (Narcotics Anonymous) for women (Linehan et al., 2002). Although both groups had positive gains, the primary finding was that those receiving DBT had more sustained positive outcomes as measured by fewer positive urines 8 months out from treatment. Other treatment effects could not be distinguished from the effects of opiate replacement medications.

In summary, although treatment outcomes are modest, the use of cognitive–behavioral therapy appears to have some research support in treating BPD. DBT in particular has garnered interest as a method that can address both BPD and substance abuse.

Substance Abuse

If Janice had begun her experience with interventions in the medical pathway, it is unlikely that her physicians would have identified substance abuse problems; even if they had noted such problems, many would have not treated them or referred her for specialized care (National Center on Addiction and Substance Abuse, 2000). Alternatively, if Janice had entered a substance abuse treatment facility without having first been assessed and treated for intimate partner violence victimization, it is unlikely that her substance abuse counselor would have even screened for victimization experiences (Collins, Kroutil, Roland, & Moore-Gurrera, 1997). Once she was in substance abuse treatment, it is unclear whether the treatment program she entered would have been grounded in research-based interventions. Furthermore, it is unclear whether she would have been placed in a gender-specific program or found herself among male substance users, many of whom might have histories of partner violence perpetration (Schumaker, Fals-Stewart, & Leonard, 2003). In addition, her history of co-occurring depression or anxiety disorder might have been associated with a higher risk for dropping out of treatment if her substance use problems were at the level of dependence (Haller, Miles, & Dawson, 2002).

In general, substance abuse treatment outcomes have been positive, with outcome studies showing reductions in substance use, criminal activity, and mental health problems and increases in employment (Anglin & Hser, 1990; Hubbard, Craddock, Flynn, Anderson, & Etheridge, 1997; McLellan et al., 1994; McLellan, Lewis, O'Brien, & Kleber, 2000; McLellan, Woody, & Metzger, 1996; N. Miller & Hoffman, 1995). However, the literature on treatment outcomes for women with substance abuse problems is more limited because of a traditional focus on male users in treatment interventions and in research (Clark & Zweben, 1994). Information is particularly limited on the effectiveness of substance abuse treatment interventions specifically designed for women and women with co-occurring disorders, such as victimization and depression (Sinha & Rounsaville, 2002; Winhusen & Kropp, 2003). Substance abuse treatment programs that match services to specific needs or offer a wider array of services tend to be more effective for women (Ashley, Marsden, & Brady, 2003; Comfort & Kaltenbach, 2000; B. Smith & Marsh, 2002).

More specifically, there is a lack of attention to the potential differences in responses to substance abuse treatment among women and men, even though there has been a slight increase in the number of research articles addressing women in treatment (Swearingen, Moyer, & Finney, 2003). Swearingen et al.'s (2003) review of alcoholism treatment outcome studies revealed a wide array of clinical interventions (58 approaches or modalities) being used to treat substance abuse. The interventions include aversive therapies, cognitive therapy, behavioral contracting, systematic desensitization, and medications such as antidepressants and anxiolytic agents for co-occurring disorders. Cognitive therapy has probably received the most attention (22 studies) according to Swearingen et al.'s (2003) review. Unfortunately, this review of alcoholism treatment studies did not specifically identify studies targeting or including women with sexual assault or intimate partner violence experiences. Information about how women with victimization experiences may or may not respond to substance abuse treatment is crucial in substance abuse treatment models and outcomes. A recent issue of the *Journal of Substance Abuse Treatment* (Simpson & Brown, 2002) was exclusively devoted to articles on transferring substance abuse research to practice. Not one article focused entirely on treatment outcomes for women, let alone women with interpersonal victimization experiences. Further, a study (also in the *Journal of Substance Abuse Treatment*) of 1,123 female and 2,019 male substance abuse clients in the National Treatment Improvement Evaluation Study for 1992–1997 found that women received more services and were less apt to use drugs after treatment. It also found that receipt of mental health services was positively associated with treatment outcomes for women but not for men (Marsh, Cao, & D'Aunno, 2004).

A further example of the difficulty in interpreting substance abuse treatment responses by gender can be found in the study by McCaul, Svikis, and Moore (2001), in which 268 outpatient substance abuse clients were examined for treatment retention and treatment participation. These authors found that women (28% of the sample), both White and African American, did worse than White men. Unfortunately, this study did not report whether the treatment groups were mixed gender, gender specific, or a combination. Hence, women may have been in treatment alongside male clients with histories of perpetrating violence against women, thus adding complexity to the treatment milieu that is not accounted for in the study. The study also did not report whether women might stay in treatment longer in women-specific treatment versus mixed-gender outpatient groups. This study's findings are, in fact, contrary to others showing better treatment outcomes for women in gender-specific treatment settings (Dahlgren & Willander, 1989; Marsh et al., 2004). Women-specific programs, however, are quite varied, and little research has defined the treatment elements that should be included (Center for Substance Abuse Treatment, 1994). Such treatment programs are more likely to offer a comprehensive approach that will address sexual assault and intimate partner violence along with substance abuse issues (Uziel-Miller & Lyons, 2000). In examining reductions in overall drug use, mixed-gender methadone and drug-free clinics have been shown to have positive outcomes for women, although it is uncertain whether women's victimization histories were addressed in these treatment settings (J. Johnson, Wiechelt, Ahmed, & Schwartz, 2003).

Although there is a growing body of research on the co-occurrence of PTSD and substance abuse and of clinical guidelines, there are few empirically supported interventions for these co-occurring disorders (Ruzek, Polusny, & Abueg, 1998). Co-occurring PTSD and substance abuse signals a greater risk for early relapse than substance abuse alone because the two conditions are likely to be interactive and thus affect treatment outcomes (Brown, Stout, & Mueller, 1996; Ouimette, Brown, & Najavits, 1998). Preliminary studies have shown that a cognitive–behavioral therapy targeting co-occurring PTSD and substance abuse among women (a program known as "Seeking Safety") may be effective in reducing substance use, PTSD symptoms, and depression (Najavits, Weiss, Shaw, & Muenz, 1998; Zlotnick, Najavits, Rohsenow, & Johnson, 2003). This intervention includes 80 safety and health coping skills and is cognitive in the sense that it teaches patients a "new understanding of their problems" (Najavits, 2002, p. 111). Two outcome studies of Seeking Safety included only 17 women in each study completing the 24-session protocol; one study had a very high dropout rate from the intent-to-treat sample, and the other used incarcerated women. Neither study documented sexual assault or intimate partner violence as the traumatic event or circumstance (Najavits et al., 1998; Zlotnick et al., 2003). Although reduction of symptoms was found in both studies, about half of the participants in one of the studies still met criteria for PTSD posttreatment and 3 months after treatment, whereas one third had used substances within 3 months after release from prison (Zlotnick et al., 2003). A more recent study of 107 women with co-occurring PTSD and substance use disorders compared Seeking Safety and relapse prevention with a nonrandomized community treatment group (Hien et al., 2004). Treatments in the two manualized cognitive approaches were conducted in twice weekly, 1-hour sessions for 12 weeks, and participants received other treatments, such as medication (Hien et al., 2004). Both the Seeking Safety and the relapse prevention groups achieved positive outcomes in reduced substance use and decreased PTSD severity, although relapse prevention does not specifically address trauma issues (Hien et al., 2004). Hien et al. (2004) surmised that techniques learned in relapse prevention could generalize to other areas such as self-care and mood regulation.

Marital approaches to substance abuse treatment may be effective for some women, although there is limited research on these approaches for women (Winters, Fals-Stewart, O'Farrell, Birchler, & Kelley, 2002). The majority of studies of the use of marital approaches to treat substance abuse have targeted White male veterans, and thus findings are of questionable relevance to women— particularly those with victimization histories (Thomas & Corcoran, 2001). In one study, 75 women substance abusers in an intensive treatment program were randomized into a behavioral couples therapy (BCT) or individual-based treatment. Although there were short-term increases in treatment gains for the BCT group, those increases diminished 6 months postintervention such that both groups showed roughly equal outcomes (Winters et al., 2002). Despite evidence of at least short-term effectiveness, less than 5% of programs that provide couples-based treatment for substance abuse use BCT. This is attributable to an overreliance on disease-model treatment philosophies (Fals-Stewart & Birchler, 2001).

In summary, there is a wide range of interventions for substance abuse and many philosophies of care. Substance abuse treatment has received more attention in research than many other problem areas and has a more than 30-year record of showing positive outcomes. However, for women with victimization histories, research-based treatment options are limited. The findings that have the closest fit to this need are from studies of co-occurring substance abuse and PTSD. As has been described throughout this book, however, there are many other co-occurring disorders that are associated with substance use and victimization among women. Although targeting PTSD and substance abuse, Najavits's (2002) approach, Seeking Safety, is likely to be applicable to the broader issue of victimization, particularly with its inclusion of a wide array of health and safety themes that can respond to diverse needs.

Summary of Longer Term Interventions

A number of interventions to address specific disorders have been described in the literature and have been given at least a moderate degree of research attention. Among the treatments that have demonstrated effectiveness, the group of cognitive or cognitive–behavioral therapies appears most likely to be of benefit. For some persons with PTSD or depression, medication clearly brings additional benefits, particularly in combination with cognitive therapies. There are, however, limited findings, particularly for women with sexual assault and intimate partner violence experiences. Other disorders, such as eating disorders and BPD, have much more limited-outcome research. Substance abuse treatment programs have shown relatively good outcomes; however, less attention has been paid to examining outcomes specifically for women, and especially women with the comorbid disorders that are often associated with victimization. Overall, this review of the literature shows that cognitive therapies have received the most attention in outcome studies and that overall, cognitive approaches are effective. However, the clinical intervention outcome literature for longer term interventions suffers from numerous methodological problems, which greatly limit confidence about findings.

Summary

This review has focused on three general categories of interventions: crisis interventions, brief interventions, and longer term interventions. Several components seem to be common across all of the interventions, including education, validation, and referrals to address needs that may include mental health, health, substance use, or other external needs.

More specifically, clinical practice literature on intimate partner violence and sexual assault victimization have stressed the importance of providing women with information about violence and giving women an opportunity to choose among interventions (J. Campbell, 1998; Ulbrich & Stockdale, 2002). For women with major mental health problems related to victimization, management of and recovery from their experiences may involve the need for information and education about their conditions. These women should also be given the opportunity to play active roles in recovery interventions. A trauma recovery and empowerment model has been developed to teach participants about the disorders arising from trauma and the risks from exposure to it (Fallot & Harris, 2002), but no empirical support has been presented for this type of approach. In a related area, Mueser et al. (2002) reviewed 40 randomized controlled studies on management of mental health problems. They found that psychoeducation, coupled with social skills training and active client involvement in treatment planning and execution, are associated with positive outcomes. Thus, education and coping skills components may be important in reducing the risk of revictimization (Marx, Calhoun, Wilson, & Meyerson, 2001).

Another significant aspect across interventions is related to increased social support. For example, Riggs, Rukstalis, Volpicelli, Kalmanson, and Foa (2003) examined treatment responses for clients with PTSD only, alcohol dependence only, and comorbid PTSD and alcohol dependence. They found that the comorbid group was far more impaired in terms of education and overall functionality than either the alcohol dependence or the PTSD groups and that there was a "relative dearth of stable social support" (Riggs et al., 2003, p. 1726). These authors suggested this to be a major factor impeding recovery for the comorbid group. Other studies also indicate that social support may help women with victimization histories (Crane & Constantino, 2003; Hogan, Linden, & Najarian, 2002; Tan et al., 1995) and that negative reactions—that is, a lack of support—from service providers toward victims may be associated with increased mental health symptoms (R. Campbell et al., 1999, 2001; Ullman, 1996; Ullman & Siegel, 1995). Thus, it may be important in developing interventions to include components that focus on increasing social support for women.

A primary outcome common to all the disorder-focused interventions is better management of negative affect. Cognitive therapy has long held this as a principal treatment goal. In general, cognitive therapies have received the most consistent empirical support across a wide range of treatment categories, and emerging research does not appear to have found reason to dispute earlier findings (Hollon & Beck, 2004). Given the evidence on the effectiveness of cognitive approaches for managing moods, preventing substance abuse relapse, and managing negative affect and anxiety, it is likely that women with partner violence and sexual assault victimization could benefit from this type of treatment.

Sexual assault and partner-violence victimization responses include such a wide array of related problems and manifestations that one discrete intervention is unlikely to be effective, regardless of how effectiveness is defined. Foa, Cascardi, Zoellner, and Feeny (2000) suggested that a comprehensive, multifaceted set of interventions is necessary to help women with victimization experiences, given the complex interface of factors contributing to and resulting from the victimization experience. Women, more so than men, appear to use more and more varied services in substance abuse treatment settings (Marsh et al., 2004). Therefore, a constellation of services provided either concurrently or sequentially and based on individual need is likely to be the most appropriate approach to intervening with women who have victimization histories (Lundy & Grossman, 2001). Integrated approaches for treating mental health problems and substance abuse have received increased support in outcomes literature (Drake, Mercer-McFadden, Mueser, McHugo, & Bond, 1998) and have shown a reduction in substance use as well as improvement in mental health symptom severity (Herman et al., 2000). Given the complexities of victimization-related disorders and problems, integrated approaches that provide information, validation, support, and skills to improve emotional regulation may be the most relevant direction for interventions. Nonetheless, complex, multimodal approaches are difficult to evaluate and would require a large number of participants to account for individual differences.

Strengths and Weaknesses of the Literature

This review of the literature on effective interventions has covered treatments from the crisis stage to those focused on sustained disorders that require intensive treatment. A growing literature seeks to ground interventions for women with sexual assault and partner violence victimization in empirical findings. Our continual caveats and limitations, however, are due to the complexity of research on interventions, particularly with women who experience co-occurring disorders within various social conditions. In all the studies reviewed for this chapter, only two or three had truly robust designs (including randomization), multiple interventions and control groups, diverse samples to account for cultural variation, adequate measures and differentiation of types of abuse or victimization, and sample sizes large enough to allow inclusion of key co-occurring conditions. Control or comparison groups are necessary to gain a better understanding of the impact an intervention may have on symptom reduction because improvement may occur naturally over time, as evidenced by many studies described here that report symptom reductions regardless of intervention. Furthermore, D. Wilson and Lipsey (2003) warned that intervention study outcomes must be replicated, because outcomes can be greatly influenced by methods. Thus, positive outcomes for interventions with only one outcome study should be interpreted cautiously.

Outcome studies are often methodologically constricted for a variety of reasons. The gaps in treatment outcomes research may be due, in part, to federal research-funding policies. The typical research grant from one of the major health institutes is for a 5-year period, and this is simply too little time to organize substantive treatment-effectiveness studies. Treatment outcomes studies with robust designs and representative samples require considerable time for recruitment, allowance for dropouts (and possible replacement samples), and long-term follow-up. The preponderant question in outcomes research has tended to be the bottom line at some arbitrary postintervention date. Research should be exploring the various activities and life experiences that occur after (and preferably long after) interventions to see the degree to which certain interventions have inoculative effects or have only short-term symptom ameliorative effects. How interventions prepare women to face new challenges to their safety and health versus the traditional question about whether they resolved the presenting problem may be an important focus for future research.

In addition, follow-up periods should not only be long term but should include frequent data collection intervals to determine what goes on during the treatment process. Thus, a series of studies that carefully examine the processes of intervention systems, independent of their specific intervention content, might help in the design of more meaningful interventions, or at least intervention components. For example, the emphasis on manual-based treatment interventions may need closer examination. Although manualized treatment provides details regarding treatment guidelines that may help in understanding what occurs during the treatment process, there is some controversy around treatment manuals because therapists in "applied" settings do not usually use manuals; thus, focusing on manualized interventions ignores other important components of the treatment process, such as therapist and client characteristics and interactions (Addis & Krasnow, 2000; Addis, Wade, & Hatgis, 1999; Chambless & Ollendick, 2001; Garfield, 1996). A concern has also been raised about whether manualized treatment approaches allow flexibility to address individual needs and the diversity of problems that may need to be addressed with clients (Addis et al., 1999; Chambles & Ollendick, 2001; Garfield, 1998). In other words, manualized interventions may narrow the focus of the intervention to specific problem areas rather than meeting the complex needs of individuals who seek treatment. This narrow focus is contraindicated for women with victimization histories, given the overlap of co-occurring problems and individual diversity in experiences and responses to victimization. More process-oriented treatment studies are needed to address the issues of how and which components of treatment really work.

Furthermore, although numerous health, mental health, and substance abuse problems related to victimization have been identified in the literature, and the literature generally agrees that the context of victimization experiences is important, interventions tend to have a narrow focus. Intervention outcome research does not always distinguish between types of victimization or trauma events but may focus on overall symptomatic presentation. In other words, the literature on cognitive interventions for PTSD does not always differentiate outcomes by type of trauma exposure; rather, it often focuses narrowly on symptom reduction or on change in diagnosis more generally (Foa & Cahill, 2002). For example, women who have experienced a natural disaster may respond very differently to the event and to treatment than a woman who has been repeatedly raped, but both women might be included in the same study of PTSD. Studies that do not differentiate the sample by type of trauma may have very different outcomes compared with studies that do make this distinction.

Another issue is that research on longer term interventions is generally focused on women who meet the criteria for a specific psychiatric disorder. Limited research has focused on interventions for women with partner violence or sexual assaults who do not meet criteria for psychiatric disorders. There has been some criticism of focusing too narrowly on diagnosis for women with trauma histories. For example, diagnoses, including PTSD, that are tied to specific traumatic events may not capture the full nature of the victimization experience (P. Smith, Smith, & Earp, 1999). The victimization may be a continuous process rather than a series of discrete events (Kaysen, Resick, & Wise, 2003). Because PTSD is event bound, it cannot capture the true nature of, for example, a woman who has experienced partner violence over a number of years (P. Smith et al., 1999). Treatment should focus on the experience as a whole, not just the discrete definable events that help to define diagnosis (P. Smith et al., 1999; Wasco, 2003). As a more specific example, Wasco (2003) suggested that commonly used trauma frameworks are too narrow to accurately capture the complexities of victimization such as sexual assault experiences. They can legitimize some responses while excluding others. The better approach might be to use a broader understanding of the "process" of sexual assault to include "victims' strategies to survive the assault, their strategies (e.g., coping, disclosure, and help-seeking) to negotiate their post-assault experiences . . . and society's responses to the assault which often absolve the perpetrator of blame" (Wasco, 2003, p. 312). The traumatic context for women with partner violence histories may include psychological abuse, stalking, and perceptions of danger throughout their experience as opposed to single, discrete events (Kaysen et al., 2003). In addition, the narrow focus on diagnosis may not consider the ongoing negotiation of external factors that a woman may face in day-to-day life (Burstow, 2003).

Others have suggested that negative labels (such as "borderline personality disorder") "continue the trend of overpathologizing women's issues and reinforcing a patriarchical system of diagnosis and treatment" (Hodges, 2003, p. 409). Focusing only on diagnosis may be disempowering for women because diagnosis implies a pathology that can only be "cured" by professionals (Burstow, 2003; Gilfus, 1999; Mirowsky & Ross, 2002). Thus, the narrow focus on diagnosis may not only trivialize or miss the true nature of individual trauma experiences, it may also pathologize women for experiences that they could not control and for their reactions to these experiences, which in many cases may be defined as "normal" reactions to abnormal events.

Furthermore, although many studies have reported significant reductions in depression, panic, and anxiety symptoms after a variety of interventions, about 50% of patients have remained symptomatic for depression or anxiety (Westen & Morrison, 2001), suggesting that treatment effectiveness is limited for some clients. R. Bryant (2000) pointed out that it is important to better identify which individuals are most likely to benefit from cognitive therapy. Depression, as discussed in chapter 2, often co-occurs with substance abuse (Swendsen & Merikangas, 2000), and thus treatment should consider a focus on co-occurring disorders as well as the context within which the disorders are developed and managed. The exclusion of co-occurring conditions (particularly substance abuse) from most effectiveness and efficacy studies of treatments for depression or anxiety disorders raises serious questions about the applicability of findings to real-world clinical practice (Westen & Morrison, 2001). Another confounding factor may be that the context within which the depression occurs may affect treatment outcomes. For example, one study ($N = 53$, 41 of whom were women) of the effects of cognitive therapy found that the intervention was less effective for patients whose depression was related to severe negative life events, thus suggesting that depression was in some sense a "normal" response to difficult circumstances versus an abreaction to events (Simons, Gordon, Monroe, & Thase, 1995). Simons et al. (1995) speculated that "the differences in treatment course and outcome between groups of patients with differing combinations of dysfunctional attitudes and life stress may reflect differences in etiology and, therefore, subtype of depression" (p. 376). In addition, although female clients have been studied, the specific contribution of partner violence or sexual assault victimization has had limited consideration in the design of substance abuse treatment or in the evaluation of treatment outcomes. Intimate partner violence has received limited attention as a factor affecting either how treatment should be delivered or how it should be evaluated. Also lacking are studies examining clinical interventions for different racial and ethnic groups and for immigrant women, who may have different needs, barriers, and responses to victimization and various interventions.

The presence of co-occurring disorders greatly complicates interventions as well as intervention outcome research. There is a lack of theoretical models to inform interventions for women with victimization experiences, especially models that address diversity and complexity, that are empowering, and that consider the strengths and needs that are unique to women. One popular intervention for women with PTSD and substance abuse is actually a collection of cognitive and behavioral techniques, specific issues or themes, and behavioral assignments (Najavits, 2002). Future research on developing effective interventions for co-occurring substance abuse and victimization may have to follow this lead with more of a shotgun array of service elements rather than a specific treatment bullet. However, it is difficult to examine the specific efficacy of an intervention array compared with a specific technique targeted on a specific problem. Consequently, many intervention effectiveness studies narrow the focus to study participants who meet criteria for one discrete disorder while either ignoring other symptoms or completely excluding individuals with co-occurring disorders because additional disorders can confound outcomes. The emergence of co-occurring disorders in the epidemiological literature cannot be ignored in treatment outcomes research, yet it clearly adds complexity that can threaten even the most rigorous research designs. Future research could benefit from more complex designs that examine multiple areas of women's functioning pre- and postintervention.

Finally, understanding when to use brief or longer term interventions can be critical for several reasons. First, given that individual women respond differently to victimization experiences, not all women may need longer term interventions. In these cases, brief interventions may be beneficial. More research is needed to determine the optimal delivery time, place, and content of brief interventions. Second, given limited individual and societal resources, it may be important to consider brief interventions for women who are unable to access longer term interventions. The costs and benefits of long-term treatment versus brief interventions should be evaluated with rigorous outcome research methods and careful cost–benefit analysis. Limited information is available regarding characteristics of individuals who may or may not be amenable to help from brief interventions versus longer term interventions and how women with various co-occurring problems such as depression and substance use may benefit from brief interventions.

Conclusion

For women with victimization experiences and mental health problems or severe situational distress, interventions may be helpful in facilitating their adaptation to adverse experiences. Clinical and social service literature has described a number of interventions to treat various problems associated with victimization experiences; however, there is less information about how effective these interventions are when clients have multiple problems. As indicated in earlier chapters, factors contributing to victimization, mental health, and substance abuse are complex. This complexity surrounding the context of victimization and responses to it has not yet been articulated in comprehensive theories. Thus, interventions that depend on theory to guide their development may lack direction in how to accommodate the complexity of problems related to victimization. There are some intervention components that the existing literature indicates should be incorporated into professional services for victims, but the outcome evidence on these is limited. Differences in cultures among researchers and clinicians must be resolved through dialogue before significant strides can be taken to bridge the gap between science and service (Marinelli-Casey, Domier, & Rawson, 2002). Clinicians need to make greater use of the few science-based interventions that have been identified in the literature. More important, outcome research needs to be more aggressively pursued to better guide practice.

This chapter does not include a review of all mental health or substance abuse treatment-effectiveness studies. Studies were selected for their relevance to delivering services to women with either partner violence or sexual assault victimization. Some studies were necessarily included that were not specific to this point but that illustrated a lack or limitation in the literature that was critical to the review of victimization-specific studies. A comprehensive review of treatment and human service intervention effectiveness can be found in other recent publications (Lambert, 2004; A. Roberts & Yeager, 2004).

In summary, this chapter has described social and clinical interventions that can be considered in treating women with victimization issues. However, the achievement of greater safety and emotional health is contingent on changes in the environments that cause the violence in the first place. The next chapter considers this by describing the literature on how the justice system responds to victimization problems, how women access protections from law enforcement and the courts, and the effectiveness of those protections.

7

Justice System Options and Responses

The Case of Karen G.

Both Karen and Richard G. filed petitions for protective orders against each other for alleged physical abuse. Karen also filed for divorce, custody, and child support. She indicated in her protective order petition that her husband had pulled the phone out of the wall when she tried to call for help and had recently threatened to kill her. There was also a history of physical abuse toward Karen by her husband, including one incident when he hit her so hard with her son's car seat that she had trouble walking. On another occasion he "stomped" on her ear, and on yet another occasion, he hit her when she refused to have sex. Richard had been involved in three separate court-ordered counseling programs over the course of about a year, including two for drug and alcohol treatment and one anger management program. The anger management program pronounced a successful completion. Even so, the violence escalated, with ongoing and repeated threats, and even included a shooting incident when Richard fired a bullet into the ground near Karen's new boyfriend. At one point, Karen became so frustrated with the court system that she wrote a letter stating the following:

> I beg this court and all other courts involved to put this case to rest . . . . I beg the courts to make Richard follow your orders, and when he doesn't, give consequences for his actions. I beg the courts to read the entire file from beginning to end before making a decision. I beg the courts to protect me, and my children.

Six months after Karen wrote the letter, Richard shot and killed both Karen and himself.

According to the investigation of the Mortality Review Committee (see Epstein, 1999), over the course of approximately 1 year, this couple had attended 16 hearings in the local criminal and family courts that were heard by 10 judges. Each of the six warrants issued for Richard's arrest were eventually set aside, often by a different judge than the one who had initiated it. Two police departments responded to 22 calls for help for this case. Apparently none of the responding police officers was aware of any previous calls when they arrived on the scene; the 10 judges were also unaware of the others' cases and rulings.[1]

---

[1]This case is from a report of the Jefferson County Office for Women Mortality Review Committee, as summarized in Epstein (1999).

*   *   *

Clinical interventions are important in helping women cope with the psychological and social aspects of victimization experiences. The fundamental reality, however, is that women are not responsible for the interpersonal violence inflicted on them, nor are they in a position to control it. Interpersonal violence is a crime. Clinical or social service interventions can only do so much to enhance women's safety. The critical step in bolstering safety comes with protections under the law—both civil, through protective orders, and criminal, through court-imposed sanctions. Ideally, the justice system can help protect women from future violence and punish offenders for their crimes. Yet using the justice system in partner violence or sexual assault cases is not easy for women. It can be complicated and frustrating, and it may incur great personal costs, such as those highlighted in the case study. Historically, the justice system response to violence against women has been clouded by ambivalence about how to protect the right of women to be safe.

> One might sum all this up by saying that all too often women are not treated as ends in their own right, persons with a dignity that deserves respect from laws and institutions. Instead, they are treated as mere instruments of the ends of others—reproducers, caregivers, sexual outlets, agents of a family's general prosperity. (Nussbaum, 2000, p. 2)

Societies, even "enlightened" ones, have not always supported the idea that women are "ends in their own right" or that violence against women is a crime. At one time, violence by husbands to keep their wives "in line" was actually supported by the law (Dobash & Dobash, 1979). Most readers are familiar with the commonly reported history of "the rule of thumb," which some believe provided husbands the right to physically punish their wives in "moderation" with a stick no thicker than their thumb. A Mississippi State Supreme Court case in 1824 (*Bradley v. State*) affirmed the right of a husband to exercise physical punishment toward his wife for discipline purposes. In fact, there is a history of court cases in which violence by the husband toward the wife was upheld as legal and a private matter unless there was a lasting injury or excessive violence (Dobash & Dobash, 1979; Erez, 2002; Worden, 2000). In other words, "women's status as subordinate family members in male-run households trumped their status as crime victims or claimants for protection by the legal system" (Worden, 2000, pp. 248–249). Although today, society and the justice system do not endorse these male-dominant views, there is some speculation that artifacts of 18th- and 19th-century values continue to influence justice system responses to violence against women (Epstein, 1999; Erez, 2002; Worden, 2000). Worden (2000) summarized the situation thus: "Despite considerable evolution in public values and beliefs, society remains ambivalent about the appropriateness of labeling domestic violence as unambiguously criminal behavior" (p. 249).

The history of rape as a crime is also convoluted, and some believe that the historical ambiguity about how sexual crimes should be viewed among adults still influences legal practice today. Early rape laws were used to protect the property of a husband or father (i.e., a daughter or a wife) rather than to protect women per se (Pagelow, 1984). For example, in early times, a daughter's loss of virginity lowered her "value." Bohmer (1991) summarized the history and current status of rape laws as follows:

> Rape was originally viewed as an insult to family honor rather than an act that caused trauma to the woman. Despite the fact that rape is now an offense against the women herself (or against a man, in states that have made their laws applicable to acts against both sexes) rather than against her "owner," vestiges of this old view remain in our current attitudes toward the law of rape. (p. 318)

Even more complex is the response of the justice system to intimate partner rape. As noted elsewhere in this book, some studies indicate that the largest category of rape offenders for adult women is intimate partners (Tjaden & Thoennes, 2000a). Women raped by partners or ex-partners are more likely to experience multiple assaults as well more physical assaults and greater injury than women assaulted by others (Mahoney, 1999; Stermac, Del Bove, & Addison, 2001). Even so, until very recently, rape laws excluded the rape of wives as a crime. It was not until 1993 that marital rape became a crime in all states (Bennice & Resick, 2003), but courts vary widely in the interpretation and application of rape laws, depending on the victim–offender relationship (Bennice & Resick, 2003; Bergen, 1996, 1999; Bohmer, 1991; Bryden & Lengnick, 1997; X, 1999). In other words, it is more difficult for a stranger to claim there was a consensual sex act when there was no prior relationship between the parties, and it may be easier to question the victim's character and motive in acquaintance and intimate partner rape cases (Bohmer, 1991; Bryden & Lengnick, 1997).

Given the history of partner violence and rape in U.S. society, it is easy to understand why seeking justice for these crimes might be challenging for women who are living with the aftermath of violence, ongoing violence, and the many other problems outlined in this book. This chapter provides an overview of the justice system to increase the understanding of legal options, justice system responses, and the impact those responses may have for women with partner violence and sexual assault victimization experiences. More specifically, police intervention, protective orders, prosecution, conviction, and sentencing, which encompass both criminal and civil remedies (see Figure 7.1) in response to physical and sexual assault, are reviewed. This chapter also reviews the justice system research on stalking; however, the discussion on stalking is separated from the general discussion because it has only recently been defined in state laws as a crime and has received less research attention. Before reviewing specific justice system remedies, we discuss the barriers or personal costs that many women may experience in trying to gain access to the justice system or after engaging in the system.

Some important caveats must be mentioned in regard to the literature on justice system responses. First, unlike research on clinical interventions, justice system interventions are rarely examined under experimental conditions. Most of the research on court and justice system actions has been naturalistic and descriptive. That is, there are virtually no studies with cases randomly assigned to an innovative or experimental justice system approach compared

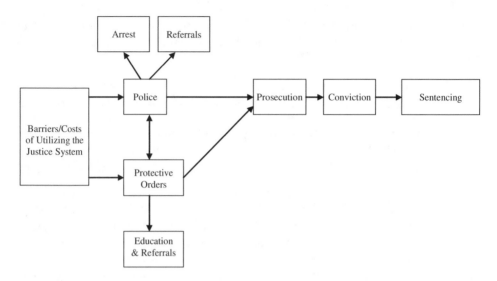

Figure 7.1. Overview of possible justice system options and responses.

with a control group of no court response or a "court sanctions as usual" condition. This makes the assessment of outcomes that can be attributed to specific court or legal processes difficult. Second, laws vary from state to state, and there are jurisdictional variations in interpretations and responses to certain criminal actions, even within states, that can exert subtle variation on legal processes, thus greatly limiting the generalizability of justice system responses. Third, studies often differ in definitions and measurement for "effectiveness." For example, one frequently cited measure of justice system effectiveness is offender recidivism. However, recidivism can be measured by examining official records of arrests or by victim reports of case outcomes or continued violence. These varying measurement strategies will likely yield very different assessments of recidivism or effectiveness.

Barriers and Costs to Use of the Justice System

There are personal costs as well as benefits for victims using the justice system. Benefits of using the justice system for a victim of interpersonal violence may include (a) increasing personal safety, (b) keeping the offender from hurting others in the future, (c) deterring others from committing similar crimes or to proclaim publicly that the behavior is wrong, (d) securing validation that a crime had been committed, and (e) retribution or "payback" for the injustice suffered (R. Bachman, 1998; Herman, 2003; Orth, 2003). Once action is initiated, any or all of these outcomes may occur. Women may be interested in only one of these goals, such as stopping the violence, however, and may not want to punish the offender for past behavior. Once the petition or criminal complaint is made, control over the selection of these goals becomes limited. In addition, personal costs—or perceived costs—to using the justice system must be considered. Research has primarily focused on barriers rather than systematically examining the cost–benefit analysis or trade-offs that victims may consider before making the decision to use the justice system. Thus, the following section is framed around barriers rather than costs. The barriers are classified into three main categories: availability, accessibility, and acceptability. Barriers exist at every point in the process of using the justice system, and these may change over time and at different stages.

Availability

Only a few qualitative studies mention limited services as a barrier to accessing the justice system. A few studies in rural areas mentioned limited police officers available to protect large geographic areas (Logan, Evans, Stevenson, & Jordan, 2004; Logan, Stevenson, Evans, & Leukefeld, 2004). Service availability barriers may also be reflected in some of the studies, with results showing that police do not always respond even when they are called (Jasinski, 2003; Logan, Stevenson, et al., 2004). One study, for example, found that police responded to 80% of the calls made for physical assault (Jasinski, 2003).

Accessibility

Accessibility to the justice system may be limited in several ways. This section focuses on two accessibility barriers addressed in the literature: the bureaucratic nature of the system and attitudes of its personnel.

BUREAUCRACY. Although the case presented at the beginning of this chapter is an extreme example with the worst possible outcome, many women with partner violence and sexual assaults experience varying in degrees of difficulty in navigating the justice system because of a lack of coordinated justice responses as well as a number of procedural barriers (Bennett, Goodman, & Dutton, 1999; Epstein, 1999; Fisher, Cullen, & Turner, 2000; Harrell & Smith, 1996; Lemon, 2001; Logan, Shannon, & Walker, 2005). For example, Fisher et al. (2000) found that about 14% of rape survivors did not report the crime because they did not know how to make a report. Partner violence cases may require multiple legal actions and may include criminal court to prosecute and sanction assaultive acts and civil court for protective orders and divorce and custody issues—all of which may be separate actions (Epstein, 1999). Furthermore, women may not have a clear understanding of the procedural differences in pursuing justice interventions, such as the difference between civil and criminal court proceedings or how to ensure the enforcement of protective orders (Bennett et al., 1999; Harrell & Smith, 1996; Lemon, 2001). Women may also have misperceptions about how the system works. For example, in partner violence situations, women may believe that they will be arrested along with the offender if the police are called to the scene or that their children may be taken into state protective services (Logan, Stevenson, et al., 2004; Wolf, Ly, Hobart, & Kernic, 2003). Immigrant and foreign-born women may also misunderstand or have a lack of knowledge about the system, as well as language barriers, that reduce access to the justice system (Dutton, Orloff, & Hass, 2000; Fleury, Sullivan, Bybee, & Davidson, 1998; West, Kaufman Kantor, & Jasinski, 1998).

Procedural barriers also make accessing the justice system difficult for some women. For example, Logan, Shannon, and Walker (2005) found that rural women were often expected to hand deliver orders to judges to be signed and enable service. In addition, advocates were unavailable in most of the rural areas to explain procedures when filing for the order and during the court hearing, and one court required the petitioner to sign a statement promising to appear in court or a warrant would be issued for her arrest. These procedural difficulties may seem small, but they exemplify what petitioners for protective orders can experience. One study found that perceptions of the effectiveness of protective orders were largely based on views about the accessibility of the court system and support services (Keilitz, Hannaford, & Efkeman, 1997). Sexual assault victims have reported difficulty in prosecuting the assailant because of procedural barriers as well (J. Dunn, 2001; Frazier & Haney, 1996; Konradi, 1996a, 1996b; Logan, Stevenson, et al., 2004).

JUSTICE SYSTEM PERSONNEL ATTITUDES. Some women believe that interacting with the justice system will be negative; some may actually have had prior negative experiences. These perceptions can serve as barriers to using the justice system (Byrne, Kilpatrick, Howley, & Beatty, 1999; Erez & Belknap, 1998b). Fisher et al. (2000) found that 26% of rape victims (assaulted by intimate partners, acquaintances, and strangers) indicated that one reason they did not report the crime was because they were concerned that police would not want to be bothered. Women may also be concerned that justice system personnel will minimize the seriousness of the victimization experience or that they themselves will be blamed for the incident (Erez & King, 2000; Fischer & Rose, 1995; Fisher et al., 2000; Van Hightower & Gorton, 2002; Wolf et al., 2003). Studies with service providers have reported similar perceptions of the negative attitudes of justice system representatives. These include the perceptions that justice system officials do not take partner violence seriously, may blame the victim for the situation, or may believe that women are using protective orders to punish or retaliate against their partner or as a way to short-circuit regular divorce and custody proceedings (Erez & Belknap, 1998a; Logan, Cole, Shannon, & Walker, in press). These perceptions may discourage victims from pursuing justice system options. Other studies have examined more tangible evidence of diminished seriousness of violence by the justice system. For example, by examining police reports and protective order petitions (written by victims), S. Harris, Dean, Holden, and Carlson (2001) found that victims reported significantly more physical violence than police recorded. Belknap (1995) surveyed more than 300 police officers about their attitudes toward partner violence. The majority of officers indicated they preferred handling partner violence cases using mediation rather than arrest. Also, some of the officers did not believe victims were always credible or that partner violence was a serious problem.

There is also a perception that police and the justice system personnel are biased (R. Bachman, 1998; Logan, Shannon, & Walker, 2005; Rennison, 2002). For example, Logan, Stevenson, et al. (2004) found from focus groups that in some jurisdictions, the offender may be treated more leniently because of his connections or status in the community. Another reason women felt that bias existed was the perception that the justice system still holds traditional gender-role notions about relationships and that violence against women is a lower priority than other crimes (Logan, Evans, et al., 2004; Logan, Stevenson, et al., 2004; Van Hightower & Gorton, 2002; Wolf et al., 2003). Stereotypes may play a role in the justice system response toward sexual assault as well. For example, R. Campbell and Johnson (1997) examined 91 police officer definitions of rape and found that about half of the sample missed key points of the legal definitions in their descriptions, and some of the officers integrated stereotypes and victim responsibility into their definitions of rape. Women from different cultural and ethnic groups may also feel that police are biased against helping them or that they or the offender will be treated unfairly in the justice system on the basis of their race or ethnicity (Bent-Goodley, 2001; Joseph, 1997; Krishnan, Hilbert, VanLeeuwen, & Kolia, 1997; Lefley, Scott, Llabre, & Hicks, 1993). This especially may be an issue for immigrant women, who may fear unfair treatment as well as deportment for themselves or the offender (Dutton et al., 2000).

Acceptability

Acceptability is probably the largest category of barriers or personal costs that can inhibit victims' use of the justice system. Five examples of this barrier are discussed in the sections that follow: embarrassment and shame, fear of offender retaliation, lack of alternative living arrangements, perceived lack of efficacy, and personal credibility.

EMBARRASSMENT AND SHAME. One frequently mentioned reason for not using the justice system is embarrassment and shame (Feldhaus, Houry, & Kaminsky, 2000; Fischer & Rose, 1995; Logan et al., 2005). For example, Wolf et al. (2003) conducted focus groups with women who experienced victimization and reported that embarrassment was a barrier, especially in rape situations where they might have to show an officer or other investigators private body parts to prove there was violence. Logan, Stevenson, et al. (2004) found that protective order petitions are published in the local newspaper in some jurisdictions, which women perceived as adding to the embarrassment of the situation. Many women believe that they should keep violence to themselves because it is a private matter or they do not want friends and family to find out what happened to them (R. Bachman, 1998; Feldhaus et al., 2000; Fleury et al., 1998; Rennison, 2002). Fisher et al. (2000) found that almost half of the rape survivors who did not report to the police indicated they did not report the crime because they did not want friends, family, or others to know about the assault. In fact, some studies have reported that both physical assault and rape survivors were told by friends and family members not to report the crime to the police (Logan, Evans, et al., 2004; Logan, Stevenson, et al., 2004c). Embarrassment and shame may also be especially salient barriers for African American, Hispanic, and immigrant women, depending on cultural norms and social support network responses (Dutton et al., 2000; Perilla, 1999; J. Taylor, 2002). Social support networks can facilitate or hinder help seeking through the justice system (Logan, Stevenson, et al., 2004; Ruback, 1994). Furthermore, women sometimes believed they were to blame, or partly to blame, for the sexual assault, which may be a barrier to reporting the crime (Feldhaus et al., 2000).

FEAR OF OFFENDER RETALIATION. Another pronounced barrier is the fear of offender retaliation for involving the justice system in the situation (Bennett et al., 1999; Feldhaus et al., 2000; Fisher et al., 2000; Fleury et al., 1998; Wolf et al., 2003). As noted in chapter 5, partner violence is often ongoing even after separation and may include threats (J. Campbell, 1995; Hall Smith et al., 1998; Hotton, 2001; McFarlane et al., 1999), verbal abuse (Gondolf et al., 2002), and stalking (McFarlane et al., 1999). Approximately one third of female murder victims are killed by an intimate partner, and intimate partner homicide is the largest category of femicides (R. Bachman & Saltzman, 1995; Bailey et al., 1997; National Institute of Justice, 1997). Rape survivors also mention fear of offender reprisal as a barrier (Fisher et al., 2000; Logan, Evans, et al., 2004). Violent partners may also threaten to seek custody of their children or may threaten to take the children, which can be a barrier for women in pursuing justice system options (Brewster, 2003; Mechanic, Weaver, & Resick, 2000; Wuest, Ford-Gilboe, Merritt-Gray, & Berman, 2003).

LACK OF ALTERNATE LIVING ARRANGEMENTS. Women experiencing partner violence may not initiate contact with the justice system unless they feel they have resources to live independently or without a partner's financial assistance (Fischer & Rose, 1995; Fleury et al., 1998; Wolf et al., 2003). For example, in partner violence situations, women may perceive that if they seek legal remedies, they should be prepared to separate from the partner, and this means that they must have alternate living arrangements (Logan, Stevenson, et al., 2004). Wolf, Holt, Kernic, and Rivara (2000) examined 448 women with police or court contact for partner violence and compared those who did and did not obtain a protective order. Financial independence was found to be an important factor associated with the decision to pursue a protective order, and women with more tangible support are more likely to follow through with prosecuting their partner for violence than women with less tangible support (L. Goodman, Bennett, & Dutton, 1999). A woman may also be concerned that if her partner goes to jail, he will be unable to provide financial assistance for her or the children (or both), which may keep her from calling the police (Bennett et al., 1999).

PERCEIVED LACK OF EFFICACY. Women do not always believe that involving the justice system will make any difference in their safety or change in any way what will happen to them (Fischer & Rose, 1995; Fleury et al., 1998; Logan, Evans, et al., 2004; Logan, Stevenson, et al., 2004; Van Hightower & Gorton, 2002; Wolf et al., 2003). Studies have noted that, one reason women did not report the crime was because they did not believe the police could or would do anything about it (R. Bachman, 1998; Logan, Evans, et al., 2004a; Tjaden & Thoennes, 2000b). Other studies found that women believe protective orders are nothing more than a piece of paper, and if a man is going to hurt his partner, a piece of paper is not going to stop him (Logan, Evans, et al., 2004; Logan, Shannon, et al., 2004; Logan, Stevenson, et al., 2004). Finn (1991) suggested that protective orders are not effective without enforcement. Van Hightower and

Gorton (2002) found from interviews with police that they often did not arrest offenders because they were unsure whether probable cause had been satisfied and because there were doubts about the credibility of the victims. One factor in the perception about the lack of justice system efficacy may be the way that the media portrays women killed by their partners, often with details about how the justice system failed to protect them (Logan, Stevenson, et al., 2004).

PERSONAL CREDIBILITY. Several studies suggest that women may not engage the justice system because they are either unsure the incident was serious enough to report or they did not feel they had sufficient evidence that a crime was committed (R. Bachman, 1998; Rennison, 2002; Wolf et al., 2003). For example, from a sample of 207 African American women who reported partner violence to the police, Weisz (2002) found that the most common reason women opposed prosecution was that they did not believe the incident was serious or because it was the first incident of violence. Fisher et al. (2000) found that 65% of completed rape victims who did not report to the police believed their experiences were not serious enough to report, 44% were not sure that it was really a crime or that harm was intended, and 42% did not feel they had enough proof of the incident to report the crime.

However, other victims may be concerned that justice system personnel will not believe them or will minimize their situation. In fact, some sexual assault survivors report having been polygraphed by the police department to determine whether they were telling the truth (Sloan, 1995). Personal credibility may come into question more often because of certain personal characteristics such as socioeconomic status (Richman, 2002), race (W. George & Martinez, 2002), or behaviors that might violate norms about appropriate female conduct (e.g., drinking or drug use, infidelity, or other risk-taking behavior; Carmody & Washington, 2001; L. Goodman et al., 1999; Ruback et al., 1999; Spohn & Holleran, 2001; Viki & Abrams, 2002; Whatley, 1996).

Several studies show that victims of partner sexual and physical assaults are often blamed for their victimization (S. Bryant & Spencer, 2003; White & Kurpius, 1999), especially when victims were drinking alcohol at the time of the assault (Fisher, Daigle, Cullen, & Turner, 2003b; Harrison & Esqueda, 2000; Jasinski & Mustaine, 2001). Stewart and Maddren (1997) studied police officer attitudes about the criminal aspects of partner violence, using vignettes. Their results indicated that officers blamed victims more for the violence if the victims were drinking at the time of the assault; they were also less likely to report that they would charge the offender with a crime the more they blamed the victim. Schuller and Stewart (2000), in a study of police officer attitudes using vignettes, reported that victim intoxication, which may affect victim credibility in court, influenced negative perceptions of sexual assault victims.

Blaming victims for sexual assault and rape is also more likely when victims have been acquainted or intimate with the offender (Cowan, 2000; Ewoldt, Monson, & Langhinrichsen-Rohling, 2000). For example, Monson, Byrd, and Langhinrichsen-Rohling (1996) used vignettes to assess college student attributions of victim blaming for rape and found that attributions of victim blaming were greater in spousal (including separated or ex-spouses) rape scenarios than stranger rapes. In a qualitative study of 32 women who had survived rape and participated in the prosecution of their assailants, Konradi (1996b, 1999) found that women use a variety of strategies to prepare for their courtroom experience. However, those who had been raped by a stranger, who felt their case met societal perceptions of a "real rape," or who felt they met the definition of a "good victim," used fewer strategies to prepare for their courtroom experience and felt more confident about their testimony than women who had a prior relationship with their assailant or who felt there would be more questions about their character. These studies suggest that women who go through the court system analyze the strength of their case by assessing questions and doubts about their character and believability. In fact, in some cases victims may have to work very hard throughout the court process to show that they are not responsible for their victimization (J. Dunn, 2001).

Summary of Barriers

Before women can use the justice system, they must overcome a number of barriers and analyze both the costs and benefits of using the justice system. The benefits of involving the justice system when an individual has been physically or sexually violated seem obvious to many who have not been through the experience, but there are many barriers or costs that must be considered in understanding the full context of victimization. In addition, barriers that are evident before becoming involved in the justice system may or may not be relevant once contact is initiated. Some barriers may diminish, but others may become more prominent. Unfortunately, much of what we know about barriers to using the justice system for partner violence and sexual assault is qualitative and anecdotal, rather than systematic.

Police

As Figure 7.1 suggests, there are two main pathways to accessing the justice system: the police and civil protective orders. It is not clear how frequently women pursue protective orders without using the police; however, victims can petition the court for protective orders in all 50 states (Eigenberg, McGuffee, Berry, & Hall, 2003). One random-digit-dialing household study found that 68% of women receiving police assistance for partner violence also obtained a protective order (Centers for Disease Control [CDC], 2000). Once a protective order is obtained, police may be called when an order is violated. Also, the most likely access to the justice system for sexual assault victims is through the police. This section begins by reviewing research on the use of police intervention and then discusses the use of civil protective orders in partner violence cases.

Reporting Rates

Assessing rates at which victims use police services is more complicated than it seems. Research to date has not provided a clear picture of the prevalence of police involvement. Reported rates of police involvement may differ, depending on where participants were recruited (e.g., shelter vs. community samples), the time frame used (e.g., ever vs. last incident of abuse), the exposure period (e.g., including incidents occurring at age 14 and older or age 18 and older), and how the question is framed (e.g., whether the women themselves called the police or if police were involved, regardless of who initiated the call). Thus, these caveats must be kept in mind when reading the literature on police involvement in partner violence and sexual assault victimization.

PARTNER PHYSICAL ASSAULT. Several national household surveys have examined partner violence rates and police involvement. One study found that 50% of the women who experienced partner violence beginning at age 12 reported police involvement during the last incident of abuse (regardless of who called the police; Jasinski, 2003). Another study found that 27% of the women who experienced partner physical assault beginning at age 18 reported police involvement for their most recent assault (Tjaden & Thoennes, 2000b). Studies of court-involved women reported a wider range in rates of police involvement. For example, Keilitz et al. (1997) studied a sample of women (N = 285) who received protective orders in three different jurisdictions and found only 28% reported having used the police in response to the violence before obtaining the protective order. On the other hand, several other studies of women involved in the court system, either for protective orders or criminal prosecution of their partners for violence, reported much higher rates of police use (72%–82%; Dutton, Goodman, & Bennett, 1999; Logan, Cole, et al., 2004; Ptacek, 1999). Several studies have found, from samples of more than 400 women in shelters, that about half (45%–58%) reported police involvement at some point during the relationship (Coulter, Kuehnle, Byers, & Alfonso, 1999; I. Johnson, 1990). Another study of women at a shelter with a smaller sample size (N = 137) found that about two thirds (67%) had contact with the police at least once in the prior 6 months (Fleury et al., 1998). In a sample of women seeking victim services for partner violence, M. Anderson et al. (2003) found that 77% called the police in response to the violence, and 61% actually filed a complaint against the offender.

There is some evidence that even when women do report partner assault to the police, they do not report every incident. Hutchison (2003) examined exposure to partner violence and police reporting in 419 women involved in misdemeanor partner violence cases with at least one call to the police. Women were threatened an average of 4.4 times and assaulted an average of 3.5 times but only called the police an average of 1.8 times over a 6-month period. This study also found that over the course of the relationship, women reported having been threatened an average of 22.5 times and assaulted an average of 10.4 times, yet only reported having involved the police an average of 3.3 times. According to some studies, Hispanic and African American women are less likely than the general female population to call the police in response to partner violence (Joseph, 1997; Krishnan et al., 1997), whereas other studies suggest similar or higher rates of police use for these groups of women (R. Bachman & Coker, 1995; Greenfeld et al., 1998).

SEXUAL ASSAULT AND RAPE. Research on rates of police reports of sexual assaults may vary for some of the same reasons mentioned earlier for partner assault. These cases also have unique features that should be considered in assessing prevalence rates for police calls, however (I. Johnson & Sigler, 2000). One of the additional complications is how sexual assault and rape are defined. Some studies have defined rape or sexual assault very narrowly, whereas others have included broader experiences such as psychological coercion to have sex along with physically forced sex (I. Johnson & Sigler, 2000). A woman who was verbally or psychologically coerced into having sex may perceive the justice system response to reporting that experience very differently than a woman who was physically forced to have sex. Thus, reporting rates for groups of women with more broadly defined sexual assault experiences may be much lower than reporting rates for women with more narrowly defined sexual assault experiences.

Furthermore, as mentioned in chapter 5, many rape survivors do not label their experiences as rape. Fisher et al. (2000, 2003a), for example, surveyed a large national sample of college women on sexual assault experiences. The authors asked questions about whether very specific behaviors had occurred. When women answered yes to questions that could be classified as rape, they were then asked whether they considered the incident to be a rape. Only about half of the women labeled their experiences as rape, and about 5% indicated that they were not sure. Studies that have asked women about specific behaviors that meet the definition of sexual assault or rape may show different reporting rates than studies that asked women directly about being sexually assaulted or raped. Another issue that can influence reporting rape victimization incidents is how the sample was selected. Samples of rape survivors may be biased, depending on recruitment, because women may be more or less likely to seek certain services or to report to the police, depending on their prior relationship with the offender.

In general, between 5% and 39% of rape victims report the crime to police (R. Campbell, Wasco, Ahrens, Sefl, & Barnes, 2001; L. George, Winfield, & Blazer, 1992; Kilpatrick, Edmunds, & Seymour, 1992; Mahoney, 1999; Rennison, 2002). For example, Resnick, Holmes, et al. (2000) found from a large national household survey that 19.6% of women with sexual assault experiences had reported their most recent or only adult rape incident (at age 18 or older) to the police. Ullman and Filipas (2001), who recruited women from the community through flyers and other media, through college campuses, and through mental health agencies, found that of the women in their study who had experienced a sexual assault since age 14, 26.4% reported the incident "they remembered best" to the police. Feldhaus et al. (2000) surveyed 360 eligible and consenting women entering an emergency room during randomized 4-hour blocks of time over a 4-week period. Of these, 27% reported adult (incident happened at age 15 or older) sexual assault (including coercion, threats, and forced sex), and about half (46%) indicated that they had reported the assault to the police. Fisher et al. (2000) conducted a national random survey of almost 4,500 college women, asked whether they had been sexually assaulted since school began (an average of a 7-month period), and found that less than 5% of completed or attempted rapes had been reported to police. Additionally, the National Violence Against Women

(NVAW) study found that less than one fifth (17.2%) of the women raped by an intimate reported their most recent rape to the police (Tjaden & Thoennes, 2000b). R. Bachman (1998) used data from the National Crime Victimization survey and found that although the police became involved in 25% of the cases in which women reported rape as an adult (18 years or older), only about two thirds of those women had called the police themselves.

Factors Influencing Reporting

Three main factors are consistently associated with reporting assaults to the police. The first is the frequency and severity of the physical or sexual assault. The second is related to whether there were witnesses to the crime. The third is the relationship of the victim to the offender. Both severity and frequency of violence have been found to correlate positively with the likelihood of police contact (Du Mont, Miller, & Myhr, 2003; Fisher et al., 2003b; Hutchison, 2003; I. Johnson, 1990; Rennison, 2002). For example, R. Bachman (1998) found that rape cases involving physical injury to the victim and those in which the offender used a weapon were more likely to be reported to police. From a study of women with physical assault experiences, Jasinski (2003) reported that regardless of victim–offender relationship, injury and the use of a weapon were associated with police involvement. According to other research, when there are witnesses to assaults, it is more likely that the crimes will come to the attention of the police (Felson, 2000; Felson & Ackerman, 2001).

It has also been noted that there is a lower likelihood of the crime being reported to the police when there is a prior connection between the offender and victim (Jasinski & Mustaine, 2001; Mahoney, 1999; Rennison, 2002). Kaukinen (2002) found that women victimized by known offenders were more likely to report the crime to family and friends rather than the police, compared with women victimized by strangers. From a sample of women seen in an emergency room for any reason, Feldhaus et al. (2000) found that women with stranger assault experiences were significantly more likely to have reported the assault to the police (79%) than those assaulted by partners (18%) or other known assailants (32%). Tjaden and Thoennes (2000b) reported that most sexual, physical, and stalking partner victimizations are not reported to the police. They noted, "These findings suggest that most victims of intimate partner violence do not consider the justice system an appropriate vehicle for resolving conflicts with intimates" (Tjaden & Thoennes, 2000b, p. v).

Arrest and Referrals

As Figure 7.1 suggests, there are two major actions police can take when responding to violence against women. The primary action that most people think of when police become involved in a crime is to arrest the offender, but police can also refer the victim to other justice system options (e.g., protective orders) and victim services (e.g., rape crisis center, shelters). Both police responses have received attention in the literature, although more is known about arrest than referral processes. When considering arrests, four primary questions come to mind: How often are arrests made in incidents of physical and sexual assault? Do arrest rates differ depending on the victim–offender relationship? What factors influence arrest rates? Finally, does arrest increase victim safety?

ARREST. Research on any topic must be evaluated carefully because methods can have a profound impact on findings, and there is no exception to this caveat when examining arrest rates. In partner violence cases, arrest rates range from a low of 13% to a high of 37% (Felson & Ackerman, 2001; Fyfe, Klinger, & Flavin, 1997; Jasinski, 2003). Various data can be used to assess arrest rates for partner assaults, including self-report data from domestic violence shelter residents (18%; I. Johnson, 1990), self-report data from large national household surveys (ranging from 19.3% to 39% of cases where police made arrests; Avakame & Fyfe, 2001; R. Bachman & Coker, 1995; CDC, 2000; Felson & Ackerman, 2001; Jasinski, 2003; Tjaden & Thoennes, 2000b), and official police department data (between 13% and 36% of cases indicated an arrest; Buzawa, Austin, & Buzawa, 1996; Feder, 1998; Fyfe et al., 1997; I. Johnson, 1990; Robinson & Chandek, 2000). Arrest rates for rape cases also vary widely. R. Bachman (1998) reported that only 23% of rape victimizations, regardless of victim–offender relationship, resulted in arrest. Gray-Eurom, Seaberg, and Wears (2002) examined approximately 800 sexual assault cases from one police department in a 2-year period. A suspect was identified in only 44% of the cases, but there was an arrest in 76% of those cases. Tjaden and Thoennes (2000b) reported that 47% of offenders were arrested or detained in cases when women reported rapes by intimate partners to police.

Another question of interest is whether arrest likelihood varies depending on the victim–offender relationship. R. Bachman (1998) found that 17% of partner-perpetrated rapes reported to the police resulted in arrests compared with 15% of stranger rape cases, 26% of acquaintance-perpetrated rape cases, and 35% of cases in which rape was committed by another family member. Fyfe et al. (1997) examined records for responses by one police department for 392 felony assaults that involved offenders with known victims. These data were collected in late 1986, giving officers at least 2 years to close the case. This study reported that arrests occurred in 13% of the male-to-female partner assaults, whereas 28% of other assault cases included arrests. Even after controlling for the use of weapons, degree of injury sustained by the victim, whether the incident involved attacks on the responding officer, as well as race, poverty, and number of suspects, results showed that officers were less likely to arrest male felony offenders who attacked an intimate partner than other offenders who committed felony assaults. There are two striking findings from this study. First, even in very serious assault cases in which the victim could identify the offender, only about a quarter of cases resulted in arrest. Second, it seems that at least in this study, partner assaults were treated differently at the arrest level than other assault cases.

Although some studies have reported lower rates of arrest for partner assaults than other assaults (Buzawa et al., 1996; Feder, 1998), other studies have reported similar rates of arrest for partner and other assaults (Felson & Ackerman, 2001; Jasinski, 2003). For example, Felson and Ackerman (2001) and Jasinski (2003) suggested that arrest rates, not taking any other factors into account, were similar or higher in partner violence cases than other assault cases. When specific characteristics of the cases are taken into consideration, however, results may be different. For example, partner assault cases may be more likely to include an identifiable offender or an offender that is present when the police arrive than other assault cases, which may facilitate arrest. Thus, when arrest rates are compared across case types for those with identified suspects, arrest rates may be more similar than if arrest rates are compared ignoring whether a suspect was identified (Felson & Ackerman, 2001; Jasinski, 2003). Felson and Ackerman (2001) underscored the complexity of understanding arrest rates by concluding that

> the police are less likely to arrest strangers than nonstrangers for assault because they are often unable to identify them. On the other hand, when the police are able to identify the suspect they show lenience when the suspect knows the victim. Their leniency is not due to a tolerance for intimate violence or violence against women; they are more likely to make an arrest in incidents involving intimate violence than in incidents involving other nonstrangers. Rather, leniency in nonstranger incidents is due to the reluctance of victims to sign complaints, the absence of witnesses, and the unwillingness of the police to arrest suspects for minor acts of violence against people they know. (p. 673)

Although there are no studies that can conclusively indicate the situational factors that most likely result in arrest, some factors seem to be consistently associated with arrest in both sexual and physical assault cases. Generally, arrest is more likely when (a) victims are injured (R. Bachman & Coker, 1995; Buzawa et al., 1996; Du Mont et al., 2003; Feder, 1998; Mignon & Holmes, 1995); (b) weapons are involved (Bouffard, 2000; Buzawa et al., 1996; Jasinski, 2003; Kane, 1999; Mignon & Holmes, 1995); (c) there were witnesses to the crime (Bouffard, 2000; Felson, 2000; Felson & Ackerman, 2001; Mignon & Holmes, 1995); (d) victims wanted an arrest or were perceived as cooperative (Bouffard, 2000; Buzawa et al., 1996; Feder, 1998); (e) offenders were present on police arrival (Buzawa et al., 1996; Robinson & Chandek, 2000); and (f) offenders were intoxicated (Jasinski, 2003; Mignon & Holmes, 1995). Note that not all studies found these factors to predict arrest, however. For example, R. Bachman (1998) found that although weapons and injuries did affect victim reporting of sexual assaults, these factors did not affect whether there was an arrest. As another example, Robinson and Chandek (2000) found a negative association of victim injury and arrest, hypothesizing that perhaps victims were more concerned about offender retaliation when they were injured, which may have affected arrest rates.

Another question is whether arrest stops violence. Although literature on this topic is limited, there is some research, with very mixed findings, on the deterrent effect of arrest for partner violence offenders. Logan, Walker, and Leukefeld (2001) found that in 1997, 17,000 arrests in one state were classified as domestic and violent, making up approximately 9% of the total statewide arrests (including only offenses eligible for bail release). From those data, a 9% random sample of partner violence cases was examined for convictions before and 2 years after the index arrest. In male-to-female partner violence cases, 26% of the defendants had been convicted of domestic violence prior to the index arrest, and 28% of the defendants were convicted on new domestic violence charges within 2 years of the index arrest. Thus, according to one state's official data records, one in four domestic violence offenders recidivate.

The question of partner violence recidivism has been of interest for several decades. Sherman and Berk (1984) reported on the effectiveness of arrest in partner violence cases. This study used misdemeanor partner assault cases when both the suspect and the victim were present as the police arrived. This study originally focused on two Minneapolis precincts with the highest rates of partner violence reports and arrests. Once a case was determined eligible, officers applied one of three randomly assigned conditions: (a) mandatory arrest of the offender, who was to spend at least one night in jail; (b) advice, with informal mediation in some cases; or (c) an order for the offender to leave the premises for at least 8 hours. Originally 314 cases were included in the study, and outcomes were measured through police records of subsequent interactions for partner violence and through victim reports. Although there were lower recidivism rates for those arrested than the other two interventions, there were many methodological problems with this study, including difficulty with implementation (e.g., low participation from officers), problems with treatment fidelity (e.g., only 73% of those who were supposed to be ordered to leave the premises were actually ordered to leave), problems with response rates from victims (e.g., there was a 62% completion rate for interviews), and the small sample size (Gelles, 1996; Sherman & Berk, 1984).

Several subsequent studies were conducted to replicate the Minneapolis study, although they were not exact replications. These studies began in 1986 and early 1987 in Colorado Springs, Colorado; Charlotte, North Carolina; Milwaukee, Wisconsin; Miami–Dade County, Florida; and Omaha, Nebraska (J. Schmidt & Sherman, 1996). The five studies had varied results, with several suggesting that arrest deterred subsequent violence, at least in the short term, depending on factors such as offender employment patterns (Berk, Campbell, Klap, & Western, 1992; Pate & Hamilton, 1992; Sherman et al., 1992). In several of these locations, arrest actually increased violence for a subgroup of offenders (Berk et al., 1992; Sherman et al., 1992), whereas in others, arrest had little or no effect (Dunford, 1992; J. Hirschel & Hutchison, 1992). Maxwell, Garner, and Fagan (2001) examined the results from these five studies by pooling the data, computing comparable independent and outcome measures, and standardizing the statistical models. They found that regardless of intervention type or outcome used to assess effectiveness, subsequent violence was not reported in the majority of cases; arrest was consistently related to reduced violence, although not all comparisons were significant; and there was little evidence that arrest increased the risk of subsequent violence. This last finding had been noted earlier in studies observing that increased violence was associated with arrest only for subgroups of offenders, such as offenders who were unemployed or who had previous criminal histories (Berk, 1993; Buzawa & Buzawa, 1993).

Studies conducted subsequent to the one in Minneapolis and the five replication studies continued to show conflicting outcomes for arrest. For example, one study found no change in violence after an arrest (McFarlane, Willson,

Lemmey, & Malecha, 2000). On the other hand, Willson, McFarlane, Lemmey, and Malecha (2001) reported that for the 83 women in the study, threats of abuse, actual abuse, and danger of homicide were lower 3 months after they contacted police than they were for the 3 months before police assistance. Compared with their experience prior to requesting police assistance, the study found that 96% of women reported fewer threats of abuse, 98% reported less physical abuse, and 95% reported less danger of homicide 6 months after seeking police aid. Willson et al. (2001) concluded that when abused women go to police agencies, the severity and frequency of abuse decreases. This finding is consistent with Wiist and McFarlane (1998), who found 72% of abused women who contacted law enforcement reported reduced violence. Like earlier studies, these studies suggest that certain offender, contextual, and legal intervention characteristics may impact the effectiveness of arrest (Wooldredge & Thistlewaite, 2002).

A review of the literature on mandatory arrests is complicated by the many nuances in legal process as well as victim and offender responses to the policy. There have been few systematic studies of mandatory arrest and prosecution policies, and existing studies have had methodological and generalizability problems (Hirschel & Buzawa, 2002). Yet this issue is at the heart of one of the most important debates regarding justice system interventions for partner violence today. Proponents of mandatory arrest policies believe arrest is critical in sending the message to society that this kind of behavior is criminal and will not be tolerated (Erez, 2002). Other proponents argue that at a minimum, mandatory arrest can provide victims with temporary relief from violence and give them time to consider their options (Iovanni & Miller, 2001; E. Stark, 1996). Critics argue that mandatory arrest policies do not consider differences in cases or what is best for the victim and the offender (Hirschel & Buzawa, 2002) and that spending a minimal amount of time in jail as the only punishment is not a deterrent (Erez, 2000). Also, mandatory arrest policies ignore the needs of women and take the control away from victims (Erez, 2002; Iovanni & Miller, 2001), and mandatory arrest runs the risk of dual arrests that punish the victim and may have a host of unintended and negative consequences for the victims, including a reduced likelihood of calling the police in the future (Hirschel & Buzawa, 2002; M. Martin, 1997; A. Smith, 2000). Mills (1998) reviewed the literature on mandatory arrest and concluded that arrest is effective for some offenders but not others; thus, instead of spending resources on implementing mandatory policies, it might be better to individualize intervention strategies for each case and to offer services tailored to victim needs.

REFERRALS. Regardless of the effect of arrest, the nature of the interaction between the police and victims at the scene is critical (Belknap & McCall, 1994; Erez, 2002; Fleury, 2002; Ptacek, 1999). As can be seen in Figure 7.1, police are generally victims' first point of contact with the justice system, and negative encounters can result in discouraging further pursuit of legal remedies. On the other hand, if the interaction is positive and helpful, women may find increased safety by pursuing their rights for protection under the law.

Although only a few studies have examined victim perspectives on their interaction with the police, some have found that victims generally perceived the police to be helpful and were satisfied with the help they received. For example, Buzawa and Austin (1993) concluded that most of the partner violence victims (85%) in their study were satisfied with police responses and that satisfaction was related to whether police had complied with their preference regarding arrest or no arrest. Apsler, Cummins, and Carl (2003) reported on a sample of women who came to the attention of the police for partner violence and found that victim ratings of police helpfulness were very positive, and more than 80% reported they would definitely call the police for help if needed in the future. These authors concluded that victim satisfaction with police responses was associated in part with whether the police actions had been consistent with their perceived safety needs (which in this study included arrest, referrals, and obtaining or enforcing a restraining order). Ullman and Filipas (2001), however, noted that almost half of their sample of sexual assault victims reported that the police had been unhelpful.

J. Miller and Krull (1997) conducted a reanalysis of victim interviews from three sites that attempted to replicate the Minneapolis arrest experiment. These authors found that

> police intervention can influence what the victim experiences after the police leave a scene. The actions a police officer takes, in the form of issuing protective orders or providing recommendations or transportation, explain variance in levels of recidivistic violence. These forms of police action are discretionary. Ordinances and police policy can mandate official, legalistic responses to domestic violence; the behaviors of a formal social control agent cannot be mandated. What a police officer does, how a police officer behaves, can affect what a victim experiences subsequent to police intervention. (p. 251)

The "victim experiences" that the authors described include future help-seeking actions, such as seeking a protective order or calling the police in the future, but also refer to validation of the victim's experience as a legitimate use of the justice system.

Police can play a key role in helping victims through referrals to community resources (Barnett, 2000; Finn, 1991). For example, of women who reported their partner assault to the police, Tjaden and Thoennes (2000b) found that only one fourth indicated they had received referrals to victim services or were given advice on self-protective measures. Several other studies reported an association of medical care and police use among sexual assault victims (Rennison, 2002; Resnick, Holmes, et al., 2000).

Protective Orders

As mentioned earlier, there are two main ways a woman can enter the justice system for partner violence: through the police and the criminal process or by petitioning the court for a civil protective order. Protective orders may have different labels, depending on the jurisdiction, including *restraining orders*, *emergency protective orders*, *domestic violence orders*, or *peace bonds* (Eigenberg et al., 2003). Currently, all states have enacted laws authorizing the issuance of civil protective orders for partner violence, although eligibility criteria may differ between states (Buzawa & Buzawa, 1996). Protective orders provide partner violence victims with a temporary judicial injunction that directs the offender to refrain from further abusive behavior and, frequently, to stay away from the victim. In general, obtaining a protective order involves a two-step process. The first step involves the filing of a petition by a victim for a temporary order, which is usually good for up to about 2 weeks (Eigenberg et al., 2003; Logan, Shannon, & Walker, 2005). Initial orders are typically issued on an ex parte basis, meaning the court can issue the order at the request of one party without the other party being present (Jordan, Nietzel, Walker, & Logan, 2004). The second step involves a hearing where both parties are given due process to determine whether a longer term order will be issued (Eigenberg et al., 2003). Orders following a hearing are usually issued for a longer period than emergency and temporary orders, although the length of time an order is in effect depends on state law, the jurisdiction, and specific components of the case (Eigenberg et al., 2003).

Protective orders, as a civil remedy, differ from traditional criminal procedures in several ways (Buzawa & Buzawa, 1996; Finn, 1989, 1991). Because they do not involve criminal cases, protective orders function to prevent future unlawful conduct as opposed to punishing past crimes. Criminal court actions require the highest level of proof—beyond reasonable doubt (Buzawa & Buzawa, 1996; Finn, 1989), whereas civil protective orders only require a preponderance of evidence, which is a lower burden of proof than criminal processes. A lesser burden of proof means less court time, cost, and bureaucratic processes. Furthermore, protective order statutes in many states provide police with the authority to arrest for violation of its terms rather than having to determine probable cause as to whether a crime has been committed, as would be required in other circumstances. Punishment for violation of protective orders is relatively rapid because contempt hearings can be concluded quicker than criminal trials (Lemon, 2001). Additionally, protective orders allow judges to provide relief that can be tailored for each specific case, including provisions for children, child support, and counseling in addition to provisions about threats, physical harm, and stalking. Also, protective orders may be a source of empowerment for women because they allow more flexibility in gaining specific protections from the justice system, they provide public validation that the violence is wrong, and they allow for a graduated legal response rather than immediate arrest and incarceration (Buzawa & Buzawa, 1996; Eigenberg et al., 2003; Finn, 1991; Fischer & Rose, 1995). For example, women may only be interested in relief from future violence and may not be interested in punishing the offender for past violence. Critics of protective orders, on the other hand, have pointed out that they are meaningless without full support and enforcement (Finn, 1991) and that it is the combination of the criminal and civil process that may be the most effective remedy for partner violence (Keilitz et al., 1997).

There are limited data on the number of women with victimization histories who actually obtain protective orders. The NVAW survey asked women whether they had received a protective order after their last incident of intimate partner victimization (Tjaden & Thoennes, 2000b). Only 16.4% of rape victims, 17.1% of physical assault victims, and 36.6% of stalking victims reported obtaining a protective order in response to their last incident of intimate partner violence. In another household survey from one state, 18% of respondents aged 18 to 59 reported partner violence having occurred during the preceding 5 years, and 34% of those respondents reported having obtained a protective order (CDC, 2000). One challenge in interpreting data on the number of women seeking protective orders is that these rates may be affected by several factors, including whether they are eligible to receive protective orders in the jurisdictions in which they live and procedural barriers that may differ by jurisdiction.

Two aspects of protective orders have been established relatively clearly in the literature. First, most women who seek protective orders report past violence, with a substantial proportion reporting a severe violence history (Buzawa, Hotaling, & Klein, 1998; Gondolf, McWilliams, Hart, & Stuehling, 1994; Harrell & Smith, 1996; Keilitz, Davis, Efkeman, Flango, & Hannaford, 1998; Klein, 1996; Ptacek, 1999). In fact, Zoellner, Feeny, et al. (2000) found that most of the women in their sample who had sought protective orders reported that it was not the first incident of abuse (81%), and only about one third (36%) reported that the most recent episode was the worst. According to Harrell and Smith (1996),

> these statistics reveal that these women have had a very burdensome history of abuse with their partners and suggest that formal intervention through a petition to the court for relief is used, not as a form of early intervention, but rather as a signal of desperation following extensive problems. (p. 231)

Fischer and Rose (1995) found that the majority of their sample of women sought protective orders in part because they felt the abuse was becoming more frequent and severe (60%).

Second, a large proportion of men (75%–85%) with protective orders against them have prior criminal histories with a variety of charges (Isaac, Cochran, Brown, & Adams, 1994; Klein, 1996; Logan, Nigoff, Jordan, & Walker, 2002). In fact, Buzawa et al. (1998) found that "the greater the number of prior restraining orders, the greater the criminal history" (p. 202). Other research has found that prior criminal histories predicted reabuse (Klein, 1996). Keilitz et al. (1997) indicated that women with partners who had prior criminal records, especially violent criminal histories, had more problems after obtaining a protective order than women with partners without criminal histories. They concluded that

> because protection orders provide petitioners with less protection against respondents with a high number of arrests, and more specifically with a history of violent crime, the need for aggressive criminal prosecution policies becomes more critical. Criminal prosecution of such individuals may be required to curb their abusive behavior. Reliance on a protection order as the sole intervention in these cases may not be the most effective deterrence against further abuse. (p. 43)

The Efficacy of Civil Orders of Protection

The efficacy of protective orders can be defined in several ways: (a) examining the proportion of women with victimization who obtain protective orders;

(b) determining reductions in violence after the order, defined either through official recidivism measures or by victim report; (c) examining the likelihood of arrests for partner violence among those with and without protective orders; and (d) victim's satisfaction with the protective order.

With regard to the first definition of efficacy, there is wide variation in the number of women who obtain full protective orders, with 20% to 63% of women who seek protective orders actually obtaining a full order (Gist et al., 2001; Gondolf et al., 1994; Harrell & Smith, 1996; Holt, Kernic, Lumley, Wolf, & Rivara, 2002; Klein, 1996; Zoellner, Feeny, et al., 2000). Reasons for not obtaining a protective order vary from not meeting statutory criteria for eligibility to withdrawal of the petition by the victim (Gist et al., 2001; Gondolf et al., 1994; Harrell & Smith, 1996; Logan et al., 2005). For example, McFarlane et al. (2004) reported that 58% of those who did not obtain a temporary protective order in their sample did not follow through in seeking the full protective order; 26% of offenders were not served with the order, which is required before protective orders can go into effect; and 16% were dismissed. Harrell and Smith (1996) found that 40% of the women in their sample did not return to request the full protective order. The primary reasons included the following: did not need one (partner stopped bothering her, was in jail, moved, or they reconciled), other interventions (he went to counseling or was arrested), the order was not served, inconvenience, lack of information, or the temporary order was not effective so they did not feel there was a reason to pursue the full order.

Furthermore, various studies reported that between 23% and 70% of women experience a violation of the protective order, which means either that 30% to 77% of women do not experience violence from the offender after obtaining a protective order or that they do not report it (Carlson, Harris, & Holden, 1999; Harrell & Smith, 1996; Keilitz et al., 1997; McFarlane et al., 2004; Tjaden & Thoennes, 2000b). For example, one study used police records and found that having a permanent protective order was associated with an 80% reduction in police-reported physical violence in the 12 months following the initial incident (Holt et al., 2002). From a meta-analysis of studies examining protective order effectiveness, Spitzberg (2002) found that orders were violated approximately 40% of the time. Several studies have reported that much of the violation activity is initiated within the first 3 months of receiving a protective order (Harrell & Smith, 1996; Keilitz et al., 1997). The wide range for both obtaining and enforcing orders probably varies across studies for multiple reasons, including methodological as well as contextual and environmental (e.g., jurisdictional variation) reasons. More specifically, violation rates are likely to differ across studies, depending on how new incidents of abuse ("reabuse") were measured. Police reports are likely to show a lower rate of reabuse than victim reports. In fact, one study found that only about half of protective order violations were reported to police when victim reports were compared with official data (Hotaling & Buzawa, 2003).

Another index of protective order effectiveness is whether the likelihood of arrest in partner violence cases is increased when there is a protective order in effect. Harrell and Smith (1996) reported that for their sample of 355 women with protective orders, 290 incidents of protective order violations were reported to the police, but only 59 arrests (20%) were actually made within 1 year. From a study of police responses to protective order violations in a jurisdiction with mandatory arrest policies for violation of protective orders, Kane (2000) found that when a protective order was violated and victim risk was high (level of threats and injury potential for harm), the arrest rate was about 76%. When a protective order was violated and victim risk was low, however, the arrest rate was 44%. Mignon and Holmes (1995) found that although implementing a mandatory arrest law significantly increased arrests in partner violence incidents, especially in cases when there was a violation of a protective order, cases of protective order violations led to arrest in only about half of the incidents. Consequently, even in a mandatory arrest jurisdiction, having a protective order does not guarantee that police will arrest the offender when the order has been violated. In general, Kane (1999) found that the violation of a protective order led to about a 5% higher arrest rate when compared with the arrest rate in cases without a protective order. In essence, these findings suggest that other factors may be important in arrest rates for partner violence regardless of whether a protective order is in place, such as victim risk.

Women also have reported life improvements, feeling better about themselves, and feeling safer after obtaining a protective order (Keilitz et al., 1997). Specifically, Harrell, Smith, and Newmark (1993) reported that 86% of their sample of women who obtained protective orders believed the order was helpful in documenting that the abuse occurred, 79% reported the protective order was helpful in sending their partner a message that his actions were wrong, 62% reported that they believed the order was helpful in punishing their partner, and 88% reported they believed the judge did the right thing for them and their children. Logan, Cole, et al. (2004) found that about half (51%) of their sample of 757 women with protective orders believed the order was extremely effective; about one quarter (23%) believed the order was fairly effective.

Education and Referral

As mentioned earlier, one important barrier to making use of the justice system is the lack of knowledge and information women have or may feel they have. There is confusion around the protective order process, with women reporting they do not understand the differences between a temporary and full protective order (Harrell & Smith, 1996), the difference between criminal and civil proceedings, or how to ensure the enforcement of an order (Bennett et al., 1999; Lemon, 2001). There are also procedures and qualifications that must be followed to obtain an order that may need explanation, including the statute about who and under what circumstances an order can legally be issued (Lemon, 2001; Logan, Shannon, et al., 2004). In addition, the time of petitioning for protective orders might be an important point for referrals to other services such as shelters, legal representation, and counseling (Keilitz, 1994; Lemon, 2001).

Prosecution

Once an offender is arrested or brought to the attention of the court, the prosecutor must decide whether to pursue the charges. Although prosecutors typically have great leeway in deciding whether to prosecute offenders (Kerstetter, 1990; Spohn & Holleran, 2001), there is some convincing research that specific factors are associated with prosecution.

Few studies have examined prosecution rates for partner violence. McFarlane, Willson, et al. (2000) interviewed 90 women seeking help for partner violence through the justice system. Forty-eight percent of the cases had insufficient evidence for charges; of the 52% that did have enough evidence for charges, 37% of the offenders were arrested, 4% were fugitives, and 11% had charges dropped by the court. Of the cases in which officials determined that there was insufficient evidence for filing or accepting charges, levels of violence were comparable to those in which charges were accepted or in which the offender was arrested. It is interesting to note that at the 3-month follow-up, women who were told their cases had insufficient evidence for charges to be filed reported significantly more risk for violence compared with the women whose cases were not classified into this group. From the NVAW survey, Tjaden and Thoennes (2000b) found that about 7.3% of women who reported partner physical assault to the police also reported that the offender was prosecuted.

Several relatively consistent factors have been associated with the decision to prosecute for partner violence, including victim injury and cooperation (Dawson & Dinovitzer, 2001; Hirschel & Hutchison, 2001; Kingsnorth, MacIntosh, Berdahl, Blades, & Rossi, 2001). For example, Dawson and Dinovitzer (2001) examined partner violence case files from charges to final disposition for 474 cases in a Canadian court system. These authors found the odds that a case would be prosecuted were 7 times higher if a victim was perceived as cooperative rather than uncooperative. L. Goodman et al. (1999) interviewed women with partners arrested for violence against them and found that the severity of violence in the relationship was associated with cooperation in the prosecution of their abuser. Even though few studies have focused on prosecution rates of partner violence offenders, the completed studies do not show a strong relationship between offenders' prior history of partner violence or other justice system involvement and prosecution of current partner violence (Dawson & Dinovitzer, 2001; Hirschel & Hutchison, 2001; Kingsnorth et al., 2001).

According to studies that have examined prosecution rates of rape, regardless of victim–offender relationship, between one third and about one half of cases overall are prosecuted (Frazier & Haney, 1996; Gray-Eurom et al., 2002; McGregor, Du Mont, & Myhr, 2002; Spohn & Holleran, 2001). However, Tjaden and Thoennes (2000b) found that 7.5% of women who reported partner sexual assault to the police reported that the offender was prosecuted—almost the same percentage who were prosecuted for physical assault (7.3%).

An interesting question is whether rape cases are treated differently from other violent crimes. That is the question that Maxwell, Robinson, and Post (2003) examined in a stratified random sample of felony cases from 75 of the most populated counties in the United States reporting to the National Pretrial Reporting Program. Over 41,000 cases were adjudicated between 1990 and 1996. These researchers compared sexual assault with physical assault, robbery, and murder case outcomes and found that sexual assault outcome patterns most closely resembled murder outcome patterns. They suggested that "sexual assault was and continues to be appropriately placed on a continuum of sanctions where it is treated leniently compared to murder but more punitively compared to other violent felonies" (Maxwell et al., 2003, p. 534).

As with partner assaults, however, there are questions about whether acquaintance rape cases are treated differently than stranger rape cases in the justice system. To address this issue, Kingsnorth, MacIntosh, and Wentworth (1999) tracked 467 sexual assault cases in one court system from prosecutorial intake through sentencing disposition. They found no differences attributable to offender–victim relationship in the decision to prosecute, the decision to go to trial rather than plea, or trial outcomes. Spohn and Holleran (2001) also found no difference between cases by victim–offender relationship in the decision to prosecute. On the other hand, Frazier and Haney (1996) found that in general, suspects were less likely to be identified in stranger rape cases than acquaintance rape cases; however, when only cases with identified suspects were examined, suspects were less likely to be questioned in acquaintance (65%) than stranger (81%) rape cases, and there was a similar trend in prosecutor referrals.

Research has also tried to determine which factors influence the decision to prosecute in rape cases. Some factors that seem consistently associated with prosecution decisions include severity of the crime (Frazier & Haney, 1996), physical evidence (McGregor, Le, Marion, & Wiebe, 1999; Spohn & Holleran, 2001), and questions about victim character or risky behaviors at the time of the assault (Spears & Spohn, 1997). The question about victim character, especially in cases of acquaintance rape cases, was mentioned at the beginning of this chapter.

Several studies have highlighted the impact of victim character on rape case outcomes. For example, Spohn, Beichner, and Davis-Frenzel (2001) examined data on all sexual battery cases ($N = 140$) involving victims 12 years and older with an offender who was arrested in 1997 in one police department. Secondary data (e.g., the closeout memorandums) and interviews with prosecutors were used to examine prosecutorial reasons for charge rejection. Spohn et al. concluded that prosecutors were concerned about reducing uncertainty and securing convictions, which increases the likelihood of prosecuting cases. The perceived seriousness of the crime, victim injury, and strong evidence against the suspect were all factors considered in whether to prosecute. They also concluded that because victim credibility plays a particularly important role in sexual assault cases, prosecutor perceptions of convictability often rest on stereotypes about rape, rape victims, and rape-relevant behavior. They summarized their findings as follows:

> The fact that over half of the sexual battery cases were not prosecuted, coupled with the fact that prosecutors questioned the victim's credibility in a substantial number of cases that were rejected, suggests that the prosecution of sexual assault cases remains problematic. The rape law reforms notwithstanding, prosecutors continue to use a decision making calculus that incorporates stereotypes of real rape and legitimate victims. (p. 233)

Other studies have also found that victim credibility has important effects on prosecution rates. For example, Spears and Spohn (1997) examined a sample of adult sexual offense cases in which an arrest was made. They found that prosecutors were about 5 times more likely to file charges if there were no questions about the victim's moral character and about 2.5 times more likely to charge if the victim was not engaging in any risky behavior at the time of the assault. Prompt reporting of the incident was also associated with a prosecutorial decision to charge. Spohn and Holleran (2001) found that physical evidence was an important predictor in charging, regardless of offender–victim relationship. In cases involving strangers, however, the odds of charging were increased if there was physical evidence or the involvement of a weapon, whereas in acquaintance cases, the odds were reduced if there were questions about victim reputation, character, or risky behavior. The interesting thing was that more of the stranger rape cases had notations about victim risk behavior compared with acquaintance rape cases, yet this issue had less of a role in the decision to charge in stranger rape cases but was an important factor in the decision to charge in acquaintance rape cases.

Conviction

Conviction rates are fairly low for both partner violence and rape cases. For example, Tjaden and Thoennes (2000b) found, using the NVAW survey data, that women who reported that their intimate partner offenders were prosecuted for assault also reported that 47.9% were convicted and that 35.6% of those convicted were actually sentenced to jail or prison. Ventura and Davis (2005) found that of the 1,982 cases of domestic violence charges tracked in one jurisdiction from April 2000 to March 2001, 67.6% resulted in dismissal, 23.8% resulted in conviction, and 8.6% of the cases were still pending. Cramer (1999) found that of the 140 partner violence cases they examined, 25% had guilty verdicts, and a previous criminal history and documentation of the injury were associated with a guilty verdict in partner violence cases. Kingsnorth et al. (2001) reported that documentation of injury, prior partner violence arrest, and victim injury were all associated with a felony conviction in partner violence cases. Factors such as severity of injury, use of a weapon, and victim age have also been associated with convictions in rape cases (Gray-Eurom et al., 2002; McGregor et al., 2002).

Similarly, McGregor et al. (2002) found that a conviction was secured in only 11% of the sexual assault cases they examined. Frazier and Haney (1996) examined rape cases reported to police in 1991 that involved a female victim aged 16 or older. Of those cases, suspects were only identified in about half (48%), and about 68% of those identified were questioned by the police. Of those questioned by the police, 68% were referred to the prosecutor, 72% were charged, 54% were convicted, and 57% were sentenced to prison. In all, of the 273 cases with an identified suspect, 91 were charged, 69 were convicted, and 39 were sentenced to incarceration. Tjaden and Thoennes (2000b) found from victim reports that of the intimate partner offenders prosecuted for sexual assault, 41.9% were convicted and 69.2% of those convicted were sentenced to jail or prison.

Prosecution and Conviction Effectiveness

Several studies have examined the impact of prosecution, conviction, and sentencing on reoffending in partner violence cases; however, no studies were located that examined prosecution effectiveness for rape cases. One of the first studies to examine differences in prosecutorial strategies in partner violence cases found that victims who had charges filed under the no-drop policy had an increased risk of abuse compared with victims who had charges filed under a drop-permitted policy but who chose not to drop the charges (Ford & Regoli, 1993). Tolman and Weiscz (1995) examined recidivism for partner violence cases in which offenders were convicted compared with cases that were dismissed or acquitted and found no differences in subsequent police reports or arrests over an 18-month period. Wooldredge and Thistlewaite (2002) conducted a study of offenders arrested for partner violence in one county. These authors found that arrestees who did not have any charges filed had higher rearrest rates (24.1%) than offenders with other arrest outcomes (14%); among those with other arrest outcomes, however (charges were dropped, acquitted at trial, mandated to counseling, or probation/jail term), there were no differences in rearrest rates. Mears, Carlson, Holden, and Harris (2001) found that there were no differences in partner violence cases with an arrest, a protective order, or both in subsequent police reports of partner physical assault. On the other hand, from random samples of domestic violence offender cases, Ventura and Davis (2005) found that offenders who were convicted were less likely to be arrested on a new domestic violence charge 1 year after the disposition compared with those who were arrested but not convicted. These authors also indicated that recidivism was associated with offender age (younger offenders were more likely to be reconvicted) and a longer history of partner violence perpetration (offenders with a longer history of partner violence were more likely to be reconvicted).

R. Davis, Smith, and Taylor (2003) concluded from their study of cases in one court that expanding prosecutorial efforts on partner violence to include cases with and without victim cooperation leads to results that

> do not support the idea that domestic violence cases can be readily prosecuted without regard for victim desires. To commit to such a policy would require a substantial commitment of additional staff, resources to collect additional types of evidence, and a willingness to try a substantially larger number of cases. (p. 263)

In essence, these authors concluded that implementing less selective prosecution policies must include increased resources at all levels to be more successful than the current system.

Sentencing

Once an offender is found guilty, there is one more important step in the criminal process—sentencing. Partner violence and rape offenders can be sentenced to a variety of sanctions, including fines, community service, treatment, probation, incarceration, or some combination of these (Gross et al., 2000). One major question is whether incarceration is an effective sanction for offenders. General recidivism rates are high across all kinds of criminal offenders who have been incarcerated. For example, among the approximately 270,000 prisoners released in 15 states in 1994, almost 68% were rearrested for a new offense within 3 years, and there was no evidence from these data that longer sentences reduced recidivism rates (Langan & Levin, 2002). Another important question regarding sentencing is whether incarceration is a more effective sanction than other kinds. Gottfredson (1999) conducted an analysis of felony offenders sentenced in 1976 and 1977 to examine rearrest rates by sentence type over a 20-year period. Incarceration, when compared with nonincarceration sentences, had no effect on subsequent justice system involvement for this group of offenders, nor did sentence length.

Only a few studies have examined sanctions for partner violence and rape offenders specifically. R. Davis, Smith, and Nickles (1998) examined recidivism rates for misdemeanor partner violence cases when the prosecutor declined the case, the case was dismissed, the offender received probation, or the offender received jail time. These researchers reported no evidence that receiving probation or jail time affected recidivism compared with no prosecution within the 6-month follow-up period. Olson and Stalans (2001) compared probationers convicted of partner violence with probationers convicted for other violent offenses. Partner violence offenders were more likely to be charged with misdemeanor charges than other offenders, thus, overall, their probation sentences were shorter. When only misdemeanants were compared, sentence length did not differ. Offenders on probation for partner violence charges were more likely to have also been sentenced to pay fines or to go to treatment than other probation offenders. Olson and Stalans found no differences in reoffending rates except that partner violence probationers were more likely to revictimize the original victim compared with the other probation offenders.

Other sentencing options for partner violence offenders can include mandated treatment for violent behavior (Gondolf, 2000a, 2001). Offender treatment is more than a justice system intervention and may focus on offenders' basic beliefs about gender roles, cognitions, personality characteristics, substance use, and overall antisocial behavior (Aldorondo, 2002; Fishbein, 2000). Although a review of research on offender treatment approaches lies outside the scope of this book, it is important to note that the few studies comparing offender treatment to other sanctions have inconsistent findings in regard to decreased violence after participation (Babcock, Green, & Robie, 2004). Some studies have shown no differences between treatment and other sanctions as measured by victim reports (B. Taylor, Davis, & Maxwell, 2001), official records (Dobash & Dobash, 2000; Gross et al., 2000) or both (Feder & Dugan, 2002). Other studies have shown significant differences between offenders ordered to treatment compared with offenders who received other sanctions, as measured by official reports (Babcock & Steiner, 1999; Murphy, Musser, & Maton, 1998; B. Taylor et al., 2001) and victim reports (Dobash & Dobash, 2000). There are many methodological problems with the research on batterer treatment programs, suggesting a need for more research so that justice system sanctions can be better tailored to address partner violence (Bennett & Williams, 2001; Buttell & Carney,

2004; Gondolf, 2001). Gondolf (2000b) also suggested that batterer treatment programs may be most effective when courts review compliance with treatment orders.

Examination of sentence outcomes or recidivism for rape offenders, excluding child molester offender research, is also difficult because it has received limited research attention (Polaschek & King, 2002; Polaschek, Ward, & Hudson, 1997). One study found that almost 50% of convicted rapists who had been released from prison committed an offense by the 5th year following release from prison, with 16% committing sexual crimes, 26% committing violent crimes, and 53% committing any crime (Firestone et al., 1998). Another study found that among convicted rapists (not including child molesters), 21% were reconvicted over an average follow-up of about 5 years (Proulx et al., 1997). Langstrom (2002) followed a sample of adolescent and young adult identified sex offenders (including child molesters) from Sweden for almost 10 years and found that 30% were reconvicted for sexual offenses and 42% were reconvicted for nonsexual offenses. P. Hall (1995) conducted a meta-analysis of treatment versus comparison conditions for 12 studies of sex offenders (which included child molesters) and found that overall, 19% of the treatment group had committed additional sexual offenses compared with 27% of the comparison group. Marx, Miranda, and Meyerson (1999) suggested that treatment may be limited, in part, when studies and treatment programs fail to assess typological differences among sex offenders. For example, child molesters are likely very different from rapists who target adults. Again, a review of research on sex offender treatment approaches lies outside the scope of this book, but more research (including studies with control comparison groups) clearly is needed about justice system response.

A few studies have also examined sentence differences by type of rape offender. For example, Frazier and Haney (1996) found that stranger rapists were more than twice as likely to receive prison sentences and that acquaintance rapists were more likely to be placed on probation or receive other forms of punishment. Kingsnorth et al. (1999) found that when selection bias and relevant legal factors were controlled in sexual assault cases, the existence of a prior relationship reduced sentence length by 35 months; each additional negative victim characteristic (e.g., victim substance use, prostitution) reduced incarceration by 17 months. McCormick, Maric, Seto, and Barbaree (1998) examined incarcerated rapists in Canada and found that stranger rapists were given the longest sentences compared with acquaintance and partner rapists. L. Simon (1996) also examined Canadian incarcerated violent offenders and found that although nonstranger offenders were charged and convicted of more serious crimes, stranger offenders received significantly longer sentences.

Stalking

Stalking is another dimension of violence against women that has an interesting history with the justice system. The first publicized cases of stalking were of celebrities who had crazed fans pursuing them (R. Saunders, 1998). Stalking was determined to be a crime in California in 1990 (Spitzberg, 2002), and by

1999 all states had enacted laws making stalking a crime (N. Miller, 2001). While these laws were being drafted, there was little empirical information available about these issues except what was being reported on the news or other media outlets (Bjerregaard, 2000). Often what was reported was about celebrity stalking rather than the more frequent occurrence of women being stalked by a current or ex-partner (Tjaden & Thoennes, 1998).

More specifically, one of the largest groups of stalking offenders who prey on women comprises intimate or ex-intimate partners (62%; Tjaden & Thoennes, 1998). Such stalkers, compared with others, have been more likely to threaten the victim and her property and to commit more violence against her and her property (Palarea, Zona, Lane & Langhinrichsen-Rohling, 1999; B. Rosenfeld, 2004; Sheridan & Davies, 2001; Sheridan, Blaauw, & Davies, 2003). In addition, stalking victimization has been associated with significant victim distress (Blaauw, Winkel, Arensman, Sheridan, & Freeve, 2002; Mechanic, Weaver, & Resick, 2000; Sheridan, Blaauw, et al., 2003; Spitzberg, 2002). Even so, studies examining perceptions of stalking behavior and risk have found that stalking is perceived as less serious and risky when it is perpetrated by a current or former partner rather than by a stranger or acquaintance (Phillips, Quirk, Rosenfeld, & O'Connor, 2004; Sheridan, Gillett, Davies, Blaauw, & Patel, 2003).

Stalking is an especially interesting case of victimization because it is difficult to prove in criminal proceedings (Logan, Cole, Shannon, & Walker, 2006; N. Miller, 2001; Wells, 2001). As noted throughout this discussion, injury and injury severity seem related to the likelihood of justice system responses such as arrest, prosecution, conviction, and sentencing. In fact, Robbennolt (2000) conducted a meta-analysis on judgments of responsibility for all kinds of events (e.g., accidents, rapes, test scores) and found that more negative outcomes were associated with a higher likelihood of attributing responsibility to the other party. In other words, society often holds victims less responsible when the effects of violence are more negative. In many stalking cases, the harm may be more emotional than physical, which makes the case more difficult to prove, validate, and prosecute (N. Miller, 2001; Wells, 2001).

A few studies have examined the appeals for police protection by stalking victims and found that rates vary from a low range of 17% to 35% (Bjerregaard, 2000; Fisher et al., 2000) to a higher range of 72% to 89% (Blaauw et al., 2002; Brewster, 2001). Studies on stalking have paralleled studies on physical and sexual assault, with requests for police protection more likely among those who experience more severe and frequent stalking (Brewster, 2001; Mechanic, Uhlmansiek, Weaver & Resick, 2000; Nicastro, Cousins, & Spitzberg, 2000). However, arrest rates of partner stalkers tend to be smaller, ranging from 25% to 39% among those that were brought to police attention (Brewster, 2001; Tjaden & Thoennes, 1998). Protective order use for stalking has also varied depending on the study. Fisher et al.'s (2000) study of college women found that only about 3% of stalking victims obtained a protective order; whereas the NVAW survey indicated that about 37% did so after their last incident of intimate partner stalking victimization (Tjaden & Thoennes, 2000b). Logan, Nigoff, et al. (2002) examined a sample of 346 men charged with stalking in 1999 in one state and found that almost two thirds had a protective order against them. Working with a sample of stalking victims, Brewster (2001) reported that about half

(51%) had filed for a protective order. Nicastro et al. (2000) found, from the city attorney's stalking case files, that the majority of cases (76%) had restraining orders but that 67% of the stalkers had violated the order.

Fewer studies have examined prosecution and conviction rates of stalkers. The NVAW survey found a prosecution rate of 24% for stalking cases with female victims who reported the stalking to law enforcement, 54% of those cases were actually convicted, and 63% of those convicted were incarcerated (Tjaden & Thoennes, 1998). Sheridan and Davies (2001) found a conviction rate of 36% from their study of victims who were seeking help for stalking. Stalkers are often charged with a variety of offenses, including harassment, menacing or threatening, vandalism, trespassing, breaking and entering, robbery, disorderly conduct, intimidation, and assault (Tjaden & Thoennes, 1998, 2000c). Even so, Jordan, Logan, Walker, and Nigoff (2003) found that dismissal was the most common disposition of stalking criminal cases even when charges were amended (49.2% of initial felony charges, 54% of amended felony charges, 61.2% of initial misdemeanor charges, and 62.2% of amended misdemeanors). Sheridan and Davies (2001) found that although intimate or ex-intimate partner stalkers were more violent than other stalkers, stranger stalkers were more likely to be convicted of stalking related offenses. Rosenfeld (2003) followed a group of 148 stalkers and harassment offenders court-ordered to a mental health evaluation and found a reoffending rate of 49%, according to official data.

Summary

This review of the literature on justice system responses to victimization describes considerable complexity. Jurisdictions differ in responses and in the ways they have accommodated changed social values about partner violence and sexual assault. The old views of women and interpersonal violence still persist in perhaps unintentional ways through cumbersome bureaucratic systems and less than aggressive enforcement for crimes of violence against women. Nonetheless, the shift from, for example, rape laws that protected the "value" of a daughter or wife to a punishment for a crime against the woman must be seen as progress despite other problems in the system. Women can now pursue civil or criminal remedies for immediate protection, punishment, protection against future crime, or social validation of the right to freedom from injury. There are, however, many costs or barriers to both initiating contact with and the ongoing use of the justice system.

Two main ways to enter the justice system were discussed in this chapter: through contact with the police and by petitioning for protective orders. Although the research is not conclusive, it seems that many women report partner violence to the police and seek protective orders at some point during their relationship with a violent partner. Rape survivors, however, may be less likely to report the crime to the police, regardless of offender–victim relationship. Interacting with the police can be helpful, but it can also be a negative experience for women who have experienced these kinds of crimes. Police can be validating, provide education and referrals, or provide immediate safety to the victim by arresting the offender; however, police interactions can also be negative and deter women from pursuing justice interventions in the future. Protective orders diminish some of the personal costs of pursuing punishment through the justice system by streamlining the process and focusing on future protection, but they have their own problems. The prevailing belief is that if an order is not supported by swift and efficient enforcement, it is essentially worthless. The frequency and severity of the violence women experience seem to be most associated with initiating justice system services.

The frequency and severity of the violence, victim injury, and victim credibility also appear to be associated with arrest rates, convictions, and sanctions for rape and partner assault crimes, even when there are protective orders in place. This is problematic when there is a threat of violence or in stalking cases because the justice system may not act until a victim is injured, whereas the victim may be using the justice system to prevent injury. The process of questioning victims' credibility may prevent women from seeking protection through the justice system and may also prevent justice system personnel from pursuing the crime.

Effectiveness of justice system responses can be measured in several ways, including diminished repeat violence and victim satisfaction with the system. Recidivism rates may be high or low, depending on how the study defined recidivism or the specific intervention. In general, however, recidivism rates for partner violence cases do not seem to be widely different from those of other crimes. The few studies that have examined satisfaction suggest that victims of partner violence are generally satisfied with the justice system process, whereas sexual assault victims are not. One study, however, compared satisfaction with various aspects of the justice system for victims of partner versus nonpartner violence. They found that the former were less satisfied with most aspects of the system (Byrne, Kilpatrick, Howley, & Beatty, 1999).

In general, improved community coordination, better enforcement of laws related to these crimes, and increased victim awareness of and input on justice system options and responses are all needed (Ford, 2003; Gregory & Erez, 2002; Konradi & Burger, 2000). Erez (2002) concluded that

> the challenge for the criminal justice system in finding an effective response to domestic violence continues as newly discovered issues emerge while accepted knowledge on this subject is questioned. This continuous search for solutions and ways to combat or reduce domestic violence requires constant revision of practices and policies as new knowledge and skills training become available. (p. 5)

This statement likely applies to both physical and sexual assault cases involving intimate partners.

Strengths and Weaknesses in the Literature

Intimate partner violence is a crime, and protections and remedies by the justice system are critical for women. This review of the literature demonstrates evidence of inroads into understanding justice system options and responses to violence against women. Nonetheless, important research gaps remain, and these are highlighted in three main areas in need of future research.

First, as noted earlier, there have been a number of studies on types of barriers to entering the justice system. However, there are critical gaps in understanding barriers more generally and the trade-offs that women with partner violence and sexual assault victimization experience in pursuing justice system contact (Herman, 2003). Most of the available information is from small qualitative studies or anecdotal reports. Large, systematic studies should be conducted on the various types of barriers that women experience across multiple and diverse jurisdictions. In addition, a better understanding is needed of how barriers differ depending on specific victimization experiences and during different phases of the justice process. Understanding differences in barriers for women who live within various social contexts is critical (D. Campbell, Sharps, Gary, Campbell, & Lopez, 2002). Furthermore, few studies have examined the effect of the justice system on the victims in terms of safety, mental health, and empowerment over the long term (Fleury, 2002; Herman, 2003; Orth & Maercker, 2004). The case study presented in the beginning of this chapter should be a wake-up call for justice system and mental health personnel as well as victim advocates. For women who have experienced partner violence and sexual assault, navigating the justice system can be frustrating, time-consuming, and demeaning; it may also be ineffective, both procedurally and in terms of outcomes. A clearer understanding of the barriers and costs to victims as well as the use of the justice system in conjunction with other service systems could help in training justice system and other service agency personnel as well as in educating women who need help from the justice system.

Second, more systematic research on violence against women and justice system responses is needed. Not only is there a need for a greater understanding of system interventions and the effectiveness of sanctions, but improved methods are also needed to examine justice system options and responses. Currently, it is difficult to compare results across studies because so many caveats pertain to each study. Conducting evaluations and comparisons require careful thought and explicit definitions of what is to be accomplished. For example, making sure that interventions are carried out similarly across various jurisdictions and that recidivism is defined consistently across studies may be important in understanding the effectiveness of justice system responses (Mears, 2003). Furthermore, methods of gathering data (e.g., official records, telephone surveys, case studies) can create differences in "effectiveness"; this can make cross-study comparisons difficult. In addition, it is difficult to develop generalizable knowledge from a patchwork of findings and seemingly conflicting results (Mears, 2003). Given the many methodological problems in extant research, multiple jurisdictional studies should become the standard in order to increase generalizability of findings. This step is important because state laws defining crimes and sanctions, local enforcement, and local cultural factors all vary. Multiple site research could help develop more global results about the justice processes and outcomes for victims.

In a different vein, Mears (2003) suggested that justice system options and responses should be considered within individual and community contexts. For example, there has been limited systematic documentation about the effectiveness of arrests or protective orders for different racial and ethnic groups or other subpopulations. As another example, Felson and Ackerman (2001) argued that researchers should not simply examine "arrest" as a global category of interventions but that the context of arrests should be considered as well. For example, comparing arrest rates in cases where the victim–offender relationship is specified compared with studies that do not specify may yield very different results, because arrest should be facilitated for offenders that have been identified for a specific crime. Furthermore, Spohn and Holleran (2001) and Decker (1993) argued that categorizing acquaintance and stranger offenders confounds case outcome results because there may be huge differences between a casual acquaintance and a partner assault, yet many studies use the simplistic classification of acquaintance rather than considering more refined categories. Other researchers have warned that how case outcomes are partitioned can bias study results. For example, examining only rejected or dismissed cases compared with cases classified as full prosecution may bias the data because the former may actually have been converted from criminal charges to probation violations (Kingsnorth, MacIntosh, & Sutherland, 2002). Kingsnorth et al. (2002) and others (Farnsworth & Teske, 1995; Spohn & Spears, 1996) have suggested that analyzing the earlier, informal, decision-making points prior to sentencing is important. In addition, intervention evaluations must consider unintended negative effects as well as positive outcomes, which may be critically important in cases of violence against women. Adequate follow-up time is also important for a true understanding of justice system responses and outcomes. Conducting evaluations of justice system responses requires not only the justice system's cooperation but also its understanding about the long-term value of scientific evaluation of the system. Feder, Jolin, and Feyerherm (2000) provided an excellent discussion of the difficult lessons learned in conducting evaluations of justice system options and responses using research conditions.

Third, careful analysis of various policies is needed and should be integrated with victims' perceptions of the policies as well as their perceptions of effectiveness. Mills (1998) argued that mandatory policies remove a burden but also remove control from the victim. Information available concerning the benefits and drawbacks of mandatory prosecution is scarce (Ford, 2003; Mills, 1998). Other researchers have called for a better understanding of how violence against women is treated within the justice system, and they have suggested that well-intentioned arrest and prosecution policies alone will not go far enough to curb violence against women (Hanna, 1998). Mills (1998) made the point that few of the mandatory arrest or prosecution studies actually have examined victim empowerment. Other questions still need to be answered, such as whether the court system can empower a victim and under what circumstances. Gregory and Erez (2002) highlighted the importance of incorporating victims' voices into program evaluations of batterer treatment programs. Barata and Senn (2003) argued that research on partner violence within the justice system needs to consider the victims, even when they are not the primary research focus. Finally, understanding offender perceptions of justice system options and responses may be important to consider in a full understanding of justice system responses and outcomes (Mills, 1998).

Conclusion

This chapter has focused on justice system options and responses for women with victimization experiences. Unfortunately, there is some evidence that women with partner violence, rape, and stalking victimization still face problems and difficulties in seeking help from the justice system. Furthermore, outcome studies on arrest, prosecution, and civil protective orders have offered inconsistent findings about which remedies are the most effective for victims. These inconsistencies present challenges in studying the complex phenomena of victimization and justice system options and responses. Even so, several promising justice system options for women should be pursued with more research and presented to women as options. These include protective orders in conjunction with using the police to provide immediate protection as well as criminal prosecution when women are willing to pursue this strategy. There are drawbacks to each of these options, and educating women about the drawbacks as well as the possible benefits is important. In addition, advocates may be critical in helping women negotiate the justice system in a way that meets their needs and desires and provides for their safety (Bell & Goodman, 2001; Pence, 2001; Weisz, 1999).

Three themes from the literature were reviewed in this chapter. First, no simple answer or model applies to every case when it comes to justice system options. For example, Natalie from chapter 2 may decide to pursue a protective order or even criminal charges if her ex-partner continues to stalk her. Sara, from chapter 3, may decide to prosecute the men who raped her through criminal court. Maria, from chapter 4, may decide against using any part of the justice system given her social environment and circumstances. Susannah, from chapter 5, may pursue a protective order and try to work things out with her husband, whereas Janice, from chapter 6, may choose to file for divorce and pursue a protective order to increase her safety. As these examples highlight, each individual case should be considered independently of others. Situations, goals, and needs differ for every woman, and these factors must be considered in deciding which avenues in the justice system to pursue. Second, future research on the justice system must be conducted with clear definitions and careful methods. Third, negotiating the justice system takes a great amount of energy, courage, and determination. Chapter 5 discussed the importance of internal resource depletion in coping effectively with stress. Women with victimization experiences often have extremely depleted internal and external resources, and negotiating the justice system may take an inordinate level of energy. Women who begin the process should be admired for their courage and strength; external resources should be rallied to help them continue through the process.

8

Final Thoughts: Past, Present, and Future

Knowledge comes by taking things apart: analysis. But wisdom comes by putting things together.
—John A. Morrison (quoted in Forbes Leadership Library, 1997, p. 130)

The investigation of the truth is in one way hard, in another easy. An indication of this is found in the fact that no one is able to attain the truth adequately, while, on the other hand, no one fails entirely, but every one says something true about the nature of things, and while individually they contribute little or nothing to the truth, by the union of all, a considerable amount is amassed.
—Aristotle (Barnes, 1984, p. 1569)

We began the Preface by asking, "Why write another book on victimization, trauma, and related problems?" The answer to this question can be found with reference to the tale of the blind men describing an elephant. In that story, each blind man described a very different animal from the others because each had but one narrow view without the benefit of "seeing" the big picture. That is what has been attempted in this book—to consolidate and assimilate findings from hundreds of studies into a more complete view of the "elephant." As Aristotle said, no one description of reality is likely to be adequate, but the sum of findings amount to something more important. Whatever truths are to be learned about interpersonal victimization must come from the ever-expanding universe of research. Yet the range and extent of literature related to intimate partner violence and sexual assault victimization is so large that it is difficult for clinicians, teachers, trainers, students, researchers, and policymakers to hold a comprehensive view of the problem. The diversity of views and complexity of the problem require a broader conceptual framework that contextualizes the abundance of information that is out there. Without an overarching framework, there is always the danger of falling into specialized academic niches that can obscure a broader understanding of the human condition. For example, several recent trends in the victimization literature suggest that using the posttraumatic stress disorder (PTSD) paradigm for understanding responses to partner violence and sexual assault victimization is inadequate (Burstow, 2003; Koss, Bailey, Yuan, Herrera, & Lichter, 2003; Mirowsky & Ross, 2002; Wasco, 2003). Given all that has been reviewed, this concern deserves serious thought. By examining a wide array of factors, this book has shown the limitations of relying on any single way of "explaining" victimization antecedents or effects. One danger of relying on one paradigm to embrace complex phenomena is that there is inevitable "conceptual bracket creep"—that is, simplistic categorizations of complex issues and potential misapplication of the concept (McNally, 2003b). Using the example of PTSD as a framework for understanding victimization, it is easy to see the term gradually including more and more phenomena until it loses clear meaning. This book encourages expanding awareness to include domains that may lie outside customary discipline orientations, which may help to avoid the pitfall of results that have an incomplete correspondence to reality.

This last chapter discusses the conceptual model that was described in stages through chapters 1–5. In addition, we discuss implications of research for practice and the areas needing future research. To cover these topics, the chapter is organized around three broad questions. (a) What is the current state of knowledge about victimization, physical and mental health, and substance use among women? (b) What can be done within the framework of current knowledge to help women with victimization experiences? (c) Where should future research on victimization, mental health, and substance use focus?

What Is the Current State of Knowledge About Victimization, Physical and Mental Health, and Substance Use Among Women?

Throughout the book, a conceptual model was been used to organize the literature contributing to victimization, mental health, and substance use among women. The overall model was introduced in chapter 1 with four major domains: (a) victimization manifestations and vulnerabilities, (b) lifestyle factors, (c) social factors, and (d) internal contextual factors. Chapters 2 through 5 each focused on one of the four domains and provided a more detailed description of factors within each domain. The complete conceptual model in Figure 8.1 shows 32 bidirectional interactions among 11 factors and 3 major outcomes. The model shows circular paths among factors, but there are also interactions (not shown) that can link diametrically across the oval, thus resulting in a virtual cat's cradle of interactional lines. This model is neither a causal model nor one that has been tested in terms of relative risk among factors. Nonetheless, it provides a way to understand the complexity that is identified in the literature. Although complexity has been repeatedly emphasized, and research still has a long way to go, much has been learned. The research of the past decade or so has resulted in a wealth of information that has great relevance to practice and to future research.

Taking the conceptual model as a whole as shown in Figure 8.1, victimization, mental health problems, and substance abuse are displayed as central phenomena that are influenced by all the factors at the circumference of the oval. Each factor domain interacts within itself and with the other domains as well as with the central phenomena. For example, a genetic predisposition can influence the expression of a mental health problem, and the resulting combination of genetic influence plus mental health problems can influence cognitive appraisals; these factors can in turn interact with social environments and

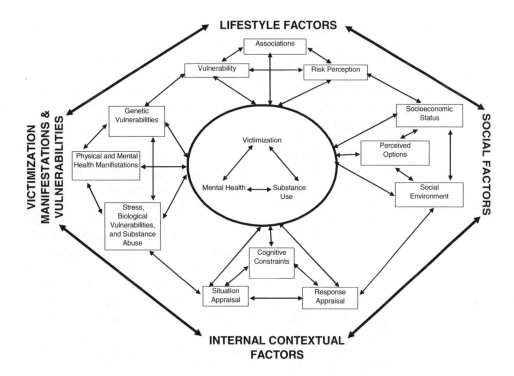

Figure 8.1. Conceptual model of factors contributing to victimization, mental health, and substance use.

lifestyle activities. The entire cycle of interactions can greatly shape how victimization is experienced and how the risk of revictimization might be increased.

Victimization Manifestations and Vulnerabilities: Physical and Mental Health, Genetic, Stress Related, Biological, and Substance Abuse

The literature has examined numerous health problems that have been associated with victimization experiences among women. Health problems can be categorized into three main areas: acute, chronic, and stress related. Certainly, these conditions are not all caused by intimate partner violence and sexual assault victimization, but their expression may be exacerbated by these factors. Health problems are often linked to stress, as are mental health problems. Furthermore, a serious review of the literature on victimization quickly dispels the idea of a clear boundary between physical and mental health and stress unites the two in disturbing ways.

The literature on mental health problems associated with victimization experiences among women, especially PTSD, anxiety, and depression, has been very rich over the past decade. The use of brain imaging has made enormous contributions to the understanding of how mental disorders affect brain regions and how experiences may lead to changes in brain functioning. The importance of these findings for victimization cannot be underestimated. The neuroanatomical and neurochemical characteristics associated with depression and PTSD suggest that simple solutions with regard to seeking safety; making clear, rational decisions; and avoiding risks are naive. The biological constraints that may accompany victimization cannot be easily or quickly dismissed. They constitute substantial problems in their own right and add burdens as women cope with their victimization experiences.

To make matters more complicated, it appears that the types of mental health problems that accompany victimization are themselves interactive, creating multiple risk factors for co-occurring mental health problems. For example, having an anxiety disorder may be associated with additional risk for depression. Having depression can be a risk factor for substance related disorders. Having a Cluster B personality disorder is associated with risk for depression, anxiety, substance-related disorders, and eating disorders. It is as if having one condition opens doors to many others, and treatment for one problem may or may not reduce the risk for other problems. It is also clear that mental health problems, at least for women, have robust associations with victimization and that victimization should be considered in any clinical exploration of mental health problems among women.

Stress clearly activates the potential for the expression of mental health problems. As discussed in chapter 2, victimization stress differs from other stress because it is continuous and affords no safe respite. With work-related stress, one might experience some respite on coming home after a stressful day at work; not so with victimization. With high levels of stress, the risk for depression and anxiety disorders increases; stress levels are also associated with the risk for substance abuse, and substance abuse becomes a risk factor for depression and anxiety. Substance use and abuse can also contribute to stress, even though substances may initially be used to relieve stress.

All of these factors interact, and stress may be a common trigger for physical and mental health problems that may have genetic underpinnings. Physical and mental health problems reduce the ability to cope and to make informed, clear, and assertive decisions. Hence, these factors may contribute to revictimization in the sense that safety seeking and other actions may be limited by depression, substance abuse, or the secondary effects of these conditions. Safety seeking behavior can also be constrained by women's concern that their depression, anxiety, or substance abuse will be viewed pejoratively by others.

Lifestyle Factors: Associations, Vulnerability, and Risk Perception

This review of the literature shows that certain lifestyle activities pose a risk for victimization. For example, individuals who are involved in illegal drug use are more likely to be victimized than those who are not involved with drugs. This may be due to associations or to perceived vulnerability by potential offenders. Furthermore, certain activities can influence risk perceptions. For example, substance use clearly influences judgment and behavior. Reduced cognitive ability while intoxicated decreases the ability to recognize danger. Certain expectations for situations can also influence risk perceptions, such as expectations for social activities or expectations about how much an acquaintance should be trusted. Furthermore, women who are intoxicated at the time of assault may feel less confident about reporting their victimization. Drug and alcohol use carry a powerful stigma—particularly for women—and this stigma itself can be a risk factor because women may fear being dismissed or rejected when seeking safety or help through the justice system. The research within this domain must be interpreted carefully. Unfortunately, lifestyles may be conflated with "choices" in the active intentional sense. Contrary to this view of "life by design," lifestyles research has indicated that unanticipated risks accrue from certain patterns of socialization.

Social Factors: Socioeconomic Status, Social Environment, and Perceived Options

Although physical and mental health problems and substance use are important manifestations of victimization, other robust contributions have been identified in the literature as well. The growing literature on social and cultural contexts demonstrates that external factors also play a major role in victimization experiences and responses. In the broadest context, social factors such as socioeconomic status, family characteristics, and social norms form areas of protection or vulnerability for women.

In chapter 4, several theories were advanced to explain the association of socioeconomic status and health and mental health, including the notion that individuals move into lower socioeconomic status because of physical or mental health problems that reduce their ability to work and earn a living. A lower income environment also is considered a factor that increases the risk for physical or mental health problems. Furthermore, early childhood experiences of low socioeconomic status may have multiple effects on later adult socioeconomic status as well as on physical and mental health. It may be that individuals living in lower socioeconomic conditions have higher stress levels and reduced access to resources that have an impact on both physical and mental health. The implications for victimization are great; as women in lower income environments experience victimization, they experience increased risk of negative consequences from the violence than women in higher income areas.

In addition, social environments consist of multiple layers, including family-of-origin experiences, neighborhood environment, cultural norms, peer norms, and partner norms. Family-of-origin experiences are an important part of socialization, and they shape expectations and social roles as well as the norms for relationships. Likewise, neighborhoods can significantly affect both the prevalence and the effects of victimization, mental health, and substance use. Neighborhoods can contribute to stress and distress through fear and social isolation. Victimization can also be profoundly affected by neighborhood cultural norms that can insulate men from being seen as criminal for their violence. Close social networks help to define reality in terms of what is "normal" and acceptable behavior and reactions to events. These social contexts can either promote safety or contribute to further victimization, depending on the socio-cultural environment.

The research is still unsettled about the effects of race and ethnicity on victimization, and it remains difficult to draw conclusions about how they might influence victimization experiences and responses. Race and ethnicity are not homogeneous phenomena, and they can be confounded with many other socio-logical factors, including poverty and living conditions (e.g., neighborhoods). Race and ethnicity are also not synonymous with cultural factors. Other socio-cultural norms must be evaluated along with race and ethnicity in understand-ing victimization. In other words, certain cultures cut across racial and ethnic groups.

Perceived and actual options for seeking safety or change in relationship status are diminished by low socioeconomic status and limited social, economic, and personal mobility. Women who perceive few options in their environment or who perceive a dismal future for themselves may also be less vigilant about their safety or less able to leave risky environmental situations such as abusive relationships. It is precisely this dynamic that may be important in recognizing what may look like a "cycle of violence" for individuals within certain socioeco-nomic strata; that is, the socioeconomic environment may give women limited options for change and increase their exposure to further harm.

In light of the conceptual model used in this book, it becomes apparent that social factors can greatly affect lifestyle and that the combination of these two can contribute to physical and mental health problems as well as victimization. The reciprocity between social environment, lifestyle, and health is perhaps best characterized as synergistic because as social and economic resources de-crease, risks of physical and mental health problems increase, and these prob-lems reduce the social resources associated with protection and safety for women. Social factors profoundly affect situation and response appraisals, which are the main focus of the next domain of factors.

Internal Contextual Factors: Situation Appraisals, Response Appraisals, and Cognitive Constraints

With the abundance of research about negative effects of victimization and vul-nerabilities, it may seem that every woman who has experienced intimate part-ner violence or sexual assault victimization would be severely impaired. How-ever, not all women experience and respond to traumatic events in the same way. One important set of factors that may have a critical protective quality is women's internal cognitions and perceptions that determine how violence is understood. This constitutes the psychological lens through which the world is perceived—the internal context of information processing.

The internal life surrounding intimate partner violence and sexual assault victimization has received only limited research attention, yet it may contain the most important areas for future research in understanding coping responses. The appraisal literature from other disciplines outside of victimization studies offers many useful ideas that can be applied to women coping with victimiza-tion experiences. In general, this literature suggests that individuals assess situations for the degree to which they present opportunities or threats. More specifically, the appraisal process includes individuals' evaluation of events in terms of their survival or perceived best interests. Appraisals are not always based on objective information processing; rather, they are grounded in a highly individualized sense of meaning. This means that two similar women may respond very differently to almost identical violent events or that an individual may respond differently to the same type of event over time. Appraisals are also influenced by memories and understanding of past events and outcomes, cognitive biases, agency (i.e., the belief that one's behavior can influence both desired and undesired effects), mood and personality, and personal goals. Personal goals exert a strong influence over behavior. For example, affiliation has been identified as one of the most basic and fundamental human needs, and it has special relevance for women. The importance of relationships for women is a strong driving force behind their self-concepts and behavior, and women's relational self-concepts strongly influence their appraisals and responses.

Once a situation is appraised, then response appraisals are made. These are influenced by blame, anticipated outcomes, and self-efficacy. Cumulative stress, multiple victimization experiences, and psychological abuse greatly affect appraisals and responses in a stepwise manner. The greater the number and intensity of victimization experiences, the greater the impact on thought processes. Cumulative stress affects both the psychological and physiological systems, which in turn affect attention, judgment, and decisions. Furthermore, internal coping resources are limited, and concentrated use of them in one major area of life (e.g., regulating emotions, making decisions) may deplete them for a period of time, which can influence appraisals and behavior.

Again, in looking at the conceptual model, the domain of internal factors of appraisal and cognition interact synergistically with all the other domains. Appraisals are affected by sociocultural environments (norms) and by lifestyles. They are also profoundly affected by overall physical and mental health status. Depression, for example, can greatly alter appraisals and perceptions about the future. Likewise, these internal factors affect mental health (both positively and negatively); they clearly influence lifestyle behaviors and can motivate changes in social affiliations and environments.

The Conceptual Model as a Framework

The conceptual model that has been used throughout this book is intended as a heuristic or as a way to guide the organization of the literature from many domains. There are three important aspects to the model: (a) All the four domains are essential to a complete understanding of intimate partner violence and sexual assault victimization; (b) all four domains are interactive or synergistic, with multiple reiterative loops among factors; and (c) the interactions are not linear and, at the individual level, probably function more in accordance with chaos models in which a new event can act as the proverbial straw that breaks the camel's back and result in more symptoms. Thus, this model has a framework that is constantly in motion with no set paradigm having complete or comprehensive explanatory power. The complexity of intimate partner violence and sexual assault victimization demands a broader view with an eye open to all these domains in research, teaching, and clinical practice.

What Can Be Done Within the Framework of Current Knowledge to Help Women With Victimization Experiences?

Much has been written about how to treat or provide interventions for women with partner violence and sexual assault victimization. Chapter 6 reviewed the clinical intervention outcome research. Chapter 7 reviewed justice system interventions. Overall, interventions seem to result in important gains for a significant percentage of clients. Nonetheless, it is unclear whether these same gains under experimental conditions can be achieved in routine clinical practice (Lambert & Ogles, 2004). Furthermore, despite the occasional competition between therapies as to which is "best," differences in outcomes among clinical approaches remain modest (Lambert & Ogles, 2004). It is also clear from the literature that the justice system is a critical element in ensuring the future safety of women. Many barriers and problems exist that make access to the system difficult for many women, so it is important to continue to improve on it to widen access and strengthen accountability of offenders. Finally, clinical and justice system interventions should be used together for the benefit of women who have victimization experiences, and these interventions should be tailored to each woman's needs.

In summary, several points stand out in what we know about helping women who are experiencing victimization. The complexity of problems that women who are victimized may experience makes it difficult to point to any specific intervention and claim its effectiveness. What chapters 6 and 7 presented was a review of clinical, social service, and legal interventions that have been identified in the literature. In addition, particularly in clinical areas, it may be important to rely on research about the treatment of clinical disorders that women with and without victimization might experience. For example, findings about the effectiveness of cognitive therapy for depression may have application to women with victimization, even though many of the studies have not specifically examined intervention effectiveness for such clients. In other words, other general outcomes literature may have relevance to interventions for women with victimization.

On the basis of the literature reviewed, five major service components or responses are identified and discussed here: (a) comprehensive assessment; (b) responding to the specific individual context of violence; (c) continual assessment; (d) validating experiences, recognizing needs, and educating women about options; and (e) building internal and external resources.

Comprehensive Assessment

The wide and diverse array of co-occurring problems that victims can experience, underscored by the literature reviewed in chapter 2, supports the importance of conducting comprehensive assessments to explore individual responses to victimization. For example, women with victimization histories should be routinely assessed for substance abuse and mental health problems. Likewise, women with substance abuse problems should be routinely assessed for victimization exposure and related mental health consequences. Health problems such as pain and sleep problems should also be assessed, especially given the interrelationships of physical and mental health, substance use, and stress. Direct assessment of victimization experiences is critical; unless women are asked directly, they may not disclose the full range of their symptoms and experiences. For example, women may present with certain physical or mental health problems but not disclose substance use or abuse or victimization. Likewise, women may disclose victimization but not talk about other physical or mental health or substance use problems for a number of reasons. In fact, when physicians in an emergency department used direct questioning, women's disclosure of victimization increased substantially (Briere & Zaidi, 1989).

Responding to the Specific Individual Context of Victimization

Although research on victimization is typically focused on groups of women with shared characteristics, interventions target individuals. Thus, in translating research findings into interventions, the research implications must be tailored to individual circumstances. Responding to the individual context of victimization may be handicapped by overly rigid application of medical models that primarily focus on diagnosis. Mirowsky and Ross (2002), for example, described two main problems with a focus on diagnosis:

> [Diagnoses] dichotomize the true range of feelings and emotions into crude either/or distinctions that do not reflect the reality of peoples lives, and they often exclude suffering such as that due to loss or illness that does not meet medical model preconceptions about mental disorder. (p. 152)

In other words, diagnoses, including PTSD tied to specific traumatic events, may not capture the full nature of the victimization experience (P. Smith, Smith, & Earp, 1999). Rather, it is important to focus on the total context of victimization experience, not just the discrete trauma events. Allowing women to identify their experiences along a continuum may be a less pathologizing and more empowering approach to helping women who have been victimized (Burstow, 2003).

Practitioners may need to go beyond diagnosing women with victimization histories and consider the full context of the victimization experience as well as their daily adaptation strategies (Wasco, 2003). Again, each of the chapters in this book underscores the need to recognize individual contexts and consequences that incorporate traumatic events but also the perhaps less obvious but equally draining stressors that must be faced every day.

Continual Assessments

Continual assessment of mental health, physical health, and substance use may be important over the entire course of treatment. Chapter 2 described the many co-occurring disorders or problems that women with victimization histories may experience, but these problems may emerge sequentially rather than being evident all at once. Success at one stage of intervention may be related to the disclosure or identification of new symptoms. Safety assessments are particularly important over time, given the high risk of revictimization for women who have experienced prior victimization, as noted in chapter 5. Few empirical studies have shown the effectiveness of safety planning with victims, but safety assessments, safety planning, and support activities have become a commonsense standard of care.

Validating Experiences, Recognizing Needs, and Educating Women About Options

Validating women's experiences of violence and their responses may be especially important. As noted in chapter 5, acknowledging and supporting women when they disclose victimization is important (Brand, 2003). Women may fear being blamed for their circumstances or feel that what they are experiencing is "normal" on the basis of their understanding of male–female rules in relationships and avoid disclosing victimization to clinicians and other practitioners (Hamberger, Ambuel, Marbella, & Donze, 1998; Lutenbacher, Cohen, & Mitzel, 2003; Rodriguez, Sheldon, Bauer, & Perez-Stable, 2001). Direct questioning can open a Pandora's box and create opportunity for affirming women's experiences. By respecting and validating disclosed experiences, women may begin to appraise their situation and the possible responses to it differently or in a way that fits more closely with their self-concept goals. Validation does not rely on a deficit model but is based on compassion, recognition, and respect for women's life histories, their strengths, their difficulties, and their understanding of their experiences (Black, 2003; Burstow, 2003; Gilfus, 1999). Validation also includes acknowledging each woman as having expert knowledge about herself, her history and needs, and what she wants in the future, including strengths and survival skills (Gilfus, 1999).

The coping and adaptive skills that women in violent relationships and those who have survived rape have developed to keep themselves and their children safe are important to emphasize as strengths that may increase agency and self-efficacy (Browne, 1998; Hamby & Gray-Little, 1997). Furthermore, recognizing the importance of relationships for women as a strength rather than a deficit may be important to successful intervention.

Clinicians may also need to recognize that women may not initially be able to take advantage of advice or referrals (Davies, Lyon, & Monti-Catania, 1998). Simply making a referral may be fine for some women, but others may be unable to follow through with such recommendations. Some may need more information or enhanced advocacy to utilize advice or referral information, and other women may not be ready to take certain actions. Clinicians should also recognize the frustrating limitations of service agencies that frequently present barriers to safety and health. For example, women making use of the justice system may experience increased stress and frustration, as noted in chapter 7. In addition, interactions with other service providers, such as physical or mental health care providers, can sometimes be negative for a variety of reasons, including bureaucracy, stigma, or lack of confidentiality (Logan, Shannon, & Walker, 2005; Logan, Stevenson, Evans, & Leukefeld, 2004).

The literature reviewed in chapters 6 and 7 highlights education as an important component of interventions. Educating women about violence, safety planning, and service options may all be important to include. Also, educating women about justice-system options and responses may be critical to their safety. This may include more than simply making a referral. Providing education about symptoms and responses to trauma as well as factors that increase risk of health and mental health problems may help clients to feel less isolated and alienated; it may also help them see that their responses to what happened to them are normal (Brand, 2003). Also, providing information to clients about factors that can increase the risk of revictimization, such as those outlined in chapters 3 and 4, may be important in helping women as well as educating them about how social factors may influence perceptions, appraisals, and responses.

Building Internal and External Resources

As noted in chapters 4 and 5, traumatic and stressful experiences can deplete the internal cognitive and emotional resources needed for coping as well as external, environmental resources. Chapter 5 in particular reviewed the literature that perhaps has the greatest relevance for interventions. As one can quickly surmise from this book, the literature paints a bleak view of women's lives in the wake of victimization. Yet, as mentioned in chapter 1, many women are able to move beyond this experience without severe harm to their physical health, mental health, or social functioning. It is likely that the world of internal cognitive and emotional resources may lie at the heart of women's resilience and eventual attainment of safety. This is a domain of research that has not been fully integrated into victimization studies, and consequently, little is understood about how internal resources can be bolstered or supported among women who have been victimized.

In addition to the description of modalities or general clinical approaches outlined in chapter 6, the literature identifies key content or action areas that can be explored in counseling or other intervention contact with women. Some of these ideas about strengthening internal and external resources are summarized in Figure 8.2. The internal resources are the typical subject matter for clinical practice, and the external resources are more like what has been addressed in case-management literature. One of the major implications of our literature review is that multiple approaches must be used to deal with a problem that has so many facets. Hence, a dual focus on internal and external coping resources may be critical.

The issue of resilience, not as an attribute of personality but as a behavioral adaptation, is a rich one that deserves attention in working with women who experience victimization (Luthar, Cicchetti, & Becker, 2000). The problem with seeing resilience as a personality attribute is that clinicians may assess clients as lacking this quality and therefore dismiss opportunities to build on coping capacities. It would appear likely that the internal resources

Internal Resources	External Resources

Health Practices
  ➤ Exercise
  ➤ Sleep
  ➤ Eating healthy
  ➤ Reduce poor health habits (e.g., smoking, substance use)
  ➤ Reduce stressful circumstances if possible
  ➤ Increase stress-coping skills
  ➤ Meditation
 	
Social Support
  ➤ Increase connections with others and with the community
  ➤ Increase skills for connecting with others
  ➤ Validate the importance of relationships as a strength
 	
Agency
  ➤ Identify "safe" places or people
  ➤ Find a sense of meaning or purpose in life
  ➤ Increase autonomy
  ➤ Identify and build on strengths, especially strengths exhibited in surviving trauma
  ➤ Set challenging but achievable goals
 	
Self-Regulation
  ➤ Reduce negative thought processes
  ➤ Increase positive thought and emotional processes
  ➤ Increase self-monitoring and self-regulation skills
  ➤ Allocate internal resources judiciously
  ➤ Increase skills for appropriate upward and downward social comparisons for coping, well-being, and emotional regulation
 	
Efficacy
  ➤ Increase self-acceptance/self-esteem/self-efficacy
  ➤ Acknowledge positive actions, even small ones
  ➤ Identify and increase competence in areas of importance
  ➤ Focus on domains in life in which women can or do feel a sense of mastery and personal control
	Justice system services
	
	Health care
	
	Dental care
	
	Mental health care
	
	Victim services
	
	Social support
	
	Community support
	
	Financial
	
	Education
	
	Employment
	
	Safe and appropriate housing
	
	Parenting, child care, and resources for children's needs

Figure 8.2. Recommendations for building internal and external resources.

that could be enhanced in an intervention setting would have lasting or inoculative effects much like what has been seen with cognitive therapy (Hollon & Beck, 2004). Individually adapted, these intervention ideas provide an expanded array of possibilities for strengthening women's coping capacities and opportunities.

This listing of internal and external resources is gleaned from all that has been reviewed in this book. The figure has been constructed to parallel in some way the conceptual model of problems related to victimization. Although the complexity of factors and problems makes it impossible to recommend a uniform intervention for women with victimization, this figure provides a menu of intervention component options and themes that should at least be considered, given all that has been learned about the problems that victimization is likely to involve.

What Should Be the Focus of Future Research on Victimization, Mental Health, and Substance Use?

Each chapter in this book discussed gaps in the research within a given area. However, several general themes for future research also emerged. (a) There is a need to develop and test theories that can describe the mechanisms and pathways of victimization experiences, responses, and contexts. (b) There is a need for research on the cumulative lifetime impact of victimization experiences, responses, and contexts. (c) There is a need for more study of adaptations to stress and trauma. (d) There is a need for more interdisciplinary approaches that also incorporate viewpoints and experiences of community agencies and women who have experienced victimization. (e) There is a need for interventions that are based on research findings and theory and for better outcome evaluations of new and existing interventions and intervention components.

Develop and Test Theories That Can Describe the Mechanisms and Pathways of Victimization Experiences, Responses, and Contexts

More sophisticated theories could guide the exploration of pathways and mechanisms of victimization antecedents, experiences, consequences, and responses. Unfortunately, theory development has been difficult, given the complexity of victimization-related problems and the "silo effect" (i.e., the narrow and often discipline-specific approach that ignores broader contexts) of the disciplines. Yet the vast research literature that currently exists may provide a foundation for a comprehensive theory or set of theories to better understand the interrelationships of victimization, mental health, and substance use. More comprehensive theories can help both to explain existing findings and to identify new areas for empirical testing. The conceptual model that guided the review of the literature in this book could be used as a road map of factors that may be important to consider in theory development.

Research on the Cumulative Lifetime Impact of Victimization Experiences, Responses, and Contexts

Research is needed to differentiate between chronic and acute victimization experiences to better understand the cumulative life impact of victimization experiences, responses, and contexts. For example, longitudinal research should incorporate the developmental stage in which the victimization occurs, the specific nature of the victimization, the environmental context in which the victimization and reactions occur (including all types of victimization experiences), the cumulative impact of victimization and other trauma, the relationship between the individual and the environment, change over time as the individual copes with the experience, vulnerability to future victimization, and the physiological consequences of victimization (Crowell & Burgess, 1996; Gilfus, 1995; Kendler, Thornton, & Gardner, 2000). Understanding the impact of victimization and chronic or repeated victimization on information processing, social functioning, and other consequences, as well as combining neurobiological measures with psychosocial approaches to gain a better understanding of the relationship of brain–behavior–environment interactions among victims, especially within a developmental context, is important for future research and for interventions. The distinction between chronic and acute victimization is not well articulated in the literature. Future research should discriminate between acute, long-term but episodic, and long-term continual victimization to increase the understanding of cumulative effects of violence over time. In fact, understanding the cumulative lifetime impact of victimization may require different paradigms or models as well as new research methods and tools.

In addition, the research knowledge on cumulative life effects of victimization cannot be advanced without clearer and more consistent definitions and distinctions of victimization, types of victimization, and revictimization (Arata, 2002; Kruttschnitt, McLaughlin, & Petrie, 2004). Definitions must be considered within the cultural context as well. Even seemingly simple definitions of terms may vary widely for different groups of women. For example, rape or sexual assault may have different meanings for White women, African American women, Hispanic women, and women from developing countries (Hamby & Koss, 2003; Lira, Koss, & Russo, 1999).

Because much of the literature on victimization consequences has focused on PTSD, it is critical for future research to understand more fully how PTSD relates to interpersonal victimization incidents and chronic victimization compared with natural disasters, wartime experiences, and other threatening circumstances. Furthermore, vulnerability and protective factors that contribute to the initiation and exacerbation of PTSD among women with victimization is needed, as is a greater understanding of the overlap of PTSD, depression, and substance abuse (Friedman, Charney, & Deutch, 1995).

There also remains a great need for research on the cumulative life experiences of victimization and the factors that contribute to and result from it for women from different cultures (Shalev, Yehuda, & McFarlane, 2000). Our review suggests that all we know about interpersonal victimization, PTSD, and other disorders has been understood primarily among Western White women, largely of European origin. There is limited information about victimization experiences and responses over the life course specifically among women in different ethnic and racial groups and how various interventions might affect them. Furthermore, there is a need for future research to focus on the developmental and cumulative effect of victimization on women in non-Judeo–Christian cultures and in developing countries, where other hardships may have a major impact on the perception of partner violence and its outcomes. For example, research on partner violence among Islamic women, women in China, and women in African countries who have been affected by many other forms of violence could help ground a more universal understanding of the effects of violence against women. Without research among diverse world cultures, it remains difficult to know whether victimization experiences or their contributing factors are universal or whether they are colored or entirely shaped by culture.

More Study of Adaptations to Stress and Trauma

As noted throughout this book, women respond to stress and trauma differently; for some women, trauma has long-lasting effects, whereas others seem to adapt to negative experiences with fewer or shorter term effects. Although this book and much of the literature have focused on the more negative outcomes of victimization, there is a need for research that focuses on positive adaptations among women who are exposed to interpersonal victimization (Seligman & Csikszentmihalyi, 2000). In other words, research on adaptation to victimization experiences, mental health, and substance use should examine the biological, psychological, sociological, and behavioral processes underlying protective and vulnerability factors and interactions between these factors (Luthar & Cicchetti, 2000; Luthar et al., 2000; Urry et al., 2004). Adaptation mechanisms may have important implications for interventions. Unfortunately, examining the biological, psychological, and sociological aspects of adaptation is difficult and has received limited research attention, in part because it is difficult to quantify adaptation in real-world situations (Aspenwall & Staudinger, 2003; Folkman & Moskowitz, 2000a, 2000b; Fredrickson & Levenson, 1998).

Furthermore, there is a paucity of empirical research on interventions addressing victimization, mental health problems, and substance abuse that incorporate strengths and coping as protective factors. There may be a misconception that "the absence of negative processes connotes adaptive functioning" (Urry et al., 2004, p. 367), which may focus research and treatment attention intently on "treating" problems rather than on strengths. Fredrickson (2000), however, argued that interventions could target and build on positive emotions such as optimism, hopefulness, and happiness as well as on helping individuals to find positive meaning in their lives to enhance coping; this is essential, because individuals with positive emotions tend to use more effective coping strategies (Aspenwall & Taylor, 1997; Irving, Snyder, & Crowson, 1998). Protective factors may also vary for different racial and ethnic groups, and these differences should be given more research attention.

Interdisciplinary Approaches That Incorporate Viewpoints and Experiences of Community Agencies and Women Who Have Experienced Victimization

Multidisciplinary perspectives are needed to enhance understanding and to elucidate pathways and mechanisms of victimization and adaptation. Single disciplinary approaches may narrow methods, findings, and interpretations of results while ignoring other important contributing factors (Salazar & Cook, 2002). This narrow focus can affect intervention development as well, which may explain the lack of robust or enduring and positive intervention outcomes in many studies.

Developing research in collaboration with community participants and key informants may provide more appropriate interpretations of study results and implications for treatment. Perhaps even more important, research should include community providers and women who are knowledgeable about the issues in formulating research questions, because the day-to-day experiences of victimization may suggest very different research agendas from the typical proposals. Research conducted in collaboration with target communities may also facilitate more rapid dissemination and implementation of research implications for practice (J. Campbell, Dienemann, Kub, Wurmser, & Loy, 1999; Edleson & Bible, 2001; Hebert, 2003; Sorensen, Rawson, Guydish, & Zweben, 2003). It is essential, too, that communities develop interventions that are uniquely tailored to their specific needs and that interventions be implemented with community support (Plested, Smitham, Thurman, Oetting, & Edwards, 1999; Sorensen et al., 2003).

Future research should also incorporate ideas from the women who will be most affected by the victimization research. Women who have been victimized should be invited into the formulation of research questions, designs, and study implementation. This recommendation goes beyond the customary qualitative studies that exhibit remarks or ideas by women who have been victimized; it is a recommendation that recognizes that victim perspectives on these factors may differ greatly from traditional academic views and standard researcher questions. The views of women who have been victimized should be integrated into research development and execution, not be simply a component of investigation.

Interventions That Are Based on Research Findings and Theory and Better Outcome Evaluations of New and Existing Interventions and Components

IMPLICATIONS FOR INTERVENTIONS. Interventions should be developed around coherent, integrative biopsychosocial theories as well as empirical findings. Although some interventions are grounded in ideology, few comprehensive, empirically supported, (or supportable) theories exist that can robustly explain relationships between victimization antecedents and consequences across the domains suggested in this book. Consequently, few interventions have been based on theory and scientifically sound research.

There is also limited information about the treatment process. Thus, a series of studies that carefully examines the processes of intervention systems, independent of their specific intervention content, might help in the design of more meaningful interventions or at least intervention components. For example, the emphasis on manual-based treatment interventions may need closer examination. Although there is some evidence of the feasibility and acceptance of manualized clinical approaches (Morgenstern, Keller, Morgan, McCrady, & Carroll, 2001; G. Wilson, 1996), it remains unclear whether community clinicians, outside of clinical trials or special attention during studies, will use manualized interventions as routine practice for any disorder (Addis & Krasnow, 2000). Practitioners hold divergent views about manuals, and little systemic training is available on the use of manualized treatments (Addis & Krasnow, 2000) yet considerable training is essential (Obert et al., 2005). Furthermore, it is not clear whether a manualized intervention that has positive outcomes is due to the content, the clinician, the specific kinds of clients, the study methods, or some other factor. Studies on treatment outcomes must consider a variety of factors that make up the concept of "treatment" for a full understanding of outcomes.

Additionally, science has not yet informed the practice community about when brief or longer term interventions may be more effective. There is a critical need for empirical findings to guide the development of interventions for women who are affected by both experiences of victimization and co-occurring conditions such as substance abuse. When the contributing factors outlined in Figure 8.1 are examined, it is difficult to imagine how a brief intervention could be effective. Given limited individual and societal resources, however, it may be important to consider alternatives that include brief interventions. Furthermore, the costs and benefits of long-term treatment versus brief interventions should be examined with rigorous outcome research and cost–benefit analysis.

INTERVENTION OUTCOMES. Outcome studies for most victimization-related interventions and clinical interventions tend to have major methodological problems, including small sample sizes, high intervention dropout rates, no control or adequate comparison groups, implementation problems, limited and inconsistent outcome measures, and poor follow-up rates (Abel, 2000; Foa & Meadows, 1997; Lundy & Grossman, 2001). There may be special considerations in evaluating interventions for women with victimization experiences. For example, including clearly defined outcomes using reliable and valid measures as well as considering the type and timing of outcome measure are important (Foa & Meadows, 1997; Linehan, 1999; Lundy & Grossman, 2001). Including longitudinal outcome studies is crucial because change over time may be important in the recovery process; however, improvement in one area may or may not relate to improvements in other areas of life. Also, there is a need for a wide variety of outcomes to determine whether interventions are truly effective (Westen & Morrison, 2001).

Future studies should be explicit in describing samples for victimization studies. Detailing specific sample victimization characteristics of research samples could be extremely important to future research—for example, it is difficult to justify evaluating intervention outcomes for women with very different victimization experiences (e.g., women who experienced a single rape by a stranger vs. women who experienced chronic repeated rape and abuse by an intimate partner). Not considering key differences in victimization experiences may mask true outcome results. In other words, without providing a clear description of the target population and evaluating outcomes for subgroups of women, it is impossible to discriminate outcomes for those experiencing chronic versus acute victimization. It is also important to include details about recruitment, selection, and eligibility so others can determine generalizability of results (Humphreys & Weisner, 2000). Intervention research must also measure and control for co-occurring conditions and disorders.

Finally, justice system interventions need a more rigorous research focus to determine the best ways to intervene in partner violence cases and to pursue more aggressively crimes such as rape and stalking. It is also important to continue to examine the justice system involvement and responses of women raped by nonintimate partners. Also, intervention outcomes must be replicated to be valid. D. Wilson and Lipsey (2003) conducted a meta-analysis of psychological treatment outcomes and found that

> the effect sizes observed in a typical treatment effectiveness study are in large part a function of method and sampling error. . . . The indications of substantial instability in observed treatment effects found in the analysis presented here have particular importance for the interpretation of findings from a single study . . . a single study will not typically provide a trustworthy indication of the effectiveness of a particular treatment. (pp. 606–607)

FUNDING CONSTRAINTS. Federal funding policies for intervention research should be revised to make longer term study of intervention outcomes feasible. As mentioned earlier, many outcome studies are flawed because of methodological limitations such as small sample sizes and short follow-up periods. Unfortunately, federal funding policies may inadvertently contribute to these limitations. The typical federally funded 5-year grant provides only limited time to examine the effectiveness of an intervention—particularly one designed to address complex problems associated with victimization histories. Longer term grants would allow for rigorous long-term follow-ups. In addition, limited funding may constrain studies in other ways by limiting sample sizes or requiring services to be conducted in artificial settings such as university clinics staffed with specialized providers rather than real-life clinical settings such as community-based services or private practice. This may inhibit the translation of findings to practice. In addition, service agencies may be reluctant to engage in costly evaluations of interventions when there are limited funds for both services and evaluation.

Conclusion

Current public interest in the United States appears to be keenly invested in ways to better protect citizens from the dangers of terrorism. Yet even a cursory review of national data suggests that threats from within, threats such as sexual assault and intimate partner violence, affect far more people than any terrorist attack yet suffered in the United States. The threat posed by intimate partner violence, for example, may result in more deaths and far more long-term damage to physical health, mental health, and social functioning than any act of terrorist violence to date. This point is not intended to minimize the effects of political terrorism on its victims but to awaken readers to the far greater menace that exists right within our communities across the nation. It may be easier for policymakers to focus on the foreign threat than the one that is within the family or one that is most relevant to women. This book suggests that the harm from this homegrown terror is far-reaching and extends into every sphere of life.

The book has stressed the interactive quality of victimization antecedents and consequences across a wide variety of problem areas as represented in the conceptual model. Admittedly, this view does not lend itself to easy analysis or simplistic interventions. By viewing victimization as an experience of extreme stress, the many biological, psychological, and social problems related to victimization may be better understood and, it is hoped, better treated.

Two main conclusions can be drawn from this book. The first is that the multiplicity of problems associated with victimization, mental health, and substance use suggests that it would be rare to find a woman affected by one of these contributing factors who was not affected by others as well. Societal responses to the victimization of women therefore must take into account this multiplicity of problems, or interventions will be inadequate. There is no one-size-fits-all model that can be used to intervene with women who have victimization histories. The second main conclusion from this book is that there are major gaps in the literature that need to be addressed to increase the understanding of the interplay of victimization, mental health, and substance use.

It should be noted that this review focused more intently on the problem side of victimization and trauma to identify factors that could be addressed by interventions to reduce negative adjustment. A greater appreciation of the victimization context can inform clinical practice, the justice system (including the courts), as well as future research efforts. Nonetheless, the focus on the negative aspects of victimization outcomes may be misleading in that women respond in various ways to experiences. Examining adaptation from a strengths perspective may be of critical importance for future research and practice. It is hoped that future studies will better describe the positive responses and resilience strategies used by some women who have experienced victimization.

The conceptual model used in this book was only a heuristic used to organize the literature; the division imposed on the literature reviewed was arbitrary because these concepts and their categorization are interrelated. In addition, although this book is densely packed with material, many content areas were not included that are also important in understanding the full spectrum of victimization, mental health, and substance use among women, such as child abuse, dating violence, and prevention of victimization. Furthermore, this book did not attempt a systematic critique of the extant literature, nor did it attempt to quantify results across studies. Rather, we selected research literature from peer-reviewed journals, published reports, and books that contribute to the understanding of victimization and its related factors to describe general themes in the research and identify general gaps for future study of victimization, mental health, and substance use among women. Another limitation is that in using a cross-disciplinary synthesis, subtle methodological and terminology differences may have been compromised out of a need to conflate findings and relevance to the field. Also, the breadth of literature reviewed means that many areas had to be covered more superficially than desired.

In addition, this review, although including international journals, did not purposively explore findings from other languages and cultures. The literature on cultural factors included here largely relates to diverse cultures within North America. For example, the findings about Hispanics were predominantly about Hispanics in the United States. It is important that the research findings described in this book be considered within the appropriate cultural context. Understanding victimization experiences and responses among women from different cultures requires research focused specifically on women from those cultures.

Given the breadth of this review, many studies and topics have been given only brief treatment. We hope that readers will use this review as a starting point for more focused study. Ideally, readers will go directly to many of the researchers and authors cited in this book. We hope the structure provides readers with guidance toward salient literature that can guide their pursuit of knowledge.

Finally, the research literature has advanced at an amazing pace, with many talented and committed researchers, many collaborating practitioners, and thousands of women who have volunteered their time and experiences for research. The future holds exciting possibilities for increasing the understanding of victimization experiences and responses as well as for developing interventions to help and prevent future victimization. Nonetheless, the greatest goal should be to bring about changes in our social and legal institutions and in our culture so that violence against women will be rejected in favor of approaches that view every person as an end unto herself, not as a means to someone else's ends.

References

Abbey, A. (2002). Alcohol-related sexual assault: A common problem among college students. *Journal of Studies on Alcohol, 63*(Suppl. 14) 118–128.

Abbey, A., McAuslan, P., Ross, L., & Zawacki, T. (1999). Alcohol expectancies regarding sex, aggression, and sexual vulnerability: Reliability and validity assessment. *Psychology of Addictive Behaviors, 13,* 174–182.

Abbey, A., McAuslan, P., Zawacki, T., Clinton, A., & Buck, P. (2001). Attitudinal, experiential, and situational predictors of sexual assault perpetration. *Journal of Interpersonal Violence, 16,* 784–807.

Abbey, A., Ross, L., & McDuffie, D. (1994). Alcohol's role in sexual assault. In R. Watson (Ed.), *Drug and alcohol abuse reviews* (Vol. 5, pp. 97–123). Totowa, NJ: Humana Press.

Abbey, A., Ross, L., McDuffie, D., & McAuslan, P. (1996). Alcohol and dating risk factors for sexual assault among college women. *Psychology of Women Quarterly, 20,* 147–169.

Abbey, A., Zawacki, T., Buck, P., Clinton, M., & McAuslan, P. (2001). Alcohol and sexual assault. *Alcohol Research and Health, 25,* 43–51.

Abbey, A., Zawacki, T., Buck, P., Testa, M., Parks, K., Norris, J., et al. (2002). How does alcohol contribute to sexual assault? Explanations from laboratory and survey data. *Alcoholism: Clinical and Experimental Research, 26,* 575–581.

Abbott, J., John, R., Loziol-McLain, J., & Lowenstein, S. (1995). Domestic violence against women: Incidence and prevalence in an emergency department population. *Journal of the American Medical Association, 273,* 1763–1767.

Abel, E. (2000). Psychosocial treatments for battered women: A review of empirical research. *Research on Social Work Practice, 10,* 55–77.

Acierno, R., Resnick, H., Flood, A., & Holmes, M. (2003). An acute post-rape intervention to prevent substance use and abuse. *Addictive Behaviors, 28,* 1701–1715.

Adamson, J., & Thompson, R. (1998). Coping with interparental verbal conflict by children exposed to spouse abuse and children from nonviolent homes. *Journal of Family Violence, 13,* 213–232.

Addis, M., & Krasnow, A. (2000). A national survey of practicing psychologists' attitudes toward psychotherapy treatment manuals. *Journal of Counseling and Clinical Psychology, 68,* 331–339.

Addis, M., Wade, W., & Hatgis, C. (1999). Barriers to dissemination of evidence-based practices: Addressing practitioners' concerns about manual-based psychotherapies. *Clinical Psychology: Science and Practice, 6,* 430–441.

Adimora, A., Schoenbach, V., Martinson, F., Donaldson, K., Fullilove, R., & Aral, S. (2001). Social context of sexual relationships among rural African Americans. *Sexually Transmitted Diseases, 28,* 69–76.

Adler, N., Epel, E., Castellazzo, G., & Ickovics, J. (2000). Relationship of subjective and objective social status with psychological and physiological functioning: Preliminary data in healthy White women. *Health Psychology, 19, 6,* 586–592.

Adler, N., & Snibbe, A. (2003). The role of psychosocial processes in explaining the gradient between socioeconomic status and health. *Current Directions in Psychological Science, 12,* 119–123.

Affleck, G., Tennen, H., Urrows, S., Higgins, P., & Abeles, M. (2000). Downward comparisons in daily life with chronic pain: Dynamic relations with pain intensity and mood. *Journal of Social and Clinical Psychology, 19,* 499–518.

Agnew, R. (1991). A longitudinal test of social control theory and delinquency. *Journal of Research in Crime and Delinquency, 28,* 126–156.

Agnew, R. (1992). Foundation for a general strain theory of crime and delinquency. *Criminology, 30,* 47–87.

Agnew, R. (2001). Building on the foundation of general strain theory: Specifying the types of strain most likely to lead to crime and delinquency. *Journal of Research in Crime and Delinquency, 38,* 319–361.

Airhihenbuwa, C., DiClemente, R., Wingood, G., & Lowe, A. (1992). HIV/AIDS education and prevention among African-Americans: A focus on culture. *AIDS Education and Prevention, 4,* 267–276.

Albrecht, C., Fossett, M., Cready, C., & Kiecolt, K. (1997). Mate availability, women's marriage prevalence, and husbands' education. *Journal of Family Issues, 18,* 429–452.

Aldorondo, E. (2002). Evaluating the effectiveness of interventions with men who batter. In E. Aldorondo & F. Mederos (Eds.), *Programs for men who batter: Intervention and prevention strategies in a diverse society* (pp. 3.1–3.17). Kingston, NJ: Civic Research Institute.

Alegria, M., Canino, G., Rios, R., Vera, M., Calderon, J., Rusch, D., & Ortega, A. (2002). Inequalities in use of specialty mental health services among Latinos, African Americans, and non-Latino Whites. *Psychiatric Services, 53,* 1547–1555.

Alexander, K., Quas, J., Goodman, G., Ghetti, S., Edelstein, R., Redlich, A., et al. (2005). Traumatic impact predicts long-term memory for documented child sexual abuse. *Psychological Science, 16,* 33–40.

Alexander, R., Bradely, L., Alarcon, G., Triana-Alexander, M., Aaron, L., Alberts, K., et al. (1998). Sexual and physical abuse in women with fibromyalgia: Association with outpatient health care utilization and pain medication usage. *Arthritis Care and Research, 11,* 102–115.

Allen, N., & Badcock, P. (2003). The social risk hypothesis of depressed mood: Evolutionary, psychosocial, and neurobiological perspectives. *Psychological Bulletin, 129,* 887–913.

Alpert, E. (1995). Violence in intimate relationships and the practicing internist: New "disease" or new agenda? *Annals of Internal Medicine, 123,* 774–781.

Alvi, S., Schwartz, M., DeKeseredy, W., & Maume, M. (2001). Women's fear of crime in Canadian public housing. *Violence Against Women, 7,* 638–661.

Amaro, H. (1988). Women in the Mexican-American community: Religion, culture, and reproductive attitudes and experiences. *Journal of Community Psychology, 16,* 6–20.

Amaro, H. (1995). Love, sex, and power. *American Psychologist, 50,* 437–447.

Amaro, H., & Hardy-Fanta, C. (1995). Gender relations in addiction and recovery. *Journal of Psychoactive Drugs, 27,* 325–337.

Amaro, H., Zuckerman, B., & Cabral, H. (1989). Drug use among adolescent mothers: A profile of risk. *Pediatrics, 84,* 144–151.

Amato, P. (1996). Explaining the intergenerational transmission of divorce. *Journal of Marriage and the Family, 58,* 628–640.

Amato, P. (1999). The postdivorce society: How divorce is shaping the family and other forms of social organization. In R. Thompson & P. Amato (Eds.), *The postdivorce family: Children, parenting, and society* (pp. 161–190). Thousand Oaks, CA: Sage.

Amato, P., & Booth, A. (1991). Consequences of parental divorce and marital unhappiness for adult well-being. *Social Forces, 69,* 905–914.

Amato, P., & DeBoer, D. (2001). The transmission of marital instability across generations: Relationship skills or commitment to marriage? *Journal of Marriage and Family, 63,* 1038–1051.

American Psychiatric Association. (1980). *Diagnostic and statistical manual of mental disorders* (3rd. ed.). Washington, DC: Author.

American Psychiatric Association. (1987). *Diagnostic and statistical manual of mental disorders* (3rd ed., rev.). Washington, DC: Author.

American Psychiatric Association. (1994). *Diagnostic and statistical manual of mental disorders* (4th ed.). Washington, DC: Author.

American Psychiatric Association. (2000). *Diagnostic and statistical manual of mental disorders* (4th ed., text rev.). Washington, DC: Author.

American Psychiatric Association Working Group on Eating Disorders. (2000). Practice guideline for the treatment of patients with eating disorders (revision). *American Journal of Psychiatry, 157*(Suppl. 1), 1–39.

Amir, M., Kaplan, Z., Neumann, L., Shrabani, R., Shani, N., & Buskila, D. (1997). Posttraumatic stress disorder tenderness and fibromyalgia. *Journal of Psychosomatic Research, 42,* 607–613.

Anderson, D., & Saunders, D. (2003). Leaving an abusive partner: An empirical review of predictors, the process of leaving, and psychological well-being. *Trauma, Violence, and Abuse, 4,* 163–191.

Anderson, J., Martin, J., Mullen, P., Romans, S., & Herbison, P. (1993). Prevalence of childhood sexual abuse experiences in a community sample of women. *Journal of the American Academy of Child Adolescent Psychiatry, 32,* 911–919.

Anderson, J., Wilson, R., Barker, P., Doll, L., Jones, T., & Holtgrave, D. (1999). Prevalence of sexual and drug-related HIV risk behaviors in the U.S. adult population: Results of the 1996 National Household Survey on Drug Abuse. *Journal of Acquired Immune Deficiency Syndromes, 21,* 148–156.

Anderson, J., Wilson, R., Doll, L., Jones, T., & Barker, P. (1999). Condom use and HIV risk behaviors among U.S. adults: Data from a national survey. *Family Planning Perspectives, 31,* 24–28.

Anderson, M., Gillig, P., Sitaker, M., McCloskey, K., Malloy, K., & Grigsby, N. (2003). "Why doesn't she just leave?": A descriptive study of victim reported impediments to her safety. *Journal of Family Violence, 18,* 151–155.

Andrews, B., & Brewin, C. (1990). Attributions of blame for marital violence: A study of antecedents and consequences. *Journal of Marriage and the Family, 52,* 757–767.

Aneshensel, C. (1992). Social stress: Theory and research. *Annual Review of Sociology, 18,* 15–38.

Anglin, M., & Hser, Y. (1990). Legal coercion and drug abuse treatment. In J. Inciardi (Ed.), *Handbook on drug control in the United States* (pp. 235–247), Westport, CT: Greenwood Press.

Anglin, M., Ryan, T., Booth, M., & Hyser, Y. (1988). Ethnic differences in narcotics addiction: Characteristics of Chicano and Anglo methadone maintenance clients. *International Journal of the Addictions, 23,* 125–149.

Annis, H., & Davis, C. (1988). Assessment of expectancies. In D. Donovan & G. Marlatt (Eds.), *Assessment of addictive behaviors* (pp. 84–111). New York: Guilford Press.

Anthenelli, R., & Schuckit, M. (1997). Genetics. In J. Lowinson, P. Ruiz, R. Millman, & J. Langrod (Eds.), *Substance abuse: A comprehensive textbook* (pp. 41–50). Baltimore: Williams & Wilkins.

Apsler, R., Cummins, M., & Carl, S. (2003). Perceptions of the police by female victims of domestic partner violence. *Violence Against Women, 9,* 1318–1335.

Arata, C. (1999a). Sexual revictimization and PTSD: An exploratory study. *Journal of Child Sexual Abuse, 8,* 49–65.

Arata, C. (1999b). Coping with rape: The roles of prior sexual abuse and attributions of blame. *Journal of Interpersonal Violence, 14,* 62–78.

Arata, C. (2000). From child victim to adult victim: A model for predicting sexual revictimization. *Child Maltreatment, 5,* 28–38.

Arata, C. (2002). Child sexual abuse and sexual revictimization. *Clinical Psychology: Science and Practice, 9,* 135–164.

Arata, C., & Burkhart, B. (1995). Post-traumatic stress disorder among college student victims of acquaintance assault. *Journal of Psychology and Human Sexuality, 8,* 79–92.

Arata, C., & Burkhart, B. (1998). Coping appraisals and adjustment to nonstranger sexual assault. *Violence Against Women, 4,* 224–239.

Arendell, T. (1995). *Fathers and divorce.* Thousand Oaks, CA: Sage.

Arias, I., Lyons, C., & Street, A. (1997). Individual and marital consequences of victimization: Moderating effects of relationship efficacy and spouse support. *Journal of Family Violence, 12,* 193–210.

Arias, I., & Pape, K. (1999). Psychological abuse: Implications for adjustment and commitment to leave violent partners. *Violence and Victims, 14,* 55–67.

Aron, A., Paris, M., & Aron, E. (1995). Falling in love: Prospective studies of self-concept change. *Journal of Personality and Social Psychology, 69,* 1102–1112.

Arriaga, X., & Foshee, V. (2004). Adolescent dating violence: Do adolescents follow in their friends' or their parents' footsteps? *Journal of Interpersonal Violence, 19,* 162–184.

Arriaga, X., & Rusbult, C. (1998). Standing in my partner's shoes: Partner perspective taking and reactions to accommodative dilemmas. *Personality and Social Psychology Bulletin, 24,* 927–948.

Ashley, O., Marsden, M., & Brady, T. (2003). Effectiveness of substance abuse treatment programming for women: A review. *American Journal of Drug and Alcohol Abuse, 29,* 19–53.

Aspenwall, L., & Staudinger, U. (Eds.). (2003). *A psychology of human strengths: Fundamental questions and future direction for a positive psychology.* Washington, DC: American Psychological Association.

Aspenwall, L., & Taylor, S. (1997). A stitch in time: Self-regulation and proactive coping. *Psychological Bulletin, 121,* 417–436.

Astin, M., Ogland-Hand, S., Coleman, E., & Foy, D. (1995). Posttraumatic stress disorder and childhood abuse in battered women: Comparisons with maritally distressed women. *Journal of Consulting and Clinical Psychology, 63,* 308–312.

Avakame, E., & Fyfe, J. (2001). Differential police treatment of male-on-female spousal violence: Additional evidence on the leniency thesis. *Violence Against Women, 7,* 22–45.

Ayduk, O., Downey, G., & Kim, M. (2001). Rejection sensitivity and depressive symptoms in women. *Personality and Social Psychology Bulletin, 27,* 868–877.

Babcock, J., Green, C., & Robie, C. (2004). Does batterers' treatment work? A meta-analytic review of domestic violence treatment. *Clinical Psychology Review, 23,* 1023–1053.

Babcock, J., & Steiner, R. (1999). The relationship between treatment, incarceration, and recidivism of battering: A program evaluation of Seattle's coordinated community response to domestic violence. *Journal of Family Psychology, 13,* 46–59.

Bachman, J., Wadsworth, K., O'Malley, P., Johnson, L., & Schulenbarg, J. (1997). *Smoking, drinking, and drug use in young adulthood.* Mahwah, NJ: Erlbaum.

Bachman, R. (1998). The factors related to rape reporting behavior and arrest: New evidence from the national crime victimization survey. *Criminal Justice and Behavior, 25,* 8–29.

Bachman, R., & Coker, A. (1995). Police involvement in domestic violence: The interactive effects of victim injury, offender's history of violence, and race. *Violence and Victims, 10,* 91–106.

Bachman, R., & Saltzman, L. (1995). *Violence against women: Estimates from the redesigned survey* (Publication No. NCJ 154348). Washington, DC: Bureau of Justice Statistics, U.S. Department of Justice.

Bagley, C., & Mallick, K. (2000). Prediction of sexual, emotional, and physical maltreatment and mental health outcomes in a longitudinal cohort of 290 adolescent women. *Child Maltreatment, 5,* 218–226.

Bagozzi, R., & Edwards, E. (2000). Goal-striving and the implementation of goal intentions in the regulation of body weight. *Psychology and Health, 15,* 255–270.

Bailey, J., Kellermann, A., Somes, G., Banton, J., Rivara, F., & Rushford, N. (1997). Risk factors for violent death of women in the home. *Archives of Internal Medicine, 157,* 777–782.

Bair, M., Robinson, R., Katon, W., & Kroenke, K. (2003). Depression and pain comorbidity—a literature review. *Archives of Internal Medicine, 163,* 2433–2445.

Bandura, A. (1997). *Self-efficacy: The exercise of control.* New York: Freeman.

Bandura, A. (1999). Social cognitive theory of personality. In L. Pervin & O. John (Eds.), *Handbook of personality: Theory and research* (pp. 154–196). New York: Guilford Press.

Bandura, A. (2001). Social cognitive theory: An agentic perspective. *Annual Review of Psychology, 52,* 1–26.

Banyard, V., Williams, L., & Siegel, J. (2001). The long-term mental health consequences of child sexual abuse: An exploratory study of the impact of multiple traumas in a sample of women. *Journal of Traumatic Stress, 14,* 697–715.

Barata, P., & Senn, C. (2003). When two fields collide: An examination of the assumptions of social science research and the law within the domains of domestic violence. *Trauma, Violence, and Abuse, 4,* 3–21.

Barber, J. (2000). Intergenerational influences on the entry into parenthood: Mothers' preferences for family and nonfamily behavior. *Social Forces, 79,* 319–348.

Bargh, J. (1994). The four horsemen of automaticity: Awareness, intention, efficiency, and control in social cognition. In R. Wyer & T. Srull (Eds.), *Handbook of social cognition* (pp. 1–40). Hillsdale, NJ: Erlbaum.

Bargh, J., & Chartrand, T. (1999). The unbearable automaticity of being. *American Psychologist, 54,* 462–479.

Bargh, J., Gollwitzer, P., Lee-Chai, A., Barndollar, K., & Trotschel, R. (2001). The automated will: Nonconscious activation and pursuit of behavioral goals. *Journal of Personality and Social Psychology, 81,* 1014–1027.

Barnes, G. (1990). Impact of the family on adolescent drinking patterns. In R. Collins, K. Leonard, & J. Searels (Eds.), *Alcohol and the family: Research and clinical perspectives* (pp. 137–162). New York: Guilford Press.

Barnes, J. (Ed. & Trans.). (1984). *The complete works of Aristotle: The revised Oxford translation* (Vol. 2). Princeton, NJ: Princeton University Press.

Barnett, O. (2000). Why battered women do not leave, Part 1: External inhibiting factors within society. *Trauma, Violence, & Abuse, 1,* 343–372.

Barnett, O. (2001). Why battered women do not leave, Part 2: External inhibiting factors—social support and internal inhibiting factors. *Trauma, Violence, & Abuse, 2,* 3–35.

Barnett, O., Martinez, T., & Keyson, M. (1996). The relationship between violence, social support and self-blame in battered women. *Journal of Interpersonal Violence, 11,* 221–233.

Barnett, R., Raudenbush, S., Brennan, R., Pleck, J., & Marshall, N. (1995). Change in job and marital experiences and change in psychological distress: A longitudinal study of dual-earner couples. *Journal of Personality and Social Psychology, 69,* 839–850.

Bartels, M., Van den Berg, M., Sluyter, F., Boomsma, D., & de Geus, E. (2003). Heritability of cortisol levels: A review and simultaneous analysis of twin studies. *Psychoneuroendocrinology, 28,* 121–137.

Bartholomew, K., & Horowitz, L. (1991). Attachment styles among young adults: A test of a four-category model. *Journal of Personality and Social Psychology, 61,* 226–244.

Bassuk, E., Browne, A., & Buckner, J. (1996). The characteristics and needs of sheltered homeless and low-income mothers. *Journal of the American Medical Association, 276,* 640–646.

Bassuk, E., Buckner, J., Weinreb, L., Browne, A., Bassuk, S., Dawason, R., & Perloff, J. (1997). Homelessness in female-headed families: Childhood and adult risk and protective factors. *American Journal of Public Health, 87,* 241–248.

Baumeister, R. (2003). Ego depletion and self-regulation failure: A resource model of self-control. *Alcoholism: Clinical and Experimental Research, 27,* 281–284.

Baumeister, R., Bratslavsky, E., Muraven, M., & Tice, D. (1998). Ego depletion: Is the active self a limited resource? *Journal of Personality and Social Psychology, 74,* 1252–1265.

Baumeister, R., Campbell, J., Krueger, J., & Vohs, K. (2003). Does high self-esteem cause better performance, interpersonal success, happiness, or healthier lifestyles? *Psychological Science in the Public Interest, 4,* 1–44.

Baumeister, R., Heatherton, T., & Tice, D. (1994). *Losing control: How and why people fail at self-regulation.* San Diego, CA: Academic Press.

Baumeister, R., & Leary, M. (1995). The need to belong: Desire for interpersonal attachments as a fundamental human motivation. *Psychological Bulletin, 117,* 497–529.

Baumeister, R., Reis, H., & Delespaul, P. (1995). Subjective and experiential correlates of guilt in daily life. *Personality and Social Psychology Bulletin, 21,* 1256–1268.

Baumeister, R., & Sommer, K. (1997a). Consciousness, free choice, and automaticity. In R. Wyer (Ed.), *The automaticity of everyday life: Advances in social cognition* (Vol. 10, pp. 75–81). Mahwah, NJ: Erlbaum.

Baumeister, R., & Sommer, K. (1997b). What do men want? Gender differences and two spheres of belongingness: Comment on Cross and Madson. *Psychological Bulletin, 122,* 38–44.

Baumeister, R., Stillwell, A., & Heatherton, T. (1995). Personal narratives about guilt: Role in action control and interpersonal relationships. *Basic and Applied Social Psychology, 17,* 173–198.

Bays, J. (1990). Substance abuse and child abuse. *Pediatric Clinics of North America, 37,* 881–904.

Beadnell, B., Baker, S., Morrison, D., & Knox, K. (2000). HIV/STD risk factors for women with violent male partners. *Sex Roles, 42,* 661–689.

Beauvais, F., & Oetting, E. (2002). Variances in the etiology of drug use among ethnic groups of adolescents. *Public Health Reports, 117*(Suppl. 1), S8–S14.

Beck, A., & Clark, D. (1997). An information processing model of anxiety: Automatic and strategic processes. *Behavior Research and Therapy, 35,* 49–58.

Beckham, J., Roodmann, A., Shipley, R., Hertzberg, M., Cunha, G., Kudler, H., et al. (1995). Smoking in Vietnam combat veterans with post-traumatic stress disorder. *Journal of Traumatic Stress, 8,* 461–472.

Beiser, M. (2003). Why should researchers care about culture? *Canadian Journal of Psychiatry, 48,* 154–160.

Belknap, J. (1995). Law enforcement officers' attitudes about the appropriate responses to woman battering. *International Review of Victimology, 4,* 47–62.

Belknap, J., & McCall, K. (1994). Woman battering and police referrals. *Journal of Criminal Justice, 22,* 223–236.

Bell, M., & Goodman, L. (2001). Supporting battered women involved with the court system: An evaluation of a law school–based advocacy intervention. *Violence Against Women, 7,* 1377–1404.

Bennenbroek, F., Buunk, B., van der Zee, K., & Grol, B. (2002). Social comparison and patient information: What do cancer patients want? *Patient Education and Counseling, 47,* 5–12.

Bennett, L., Goodman, L., & Dutton, M. (1999). Systemic obstacles to the criminal prosecution of a battering partner. *Journal of Interpersonal Violence, 14,* 761–772.

Bennett, L., & Williams, O. (2001). Intervention programs for men who batter. In C. Renzetti, J. Edleson, & R. Bergen (Eds.), *Sourcebook on violence against women* (pp. 261–277). Thousand Oaks, CA: Sage.

Bennice, J., & Resick, P. (2003). Marital rape: History, research, and practice. *Trauma, Violence, & Abuse, 4,* 228–246.

Bensley, L., Van Eenwyk, J., & Simmons, K. (2000). Self-reported childhood sexual and physical abuse and adult HIV-risk behaviors and heavy drinking. *American Journal of Preventive Medicine, 18,* 151–158.

Benson, M., Fox, G., DeMaris, A., & Van Wyk, J. (2000). Violence in families: The intersection of race, poverty, and community context. *Contemporary Perspectives in Family Research, 2,* 91–109.

Bent-Goodley, T. (2001). Eradicating domestic violence in the African American community: A literature review and action agenda. *Trauma, Violence, & Abuse, 2,* 316–330.

Bent-Goodley, T. (2005). Culture and domestic violence: Transforming knowledge development. *Journal of Interpersonal Violence, 20,* 195–203.

Bergen, R. (1996). *Wife rape: Understanding the response of survivors and service providers.* Thousand Oaks, CA: Sage.

Bergen, R. (1999). *Marital rape.* Retrieved January 1, 2004, from http://www.vaw.umn.edu/documents/vawnet/mrape/mrape.html

Berk, R. (1993). What the scientific evidence shows: On the average, we can do no better than arrest. In R. Gelles & D. Loeske (Eds.), *Current controversies on family violence* (pp. 323–336). Newbury Park, CA: Sage.

Berk, R., Campbell, A., Klap, R., & Western, B. (1992). A Bayesian analysis of the Colorado Springs Spouse Abuse Experiment. *Journal of Criminal Law and Criminology, 83,* 170–200.

Berkley, K. (1997). Sex differences in pain. *Behavioral and Brain Sciences, 20,* 371–380.

Bertram, E., Blachman, M., Sharpe, K., & Andreas, P. (1996). *Drug war politics: The price of denial.* Berkeley: University of California Press.

Biederman, J., Faraone, S., Monuteaux, M., & Feighner, J. (2000). Patterns of alcohol and drug use in adolescents can be predicted by parental substance use disorders. *Pediatrics, 106,* 792–797.

Birditt, K., & Fingerman, K. (2003). Age and gender differences in adults' descriptions of emotional reactions to interpersonal problems. *Journal of Gerontology, 58B,* 237–245.

Bjerregaard, B. (2000). An empirical study of stalking victimization. *Violence and Victims, 15,* 389–406.

Blaauw, E., Winkel, F., Arensman, E., Sheridan, L., & Freeve, A. (2002). The toll of stalking: The relationship between features of stalking and psychopathology of victims. *Journal of Interpersonal Violence, 17,* 50–63.

Black, C. (2003). Translating principles into practice: Implementing the feminist and strengths perspectives in work with battered women. *Affilia, 18,* 332–349.

Blake, D., & Sonnenberg, R. (1998). Outcome research on behavioral and cognitive–behavioral treatments for trauma survivors. In V. Follette, J. Ruzek, & F. Abueg (Eds.), *Cognitive–behavioral therapies for trauma* (pp. 15–47). New York: Guilford Press.

Blazer, D. (2000). Mood disorders: Epidemiology. In B. Sadock & V. Sadock (Eds.), *Kaplan and Sadock's comprehensive textbook of psychiatry* (7th ed., pp. 1298–1308). Philadelphia: Lippincott Williams & Wilkins.

Blazer, D., Kessler, R., McGonagle, K., & Swartz, M. (1994). The prevalence and distribution of major depression in a National Community Sample: The National Comorbidity Survey. *American Journal of Psychiatry, 151,* 979–986.

Boardman, J., Finch, B., Ellison, C., Williams, D., & Jackson, J. (2001). Neighborhood disadvantage, stress, and drug use among adults. *Journal of Health and Social Behavior, 42,* 151–165.

Boeschen, L., Koss, M., Figueredo, A., & Coan, J. (2001). Experiential avoidance and post-traumatic stress disorder: A cognitive mediational model of rape recovery. *Journal of Aggression, Maltreatment, and Trauma, 4,* 211–245.

Bogat, G., Levendosky, A., Theran, S., von Eye, A., & Davidson, W. (2003). Predicting the psychosocial effects of interpersonal partner violence (IPV): How much does a woman's history of IPV matter? *Journal of Interpersonal Violence, 18,* 1271–1291.

Bohmer, C. (1991). Acquaintance rape and the law. In A. Parrot & L. Bechhofer (Eds.), *Acquaintance rape: The hidden crime* (pp. 317–333). New York: Wiley.

Bohus, M., Haaf, B., Simms, T., Limberger, M., Schmahl, C., Unckel, C., et al. (2004). Effectiveness of inpatient dialectical behavioral therapy for borderline personality disorder: A controlled trial. *Behavior Research and Therapy, 42,* 487–499.

Bonanno, G. (2004). Loss, trauma, and human resilience: Have we underestimated the human capacity to thrive after extremely aversive events? *American Psychologist, 59,* 20–28.

Borrill, J., Rosen, B., & Summerfield, A. (1987). The influence of alcohol on judgment of facial expressions of emotion. *British Journal of Medical Psychology, 60,* 71–77.

Bostock, L. (2001). Pathways of disadvantage? Walking as a mode of transport among low-income mothers. *Health and Social Care in the Community, 9,* 11–18.

Bouchard, T., McGue, M., Hur, Y., & Horn, J. (1998). A genetic and environmental analysis of the California Personality Inventory using adult twins reared apart and together. *European Journal of Personality, 12,* 307–320.

Bouffard, J. (2000). Predicting type of sexual assault case closure from victim, suspect, and case characteristics. *Journal of Criminal Justice, 28,* 527–542.

Bouffard, J. (2002). The influence of emotion on rational decision making in sexual aggression. *Journal of Criminal Justice, 30,* 121–134.

Bowlby, J. (1982). *Attachment and loss: Vol. 1. Attachment* (2nd ed.). New York: Basic Books.

Bradley v. State, 1 Miss. 156, 157 (1824).

Brady, K., & Lydiard, R. (1992). Bipolar affective disorder and substance abuse. *Journal of Clinical Psychopharmacology, 12*(Suppl. 1), 17S–22S.

Brand, B. (2003). Trauma and women. *Psychiatric Clinics of North America, 26,* 759–779.

Brandt, L., Locke, G., Olden, K., Quigley, E., Schoenfeld, P., Schuster, M., & Talley, N. (2002). *An evidence-based approach to the management of irritable bowel syndrome in North America.* Arlington, VA: American College of Gastroenterology Functional Gastrointestinal Disorders Task Force.

Bray, J., Adams, G., Getz, J., & Baer, P. (2001). Developmental, family, and ethnic influences on adolescent alcohol usage: A growth curve approach. *Journal of Family Psychology, 15,* 301–314.

Bray, J., Zarkin, G., Dennis, M., & French, M. (2000). Symptoms of dependence, multiple substance use, and labor market outcomes. *American Journal of Drug and Alcohol Abuse, 26,* 77–95.

Bremner, J. (1999). Alterations in brain structure and function associated with post-traumatic stress disorder. *Seminars in Clinical Neuropsychiatry, 4,* 249–255.

Bremner, J., Krystal, J., Southwick, S., & Charney, D. (1995). Functional neuroanatomical correlates of the effects of stress on memory. *Journal of Traumatic Stress, 8,* 527–554.

Bremner, J., Scott, T., Delaney, C., Southwick, S., Mason, J., Johnson, D., et al. (1993). Deficits in short-term memory in posttraumatic stress disorder. *American Journal of Psychiatry, 150,* 1015–1019.

Bremner, J., Southwick, S., & Charney, D. (1997). Neuroanatomical correlates of the effects of stress on memory: Relevance to the validity of memories of childhood abuse. In P. Appelbaum, L. Uyehara, & M. Elin (Eds.), *Trauma and memory: Clinical and legal controversies* (pp. 61–92). New York: Oxford University Press.

Bremner, J., Southwick, S., Johnson, D., Yehuda, R., & Charney, D. (1993). Childhood physical abuse and combat-related posttraumatic stress disorder in Vietnam veterans. *American Journal of Psychiatry, 150,* 235–239.

Bremner, J., Staib, L., Narayan, M., Southwick, S., McGlashan, T., & Charney, D. (1999). Neural correlates of memories of childhood sexual abuse in women with and without posttraumatic stress disorder. *American Journal of Psychiatry, 156,* 1787–1794.

Bremner, J., Vithylingam, M., Vermetten, E., Southwick, S., McGlashan, T., Nazeer, A., et al. (2003). MRI and PET study of deficits in hippocampal structure and function in women with childhood sexual abuse and posttraumatic stress disorder. *American Journal of Psychiatry, 160,* 924–932.

Bremner, J., Vythilingam, M., Vermetten, E., Vaccarino, V., & Charney, D. (2004). Deficits in hippocampal and anterior cingulate functioning during verbal declarative memory encoding in midlife major depression. *American Journal of Psychiatry, 161,* 637–645.

Breslau, N., Chilcoat, H., Kessler, R., & Davis, G. (1999). Previous exposure to trauma and PTSD effects of subsequent trauma: Results from the Detroit area survey of trauma. *American Journal of Psychiatry, 156,* 902–907.

Breslau, N., Davis, G., & Andreski, P. (1995). Risk factors for PTSD-related traumatic events: A prospective analysis. *American Journal of Psychiatry, 152,* 529–535.

Breslau, N., Davis, G., Andreski, P., & Peterson, E. (1991). Traumatic events and posttraumatic stress disorder in an urban population of young adults. *Archives of General Psychiatry, 48,* 216–222.

Breslau, N., Davis, G., Peterson, E., & Schultz, L. (1997). Psychiatric sequelae of posttraumatic stress disorder in women. *Archives of General Psychiatry, 54,* 81–87.

Breslau, N., Davis, G., Schultz, L., & Peterson, E. (1994). Migraine and major depression: A longitudinal study. *Headache, 34,* 387–393.

Breslau, N., & Kessler, R. (2001). The stressor criterion in *DSM–IV* posttraumatic stress disorder: An empirical investigation. *Biological Psychiatry, 50,* 699–704.

Breslau, N., Merikangas, K., & Bowden, C. (1994). Comorbidity of migraine and major affective disorders. *Neurology, 44*(Suppl. 7), S17–S22.

Breslau, N., Roth, T., Rosenthal, L., & Andreski, P. (1996). Sleep disturbance and psychiatric disorders: A longitudinal epidemiological study of young adults. *Biological Psychiatry, 39,* 411–418.

Brewer, D., Fleming, C., Haggerty, K., & Catalano, R. (1998). Drug use predictors of partner violence in opiate-dependent women. *Violence and Victims, 13,* 107–115.

Brewerton, T., & Dansky, B. (1995). Bulimia nervosa, victimization, and PTSD. *Eating Disorder Review, 6,* 1–4.

Brewin, C., Andrews, B., & Valentine, J. (2000). Meta-analysis of risk factors for posttraumatic stress disorder. *Journal of Consulting and Clinical Psychology, 68,* 748–766.

Brewster, M. (2001). Legal help-seeking experiences of former intimate-stalking victims. *Criminal Justice Policy Review, 12,* 91–112.

Brewster, M. (2003). Power and control dynamics in prestalking and stalking situations. *Journal of Family Violence, 18,* 207–217.

Briere, J. (1988). The long-term clinical correlates of childhood sexual victimization. In *Annals of the New York Academy of Sciences: Vol. 528. Human sexual aggression: Current perspectives* (pp. 327–334). New York: New York Academy of Sciences.

Briere, J. (1996). *Therapy for adults molested as children* (2nd ed.). New York: Springer Publishing Company.

Briere, J., & Runtz, M. (1987). Post-sexual abuse trauma: Data and implications for clinical practice. *Journal of Interpersonal Violence, 2,* 367–379.

Briere, J., & Runtz, M. (1988). Symptomatology associated with childhood sexual victimization in a non-clinical adult sample. *Child Abuse and Neglect, 12,* 51–59.

Briere, J., & Zaidi, L. (1989). Sexual abuse histories and sequelae in female psychiatric emergency room patients. *American Journal of Psychiatry, 146,* 1602–1606.

Brody, G., Ge, X., Katz, J., & Arias, I. (2000). A longitudinal analysis of internalization of parental alcohol-use norms and adolescent alcohol use. *Applied Developmental Science, 4,* 71–79.

Broman, C. (1996). Coping with personal problems. In H. Neighbors & J. Jackson (Eds.), *Mental health in Black America* (pp. 117–129). Thousand Oaks, CA: Sage.

Bromet, E., Sonnega, A., & Kessler, R. (1998). Risk factors for *DSM–III–R* posttraumatic stress disorder: Findings from the National Comorbidity Survey. *Archives of General Psychiatry, 54,* 1044–1048.

Brook, J., Cohen, P., Whiteman, M., & Gordon, A. (1992). Psychosocial risk factors in the transition from moderate to heavy use or abuse of drugs. In M. Glantz & R. Pickens (Eds.), *Vulnerability to drug abuse* (pp. 359–388). Washington, DC: American Psychological Association.

Brookes, M., & Buckner, J. (1996). Work and welfare: Job histories, barriers to employment, and predictors of work among low-income single mothers. *American Journal of Orthopsychiatry, 66,* 526–537.

Brown, C., Reedy, D., Fountain, J., Johnson, A., & Dichiser, T. (2000). Battered women's career decision-making self-efficacy: Further insights and contributing factors. *Journal of Career Assessment, 8,* 251–265.

Brown, E., Ojeda, V., Wyn, R., & Levan, R. (2000). *Racial and ethnic disparities in access to health insurance and health care.* Los Angeles: UCLA Center for Health Policy Research and the Henry J. Kaiser Family Foundation.

Brown, E., Rush, A., & McEwen, B. (1999). Hippocampal remodeling and damage by corticosteriods: Implications for mood disorders. *Neuropsychopharmacology, 21,* 474–484.

Brown, P., & O'Leary, K. (1997). Wife abuse in intact couples: A review of couples treatment programs. In G. Kantor Kaufman & J. Jasinski (Eds.), *Out of the darkness: Contemporary perspectives on family violence* (pp. 194–207). Thousand Oaks, CA: Sage.

Brown, P., Stout, R., & Mueller, T. (1996). Posttraumatic stress disorder and substance abuse among women: A pilot study. *Psychology of Addictive Behaviors, 10,* 124–128.

Brown, T., & Barlow, D. (1992). Comorbidity among anxiety disorders: Implications for treatment and *DSM–IV. Journal of Consulting and Clinical Psychology, 6,* 835–844.

Brown, T., Werk, A., Caplan, T., Shields, N., & Seraganian, P. (1998). The incidence and characteristics of violent men in substance abuse treatment. *Addictive Behaviors, 23,* 573–586.

Browne, A. (1993). Violence against women by male partners: Prevalence, incidence, and policy implications. *American Psychologist, 48,* 1077–1087.

Browne, A. (1998). Recognizing the strengths of battered women. In E. Gondolf (Ed.), *Assessing woman battering in mental health services* (pp. 95–109). Thousand Oaks, CA: Sage.

Browne, A., & Bassuk, S. (1997). Intimate violence in the lives of homeless and poor housed women: Prevalence and patterns in an ethnically diverse sample. *American Journal of Orthopsychiatry, 67,* 261–278.

Browning, C. (2002). The span of collective efficacy: Extending social disorganization theory to partner violence. *Journal of Marriage and Family, 64,* 833–850.

Brownridge, D., & Halli, S. (2001). *Explaining violence against women in Canada.* Oxford, England: Lexington Books.

Bryant, R. (2000). Cognitive behavioral therapy of violence-related posttraumatic stress disorder. *Aggression and Violent Behavior, 5,* 79–97.

Bryant, R., Samaranyake, V., & Wilhite, A. (2000). The effect of drug use on wages: A human capital interpretation. *American Journal of Drug and Alcohol Abuse, 26,* 659–682.

Bryant, S., & Spencer, G. (2003). University students' attitudes about attributing blame in domestic violence. *Journal of Family Violence, 18,* 369–376.

Bryden, D., & Lengnick, S. (1997). Rape in the criminal justice system. *Journal of Criminal Law and Criminology, 87,* 1194–1384.

Buddie, A., & Parks, K. (2003). The role of the bar context and social behaviors on women's risk for aggression. *Journal of Interpersonal Violence, 18,* 1378–1393.

Bui, H. (2003). Help-seeking behavior among abused immigrant women: A case of Vietnamese American women. *Violence Against Women, 9,* 207–239.

Buka, S. (2002). Disparities in health status and substance use: Ethnicity and socioeconomic factors. *Public Health Reports, 117*(Suppl. 1), S118–S125.

Bulik, C., Sullivan, P., Carter, F., & Joyce, P. (1997). Lifetime comorbidity of alcohol dependence in women with bulimia nervosa. *Addictive Behaviors, 22,* 437–446.

Bullers, S., Cooper, M., & Russell, M. (2001). Social network drinking and adult alcohol involvement: A longitudinal exploration of the direction of influences. *Addictive Behaviors, 26,* 181–199.

Burch, E. (1994). Suicide attempt histories in alcohol-dependent men: Differences in psychological profiles. *International Journal of the Addictions, 29,* 1477–1486.

Bureau of Justice Statistics. (2000). *Criminal victimization in the United States, 1995* (NCJ 171129). Washington, DC: U.S. Department of Justice, Office of Justice Programs.

Burgess, A., Baker, T., Greening, D., Hartman, C., Burgess, A., Douglas, J., & Halloran, R. (1997). Stalking behaviors within domestic violence. *Journal of Family Violence, 12,* 389–403.

Burke, J., Denison, J., Gielen, A., McDonnell, K., & O'Campo, P. (2004). Ending intimate partner violence: An application of the transtheoretical model. *American Journal of Health Behavior, 28,* 122–133.

Burke, J., Gielen, A., McDonnell, K., O'Campo, P., & Maman, S. (2001). The process of ending abuse in intimate relationships: A qualitative exploration of the transtheoretical model. *Violence Against Women, 7,* 1144–1163.

Burstow, B. (2003). Toward a radical understanding of trauma and trauma work. *Violence Against Women, 9,* 1293–1317.

Busch, N., & Wolfer, T. (2002). Battered women speak out: Welfare reform and their decisions to disclose. *Violence Against Women, 8,* 566–584.

Buttell, F., & Carney, M. (2004). A multidimensional assessment of a batterer treatment program: An alert to a problem? *Research on Social Work Practice, 14,* 93–101.

Buunk, B., Gibbons, F., & Visser, A. (2002). The relevance of social comparison processes for prevention and health care. *Patient Education and Counseling, 47,* 1–3.

Buzawa, E., & Austin, T. (1993). Determining police response to domestic violence victims: The role of victim preferences. *American Behavioral Scientist, 36,* 610–623.

Buzawa, E., Austin, T., & Buzawa, C. (1996). The role of arrest in domestic versus stranger assault: Is there a difference? In E. Buzawa & C. Buzawa (Eds.), *Do arrests and restraining orders work?* (pp. 150–175). Thousand Oaks, CA: Sage.

Buzawa, E., & Buzawa, C. (1993). The scientific evidence is not conclusive: Arrest is no panacea. In R. Gelles & D. Loeske (Eds.), *Current controversies on family violence* (pp. 337–356). Newbury Park, CA: Sage.

Buzawa, E., & Buzawa, C. (1996). *Domestic violence: The criminal justice response* (2nd ed.). Thousand Oaks, CA: Sage.

Buzawa, E., Hotaling, G., & Klein, A. (1998). The response to domestic violence in a model court: Some initial findings and implications. *Behavioral Sciences and the Law, 16,* 185–206.

Bybee, D., & Sullivan, C. (2002). The process through which an advocacy intervention resulted in positive change for battered women over time. *American Journal of Community Psychology, 30,* 103–132.

Byrne, C., Kilpatrick, D., Howley, S., & Beatty, D. (1999). Female victims of partner versus nonpartner violence: Experience with the criminal justice system. *Criminal Justice and Behavior, 26,* 275–292.

Byrne, C., Resnick, H., Kilpatrick, D., Best, C., & Saunders, B. (1999). The socioeconomic impact of interpersonal violence on women. *Journal of Consulting and Clinical Psychology, 67,* 362–366.

Byrnes, J., Miller, D., & Schafer, W. (1999). Gender differences in risk taking: A meta-analysis. *Psychological Bulletin, 125,* 367–383.

Cafferata, G., & Meyers, S. (1990). Pathways to psychotropic drugs. Understanding the basis of gender differences. *Medical Care, 28,* 285.

Cahill, S., Carrigan, M., & Frueh, B. (1999). Does EMDR work? And if so, why? A critical review of controlled outcome and dismantling research. *Journal of Anxiety Disorders, 13,* 5–33.

Campbell, A. (2002). *A mind of her own: The evolutionary psychology of women.* New York: Oxford University Press.

Campbell, D., Sharps, P., Gary, F., Campbell, J., & Lopez, L. (2002). Intimate partner violence in African American women. *Online Journal of Issues in Nursing, 7.* Retrieved January 1, 2004, from http://www.nursingworld.org/ojin/topic17/tpc17_4.htm

Campbell, J. (1995). Prediction of homicide of and by battered women. In J. Campbell (Ed.), *Assessing the risk of dangerousness: Potential for further violence of sexual offenders, batterers, and child abusers* (pp. 93–113). Newbury Park, CA: Sage.

Campbell, J. (1998). Making the health care system an empowerment zone for battered women. In J. Campbell (Ed.), *Empowering survivors of abuse* (pp. 3–22). Thousand Oaks, CA: Sage.

Campbell, J. (2002). Health consequences of intimate partner violence. *The Lancet, 359,* 1331–1336.

Campbell, J., Dienemann, J., Kub, J., Wurmser, T., & Loy, E. (1999). Collaboration as a partnership. *Violence Against Women 5,* 140–156.

Campbell, J., Jones, A., Dienemann, J., Kub, J., Schollenberger, J., O'Campo, P., et al. (2002). Intimate partner violence and physical health consequences. *Archives of Internal Medicine, 162,* 1157–1163.

Campbell, J., Kub, J., Belknap, R., & Templin, T. (1997). Predictors of depression in battered women. *Violence Against Women, 3,* 271–293.

Campbell, J., Kub, J., & Rose, L. (1996). Depression in battered women. *Journal of the American Medical Women's Association, 51,* 106–110.

Campbell, J., Oliver, C., & Bullock, L. (1993). Why battering during pregnancy? *AWHONNS Clinical Issues in Perinatal and Women's Mental Health Nursing, 4,* 343–349.

Campbell, J., Pliska, M., Taylor, W., & Sheridan, D. (1994). Battered women's experiences in the emergency department. *Journal of Emergency Nursing, 20,* 280–288.

Campbell, J., & Soeken, K. (1999a). Women's responses to battering over time: An analysis of change. *Journal of Interpersonal Violence, 14,* 21–40.

Campbell, J., & Soeken, K. (1999b). Forced sex and intimate partner violence: Effects on women's risk and women's health. *Violence Against Women, 5,* 1017–1035.

Campbell, J., Webster, D., Koziol-McLain, J., Block, C., Campbell, D., Curry, M., et al. (2003). Risk factors for femicide in abusive relationships: Results from a multi-site case control study. *American Journal of Public Health, 93,* 1089–1097.

Campbell, J., Woods, A., Chouaf, K., & Parker, B. (2000). Reproductive health consequences of partner violence: A nursing research review. *Clinical Nursing Research, 9,* 217–237.

Campbell, L., Clauw, D., & Keefe, F. (2003). Persistent pain and depression: A biopsychosocial perspective. *Biological Psychiatry, 54,* 399–409.

Campbell, L., Riley, J., Kashikar-Zuck, S., Gremillion, H., & Robinson, M. (2000). Somatic affective, and pain characteristics of chronic TMD patients with sexual versus physical abuse histories. *Journal of Orofacial Pain, 14,* 112–119.

Campbell, R., Ahrens, C., Sefl, T., Wasco, S., & Barnes, H. (2001). Social reactions to rape victims: Healing and hurtful effects on psychological and physical health outcomes. *Violence and Victims, 16,* 287–302.

Campbell, R., & Johnson, C. (1997). Police officers' perceptions of rape: Is there consistency between state law and individual beliefs? *Journal of Interpersonal Violence, 12,* 255–274.

Campbell, R., & Martin, P. (2001). Services for sexual assault survivors: The role of rape crisis centers. In C. Renzetti, J. Edleson, & R. Bergen (Eds.), *Sourcebook on violence against women* (pp. 247–260). Thousand Oaks, CA: Sage.

Campbell, R., Sefl, T., Barnes, H., Ahrens, C., Wasco, S., & Zaragoza-Diesfeld, Y. (1999). Community services for rape survivors: Enhancing psychological well-being or increasing trauma? *Journal of Consulting and Clinical Psychology, 67, 6,* 847–858.

Campbell, R., Sullivan, C., & Davidson, W. (1995). Women who use domestic violence shelters: Changes in depression over time. *Psychology of Women Quarterly, 19,* 237–255.

Campbell, R., Wasco, S., Ahrens, C., Sefl, T., & Barnes, H. (2001). Preventing the "second rape": Rape survivors' experiences with community service providers. *Journal of Interpersonal Violence, 16,* 1239–1259.

Campbell, S., Marriott, M., Nahmias, C., & MacQueen, G. (2004). Lower hippocampal volume in patients suffering from depression: A meta-analysis. *American Journal of Psychiatry, 161,* 598–607.

Cantos, A., Neidig, P., & O'Leary, K. (1993). Men and women's attributions of blame for domestic violence. *Journal of Family Violence, 8,* 289–303.

Capaldi, D., Dishion, T., Stoolmiller, M., & Yoerger, K. (2001). Aggression toward female partners by at-risk young men: The contribution of male adolescent friendships. *Developmental Psychology, 37,* 61–73.

Carlson, B. (2000). Children exposed to intimate partner violence: Research findings and implications for intervention. *Trauma, Violence, & Abuse, 1,* 321–342.

Carlson, E., & Dalenberg, C. (2000). A conceptual framework for the impact of traumatic experiences. *Trauma, Violence, & Abuse, 1,* 4–28.

Carlson, M., Harris, S., & Holden, G. (1999). Protective orders and domestic violence: Risk factors for re-abuse. *Journal of Family Violence, 14,* 205–226.

Carmody, D., & Washington, L. (2001). Rape myth acceptance among college women: The impact of race and prior victimization. *Journal of Interpersonal Violence, 16,* 424–436.

Carpenter, K., & Hasin, D. (1999). Drinking to cope with negative affect and *DSM–IV* alcohol use disorders: A test of three alternative explanations. *Journal of Studies on Alcohol, 60,* 694–704.

Carter, C., Lederhendler, I., & Kirkpatrick, B. (1999). Introduction. In C. Carter, I. Lederhendler, & B. Kirkpatrick (Eds.), *The integrative neurobiology of affiliation* (pp. ix–xiv). Cambridge, MA: MIT Press.

Carver, C., & Scheier, M. (1999). Optimism. In C. Snyder (Ed.), *Coping: The psychology of what works* (pp. 182–204). New York: Oxford University Press.

Center for the Advancement of Women. (2003). *Progress and perils: New agenda for women.* New York: Author.

Center for Substance Abuse Treatment. (1994). *Practical approaches in the treatment of women who abuse alcohol and other drugs.* Rockville, MD: Department of Health and Human Services, Public Health Service.

Centers for Disease Control and Prevention. (2000). Use of medical care, police assistance, and restraining orders by women reporting intimate partner violence—Massachusetts, 1996–1997. *Journal of the American Medical Association, 284,* 558–559.

Chambless, D., & Ollendick, T. (2001). Empirically supported psychological interventions: Controversies and evidence. *Annual Review of Psychology, 52,* 685–716.

Chang, E. (1998). Dispositional optimism and primary and secondary appraisal of a stressor: Controlling for confounding influences and relations to coping and psychological and physical adjustment. *Journal of Personality and Social Psychology, 74,* 1109–1120.

Chang, E., & Strunk, D. (1999). Dysphoria: Relations to appraisals, coping, and adjustment. *Journal of Counseling Psychology, 46,* 99–108.

Chang, I., Lapham, S., & Barton, K. (1996). Drinking environment and sociodemographic factors among DWI offenders. *Journal of Studies on Alcohol, 57,* 659–669.

Charney, D. (2004). Psychobiological mechanisms of resilience and vulnerability: Implications for successful adaptation to extreme stress. *American Journal of Psychiatry, 161,* 195–216.

Charney, D., & Bremner, J. (1999). The neurobiology of anxiety disorders. In D. Charney, E. Nestler, & B. Bunney (Eds.), *Neurobiology of mental illness* (pp. 494–517). New York: Oxford University Press.

Chassin, L., Curran, P., Hussong, A., & Colder, C. (1996). The relation of parent alcoholism to adolescent substance use: A longitudinal follow-up study. *Journal of Abnormal Psychology, 105,* 70–80.

Chilcoat, H., & Anthony, J. (1996). Impact of parent monitoring on initiation of drug use through late childhood. *Journal of the American Academy of Child and Adolescent Psychiatry, 35,* 91–100.

Chodorow, N. (1978). *The reproduction of mothering: Psychoanalysis and the sociology of gender.* Berkeley: University of California Press.

Choice, P., & Lamke, L. (1997). A conceptual approach to understanding abused women's stay/leave decisions. *Journal of Family Issues, 18,* 290–314.

Chu, J., Frey, L., Ganzel, B., & Matthews, J. (1999). Memories of childhood abuse: Dissociation, amnesia, and corroboration. *American Journal of Psychiatry, 156,* 749–755.

Chua, P., & Dolan, R. (2000). Neurobiology of anxiety-related disorders: A functional neuroimaging perspective. In J. Mazziota, A. Toga, & R. Frackowiak (Eds.), *Brain mapping: The disorders* (pp. 509–522). San Diego, CA: Academic Press.

Clapp, J., & Shillington, A. (2001). Environmental predictors of heavy episodic drinking. *American Journal of Drug and Alcohol Abuse, 27,* 301–313.

Clark, D., Lesnick, L., & Hegedus, A. (1997). Traumas and other adverse life events in adolescents with alcohol abuse and dependence. *Journal of the American Academy of Child and Adolescent Psychiatry, 36,* 1744–1751.

Clark, H., & Zweben, J. (1994). Dual diagnosis in adolescent populations. In N. Miller (Ed.), *Treating coexisting psychiatric and addictive disorders* (pp. 111–126). Center City, MN: Hazelden Educational Materials.

Classen, C., Field, N., Koopman, C., Nevill-Manning, K., & Spiegel, D. (2001). Interpersonal problems and their relationship to sexual revictimization among women sexually abused in childhood. *Journal of Interpersonal Violence, 16,* 495–509.

Classen, C., Nevo, R., Koopman, C., Nevill-Manning, K., Gore-Felton, C., Rose, D., & Spiegel, D. (2002). Recent stressful life events, sexual revictimization, and their relationship with traumatic stress symptoms among women sexually abused in childhood. *Journal of Interpersonal Violence, 17,* 1274–1290.

Clements, C., & Sawhney, D. (2000). Coping with domestic violence: Control attributions, dysphoria, and hopelessness. *Journal of Traumatic Stress, 13,* 219–240.

Cloitre, M. (1998). Sexual revictimization: Risk factors and prevention. In V. Follette, J. Ruzek, & F. Abueg (Eds.), *Cognitive–behavioral therapies for trauma* (pp. 278–304). New York: Guilford Press.

Cloutier, S., Martin, S., & Poole, C. (2002). Sexual assault among North Carolina women: Prevalence and health risk factors. *Journal of Epidemiological Community Health, 56,* 265–271.

Clum, G., Nishith, P., & Resick, P. (2001). Trauma-related sleep disturbance and self-reported physical health symptoms in treatment-seeking female rape victims. *Journal of Nervous and Mental Disease, 189,* 618–622.

Coben, J., Forjuoh, S., & Gondolf, E. (1999). Injuries and health care use in women with partners in batterer intervention programs. *Journal of Family Violence, 14,* 83–94.

Cochran, S. (1990). Women and HIV infection: Issues in prevention and behavior change. In V. Mays, G. Albee, & S. Schneider (Eds.), *Primary prevention of AIDS: Psychological approaches.* Newbury Park, CA: Sage.

Coffey, P., Leitenberg, H., Henning, K., Turner, T., & Bennett, R. (1996). The relationship between methods of coping during adulthood with a history of childhood sexual abuse and current psychological adjustment. *Journal of Consulting and Clinical Psychology, 64,* 1090–1093.

Cohen, D., Mason, K., Bedimo, A., Scribner, R., Basolo, V., & Farley, T. (2003). Neighborhood physical conditions and health. *American Journal of Public Health, 93,* 467–471.

Cohen, D., Spear, S., Scribner, R., Kissinger, P., Mason, K., & Wildgen, J. (2000). "Broken windows" and the risk of gonorrhea. *American Journal of Public Health, 90,* 230–236.

Cohen, L., & Felson, M. (1979). Social change and crime rate trends: A routine activity approach. *American Sociological Review, 44,* 588–608.

Cohen, S., Gottlieb, B., & Underwood, L. (2000). Social relationships and health. In S. Cohen, L. Underwood, & B. Gottlieb (Eds.), *Social support measurement and intervention: A guide for health and social scientists* (pp. 3–25). New York: Oxford University Press.

Coker, A., Derrick, C., Lumpkin, J., Aldrich, T., & Oldendick, R. (2000). Help-seeking for intimate partner violence and forced sex in South Carolina. *American Journal of Preventive Medicine, 19,* 316–320.

Coker, A., Smith, P., Bethea, L., King, M., & McKeown, R. (2000). Physical health consequences of physical and psychological intimate partner violence. *Archives of Family Medicine, 9,* 451–457.

Coker, A., Smith, P., McKeown, R., & King, M. (2000). Frequency and correlates of intimate partner violence by type: Physical, sexual and psychological battering. *American Journal of Public Health, 90,* 553–559.

Cole, J., Logan, T., & Shannon, L. (in press). Intimate sexual victimization among women with protective orders: Types and associations of physical and mental health problems. *Violence and Victims.*

Coleman, F. (1997). Stalking behavior and the cycle of domestic violence. *Journal of Interpersonal Violence, 12,* 420–432.

Collins, J., Kroutil, L., Roland, E., & Moore-Gurrera, M. (1997). Issues in the linkage of alcohol and domestic violence services. In M. Galanter (Ed.), *Recent developments in alcoholism: Vol. 13. Alcoholism and violence* (pp. 387–405). New York: Plenum Press.

Combs-Lane, A., & Smith, D. (2002). Risk of sexual victimization in college women: The role of behavioral intentions and risk-taking behaviors. *Journal of Interpersonal Violence, 17,* 165–183.

Comfort, M., & Kaltenbach, K. (2000). Predictors of treatment outcomes for substance-abusing women: A retrospective study. *Substance Abuse, 21,* 33–45.

Compas, B., Conner, J., Osowiecki, D., & Welch, A. (1997). Effortful and involuntary responses to stress. In B. Gottlieb (Ed.), *Coping with chronic stress* (pp. 105–130). New York: Plenum Press.

Conger, R., Cui, M., Bryant, C., & Elder, G. (2000). Competence in early adult romantic relationships: A developmental perspective on family influences. *Journal of Personality and Social Psychology, 79,* 224–237.

Cook, J. (1997). *The book of positive quotations.* Minneapolis, MN: Fairview Press.

Cook, S. (1995). Acceptance and expectation of sexual aggression in college students. *Psychology of Women Quarterly, 19,* 181–194.

Coolidge, F., & Anderson, L. (2002). Personality profiles of women in multiple abusive relationships. *Journal of Family Violence, 17,* 117–131.

Cooper, M., Russell, M., Skinner, J., Frone, M., & Mudar, P. (1992). Stress and alcohol use: Moderating effects of gender, coping and alcohol expectancies. *Journal of Abnormal Psychology, 101,* 139–152.

Cooper-Patrick, L., Powe, N., Jenckes, M., Gonzales, J., Levine, D., & Ford, D. (1997). Identification of patient attitudes and preferences regarding treatment of depression. *Journal of General Internal Medicine, 12,* 431–438.

Corbin, W., Bernat, J., Calhoun, K., McNair, L., & Seals, K. (2001). The role of alcohol expectancies and alcohol consumption among sexually victimized and nonvictimized college women. *Journal of Interpersonal Violence, 16,* 297–311.

Costello, E., Pine, D., Hammen, C., March, J., Plotsky, P., Weissman, M., et al. (2002). Development and natural history of mood disorders. *Biological Psychiatry, 52,* 529–542.

Coulter, M., Kuehnle, K., Byers, R., & Alfonso, M. (1999). Police-reporting behavior and victim–police interactions as described by women in a domestic violence shelter. *Journal of Interpersonal Violence, 14,* 1290–1298.

Covington, S. (1997). Women, addiction, and sexuality. In L. Straussner & E. Zelvin (Eds.), *Gender and addictions: Men and women in treatment* (pp. 79–95). Northvale, NJ: Aronson.

Covington, S., & Surrey, J. (1997). The relational model of women's psychological development: Implications for substance abuse. In R. Wilsnack & S. Wilsnack (Eds.), *Gender and alcohol: Individual and social perspectives* (pp. 335–351). New Brunswick, NJ: Rutgers Center of Alcohol Studies.

Cowan, G. (2000). Beliefs about the cause of four types of rape. *Sex Roles: A Journal of Research, 42,* 807–823.

Cox, A., & Cox, D. (1998). Beyond "peer pressure": A theoretical framework for understanding the varieties of social influence in adolescent risk behavior. *Social Marketing Quarterly, 4,* 43–47.

Cox, B., Norton, G., Sinson, R., & Endler, N. (1990). Substance abuse and panic-related anxiety: A critical review. *Behavior Research and Therapy, 28,* 385–393.

Crabbe, J. (1999). Molecular genetics of addiction. In D. Charney, E. Nestler, & B. Bunney (Eds.), *Neurobiology of mental illness* (pp. 591–600). New York: Oxford University Press.

Cramer, E. (1999). Variables that predict verdicts in domestic violence cases. *Journal of Interpersonal Violence, 14,* 1137–1150.

Crane, P., & Constantino, R. (2003). Use of the interpersonal support evaluation list (ISEL) to guide intervention development with women experiencing abuse. *Issues in Mental Health Nursing, 24,* 523–541.

Craven, D. (1997). *Sex differences in violent victimization, 1994, Bureau Of Justice Statistics Special Report* (NCJ 164508). Washington, DC: U.S. Department of Justice, Office of Justice Programs.

Creamer, M. (2000). Posttraumatic stress disorder following violence and aggression. *Aggression and Violent Behavior, 5,* 431–449.

Creamer, M., Burgess, P., & McFarlane, A. (2001). Post-traumatic stress disorder: Findings from the Australian national survey of mental health and well-being. *Psychological Medicine, 31,* 1237–1247.

Crome, S., & McCabe, M. (2001). Adult rape scripting within a victimological perspective. *Aggression and Violent Behavior, 6,* 395–413.

Cross, S., Bacon, P., & Morris, M. (2000). The relational-interdependent self-construal and relationships. *Journal of Personality and Social Psychology, 78,* 791–808.

Cross, S., & Madson, L. (1997a). Models of the self: Self-construals and gender. *Psychological Bulletin, 122,* 5–37.

Cross, S., & Madson, L. (1997b). Elaboration of models of the self: Reply to Baumeister and Sommer (1997) and Martin and Ruble (1997). *Psychological Bulletin, 122,* 51–55.

Cross, S., Morris, M., & Gore, J. (2002). Thinking about oneself and others: The relational-interdependent self-construal and social cognition. *Journal of Personality and Social Psychology, 82,* 399–418.

Crowell, N., & Burgess, A. (1996). *Understanding violence against women.* Washington, DC: National Academy Press.

Crum, R., Storr, C., Chan, Y., & Ford, D. (2004). Sleep disturbance and risk for alcohol-related problems. *American Journal of Psychiatry, 161,* 1197–1203.

Cue, K., George, W., & Norris, J. (1996). Women's appraisals of sexual-assault risk in dating situations. *Psychology of Women Quarterly, 20,* 487–504.

Culbertson, K., & Dehle, C. (2001). Impact of sexual assault as a function of perpetrator type. *Journal of Interpersonal Violence, 16,* 992–1007.

Cullinan, W., Herman, J., Helmreich, D., & Watson, S. (1995). A neuroanatomy of stress. In M. Friedman, D. Charney, & A. Deutch (Eds.), *Neurobiological and clinical consequences of stress: From normal adaptation to PTSD* (pp. 3–26). Philadelphia: Lippincott-Raven.

Cunradi, C., Caetano, R., Clark, C., & Schafer, J. (2000). Neighborhood poverty as a predictor of intimate partner violence among White, Black, and Hispanic couples in the United States: A multilevel analysis. *Annals of Epidemiology, 10,* 297–308.

Cunradi, C., Caetano, R., & Schafer, J. (2002). Alcohol-related problems, drug use, and male intimate partner violence severity among US couples. *Alcoholism: Clinical and Experimental Research, 26,* 493–500.

Curran, G., White, H., & Hansell, S. (2000). Personality, environment, and problem drug use. *Journal of Drug Issues, 30,* 375–406.

Currie, E. (1994). *Reckoning: Drugs, the cities, and the American future.* New York: Hill & Wang.

Dahlgren, L., & Willander, A. (1989). Are special treatment facilities for female alcoholics needed? A controlled two-year follow-up from a specialized female unit (EWA) versus a mixed male/female treatment facility. *Alcoholism, Clinical, Experimental Research, 13,* 499–504.

Dalenberg, C., & Jacobs, D. (1994). Attributional analysis of child sexual abuse episodes: Empirical and clinical issues. *Journal of Child Sexual Abuse, 3,* 37–50.

Danielson, K., Moffitt, T., Caspi, A., & Silva, P. (1998). Comorbidity between abuse of an adult and *DSM–III–R* mental disorders: Evidence from an epidemiological study. *American Journal of Psychiatry, 155,* 131–133.

Dansky, B., Brewerton, T., Kilpatrick, D., & O'Neill, P. (1997). The National Women's Study: Relationship of victimization and posttraumatic stress disorder to bulimia nervosa. *International Journal of Eating Disorders, 21,* 213–228.

Davies, J., Lyon, E., & Monti-Catania, D. (1998). *Safety planning with battered women: Complex lives/difficult choices.* Thousand Oaks, CA: Sage.

Davis, J., Combs-Lane, A., & Jackson, T. (2002). Risky behaviors associated with interpersonal victimization: Comparisons based on type, number, and characteristics of assault incidents. *Journal of Interpersonal Violence, 17,* 611–629.

Davis, K., George, W., & Norris, J. (2004). Women's responses to unwanted sexual advances: The role of alcohol and inhibition conflict. *Psychology of Women Quarterly, 28,* 333–343.

Davis, R., Smith, B., & Nickles, L. (1998). The deterrent effect of prosecuting domestic violence misdemeanors. *Crime & Delinquency, 44,* 434–442.

Davis, R., Smith, B., & Taylor, B. (2003). Increasing the proportion of domestic violence arrests that are prosecuted: A natural experiment in Milwaukee. *Criminology and Public Policy, 2,* 263–282.

Dawson, M., & Dinovitzer, R. (2001). Victim cooperation and the prosecution of domestic violence in a specialized court. *Justice Quarterly, 18,* 593–622.

Dawson, M., & Gartner, R. (1998). Differences in the characteristics of intimate femicides: The role of relationship state and relationship status. *Homicide Studies, 2,* 378–399.

Decker, S. (1993). Exploring victim–offender relationships in homicide: The role of individual and event characteristics. *Justice Quarterly, 10,* 585–612.

DeKeseredy, W., Alvi, S., Schwartz, M., & Perry, B. (1999). Violence against and the harassment of women in Canadian public housing: An exploratory study. *Canadian Review of Sociology and Anthropology, 36,* 499–516.

DeKeseredy, W., & Kelly, K. (1995). Sexual abuse in Canadian university and college dating relationships: The contribution of male peer support. *Journal of Family Violence, 10,* 41–53.

DeKeseredy, W., & Schwartz, M. (1993). Male peer support and woman abuse: An expansion of DeKeseredy's model. *Sociological Spectrum, 13,* 393–413.

Delva, J., Neumark, Y., Furr, C., & Anthony, J. (2000). Drug use among welfare recipients in the United States. *American Journal of Drug and Alcohol Abuse, 26,* 335–342.

Dement, W., & Vaughn, C. (1999). *The promise of sleep.* New York: Random House.

Denton, R., & Kampfe, C. (1994). The relationship between family variables and adolescent substance abuse: A literature review. *Adolescence, 29,* 475–495.

Dermen, K., Cooper, M., & Agocha, V. (1998). Sex-related alcohol expectancies as moderators of the relationship between alcohol use and risky sex in adolescents. *Journal of Studies on Alcohol, 59,* 71–77.

Desai, S., Arias, I., Thompson, M., & Basile, K. (2002). Childhood victimization and subsequent adult revictimization assessed in a nationally representative sample of women and men. *Violence and Victims, 17,* 639–653.

DeSouza, E. (1995). Corticotropin-releasing factor receptors: Physiology, pharmacology, biochemistry and role in central nervous system and immune disorders. *Psychoneuroendocrinology, 20,* 789–819.

Devilly, G., & Spence, S. (1999). The relative efficacy and treatment distress of EMDR and a cognitive-behavioral trauma treatment protocol in the amelioration of posttraumatic stress disorder. *Journal of Anxiety Disorders, 13,* 131–157.

Dew, A. (1998). Psychiatric disorder in the context of physical illness. In B. Dohrenwend (Ed.), *Adversity, stress, and psychopathology* (pp. 177–218). New York: Oxford University Press.

Dewe, P. (1991). Primary appraisal, secondary appraisal and coping: Their role in stressful work encounters. *Journal of Occupational Psychology, 64,* 331–351.

Diaz-Olavarrieta, C., Campbell, J., Garcia de la Cadena, C., Paz, F., & Villa, A. (1999). Domestic violence against patients with chronic neurologic disorders. *Archives of Neurology, 56,* 681–685.

Dickinson, L., deGruy, F., Dickinson, P., & Candib, L. (1999). Health-related quality of life and symptom profiles of female survivors of sexual abuse. *Archives of Family Medicine, 8,* 35–43.

Dienemann, J., Boyle, E., Baker, D., Resnick, W., Wiederhorn, N., & Campbell, J. (2000). Intimate partner abuse among women diagnosed with depression. *Issues in Mental Health Nursing, 21,* 499–513.

Dienemann, J., Campbell, J., Landenburger, K., & Curry, M. (2002). The domestic violence survivor assessment: A tool for counseling women in intimate partner violence relationships. *Patient Education and Counseling, 46,* 221–228.

Diener, E., Oishi, S., & Lucas, R. (2003). Personality, culture, and subjective well-being: Emotional and cognitive evaluations of life. *Annual Review of Psychology, 54,* 403–425.

DiLillo, D., Giuffre, D., Tremblay, G., & Peterson, L. (2001). A closer look at the nature of intimate partner violence reported by women with a history of child sexual abuse. *Journal of Interpersonal Violence, 16,* 116–132.

Dobash, R. E., & Dobash, R. (1979).*Violence against wives: A case against the patriarchy.* New York: Free Press.

Dobash, R. E., & Dobash, R. (2000). Evaluating criminal justice interventions for domestic violence. *Crime and Delinquency, 46,* 252–270.

Dohrenwend, B., Levav, I., Shrout, P., Schwartz, S., Naveh, G., Link, B., et al. (1992, February 21). Socioeconomic status and psychiatric disorders: The causation–selection issue. *Science, 255,* 946–952.

Dohrenwend, B., Levav, I., Shrout, P., Schwartz, S., Naveh, G., Link, B., et al. (1998). Ethnicity, socioeconomic status, and psychiatric disorders: A test of the social causation–social selection issue. In B. Dohrenwend (Ed.), *Adversity, stress, and psychopathology* (pp. 285–318). New York: Oxford University Press.

D'Onofrio, C. (1997). Prevention of alcohol use by rural youth. In E. Robertson, Z. Sloboda, G. Boyd, L. Beatty, & J. Kozel (Eds.), *Rural substance abuse: State of knowledge and issues* (NIDA Research Monograph No. 168; pp. 250–363). Rockville MD: National Institute on Drug Abuse.

Drake, R., Mercer-McFadden, C., Mueser, K., McHugo, G., & Bond, G. (1998). Review of integrated mental health and substance abuse treatment for patients with dual disorders. *Schizophrenia Bulletin, 24,* 589–608.

Drossman, D. (1997). Irritable bowel syndrome and sexual/physical abuse history. *European Journal of Gastroenterology and Hepatology, 9,* 327–330.

Dufour, M., & Nadeau, L. (2001). Sexual abuse: A comparison between resilient victims and drug-
addicted victims. *Violence and Victims, 16,* 655–672.

Du Mont, J., Miller, K., & Myhr, T. (2003). The role of "real rape" and "real victim" stereotypes in
the police reporting practices of sexually assaulted women. *Violence Against Women, 9,* 466–
486.

Duncan, G. (1996). Income dynamics and health. *International Journal of Health Services, 26,*
419–444.

Duncan, G., Yeung, W., Brooks-Gunn, J., & Smith, J. (1998). How much does childhood poverty
affect the life chances of children? *American Sociological Review, 63,* 406–423.

Duncan, R., Saunders, B., Kilpatrick, D., Hanson, R., & Resnick, H. (1996). Childhood physical
assault as a risk factor for PTSD, depression and substance abuse: Findings from a national
survey. *American Journal of Orthopsychiatry, 66,* 437–448.

Duncan, S., Duncan, T., Strycker, L., & Chaumeton, N. (2002). Relations between youth antisocial
and prosocial activities. *Journal of Behavioral Medicine, 25,* 425–438.

Duncan, T., Duncan, S., & Hops, H. (1994). The effects of family cohesiveness and peer encouragement on the development of adolescent alcohol use: A cohort-sequential approach to the analysis
of longitudinal data. *Journal of Studies on Alcohol, 55,* 588–599.

Dunford, F. (1992). The measurement of recidivism in cases of spouse assaults. *Journal of Criminal Law and Criminology, 83,* 120–136.

Dunn, G., Ryan, J., & Dunn, C. (1994). Trauma symptoms in substance abusers with and without
histories of childhood abuse. *Journal of Psychoactive Drugs, 26,* 357–360.

Dunn, J. (2001). Innocence lost: Accomplishing victimization in intimate stalking cases. *Symbolic
Interaction, 24,* 285–313.

Dutton, M., Burghardt, K., Perrin, S., Chrestman, K., & Halle, P. (1994). Battered women's cognitive schemata. *Journal of Traumatic Stress, 7,* 237–255.

Dutton, M., Goodman, L., & Bennett, L. (1999). Court-involved battered women's responses to
violence: The role of psychological, physical, and sexual abuse. *Violence and Victims, 14,* 89–
104.

Dutton, M., Orloff, L., & Hass, G. (2000). Characteristics of help-seeking behaviors, resources and
service needs of battered immigrant Latinas: Legal and policy implications. *Georgetown Journal on Poverty, Law and Policy, 7,* 245–305.

Eaton, W., Badawi, M., & Melton, B. (1995). Prodromes and precursors: Epidemiologic data for
primary prevention of disorders with slow onset. *American Journal of Psychiatry, 152,* 967–
972.

Eby, K., Campbell, J., Sullivan, C., & Davidson, W. (1995). Health effects of experiences of sexual
violence for women with abusive partners. *Health Care for Women International, 16,* 563–576.

Eccles, J., & Wigfield, A. (2002). Motivational beliefs, values, and goals. *Annual Review of Psychology, 53,* 109–132.

Echlin, C., & Marshall, L. (1995). Child protection services for children of battered women: Practice and controversy. In P. Peled & J. Edleson (Eds.), *Ending the cycle of violence: Community
responses to children of battered women* (pp. 170–185). Thousand Oaks, CA: Sage.

Eckert, E., Halmi, K., Marchi, P., Grove, W., & Crosby, R. (1995). Ten-year follow-up of anorexia
nervosa: Clinical course and outcome. *Psychological Medicine, 25,* 143–156.

Edleson, J. (1999). The overlap between child maltreatment and woman battering. *Violence Against
Women, 5,* 134–154.

Edleson, J., & Bible, A. (2001). Collaborating for women's safety: Partnerships between research
and practice. In C. Renzetti, J. Edleson, & R. Bergen (Eds.), *Sourcebook on violence against
women* (pp. 73–95). Thousand Oaks, CA: Sage.

Edmonds, D., & Eidinow, J. (2001). *Wittgenstein's poker.* New York: HarperCollins.

Edwards, J., & Weary, G. (1998). Antecedents of causal uncertainty and perceived control: A prospective study. *European Journal of Personality, 12,* 135–148.

Ehlers, A., Clark, D., Hackman, A., McManus, F. Fennell, M., Herbert, C., & Mayou, R. (2003). A randomized controlled trial of cognitive therapy, a self-help booklet, and repeated assessment as early interventions for posttraumatic stress disorder. *Archives of General Psychiatry, 60,* 1024–1032.

Ehlers, A., Mayou, R., & Bryant, B. (1998). Psychological predictors of chronic PTSD after motor vehicle accidents. *Journal of Abnormal Psychology, 107,* 508–519.

Ehrenreich, H., Schuck, J., Stender, N., Pilz, J. Gefeller, O., Schilling, L., et al. (1997). Endocrine and hemodynamic effects of stress versus systemic CRF in alcoholics during early and medium term abstinence. *Alcoholism: Clinical and Experimental Research, 21,* 1285–1293.

Ehrensaft, M., Cohen, P., Brown, J., Smailes, E., Chen, H., & Johnson, J. (2003). Intergenerational transmission of partner violence: A 20-year prospective study. *Journal of Consulting and Clinical Psychology, 71,* 741–753.

Ehrhardt, A., & Wasserheit, J. (1991). Age, gender, and sexual risk behaviors for sexually transmitted diseases in the United States. In J. Wasserheit, S. Aral, K. Holmes, & P. Hitchcock (Eds.), *Research issues in human behavior and sexually transmitted diseases in the AIDS era* (pp. 73–89). Washington, DC: American Society for Microbiology.

Eichenbaum, H., Otto, T., & Cohen, N. (1994). Two functional components of the hippocampal memory system. *Behavioral and Brain Sciences, 17,* 449–518.

Eigenberg, H., McGuffee, K., Berry, P., & Hall, W. (2003). Protective order legislation: Trends in state statutes. *Journal of Criminal Justice, 31,* 411–422.

Eisenberger, N., Lieberman, M., & Williams, K. (2003). Does rejection hurt? An fMRI study of social exclusion. *Science, 302,* 290–292.

Eisenstat, S., & Bancroft, L. (1999). Domestic violence. *New England Journal of Medicine, 341,* 886–892.

El-Bassel, N., Gilbert, L., & Rajah, V. (2003). The relationship between drug abuse and sexual performance among women on methadone heightening the risk of sexual intimate violence and HIV. *Addictive Behaviors, 28,* 1385–1403.

El-Bassel, N., Gilbert, L., Rajah, V., Foleno, A., & Frye, V. (2001). Social support among women in methadone treatment who experience partner violence: Isolation and male controlling behavior. *Violence Against Women, 7,* 246–274.

El-Bassel, N., Witte, S., Wada, T., Gilbert, L., & Wallace, J. (2001). Correlates of partner violence among female street-based sex workers: Substance abuse, history of childhood abuse, and HIV risks. *AIDS Patient Care and STDs, 15,* 41–51.

Elliott, D., Mok, D., & Briere, J. (2004). Adult sexual assault: Prevalence, symptomology, and sex differences in the general population. *Journal of Traumatic Stress, 17,* 203–211.

Ellsworth, P., & Scherer, K. (2003). Appraisal processes in emotion. In R. Davidson, K. Scherer, & H. Goldsmith (Eds.), *Handbook of affective sciences* (pp. 572–595). New York: Oxford University Press.

Epel, E., McEwen, B., Seeman, T., Matthews, K., Castellazzo, G., Brownell, K., et al. (2000). Stress and body shape: Stress-induced cortisol secretion is consistently greater among women with central fat. *Psychosomatic Medicine, 62,* 623–632.

Epstein, D. (1999). Effective intervention in domestic violence cases: Rethinking the roles of prosecutors, judges, and the court system. *Yale Journal of Law and Feminism, 11,* 3–50.

Erez, E. (2002). Domestic violence and the criminal justice system: An overview. *Online Journal of Issues in Nursing, 7.* Retrieved January 1, 2004, from http://www.nursingworld.org/ojin/topic17/tpc17_3.htm

Erez, E., & Belknap, J. (1998a). Battered women and the criminal justice system: The service providers' perspective. *European Journal of Criminal Policy and Research, 6,* 37–57.

Erez, E., & Belknap, J. (1998b). In their own words: Battered women's assessment of the criminal processing system's responses. *Violence and Victims, 13,* 251–267.

Erez, E., & King, T. (2000). Patriarchal terrorism or common couple violence: Attorney's views of prosecuting and defending woman batterers. *International Review of Victimology, 7,* 207–226.

Erikson, E. (1968). *Identity, youth, and crisis.* New York: Norton.

Esterberg, K., Moen, P., & Dempster-McCain, D. (1994). Transition to divorce: A life-course approach to women's marital duration and dissolution. *The Sociological Quarterly, 35,* 289–307.

Evans, G., & English, K. (2002). The environment of poverty: Multiple stressor exposure, the psychophysiological stress, and socioemotional adjustment. *Child Development, 73,* 1238–1248.

Evans, G., & Kantrowitz, E. (2002). Socioeconomic status and health: The potential role of environmental risk exposure. *Annual Review of Public Health, 23,* 303–331.

Ewoldt, C., Monson, C., & Langhinrichsen-Rohling, J. (2000). Attributions about rape in a continuum of dissolving marital relationships. *Journal of Interpersonal Violence, 15,* 1175–1182.

Fagan, J. (1993). Set and setting revisited: Influences of alcohol and illicit drugs on the social context of violent events. In S. Martin (Ed.), *Alcohol and interpersonal violence: Fostering multidisciplinary perspectives* (NIH Publication No. 93–3496; pp. 161–191). Rockville, MD: U.S. Department of Health and Human Services.

Fairburn, C. (2002). Cognitive behavioral therapy for bulimia nervosa. In C. Fairburn & K. Brownell (Eds.), *Eating disorders and obesity* (pp. 302–307). New York: Guilford Press.

Fairburn, C., Doll, H., Welch, S., Hay, P., Davies B., & O'Connor, M. (1998). Risk factors for binge eating disorder. *Archives of General Psychiatry, 55,* 425–432.

Falck, R., Wang, J., Carlson, R., & Siegal, H. (2001). The epidemiology of physical attack and rape among crack using women. *Violence and Victims, 16,* 79–89.

Fallott, R., & Harris, M. (2002). The trauma recovery and empowerment model (TREM): Conceptual and practical issues in a group intervention for women. *Community Mental Health Journal, 38,* 475–485.

Fals-Stewart, W., & Birchler, G. (2001). A national survey of the use of couples therapy in substance abuse treatment. *Journal of Substance Abuse Treatment, 20,* 277–283.

Faravelli, C., Giugni, A., Salvatori, S., & Ricca, V. (2004). Psychopathology after rape. *American Journal of Psychiatry, 161,* 1483–1485.

Farnsworth, M., & Teske, R. (1995). Gender differences in felony court processing: Three hypotheses of disparity. *Women and Criminal Justice, 6,* 23–44.

Feder, L. (1998). Police handling of domestic and nondomestic assault calls: Is there a case for discrimination? *Crime and Delinquency, 44,* 335–349.

Feder, L., & Dugan, L. (2002). A test of the efficacy of court-mandated counseling for domestic violence offenders: The Broward experiment. *Justice Quarterly, 19,* 343–375.

Feder, L., Jolin, A., & Feyerherm, W. (2000). Lessons from two randomized experiments in criminal justice settings. *Crime & Delinquency, 46,* 380–401.

Feerick, M., Haugaard, J., & Hien, D. (2002). Child maltreatment and adulthood violence: The contribution of attachment and drug abuse. *Child Maltreatment, 7,* 226–240.

Feig, L. (1990). *Drug-exposed infants and children: Service needs and policy questions.* Washington, DC: U.S. Dept of Health and Human Services, Office of the Assistant Secretary for Planning and Evaluation.

Felder, R., & Victor, B. (1997). *Getting away with murder: Weapons for the war against domestic violence.* New York: Touchstone.

Feldhaus, K., Houry, D., & Kaminsky, R. (2000). Lifetime sexual assault prevalence rates and reporting practices in an emergency department population. *Annals of Emergency Medicine, 36,* 23–27.

Felson, M. (1998). *Crime and everyday life* (2nd ed.). Thousand Oaks, CA: Pine Forge Press.

Felson, R. (1997). Routine activities and involvement in violence as actor, witness, or target. *Violence and Victims, 12,* 209–221.

Felson, R. (2000). The normative protection of women from violence. *Sociological Forum, 15,* 91–116.

Felson, R., & Ackerman, J. (2001). Arrest for domestic and other assaults. *Criminology, 39,* 655–675.

Fergusson, D., Horwood, L., & Lynskey, M. (1997). Childhood sexual abuse, adolescent sexual behaviors and sexual revictimization. *Child Abuse & Neglect, 21,* 789–803.

Ferraro, K. (1993). Rationalizing violence: How battered women stay. *Victimology, 8,* 203–212.

Festinger, L. (1954). A theory of social comparison processes. *Human Relations, 7,* 117–140.

Field, C., & Caetano, R. (2003). Longitudinal model predicting partner violence among White, Black, and Hispanic couples in the United States. *Alcoholism: Clinical and Experimental Research, 27,* 1451–1458.

Field, C., & Caetano, R. (2004). Ethnic differences in intimate partner violence in the U.S. general population: The role of alcohol use and socioeconomic status. *Trauma, Violence, and Abuse, 5,* 303–317.

Field, N., Classen, C., Butler, L., Koopman, C., Zarcone, J., & Spiegel, D. (2001). Revictimization and information processing in women survivors of childhood sexual abuse. *Anxiety Disorders, 15,* 459–469.

Fillmore, M., Dixon, M., & Schweizer, T. (2000). Alcohol affects processing of ignored stimuli in a negative priming paradigm. *Journal of Studies on Alcohol, 61,* 571–578.

Fillmore, M., & Vogel-Sprott, M. (1998). Behavioral impairment under alcohol: Cognitive and pharmacokinetic factors. *Alcoholism: Clinical and Experimental Research, 22,* 1476–1482.

Fillmore, M., & Vogel-Sprott, M. (1999). An alcohol model of impaired inhibitory control and its treatment in humans. *Experimental and Clinical Psychopharmacology, 7,* 49–55.

Fillmore, M., & Vogel-Sprott, M. (2000). Response inhibition under alcohol: Effects of cognitive and motivational conflict. *Journal of Studies on Alcohol, 61,* 239–246.

Fillmore, M., & Weafer, J. (2004). Alcohol impairment of behavior in men and women. *Addiction, 99,* 1237–1246.

Finch, B., Vega, W., & Kolody, B. (2001). Substance use during pregnancy in the state of California, USA. *Social Science and Medicine, 52,* 571–583.

Finestone, H., Stenn, P., Davies, F., Stalker, C., Fry, R., & Koumanis, J. (2000). Chronic pain and health care utilization in women with a history of childhood sexual abuse. *Child Abuse and Neglect, 24,* 547–556.

Finkelhor, D., & Asdigian, N. (1996). Risk factors for youth victimization: Beyond a lifestyle/routine activities theory approach. *Violence and Victims, 11,* 3–19.

Finkelhor, D., Hotaling, G., Lewis, I., & Smith, C. (1990). Sexual abuse in a national survey of adult men and women: Prevalence, characteristics, and risk factors. *Child Abuse and Neglect, 14,* 19–28.

Finkelstein, N., Kennedy, C., Thomas, K., & Kearns, M. (1997). *Gender-specific substance abuse treatment.* Alexandria, VA: National Women's Resource Center for the Prevention and Treatment of Alcohol, Tobacco, and Other Drug Abuse and Mental Illness.

Finlay, K., & Trafimow, D. (1998). The relationship between the private self and helping victims of AIDS. *Journal of Applied Social Psychology, 28,* 1798–1809.

Finn, P. (1989). Statutory authority in the use and enforcement of civil protection orders against domestic abuse. *Family Law Quarterly, 23,* 43–67.

Finn, P. (1991). Civil protection orders: A flawed opportunity for intervention. In M. Steinman (Ed.), *Women battering: Policy responses* (pp. 155–189). Cincinnati, OH: Anderson.

Finn, P., Sharkansky, E., Viken, R., West, T., Sandy, J., & Bufferd, G. (1997). Heterogeneity in the families of sons of alcoholics: The impact of familial vulnerability type on offspring characteristics. *Journal of Abnormal Psychology, 106,* 26–36.

Firestone, P., Bradford, J., McCoy, M., Greenberg, D., Curry, S., & Larose, M. (1998). Recidivism in convicted rapists. *Journal of the American Academy of Psychiatry and the Law, 26,* 185–200.

Fischer, K., & Rose, M. (1995). When "enough is enough": Battered women's decision making around court orders of protection. *Crime & Delinquency, 41,* 414–429.

Fishbein, D. (2000). Introduction. In D. Fishbein (Ed.), *The science, treatment, and prevention of antisocial behaviors: Application to the criminal justice system* (pp 1.1–1.8) Kingston, NJ: Civic Research Institute.

Fisher, B., Cullen, F., & Turner, M. (2000). *The sexual victimization of college women* (NCJ 182369). Washington, DC: Office of Justice Programs, U.S. Department of Justice.

Fisher, B., Daigle, L., Cullen, F., & Turner, M. (2003a). Acknowledging sexual victimization as rape: Results from a national-level study. *Justice Quarterly, 20,* 535–574.

Fisher, B., Daigle, L., Cullen, F., & Turner, M. (2003b). Reporting sexual victimization to the police and others: Results from a national-level study of college women. *Criminal Justice and Behavior, 30,* 6–38.

Fitzpatrick, K., LaGory, M., & Ritchey, F. (1999). Dangerous places: Exposure to violence and its mental health consequences for the homeless. *American Journal of Orthopsychiatry, 69,* 438–447.

Fitzsimons, G. M., & Bargh, J. A. (2003). Thinking of you: Nonconscious pursuit of interpersonal goals associated with relationship partners. *Journal of Personality and Social Psychology, 84,* 148–164.

Fleming, J., Mullen, P., Sibthorpe, B., Attewell, R., & Bammer, G. (1998). The relationship between childhood sexual abuse and alcohol abuse in women—A case-control study. *Addiction, 93,* 1787–1798.

Fleming, J., Mullen, P., Sibthorpe, B., & Bammer, G. (1999). The long-term impact of childhood sexual abuse in Australian women. *Child Abuse & Neglect, 23,* 145–159.

Fleury, R. (2002). Missing voices: Patterns of battered women's satisfaction with the criminal legal system. *Violence Against Women, 8,* 181–205.

Fleury, R., Sullivan, C., Bybee, D., & Davidson, W. (1998). "Why don't they just call the cops?": Reasons for differential police contact among women with abusive partners. *Violence and Victims, 13,* 333–346.

Flores, B., Musselman, D., DeBattista, C., Garlow, S., Schatzberg, A., & Nemeroff, C. (2004). Biology of mood disorders. In A. Schatzberg & C. Nemeroff (Eds.), *The American psychiatric publishing textbook of psychopharmacology* (3rd ed., pp. 717–764). Washington, DC: American Psychiatric Publishing.

Flynn, P., Craddock, S., Luckey, J., Hubbard, R., & Dunteman, G. (1996). Comorbidity of antisocial personality and mood disorders among psychoactive substance-dependent treatment clients. *Journal of Personality Disorders, 10,* 56–67.

Foa, E., & Cahill, S. (2002). Specialized treatment for PTSD: Matching survivors to the appropriate modality. In R. Yehuda (Ed.), *Treating trauma survivors with PTSD* (pp. 43–62). Washington, DC: American Psychiatric Publishing.

Foa, E., Cascardi, M., Zoellner, L., & Feeny, N. (2000). Psychological and environmental factors associated with partner violence. *Trauma, Violence, and Abuse, 1,* 67–91.

Foa, E., Dancu, C., Hembree, E., Jaycox, L., Meadows, E., & Street, G. (1999). A comparison of exposure therapy, stress inoculation training, and their combination for reducing posttraumatic stress disorder in female assault victims. *Journal of Consulting and Clinical Psychology, 67,* 194–200.

Foa, E., Davidson, J., & Frances, A. (1999). The Expert Consensus Guideline Series: Treatment of posttraumatic stress disorder. *Journal of Clinical Psychiatry, 60,* 16, 4–76.

Foa, E., Hearst-Ikeda, D., & Perry, K. (1995). Evaluation of a brief cognitive–behavioral program for the prevention of chronic PTSD in recent assault victims. *Journal of Consulting and Clinical Psychology, 63,* 948–955.

Foa, E., & Meadows, E. (1997). Psychosocial treatments for posttraumatic stress disorder: A critical review. *Annual Review of Psychology, 48,* 449–480.

Foa, E., Olasov Rothbaum, B., & Molnar, C. (1995). Cognitive–behavioral therapy of post-traumatic stress disorder. In M. Friedman, D. Charney, & A. Deutch (Eds.), *Neurobiological and clinical consequences of stress: From normal adaptation to PTSD* (pp. 483–494). Philadelphia: Lippincott-Raven.

Foa, E., & Riggs, D. (1994). Posttraumatic stress disorder and rape. In R. Pynoos (Ed.), *PTSD: A clinical review* (pp. 133–163). Lutherville, MD: Sidran.

Foa, E., Rothbaum, B., Riggs, D., & Murdock, T. (1991). Treatment of posttraumatic stress disorder in rape victims: A comparison between cognitive–behavioral procedures and counseling. *Journal of Consulting and Clinical Psychology, 59,* 715–723.

Foa, E., & Street, G. (2001). Women and traumatic events. *Journal of Clinical Psychiatry, 62*(Suppl. 17), 29–34.

Foley, D., Neale, M., Gardner, C., Pickles, A., & Kendler, K. (2003). Major depression and associated impairment: Same or different genetic and environmental risk factors? *American Journal of Psychiatry, 160,* 2128–2133.

Folkman, S., & Moskowitz, J. (2000a). Stress, positive emotion, and coping. *Current Directions in Psychological Science, 9,* 115–118.

Folkman, S., & Moskowitz, J. (2000b). Positive affect and the other side of coping. *American Psychologist, 55,* 647–654.

Follingstad, D., & DeHart, D. (2000). Defining psychological abuse of husbands toward wives: Context, behaviors, and typologies. *Journal of Interpersonal Violence, 15,* 891–920.

Follingstad, D., Rutledge, L., Berg, B., Hause, E., & Polek, D. (1990). The role of emotional abuse in physically abusive relationships. *Journal of Family Violence, 5,* 107–120.

Forbes Leadership Library. (1997). *Thoughts on wisdom: Thoughts and reflections from history's greatest thinkers.* Chicago: Triumph Books.

Ford, D. (2003). Coercing victim participation in domestic violence prosecutions. *Journal of Interpersonal Violence, 18,* 669–684.

Ford, D., & Kamerow, D. (1989). Epidemiologic study of sleep disturbances and psychiatric disorders: An opportunity for prevention? *Journal of the American Medical Association, 262,* 1479–1485.

Ford, D., & Regoli, J. (1993). The criminal prosecution of wife assaulters: Process, problems, and effects. In N. Zoe Hilton (Ed.), *Legal responses to wife assault: Current trends and evaluation* (pp. 127–164). Newbury Park, CA: Sage.

Forgas, J. (2003). Affective influences on attitudes and judgments. In R. Davidson, K. Scherer, & H. Goldsmith (Eds.), *Handbook of affective sciences* (pp. 596–618). New York: Oxford University Press.

Frasier, P., Slatt, L., Kowlowitz, V., & Glowa, P. (2001). Using the stages of change model to counsel victims of intimate partner violence. *Patient Education and Counseling, 43,* 211–217.

Frazier, P. (1990). Victim attributions and postrape trauma. *Journal of Personality and Social Psychology, 59,* 298–304.

Frazier, P. (2003). Perceived control and distress following sexual assault: A longitudinal test of a new model. *Journal of Personality and Social Psychology, 84,* 1257–1269.

Frazier, P., & Haney, B. (1996). Sexual assault cases in the legal system: Police, prosecutor and victim perspectives. *Law & Human Behavior, 20,* 607–617.

Frazier, P., & Schauben, L. (1994). Causal attributions and recovery from rape and other stressful life events. *Journal of Social and Clinical Psychology, 14,* 1–14.

Fredrickson, B. (2000). Cultivating positive emotions to optimize health and well-being. *Prevention & Treatment, 3,* Article 0001a. Retrieved August 9, 2000, from http://www.journals.apa.org/prevention/volume3/pre0030001a.html

Fredrickson, B., & Levenson, R. (1998). Positive emotions speed recovery from the cardiovascular sequelae of negative emotions. *Cognition and Emotion, 12,* 191–220.

Freedman, S., & Shalev, A. (2000). Prospective studies of the recently traumatized. In A. Shalev, R. Yehuda, & A. McFarlane (Eds.), *International handbook of human response to trauma* (pp. 249–261). New York: Kluwer Academic/Plenum Publishers.

Freeman, R., Collier, K., & Parillo, K. (2002). Early life sexual abuse as a risk factor for crack cocaine use in a sample of community-recruited women at high risk for illicit drug use. *American Journal of Drug and Alcohol Abuse, 28,* 109–131.

Friedman, M., Charney, D., & Deutch, A. (1995). Key questions and a research agenda for the future. In M. Friedman, D. Charney, & A. Deutch (Eds.), *Neurobiological and clinical consequences of stress: From normal adaptation to post-traumatic stress disorder* (pp. 527–533). Philadelphia: Williams & Wilkins.

Friedman, M., & Schnurr, P. (1995). The relationship between trauma, post-traumatic stress disorder, and physical health. In M. Friedman, D. Charney, & A. Deutch (Eds.), *Neurobiological and clinical consequences of stress: From normal adaptation to post-traumatic stress disorder* (pp. 507–524). Philadelphia: Williams & Wilkins.

Friedman, M., & Southwick, S. (1995). Towards pharmacotherapy for PTSD. In M. Friedman, D. Charney, & A. Deutch (Eds.), *Neurobiological and clinical consequences of stress: From normal adaptation to post-traumatic stress disorder.* Philadelphia: Williams & Wilkins.

Friedman, M., & Yehuda, R. (1995). Post-traumatic stress disorder and comorbidity: Psychobiological approaches to differential diagnosis. In M. Friedman, D. Charney, & A. Deutsch (Eds.), *Neurobiological and clinical consequences of stress: From normal adaptation to post-traumatic stress disorder* (pp. 429–445). Philadelphia: Williams & Wilkins.

Friedrich, M. (1999). Experts describe optimal symptom management for hospice patients. *Journal of the American Medical Association, 282,* 1213–1215.

Frijda, N. (1993). Moods, emotion episodes, and emotions. In M. Lewis & J. Haviland (Eds.), *Handbook of emotions* (pp. 381–403). New York: Guilford Press.

Frintner, M., & Rubinson, L. (1993). Acquaintance rape: The influence of alcohol, fraternity membership, and sports team membership. *Journal of Sex Education and Therapy, 19,* 272–284.

Frodl, T., Meisenzahl, E., Zetzsche, T., Born, C., Groll, C., Jäger, M., et al. (2002). Hippocampal changes in patients with a first episode of major depression. *American Journal of Psychiatry, 159,* 1112–1118.

Fromme, K., D'Amico, E., & Katz, E. (1999). Intoxicated sexual risk taking: An expectancy or cognitive impairment explanation? *Journal of Studies on Alcohol, 60,* 54–63.

Fromme, K., Katz, E., & D'Amico, E. (1997). Effects of alcohol intoxication on the perceived consequences of risk-taking. *Experimental Clinical Psychopharmacology, 5,* 14–23.

Fukuda, K., Nisenbaum, R., Stewart, G., Thompson, W., Robin, L., Washko, R., et al. (1998). Chronic multisymptom illness affecting Air Force veterans of the Gulf War. *Journal of the American Medical Association, 280,* 981–988.

Fullilove, M., Fullilove, R., Haynes, K., & Gross, S. (1990). Black women and AIDS prevention: A view towards understanding the gender rules. *Journal of Sex Research, 27,* 47–64.

Furby, L., Fischhoff, B., & Morgan, M. (1990). Preventing rape: How people perceive the options for assault prevention. In E. Viano (Ed.), *The victimology handbook: Research findings, treatment, and public policy* (pp. 227–259). New York: Garland Publishing.

Furst, R., Johnson, B., Dunlap, E., & Curtis, R. (1999). The stigmatized image of the "crack head": A sociocultural exploration of a barrier to cocaine smoking among a cohort of youth in New York. *Deviant Behavior, 20,* 153–181.

Furstenberg, F., & Weiss, C. (2000). Intergenerational transmission of fathering roles in at risk families. *Fatherhood: Research, Interventions and Policies, 29,* 181–201.

Futa, K., Nash, C., Hansen, D., & Garbin, C. (2003). Adult survivors of childhood abuse: An analysis of coping mechanisms used for stressful childhood memories and current stressors. *Journal of Family Violence, 18,* 227–239.

Fyer, A. (2000). Anxiety disorder: Genetics. In B. Sadock & V. Sadock (Eds.), *Kaplan and Sadock's comprehensive textbook of psychiatry* (7th ed., pp. 1457–1463). Philadelphia: Lippincott Williams & Wilkins.

Fyfe, J., Klinger, D., & Flavin, J. (1997). Differential police treatment of male-on-female spousal violence. *Criminology, 35,* 455–473.

Galaif, E., Nyamathi, A., & Stein, J. (1999). Psychosocial predictors of current drug use, drug problems, and physical drug dependence in homeless women. *Addictive Behaviors, 24,* 801–814.

Gallagher, J., Parle, M., & Cairns, D. (2002). Appraisal and psychological distress six months after diagnosis of breast cancer. *British Journal of Health Psychology, 7,* 365–376.

Gallo, L., & Matthews, K. (2003). Understanding the association between socioeconomic status and physical health: Do negative emotions play a role? *Psychological Bulletin, 129,* 10–51.

Garfield, S. (1996). Some problems associated with "validated" forms of psychotherapy. *Clinical Psychology: Science and Practice, 3,* 218–229.

Garfield, S. (1998). Some comments on empirically supported treatments. *Journal of Consulting and Clinical Psychology, 66,* 1, 121–125.

Garis, D. (1998). Poverty, single-parent households, and youth at-risk behavior: An empirical study. *Journal of Economic Issues, 32,* 1079–1085.

Gavaler, J., & Arria, A. (1995). Increased susceptibility of women to alcoholic liver disease: Artifactual or real? In P. Hall (Ed.), *Alcoholic liver disease: Pathology and pathogenesis* (pp. 123–133). London: Edward Arnold.

Gavranidou, M., & Rosner, R. (2003). The weaker sex? Gender and post-traumatic stress disorder. *Depression and Anxiety, 17,* 130–139.

Geissler, L., Bormann, C., Kwiatkowski, C., Braucht, G., & Reichardt, C. (1995). Women, homelessness, and substance abuse: Moving beyond the stereotypes. *Psychology of Women Quarterly, 19,* 65–83.

Gelles, R. (1996). Constraints against family violence: How well do they work? In E. Buzawa & C. Buzawa (Eds.), *Do arrests and restraining orders work?* (pp. 30–42). Thousand Oaks, CA: Sage.

George, D., Carroll, P., Kersnick, R., & Calderon, K. (1998). Gender related patterns of helping among friends. *Psychology of Women Quarterly, 22,* 685–704.

George, L., Winfield, I., & Blazer, D. (1992). Sociocultural factors in sexual assault: Comparison of two representative samples of women. *Journal of Social Issues, 48,* 105–125.

George, W., Cue, K., Lopez, P., Crowe, L., & Norris, J. (1995). Self-reported alcohol expectancies and postdrinking sexual inferences about women. *Journal of Applied Social Psychology, 25,* 164–186.

George, W., Gournic, S., & McAfee, M. (1988). Perceptions of postdrinking female sexuality: Effects of gender, beverage choice, and drink payment. *Journal of Applied Social Psychology, 18,* 1295–1317.

George, W., & Martinez, L. (2002). Victim blaming in rape: Effects of victim and perpetrator race, type of rape, and participant racism. *Psychology of Women Quarterly, 26,* 110–119.

Germain, A., Buysse, D., Ombao, H., Kupfer, D., & Hall, M. (2003). Psychophysiological reactivity and coping styles influence effects of acute stress exposure on rapid eye movement sleep. *Psychosomatic Medicine, 65,* 857–864.

Gidycz, C., Hanson, K., & Layman, M. (1995). A prospective analysis of the relationships among sexual assault experiences. *Psychology of Women Quarterly, 19,* 5–29.

Gil, A., Vega, W., & Turner, R. (2002). Early and mid-adolescence risk factors for later substance abuse by African Americans and European Americans. *Public Health Reports, 117*(Suppl. 1), S15–S29.

Gilbert, L., El-Bassel, N., Schilling, R., & Friedman, E. (1997). Childhood abuse as a risk for partner abuse among women in methadone maintenance. *American Journal of Drug and Alcohol Abuse, 23,* 581–595.

Gilfus, M. (1995). *A life-span perspective on research on violence against women.* Unpublished manuscript.

Gilfus, M. (1999). The price of the ticket: A survivor-centered appraisal of trauma theory. *Violence Against Women, 5,* 1238–1257.

Gilligan, C. (1982). *In a different voice: Psychological theory and women's development.* Cambridge, MA: Harvard University Press.

Gilman, S., Kawachi, I., Fitzmaurice, G., & Buka, S. (2002). Socioeconomic status in childhood and the lifetime risk of major depression. *International Journal of Epidemiology, 31,* 359–367.

Gil-Rivas, V., Fiorentine, R., & Anglin, D. (1996). Sexual abuse, physical abuse, and posttraumatic stress disorder among women participating in outpatient drug abuse treatment. *Journal of Psychoactive Drugs, 28,* 95–102.

Gist, J., McFarlane, J., Malecha, A., Fredland, N., Schultz, P., & Willson, P. (2001). Women in danger: Intimate partner violence experienced by women who qualify and do not qualify for protective order. *Behavioral Sciences and the Law, 19,* 637–647.

Gladstone, G., Parker, G., Mitchell, P., Wilhelm, K., & Austin, M. (2004). Implications of childhood trauma for depressed women: An analysis of pathways from childhood sexual abuse to deliberate self-harm and revictimization. *American Journal of Psychiatry, 161,* 1417–1425.

Gleason, W. (1993). Mental disorders in battered women: An empirical study. *Violence and Victims, 8,* 53–68.

Gold, M., & Miller, N. (1997). Cocaine (and crack): Neurobiology. In J. Lowinson, P. Ruiz, R. Millman, & J. Langrod (Eds.), *Substance abuse: A comprehensive textbook* (3rd ed., pp. 181–198). Baltimore: Williams & Wilkins.

Gold, S., Sinclair, B., & Balge, K. (1999). Risk of sexual revictimization: A theoretical model. *Aggression and Violent Behavior, 4,* 157–170.

Goldberg, R. (1994). Childhood abuse, depression, and chronic pain. *Clinical Journal of Pain, 10,* 277–281.

Golding, J. (1994). Sexual assault history and physical health in randomly selected Los Angeles women. *Health Psychology, 13,* 130–138.

Golding, J. (1999). Intimate partner violence as a risk factor for mental disorders: A meta-analysis. *Journal of Family Violence, 14,* 99–132.

Goldman, J., & Padayachi, U. (2000). Some methodological problems in estimating incidence and prevalence in child sexual abuse research. *Journal of Sex Research, 37,* 305–314.

Goldman, M. (1999). The Violence Against Women Act: Meeting its goals in protecting battered immigrant women? *Family and Conciliation Courts Review, 37,* 375–392.

Goldman, M., Del Boca, F., & Darkes, J. (1999). Alcohol expectancy theory: The application of cognitive neuroscience. In K. Leonard & H. Blane (Eds.), *Psychological theories of drinking and alcoholism* (2nd ed., pp. 203–246). New York: Guilford Press.

Golier, J., Yehuda, R., Bierer, L., Mitropoulou, V., New, A., Schmeidler, J., et al. (2003). The relationship of borderline personality disorder to posttraumatic stress disorder and traumatic events. *American Journal of Psychiatry, 160,* 2018–2024.

Golier, J., Yehuda, R., & Southwick, S. (1997). Memory and posttraumatic stress disorder. In P. Appelbaum, L. Uyehara, & M. Elin (Eds.), *Trauma and memory: Clinical and legal controversies* (pp. 225–242). New York: Oxford University Press.

Gondolf, E. (1998). Victims of court-ordered batterers: Their victimization, helpseeking, and perceptions. *Violence Against Women, 4,* 659–676.

Gondolf, E. (2000a). A 30-month follow-up of court-referred batterers in four cities. *International Journal of Offender Therapy and Comparative Criminology, 44,* 111–128.

Gondolf, E. (2000b). Mandatory court review and batterer program compliance. *Journal of Interpersonal Violence, 15,* 428–437.

Gondolf, E. (2001). Limitations of experimental evaluation of batterer programs. *Trauma, Violence, & Abuse, 2,* 79–88.

Gondolf, E., & Heckert, D. (2003). Determinants of women's perceptions of risk in battering relationships. *Violence and Victims, 18,* 371–386.

Gondolf, E., Heckert, D., & Kimmel, C. (2002). Nonphysical abuse among batterer program participants. *Journal of Family Violence, 17,* 293–314.

Gondolf, E., McWilliams, J., Hart, B., & Stuehling, J. (1994). Court response to petitions for civil protection orders. *Journal of Interpersonal Violence, 9,* 503–517.

Goodkind, J., Gillum, T., Bybee, D., & Sullivan, C. (2003). The impact of family and friends' reactions on the well-being of women with abusive partners. *Violence Against Women, 9,* 347–373.

Goodman, E. (1999). The role of socioeconomic status gradients in explaining differences in US adolescents' health. *American Journal of Public Health, 89,* 1522–1528.

Goodman, E., & Huang, B. (2002). Socioeconomic status, depressive symptoms, and adolescent substance use. *Archives of Pediatric Adolescent Medicine, 156,* 448–453.

Goodman, L., Bennett, L., & Dutton, M. (1999). Obstacles to victims' cooperation with the criminal prosecution of their abusers: The role of social support. *Violence and Victims, 14,* 427–444.

Goodwin, F., & Blehar, M. (1993). Special edition: Toward a new psychology of depression in women. *Journal of Affective Disorders, 29,* 75–76.

Gordon, C., Carey, M., & Carey, K. (1997). Effects of a drinking event on behavioral skills and condom attitudes in men: Implications for HIV risk from a controlled experiment. *Health Psychology, 16,* 490–495.

Gore-Felton, C., Gill, M., Koopman, C., & Spiegel, D. (1999). A review of acute stress reactions among victims of violence: Implications for early intervention. *Aggression and Violent Behavior, 4,* 293–306.

Gorey, K., & Leslie, D. (1997). The prevalence of child sexual abuse: Integrative review adjustment of potential response and measurement bias. *Child Abuse and Neglect, 21,* 391–398.

Gottfredson, D. (1999). *Effects of judges' sentencing on decisions on criminal careers.* Washington, DC: National Institute of Justice.

Gottlieb, B. (1997). Conceptual and measurement issues in the study of coping with chronic stress. In B. Gottlieb (Ed.), *Coping with chronic stress* (pp. 3–42). New York: Plenum Press.

Graham, K., & Vidal-Zeballos, D. (1997). Analyses of use of tranquilizers and sleeping pills across five surveys of the same population (1985–1991): The relationship with gender, age and use of other substances. *Social Science Medicine, 46,* 381–395.

Granello, D., & Beamish, P. (1998). Reconceptualizing codependency in women: A sense of connectedness, not pathology. *Journal of Mental Health Counseling, 20,* 344–359.

Gray-Eurom, K., Seaberg, D., & Wears, R. (2002). The prosecution of sexual assault cases: Correlation with forensic evidence. *Annals of Emergency Medicine, 39,* 39–46.

Green, B., Goodman, L., Krupnick, J., Corcoran, C., Petty, R., Stockton, P., & Stern, N. (2000). Outcomes of single versus multiple trauma exposure in a screening sample. *Journal of Traumatic Stress, 13,* 271–286.

Green, C., Flowe-Valencia, H., Rosenblum, L., & Tait, A. (2001). The role of childhood and adulthood abuse among women presenting for chronic pain management. *Journal of Pain, 17,* 359–364.

Greenberg, P., Sisitsky, M., Kessler, R., Finkelstein, S., Berndt, E., Davidson, J., et al. (1999). The economic burden of anxiety disorders in the 1990s. *Journal of Clinical Psychiatry, 60,* 427–435.

Greenberg, P., Stiglin, L., Finkelstein, S., & Berndt, E. (1993). The economic burden of depression in 1990. *Journal of Clinical Psychiatry, 54,* 405–418.

Greene, D., & Navarro, R. (1998). Situation-specific assertiveness in the epidemiologist of sexual victimization among university women—a prospective path analysis. *Psychology of Women Quarterly, 22,* 589–604.

Greenfeld, L., Rand, M., Craven, D., Klaus, P., Perkins, C., Ringel, C., et al. (1998). *Violence by intimates: Analysis of data on crimes by current or former spouses, boyfriends, and girlfriends* (NCJ 167237). Washington, DC: U.S. Department of Justice, Office of Justice Programs, Bureau of Justice Statistics.

Greenfield, S. (2002). Women and alcohol use disorders. *Harvard Review of Psychiatry, 10,* 76–85.

Greenfield, S., Hufford, M., Vagge, L., Muenz, L., Costello, M., & Weiss, R. (2000). The relationship of self-efficacy expectancies to relapse among alcohol dependent men and women: A prospective study. *Journal of Studies on Alcohol, 61,* 345–351.

Greenfield, T., & Room, R. (1997). Situational norms for drinking and drunkenness: Trends in the U.S. adult population, 1979–1990. *Addiction, 92,* 33–47.

Gregory, C., & Erez, E. (2002). The effects of batterer intervention programs: The battered women's perspectives. *Violence Against Women, 8,* 206–232.

Griffin, K., Botvin, G., Scheier, L., Diaz, T., & Miller, N. (2000). Parenting practices as predictors of substance use, delinquency, and aggression among urban minority youth: Moderating effects of family structure and gender. *Psychology of Addictive Behaviors, 14,* 174–184.

Grisso, J., Schwarz, D., Hirschinger, N., Sammel, M., Brensinger, C., Santanna, J., et al. (1999). Violent injuries among women in an urban area. *New England Journal of Medicine, 341,* 1899–1905.

Gross, M., Cramer, E., Forte, J., Gordon, J., Kunkel, T., & Moriarty, L. (2000). The impact of sentencing options on recidivism among domestic violence offenders: A case study. *American Journal of Criminal Justice, 24,* 301–312.

Grossman, P. Niemann, L., Schmidt, S., & Walach, H. (2004). Mindfulness-based stress reduction and health benefits: A meta-analysis. *Journal of Psychosomatic Research, 57,* 35–43.

Gunderson, J., & Sabo, A. (1993). The phenomenological and conceptual interface between borderline personality disorder and PTSD. *American Journal of Psychiatry, 150,* 1927.

Gunthert, K., Cohen, L., & Armeli, S. (1999). The role of neuroticism in daily stress and coping. *Journal of Personality and Social Psychology, 77,* 1087–1100.

Guttentag, M., & Secord, P. (1983). *Too many women? The sex ratio question.* Beverly Hills, CA: Sage.

Haaken, J. (1990). A critical analysis of the co-dependence construct. *Psychiatry, 53,* 396–406.

Haggerty, L., & Goodman, L. (2002). Stages of change-based nursing interventions for victims of interpersonal violence. *Journal of Obstetric, Gynecologic, and Neonatal Nursing, 32,* 27–39.

Halgren, E. (1992). Emotional neurophysiology of the amygdale within the context of human cognition. In J. Aggelton (Ed.), *The amygdala: Neurobiological aspects of emotion, memory, and mental dysfunction* (pp. 191–228). New York: Wiley.

Hall, G. (1995). Sexual offender recidivism revisited: A meta-analysis of recent treatment studies. *Journal of Consulting and Clinical Psychology, 63,* 802–809.

Hall, P. (1995). Factors influencing individual susceptibility to alcoholic liver disease. In P. Hall (Ed.), *Alcoholic liver disease: Pathology and pathogenesis* (pp. 299–316). London: Arnold.

Hall Smith, P., Moracco, K., & Butts, J. (1998). Partner homicide in context: A population-based perspective. *Homicide Studies, 2,* 400–421.

Haller, D., Miles, D., & Dawson, K. (2002). Psychopathology influences treatment retention among drug-dependent women. *Journal of Substance Abuse Treatment, 23,* 431–436.

Halmi, K. (2000). Eating disorders. In B. Sadock & V. Sadock (Eds.), *Kaplan and Sadock's comprehensive textbook of psychiatry* (7th ed., pp. 1663–1676). Philadelphia: Lippincott Williams & Wilkins.

Halpern, C., Oslak, S., Young, M., Martin, S., & Kupper, L. (2001). Partner violence among adolescents in opposite-sex romantic relationships: Findings from the national longitudinal study of adolescent health. *American Journal of Public Health, 91,* 1679–1685.

Hamberger, L., Ambuel, B., Marbella, M., & Donze, J. (1998). Physician interaction with battered women: The women's perspective. *Archives of Family Medicine, 7,* 575–582.

Hamberger, L., Saunders, D., & Hovey, M. (1992). The prevalence of domestic violence in community practice and rate of physician inquiry. *Family Medicine, 24,* 283–287.

Hamby, S., & Gray-Little, B. (1997). Responses to partner violence: Moving away from deficit models. *Journal of Family Psychology, 11,* 339–350.

Hamby, S., & Gray-Little, B. (2000). Labeling partner violence: When do victims differentiate among acts? *Violence and Victims, 15,* 173–186.

Hamby, S., & Koss, M. (2003). Shades of gray: A qualitative study of terms used in the measurement of sexual victimization. *Psychology of Women's Quarterly, 27,* 243–255.

Hammen, C., Burge, D., Daley, S., Davila, J., Paley, B., & Rudolph, K. (1995). Interpersonal attachment cognitions and prediction of symptomatic responses to interpersonal stress. *Journal of Abnormal Psychology, 104,* 436–443.

Hammock, G., & Richardson, D. (1997). Perceptions of rape: The influence of closeness of relationship, intoxication and sex of participant. *Violence and Victims, 12,* 237–246.

Hammond, P. (1978). *An introduction to cultural and social anthropology.* New York: McMillan.

Hampton, R., & Gelles, R. (1994). Violence toward Black women in a nationally representative sample of Black families. *Journal of Comparative Family Studies, 25,* 105–119.

Hampton, R., Oliver, W., & Magarian, L. (2003). Domestic violence in the African American community: An analysis of social and structural factors. *Violence Against Women, 9,* 533–557.

Hanna, C. (1998). The paradox of hope: The crime and punishment of domestic violence. *William and Mary Law Review, 39,* 1505–1584.

Harford, T., Wechsler, H., & Seibring, M. (2002). Attendance and alcohol use at parties and bars in college: A national survey of current drinkers. *Journal of Studies on Alcohol, 63,* 726–733.

Harrell, A., & Smith, B. (1996). Effects of restraining orders on domestic violence victims. In E. Buzawa & C. Buzawa (Eds.), *Do arrests and restraining orders work?* (pp. 214–242). Thousand Oaks, CA: Sage.

Harrell, A., Smith, B., & Newmark, L. (1993). *Court processing and the effects of restraining orders for domestic violence victims.* Washington, DC: Urban Institute.

Harris, M. (1992). Sex and ethnic differences in past aggressive behaviors. *Journal of Family Violence, 7,* 85–102.

Harris, R., Stickney, J., Grasley, C., Hutchinson, G., Greaves, L., & Boyd, T. (2001). Searching for help and information: Abused women speak out. *Library and Information Science Research, 23,* 123–141.

Harris, S., Dean, K., Holden, G., & Carlson, M. (2001). Assessing police and protective order reports of violence: What is the relation? *Journal of Interpersonal Violence, 16,* 602–609.

Harrison, L., & Esqueda, C. (2000). Effects of race and victim drinking on domestic violence attributions. *Sex Roles, 42,* 1043–1057.

Harrison, P., Fulkerson, J., & Beebe, T. (1997). Multiple substance use among adolescent physical and sexual abuse victims. *Child Abuse and Neglect, 21,* 529–540.

Hartlage, S., Alloy, L., Vazquez, C., & Dykman, B. (1993). Automatic and effortful processing in depression. *Psychological Bulletin, 113,* 247–278.

Harvey, A., Jones, C., & Schmidt, D. (2003). Sleep and posttraumatic stress disorder: A review. *Clinical Psychology Review, 23,* 377–407.

Harwood, H. (2000). *Updating estimates of the economic costs of alcohol abuse in the United States: Estimates, update methods, and data.* Washington, DC: National Institute on Alcohol Abuse and Alcoholism.

Hawkins, J., Catalano, R., & Miller, J. (1992). Risk and protective factors for alcohol and other drug problems in adolescence and early adulthood: Implications for substance abuse prevention. *Psychological Bulletin, 112,* 64–105.

Hawkins, J., Graham, J., Maguin, E., Abbott, R., Hill, K., & Catalano, R. (1997). Exploring the effects of age of alcohol use initiation and psychosocial risk factors on subsequent alcohol misuse. *Journal of Studies on Alcohol, 58,* 280–290.

Hays, R., & Revetto, J. (1990). Peer cluster theory and adolescent drug use: A reanalysis. *Journal of Drug Education, 20,* 191–198.

Hebert, R. (2003). The first steps. *American Psychological Society, 16,* 11.

Heer, D., & Grossbard-Shechtman, A. (1981). The impact of the female marriage squeeze and the contraceptive revolution on sex roles and the women's liberation movement in the United States, 1960 to 1975. *Journal of Marriage and the Family, 34,* 49–65.

Heim, C., Ehlert, U., Hanker, J., & Hellhammer, D. (1998). Abuse-related posttraumatic stress disorder and alterations of the hypothalamic–pituitary–adrenal axis in women with chronic pelvic pain. *Psychosomatic Medicine, 60,* 309–318.

Heim, K., Newport, D., Heit, S., Graham, Y., Wilcox, M., Bonsall, R., et al. (2000). Pituitary–adrenal and autonomic responses to stress in women after sexual and physical abuse in childhood. *Journal of the American Medical Association, 284,* 592–597.

Heimer, L. (2003). A new anatomical framework for neuropsychiatric disorders and drug abuse. *American Journal of Psychiatry, 160,* 1726–1739.

Hembree, E., & Foa, E. (2003). Interventions for trauma-related emotional disturbances in adult victims of crime. *Journal of Traumatic Stress, 16,* 187–199.

Hemenover, S., & Zhang, S. (2004). Anger, personality, and optimistic stress appraisals. *Cognition and Emotion, 18,* 363–382.

Henderson, A. (1990). Children of abused wives: Their influence on their mothers' decisions. *Canada's Mental Health Journal, June/September,* 10–13.

Hendryx, M., & Ahern, M. (1997). Mental health functioning and community problems. *Journal of Community Psychology 25,* 147–157.

Heninger, G. (1995). Neuroimmunology of stress. In M. Friedman, D. Charney, & A. Deutch (Eds.), *Neurobiological and clinical consequences of stress: From normal adaptation to PTSD* (pp. 381–401). Philadelphia: Lippincott-Raven.

Henning, K., & Klesges, L. (2002). Utilization of counseling and supportive services by female victims of domestic abuse. *Violence and Victims, 17,* 623–636.

Henning, K., & Leitenberg, H. (1996). Long-term psychological and social impact of witnessing physical conflict between parents. *Journal of Interpersonal Violence, 11,* 35–52.

Herbert, T., Silver, R., & Ellard, J. (1991). Coping with an abusive relationship: I. How and why do women stay? *Journal of Marriage and the Family, 53,* 311–325.

Herman, J. (1992). *Trauma and recovery.* New York: Basic Books.

Herman, J. (2003). The mental health of crime victims: Impact of legal intervention. *Journal of Traumatic Stress, 16,* 159–166.

Herman, J., & van der Kolk, B. (1987). Traumatic antecedents of BPD. In B. van der Kolk (Ed.), *Psychological trauma* (pp. 111–125). Washington, DC: American Psychiatric Press.

Herman, S., Frank, K., Mowbray, C., Ribisl, K., Davidson, W., Bootsmiller, B., et al. (2000). Longitudinal effects of integrated treatment on alcohol use for persons with serious mental illness and substance use disorders. *Journal of Behavioral Health Services & Research, 27,* 286–302.

Hesselbrock, M., & Hesselbrock, V. (1992). Relationship of family history, antisocial personality disorder and personality traits in young men at risk for alcoholism. *Journal of Studies on Alcohol, 53,* 619–625.

Hetherington, S., Harris, R., Bausell, R., Kavanaugh, K., & Scott, D. (1996). AIDS prevention in high-risk African American women: Behavioral and psychological, and gender issues. *Journal of Sex and Marital Therapy, 22,* 9–11.

Hettema, J., Annas, P., Neale, M., Kendler, K., & Fredrickson, M. (2003). A twin study of the genetics of fear conditioning. *Archives of General Psychiatry, 60,* 702–708.

Heymann, J. (2000). What happens during and after school: Conditions faced by working parents living in poverty and their school-aged children. *Journal of Children and Poverty, 6,* 5–20.

Hickman, S., & Muehlenhard, C. (1997). College women's fears and precautionary behaviors relating to acquaintance rape and stranger rape. *Psychology of Women Quarterly, 21,* 527–547.

Hien, D., Cohen, L., Miele, G., Litt, L., & Capstick, C. (2004). Promising treatments for women with comorbid PTSD and substance use disorders. *American Journal of Psychiatry, 161,* 1426–1432.

Higgins, E. (1996). The "self digest": Self-knowledge serving self-regulatory functions. *Journal of Personality and Social Psychology, 71,* 1062–1083.

Hildebrandt, M., Steyerberg, E., Stage, K., Passchier, J., & Kragh-Soerensen, P. (2003). Are gender differences important for the clinical effects of antidepressants? *American Journal of Psychiatry, 160,* 1643–1650.

Hill, E., Ross, L., & Low, B. (1997). The role of future unpredictability in human risk-taking. *Human Nature, 8,* 287–325.

Hilton, Z. (1992). Battered women's concerns about their children witnessing wife assault. *Journal of Interpersonal Violence, 7,* 77–86.

Hindelang, M., Gottfredson, M., & Garofalo, J. (1978). Correlates of delinquency: The illusion of discrepancy between self-report and official measures. *American Sociological Review, 44,* 995–1014.

Hines, D., & Saudino, K. (2002). Intergenerational transmission of intimate partner violence. *Trauma, Violence, & Abuse, 3,* 210–225.

Hirschel, D., & Buzawa, E. (2002). Understanding the context of dual arrest with directions for future research. *Violence Against Women, 8,* 1449–1473.

Hirschel, D., & Hutchison, I. (2001). The relative effects of offense, offender, and victim variables on the decision to prosecute domestic violence cases. *Violence Against Women, 7,* 46–59.

Hirschel, J., & Hutchison, I. (1992). Female spouse abuse and the police response: The Charlotte, North Carolina experiment. *Journal of Criminal Law and Criminology, 83,* 73–119.

Hittner, J. (1995). Tension-reduction expectancies and alcoholic beverage preferences revisited: Associations to drinking frequency and gender. *International Journal of Addiction, 30,* 323–336.

Hobfall, S., Freedy, J., Green, B., & Solomon, S. (1996). Coping in reaction to extreme stress: The roles of resource loss and resource availability. In M. Zeidner & N. Endler (Eds.), *Handbook of coping: Theory, research, applications* (pp. 322–349). New York: Wiley.

Hobfall, S., & Lilly, R. (1993). Resource conservation as a strategy for community psychology. *Journal of Community Psychology, 21,* 128–148.

Hobfall, S., Schroder, K., Wells, M., & Malek, M. (2002). Communal versus individualistic construction of sense of mastery in facing life challenges. *Journal of Social and Clinical Psychology, 21,* 362–399.

Hobson, J. (1995). *Sleep.* New York: Freeman.

Hock, M., Krohne, H., & Kaiser, J. (1996). Coping dispositions and the processing of ambiguous stimuli. *Journal of Personality and Social Psychology, 70,* 1052–1066.

Hodges, S. (2003). Borderline personality disorder and posttraumatic stress disorder: Time for integration? *Journal of Counseling and Development, 81,* 409–417.

Hodgins, H., Liebeskind, E., & Schwartz, W. (1996). Getting out of hot water: Facework in social predicaments. *Journal of Personality and Social Psychology, 71,* 300–314.

Hoffman, J., Barnes, G., Welte, J., & Dintcheff, B. (2000). Trends in combinational use of alcohol and illicit drugs among minority adolescents. *American Journal of Drug and Alcohol Abuse, 26,* 311–321.

Hogan, B., Linden, W., & Najarian, B. (2002). Social support interventions: Do they work? *Clinical Psychology Review, 22,* 381–440.

Holden, C. (2003, October 31). Future brightening for depression treatments. *Science, 302,* 810–813.

Holden, G., Geffner, R., & Jouriles, E. (1998). *Children exposed to marital violence: Theory, research, and applied issues.* Washington, DC: American Psychological Association.

Hollander, E., Stein, D., DeCaria, C., Cohen, L., Saoud, J., Skodol, A., et al. (1994). Serotonergic sensitivity in borderline personality disorder: Preliminary findings. *American Journal of Psychiatry, 151,* 277–280.

Hollingshead, A., & Redlich, F. (1964). *Social class and mental illness: A community study.* Baltimore: Wiley.

Hollingshead, A., & Redlich, F. (1993). *Social stratification and psychiatric disorders.* New York: Irvington.

Hollon, S., & Beck, A. (2004). Cognitive and cognitive behavioral therapies. In M. Lambert (Ed.), *Bergin and Garfield's handbook of psychotherapy and behavior change* (5th ed., pp. 447–492). New York: Wiley.

Hollon, S., Shelton, R., & Davis, D. (1993). Cognitive therapy for depression: Conceptual issues and clinical efficacy. *Journal of Consulting and Clinical Psychology, 61,* 270–275.

Hollon, S., Thase, M., & Markowitz, J. (2002). Treatment and prevention of depression. *Psychological Science in the Public Interest, 3,* 39–77.

Holloway, F. (1995). Low-dose alcohol effects on human behavior and performance. *Alcohol, Drugs, and Driving, 11,* 39–56.

Holt, V., Kernic, M., Lumley T., Wolf, M., & Rivara, F. (2002). Civil protection orders and risk of subsequent police-reported violence. *Journal of the American Medical Association, 288,* 589–594.

Holtzworth-Munroe, A., Jacobson, N., Fehrenbach, P., & Fruzzetti, A. (1992). Violent married couples' attributions for violent and nonviolent self and partner behaviors. *Behavioral Assessment, 14,* 53–64.

Holtzworth-Munroe, A., Smutzler, N., & Sandin, E. (1997). A brief review of the research on husband violence. Part II: The psychological effects of husband violence on battered women and their children. *Aggression and Violent Behavior, 2,* 179–213.

Holtzworth-Munroe, A., & Stuart, G. (1994). Typologies of male batterers: Three subtypes and the differences among them. *Psychological Bulletin, 116,* 476–497.

Homel, R., Tomsen, S., & Thommeny, J. (1992). Public drinking and violence: Not just an alcohol problem. *Journal of Drug Issues, 22,* 679–697.

Hommer, D., Momenan, R., Kaiser, E., & Rawlings, R. (2001). Evidence for a gender-related effect of alcoholism on brain volumes. *American Journal of Psychiatry, 158,* 198–204.

Hopfer, C., Crowley, T., & Hewitt, J. (2003). Review of twin and adoption studies of adolescent substance use. *Journal of the American Academy of Child & Adolescent Psychiatry, 42,* 710–719.

Horwath, E., & Weissman, M. (1997). Epidemiology of anxiety disorders across cultural groups. In S. Friedman (Ed.), *Cultural issues in the treatment of anxiety* (pp. 21–39). New York: Guilford Press.

Horwath, E., & Weissman, M. (2000). The epidemiology and cross-national presentation of obsessive–compulsive disorder. *Psychiatric Clinics of North America, 23,* 493–507.

Horwitz, A., Widom, C., McLaughlin, J., & White, H. (2001). The impact of childhood abuse and neglect on adult mental health: A prospective study. *Journal of Health and Social Behavior, 42,* 184–201.

Hotaling, G., & Buzawa, E. (2003). *Forgoing criminal justice assistance: The non-reporting of new incidents of abuse in a court sample of domestic violence victims* (NCJ 195667). Washington, DC: U.S. Government Printing Office.

Hotton, T. (2001). Spousal violence after marital separation. *Juristat, 21,* 1–19.

Howard, A., Riger, S., Campbell, R., & Wasco, S. (2003). Counseling services for battered women: A comparison of outcomes for physical and sexual assault survivors. *Journal of Interpersonal Violence, 18,* 717–734.

Hoyt, D., Ryan, K., & Cauce, A. (1999). Personal victimization in a high-risk environment: Homeless and runaway adolescents. *Journal of Research in Crime and Delinquency, 36,* 371–393.

Hubbard, R., Craddock, S., Flynn, P., Anderson, J., & Etheridge, R. (1997). Overview of 1-year follow-up outcomes in the Drug Abuse Treatment Outcome Study (DATOS). *Psychology of Addictive Behaviors, 11,* 261–278.

Hughes, H. (1988). Psychological and behavioral correlates of family violence in child witnesses and victims. *American Journal of Orthopsychiatry, 58,* 77–90.

Hughes, M., & Thomas, M. (1998). The continuing significance of race revisited: A study of race, class and quality of life in America, 1972–1996. *American Sociological Review, 63,* 785–795.

Humphrey, J., & White, J. (2000). Women's vulnerability to sexual assault from adolescence to young adulthood. *Journal of Adolescent Health, 27,* 419–424.

Humphreys, J., Lee, K., Neylan, T., & Marmar, C. (1999). Trauma history of sheltered battered women. *Issues in Mental Health Nursing, 20,* 319–332.

Humphreys, K., & Weisner, C. (2000). Use of exclusion criteria in selecting research subjects and its effect on the generalizability of alcohol treatment outcome studies. *American Journal of Psychiatry, 157,* 588–594.

Hunt, W. (1998). Pharmacology of alcohol. In R. Tarter, R. Ammerman, & P. Ott (Eds.), *Handbook of substance abuse: Neurobehavioral pharmacology* (pp. 7–22). New York: Plenum Press.

Hutchison, I. (2003). Substance use and abused women's utilization of the police. *Journal of Family Violence, 18,* 93–106.

Hutchison, I., & Hirschel, J. (1998). Abused women: Help-seeking strategies and police utilization. *Violence Against Women, 4,* 436–456.

Hutchison, I., & Hirschel, J. (2001). The effects of children's presence on woman abuse. *Violence and Victims, 16,* 3–17.

Huth-Bocks, A., Levendosky, A., & Bogat, G. (2002). The effects of domestic violence during pregnancy on maternal and infant health. *Violence and Victims, 17,* 169–185.

Iacono, W., Carlson, S., Taylor, J., Elkins, I., & McGue, M. (1999). Behavioral disinhibition and the development of substance-use disorders: Findings from the Minnesota twin family study. *Development and Psychopathology, 11,* 869–900.

Impett, E., & Peplau, L. (2003). Sexual compliance: Gender, motivational, and relationship perspectives. *Journal of Sex Research, 40,* 87–100.

Iovanni, L., & Miller, S. (2001). Criminal justice response to domestic violence: Law enforcement and the courts. In C. Renzetti, J. Edleson, & R. Bergen (Eds.), *Sourcebook on violence against women* (pp. 303–327). Thousand Oaks, CA: Sage.

Irving, L., Snyder, C., & Crowson, J. (1998). Hope and caring with cancer by college women. *Journal of Personality, 66,* 195–214.

Irwin, C., Falsetti, S., Lydiard, R., Ballenger, J., Brock, C., & Brener, W. (1996). Comorbidity of posttraumatic stress disorder and irritable bowel syndrome. *Journal of Clinical Psychiatry, 57,* 576–578.

Irwin, H. (1999). Violent and nonviolent revictimization of women abused in childhood. *Journal of Interpersonal Violence, 14,* 1095–1110.

Isaac, N., Cochran, D., Brown, M., & Adam, S. (1994). Men who batter: Profile from a restraining order database. *Archives of Family Medicine, 3,* 50–54.

Israel, B., Farquhar, S., Schulz, A., James, S., & Parker, E. (2002). The relationship between social support, stress, and health among women on Detroit's east side. *Health Education & Behavior, 29,* 342–360.

Izard, C. (1993). Four systems for emotion activation: Cognitive and noncognitive processes. *Psychology Review, 100,* 68–90.

Jackson, C., Henriksen, L., & Dickinson, D. (1999). Alcohol-specific socialization, parenting behaviors and alcohol use by children. *Journal of Studies on Alcohol, 60,* 362–367.

Jackson, H., Philp, E., Nuttall, R., & Diller, L. (2002). Traumatic brain injury: A hidden consequence for battered women. *Professional Psychology: Research and Practice, 33,* 39–45.

Jacobi, C., Dahme, B., & Dittmann, R. (2002). Cognitive–behavioral, fluoxetine and combined treatment for bulimia nervosa: Short- and long-term results. *European Eating Disorders Review, 10,* 179–198.

Jacobson, J., Weary, G., & Edwards, J. (1999). Certainty-related beliefs and depressive symptomatology: Concurrent and longitudinal relationships. *Social Cognition, 17,* 19–45.

Jaffe, P., Lemon, N., & Poisson, S. (2003). *Child custody and domestic violence: A call for safety and accountability.* Thousand Oaks, CA: Sage.

Janoff-Bulman, R. (1992). *Shattered assumptions: Toward a new psychology of trauma.* New York: Free Press.

Jarjoura, G., Triplett, R., & Brinker, G. (2002). Growing up poor: Examining the link between persistent childhood poverty and delinquency. *Journal of Quantitative Criminology, 18,* 159–187.

Jarrett, R., Kraft, D., Doyle, J., Foster, B., Eaves, G., & Silver, P. (2001). Preventing recurrent depression using cognitive therapy with and without a continuation phase: A randomized clinical trial. *Archives of General Psychiatry, 58,* 381–388.

Jasinski, J. (2001a). Physical violence among Anglo, African American, and Hispanic couples: Ethnic differences in persistence and cessation. *Violence and Victims, 16,* 479–490.

Jakinski, J. (2001b). Pregnancy and violence against women: An analysis of longitudinal data. *Journal of Interpersonal Violence, 16,* 712–733.

Jasinski, J. (2003). Police involvement in the incidents of physical assault: Analysis of the redesigned national crime victimization survey. *Journal of Family Violence, 18,* 143–150.

Jskinski, J. (2004). Pregnancy and domestic violence: A review of the literature. *Trauma, Violence, & Abuse, 5,* 47–64.

Jasinski, J., & Mustaine, E. (2001). Police response to physical assault and stalking victimization: A comparison of influential factors. *American Journal of Criminal Justice, 26,* 23–41.

Jason, L., Taylor, R., Kennedy, C., Jordan, K., Song, S., Johnson, D., & Torres, S. (2000). Chronic fatigue syndrome: Sociodemographic subtypes in a community-based sample. *Evaluation and the Health Professions, 23,* 243–263.

Jenkins, J., & Zunguze, S. (1998). The relationship of family structure to adolescent drug use, peer affiliation and perception of peer acceptance of drug use. *Adolescence, 33,* 811–813.

John, O., & Srivastava, S. (1999). The Big Five trait taxonomy: History, measurement, and theoretical perspectives. In L. Pervin & O. John (Eds.), *Handbook of personality: Theory and research* (2nd ed., pp. 102–138). New York: Guilford Press.

Johnson, E. (1993). *Risky sexual behaviors among African-Americans.* Westport, CT: Praeger.

Johnson, H. (1996). *Dangerous domains: Violence against women in Canada.* Toronto, Ontario, Canada: Nelson Canada.

Johnson, I. (1990). A loglinear analysis of abused wives' decisions to call the police in domestic-violence disputes. *Journal of Criminal Justice, 18,* 147–159.

Johnson, I. (1992). Economic, situational, and psychological correlates of the decision-making process of battered women. *Families in Society: The Journal of Contemporary Human Services, 73,* 168–177.

Johnson, I., & Sigler, R. (2000). Forced sexual intercourse among intimates. *Journal of Family Violence, 15,* 95–108.

Johnson, J., Spitzer, R., Williams, J., Kroenke, K., Linzer, M., Brody, D., et al. (1995). Psychiatric comorbidity, health status, and functional impairment associated with alcohol abuse and dependence in primary care patients: Findings of the PRIME MD-1000 study. *Journal of Consulting and Clinical Psychology, 63,* 133–140.

Johnson, J., Wiechelt, S., Ahmed, A., & Schwartz, R. (2003). Outcomes for substance user treatment in women: Results from the Baltimore Drug and Alcohol Treatment Outcomes Study. *Substance Use and Misuse, 38,* 1807–1829.

Johnson, R., Hoffman, J., & Gerstein, D. (1996). *The relationship between family structure and adolescent substance use.* Washington, DC: Substance Abuse and Mental Health Services, Department of Health and Human Services.

Jones, D., & Houts, R. (1990). Parental drinking, parent–child communication, and social skills in young adults. *Journal of Studies on Alcohol, 53,* 48–56.

Jones, L., Hughes, M., & Unterstaller, U. (2001). Post-traumatic stress disorder (PTSD) in victims of domestic violence: A review of the research. *Trauma, Violence, & Abuse, 2,* 99–119.

Jones-Webb, R., Toomey, T., Short, B., Murray, D., Wagenaar, A., & Wolfson, M. (1997). Relationship among alcohol availability, drinking location, alcohol consumption, and drinking problems in adolescents. *Substance Use and Misuse, 32,* 1261–1285.

Jordan, C., Logan, T., Walker, R., & Nigoff, A. (2003). Stalking: An examination of the criminal justice response. *Journal of Interpersonal Violence, 18,* 148–165.

Jordan, C., Nietzel, M., Walker, R., & Logan, T. (2004). *Intimate partner violence: A clinical training guide for mental health professionals.* New York: Springer Publishing Company.

Jordan, C., & Walker, R. (1994). Guidelines for handling domestic violence cases in community mental health centers. *Hospital and Community Psychiatry, 45,* 147–151.

Joseph, J. (1997). Woman battering: A comparative analysis of Black and White women. In G. Kaufman Kantor & J. Jasinski (Eds.), *Out of the darkness: Contemporary perspectives on family violence* (pp. 161–169). Thousand Oaks, CA: Sage.

Josephs, R., Markus, H., & Tafarodi, R. (1992). Gender and self-esteem. *Journal of Personality and Social Psychology, 63,* 391–402.

Jouriles, E., Norwood, W., McDonald, R., & Peters, B. (2001). Domestic violence and child adjustment. In J. Grych & F. Fincham (Eds.), *Interparental conflict and child development* (pp. 315–336). New York: Cambridge University Press.

Jouriles, E., Norwood, W., McDonald, R., Vincent, J., & Mahony, A. (1996). Physical violence and other forms of marital aggression: Links with children's behavior problems. *Journal of Family Psychology, 10,* 223–234.

Judge, T., Erez, A., Bono, J., & Thoresen, C. (2002). Are measures of self-esteem, neuroticism, locus of control, and generalized self-efficacy indicators of a common core construct? *Journal of Personality and Social Psychology, 83,* 693–710.

Kadushin, C., Reber, E., Saxe, L., & Livert, D. (1998). The substance use system: Social and neighborhood environments associated with substance use and misuse. *Substance Use and Misuse, 33,* 1681–1710.

Kahn, A., Jackson, J., Kully, C., Badger, K., & Halvorsen, J. (2003). Calling it rape: Differences in experiences of women who do or do not label their sexual assault as rape. *Psychology of Women Quarterly, 27,* 233–242.

Kajimura, N., Nishikawa, M., Uchiyama, M., Kato, M., Watanabe, T., Nakajima, T., et al. (2004). Deactivation by benzodiazepine of the basal forebrain and amygdale in normal humans during sleep: A placebo-controlled [^{15}o]H$_2$O PET study. *American Journal of Psychiatry, 161,* 748–751.

Kalmijn, M. (1991a). Shifting boundaries: Trends in religious and educational homogamy. *American Sociological Reviews, 56,* 786–800.

Kalmijn, M. (1991b). Status homogamy in the United States. *American Journal of Sociology, 97,* 496–523.

Kalmijn, M., & Flap, H. (2001). Assortative meeting and mating: Unintended consequences of organized settings for partner choices. *Social Forces, 79,* 1289–1313.

Kamarck, T., Shiffman, S., Smithline, S., Goddie, J., Paty, J., Gnys, M., & Jong, J. (1998). Effects of task strain, social conflict, and emotional activation on ambulatory cardiovascular activity: Daily life consequences of recurring stress in a multiethnic adult sample. *Health Psychology, 17,* 17–29.

Kamphuis, J., & Emmelkamp, P. (2005). 20 years of research into violence and trauma: Past and future developments. *Journal of Interpersonal Violence, 20,* 167–174.

Kandel, D. (1995). Ethnic difference in drug use. In G. Botyin, S. Schinke, & M. Orlandi (Eds.), *Drug abuse prevention with multiethnic youth* (pp. 81–104). Thousand Oaks, CA: Sage.

Kandel, D. (1996). The parental and peer contexts of adolescent deviance: An algebra of interpersonal influences. *Journal of Drug Issues, 26,* 289–315.

Kane, R. (1999). Patterns of arrest in domestic violence encounters: Identifying a police decision-making model. *Journal of Criminal Justice, 27,* 65–79.

Kane, R. (2000). Police responses to restraining orders in domestic violence incidents: Identifying the custody-threshold thesis. *Criminal Justice and Behavior, 27,* 561–580.

Kaplan, J., & Bennett, T. (2003). Use of race and ethnicity in biomedical publication. *Journal of the American Medical Association, 289,* 2709–2716.

Karkowski, L., Prescott, C., & Kendler, K. (2000). Multivariate assessment of factors influencing illicit substance use in twins from female–female pairs. *American Journal of Medical Genetics and Neuropsychiatric Genetics, 96,* 665–670.

Kasturirangan, A., Krishnan, S., & Riger, S. (2004). The impact of culture and minority status on women's experience of domestic violence. *Trauma, Violence, & Abuse, 5,* 318–332.

Katz, J., Arias, I., Beach, S., Brody, G., & Roman, P. (1995). Excuses, excuses: Accounting for the effects of partner violence on marital satisfaction and stability. *Violence and Victims, 10,* 315–326.

Katz, L., Kling, J., & Liebman, J. (2001). Moving to opportunity in Boston: Early results of a randomized mobility experiment. *Quarterly Journal of Economics, 116,* 607–654.

Kauffman, S. (1993). *The origins of order: Self-organization and selection in evolution.* New York: Oxford University Press.

Kaufman Kantor, G., Jasinski, J., & Aldarondo, E. (1994). Sociocultural status and incidence of marital violence in Hispanic families. *Violence and Victims, 9,* 207–222.

Kaukinen, C. (2002). The help-seeking decisions of violent crime victims: An examination of the direct and conditional effects of gender and victim–offender relationship. *Journal of Interpersonal Violence, 17,* 432–456.

Kawachi, I., & Berkman, L. (2001). Social ties and mental health. *Journal of Urban Health, 78,* 458–467.

Kaye, W., Bulik, C., Thornton, L., Barbarich, N., & Masters, K. (2004). Comorbidity of anxiety disorders with anorexia and bulimia nervosa. *American Journal of Psychiatry, 161,* 2215–2221.

Kaysen, K., Resick, P., & Wise, D. (2003). Living in danger: The impact of chronic traumatization and the traumatic context on posttraumatic stress disorder. *Trauma, Violence, & Abuse, 4,* 247–264.

Kearney, M. (2001). Enduring love: A grounded formal theory of women's experience of domestic violence. *Research in Nursing and Health, 24,* 270–282.

Keilitz, S. (1994). Civil protection orders: A viable justice system tool for deterring domestic violence. *Violence and Victims, 9,* 79–84.

Keilitz, S., Davis, C., Efkeman, H., Flango, C., & Hannaford, P. (1998). *Civil protection orders: Victims' views on effectiveness.* Washington, DC: U.S. Department of Justice.

Keilitz, S., Hannaford, P., & Efkeman, H. (1997). *Civil protection orders: The benefits and limitations for victims of domestic violence* (Publication No. R-201). Williamsburg, VA: National Center for State Courts Research.

Kellett, S. (1993). *In the wake of chaos*. Chicago: University of Chicago Press.

Kelley, B., Thornberry, T., & Smith, C. (1997). *In the wake of childhood maltreatment* (NCJ 165257). Washington, DC: U.S. Department of Justice, Office of Justice Programs, Office of Juvenile Justice and Delinquency Prevention.

Kelso, J. (1995). *Dynamic patterns: The self-organization of brain and behavior*. Cambridge, MA: MIT Press.

Kelso, J. (2000). Mood disorders: Genetics. In B. Sadock & V. Sadock (Eds.), *Kaplan and Sadock's comprehensive textbook of psychiatry* (7th ed., pp. 1457–1463). Philadelphia: Lippincott Williams & Wilkins.

Kemp, K., Green, B., Hovanitz, C., & Rawlings, E. (1995). Incidence and correlates of posttraumatic stress disorder in battered women. *Journal of Interpersonal Violence, 10,* 43–55.

Kems, R., & Haythomthwaite, J. (1988). Depression among chronic pain patients: Cognitive–behavioral analysis and effect on rehabilitation outcome. *Journal of Consulting and Clinical Psychology, 8,* 101–113.

Kendall, P., Holmbeck, G., & Verdun, T. (2004). Methodology, design, and evaluation in psychotherapy research. In M. Lambert (Ed.), *Bergin and Garfield's handbook of psychotherapy and behavior change* (5th ed., pp. 16–43) New York: Wiley.

Kendall-Tackett, K. (2000). Physiological correlates of childhood abuse: Chronic hyper arousal in PTSD, depression, and irritable bowel syndrome. *Child Abuse and Neglect, 24,* 715–729.

Kendall-Tackett, K. (2002). The health effects of childhood abuse: Four pathways by which abuse can influence health. *Child Abuse and Neglect, 26,* 715–729.

Kendall-Tackett, K., Marshall, R., & Ness, K. (2003). Chronic pain syndromes and violence against women. *Women and Therapy, 26,* 45–56.

Kendler, K. (1996). Major depression and generalized anxiety disorder: Same genes, (partly) different environments—Revisited. *British Journal of Psychiatry, 30,* 68–75

Kendler, K., Bulik, C., Siberg, J., Hettema, J., Myers, J., & Prescott, C. (2000). Childhood sexual abuse and adult psychiatric and substance use disorders in women. *Archives of General Psychiatry, 57,* 953–959.

Kendler, K., Gardner, C., & Prescott, C. (2002). Toward a comprehensive developmental model for major depression in women. *American Journal of Psychiatry, 159,* 1133–1145.

Kendler, K., Heath, A., Martin, N., & Eaves, L. (1987). Symptoms of anxiety and symptoms of depression: Same genes, different environments? *Archives of General Psychiatry, 44,* 451–455.

Kendler, K., Jacobson, K., Prescott, C., & Neale, M. (2003). Specificity of genetic and environmental risk factors for use and abuse/dependence of cannabis, cocaine, hallucinogens, sedatives, stimulants, and opiates in male twins. *American Journal of Psychiatry, 160,* 687–695.

Kendler, K., Karkowski, L., & Prescott, C. (1999). Causal relationship between stressful life events and the onset of major depression. *American Journal of Psychiatry, 156,* 837–841.

Kendler, K., Kessler, R., Neale, M., Heath, A., & Eaves, L. (1993). The prediction of major depression in women: Toward an integrated etiologic model. *American Journal of Psychiatry, 150,* 1139–1148.

Kendler, K., Kessler, R., Walters, E., MacLean, C., Neale, M., Heath, A., & Eaves, L. (1995). Stressful life events, genetic liability, and onset of an episode of major depression in women. *American Journal of Psychiatry, 152,* 833–842.

Kendler, K., Kuhn, J., & Prescott, C. (2004). The interrelationship of neuroticism, sex, and stressful life events in the prediction of episodes of major depression. *American Journal of Psychiatry, 161,* 631–636.

Kendler, K., MacLean, C., Neale, M., Kessler, R., Heath, A., & Eaves, L. (1991). The genetic epidemiology of bulimia nervosa. *American Journal of Psychiatry, 148,* 1627–1637.

Kendler, K., Neale, M., Kessler, R., Heath, A., & Eaves, L. (1993). Major depression and phobias: The genetic and environmental sources of comorbidity. *Psychological Medicine, 23,* 361–371.

Kendler, K., & Prescott, C. (1999). A population-based twin study of lifetime major depression in men and women. *Archives of General Psychiatry, 56,* 39–44.

Kendler, K., Thornton, L., & Gardner, C. (2000). Stressful life events and previous episodes in the etiology of major depression in women: An evaluation of the "kindling" hypothesis. *American Journal of Psychiatry, 157,* 1243–1251.

Kendler, K., Thornton, L., & Gardner, C. (2001). Genetic risk, number of previous depressive episodes, and stressful life events in predicting major depression. *American Journal of Psychiatry, 158,* 582–587.

Kendler, K., Thornton, L., & Prescott, C. (2001). Gender differences in the rates of exposure to stressful life events and sensitivity to their depressogenic effects. *American Journal of Psychiatry, 158,* 587–593.

Kent, A., Waller, G., & Dagnan, D. (1999). A greater role of emotional than physical or sexual abuse in predicting disordered eating attitudes: The role of mediating variables. *International Journal of Eating Disorders, 25,* 159–167.

Kernic, M., Holt, V., Stoner, J., Wolf, M., & Rivara, F. (2003). Resolution of depression among victims of intimate partner violence: Is cessation enough? *Violence and Victims, 18,* 115–129.

Kerstetter, W. (1990). Gateway to justice: Police and prosecutorial response to sexual assaults against women. *Journal of Criminal Law and Criminology, 81,* 267–313.

Kessler, R. (1997). The effects of stressful life events on depression. *Annual Review of Psychology, 48,* 191–214.

Kessler, R., Berglund, P., Demler, O., Jin, R., Koretz, D., Merikangas, K., et al. (2003). The epidemiology of major depressive disorder: Results from the National Comorbidity Survey. *Journal of the American Medical Association, 289,* 3095–3105.

Kessler, R., Crum, R., & Warner, L. (1997). Lifetime co-occurrence of alcohol abuse and dependence with other psychiatric disorders in the National Comorbidity Survey. *Archives of General Psychiatry, 54,* 313–321.

Kessler, R., Crum, R., Warner, L., Nelson, C., Schulenberg, J., & Anthony, J. (1997). Lifetime co-occurrence of *DSM–III–R* alcohol abuse and dependence with other psychiatric disorders in the national comorbidity survey. *Archives of General Psychiatry, 52,* 313–321.

Kessler, R., McGonagle, K., Swartz, M., Blazer, D., & Nelson, C. (1993). Sex and depression in the National Comorbidity Survey: I. Lifetime prevalence, chronicity and recurrence. *Journal of Affective Disorders, 29,* 85–96.

Kessler, R., McGonagle, K., Zhao, S., Nelson, C., Hughes, M., Eshleman, S., et al. (1994). Lifetime and 12-month prevalence of *DSM–III–R* psychiatric disorders in the United States. *Archive of General Psychiatry, 51,* 8–19.

Kessler, R., & McLeod, J. (1984). Sex differences in the vulnerability to undesirable life events. *American Sociological Review, 49,* 620–631.

Kessler, R., Sonnega, A., Bromet, E., Hughes, M., & Nelson, C. (1995). Posttraumatic stress disorder in the National Comorbidity Survey. *Archives of General Psychiatry, 52,* 1048–1060.

Khantzian, E. (1990). Self-regulation and self-medication factors in alcoholism and the addictions: Similarities and differences. *Recent Developments in Alcoholism, 8,* 255–271.

Khantzian, E. (1997). The self-medication hypothesis of substance use disorders: A reconsideration and recent applications. *Harvard Review of Psychiatry, 4,* 231–244.

Kiecolt-Glaser, J., & Newton, T. (2001). Marriage and health: His and hers. *Psychological Bulletin, 127,* 472–503.

Killen, M., & Turiel, E. (1998). Adolescents' and young adults' evaluations of helping and sacrificing for others. *Journal of Research on Adolescence, 8,* 355–375.

Kilpatrick, D., Acierno, R., Resnick, H., Saunders, B., & Best, C. (1997). A 2-year longitudinal analysis of the relationship between violent assault and substance use in women. *Journal of Consulting and Clinical Psychology, 65,* 834–847.

Kilpatrick, D., Acierno, R., Saunders, B., Resnick, H., & Best, C. (2000). Risk factors for adolescent substance abuse and dependence: Data from a national sample. *Journal of Consulting and Clinical Psychology, 68,* 19–30.

Kilpatrick, D., Edmunds, C., & Seymour, A. (1992). *Rape in America: A report to the nation.* Arlington, VA: National Crime Victims Center.

Kilpatrick, D., Resnick, H., Saunders, B., & Best, C. (1998a). Rape, other violence against women, and posttraumatic stress disorder. In B. Dohrenwend (Ed.), *Adversity, stress, and psychopathology* (pp. 161–176). New York: Oxford University Press.

Kilpatrick, D., Resnick, H., Saunders, B., & Best, C. (1998b). Victimization, posttraumatic stress disorder, and substance use and abuse among women. In C. Wetherington & A. Roman (Eds.), *Drug addiction research and the health of women* (pp. 285–307). Rockville, MD: National Institutes of Health, U.S. Department of Health and Human Services.

Kilpatrick, D., Saunders, B., Veronen, L., Best, C., & Von, J. (1987). Criminal victimization: Lifetime prevalence, reporting to the police, and psychological impact. *Crime and Delinquency, 334,* 479–489.

Kilts, C. (2004). Neurobiology of substance abuse disorders. In A. Schatzberg & C. Nemeroff (Eds.), *The American Psychiatric Publishing textbook of psychopharmacology* (3rd ed., pp. 809–818). Washington, DC: American Psychiatric Publishing.

Kimerling, R., & Calhoun, K. (1994). Somatic symptoms, social support and treatment seeking among sexual assault victims. *Journal of Consulting and Clinical Psychology, 62,* 333–340.

Kingsnorth, R., MacIntosh, R., Berdahl, T., Blades, C., & Rossi, S. (2001). Domestic violence: The role of interracial/ethnic dyads in criminal court processing. *Journal of Contemporary Criminal Justice, 17,* 123–141.

Kingsnorth, R., MacIntosh, R., & Sutherland, S. (2002). Criminal charge or probation violation? Prosecutorial discretion and implications for research in criminal court processing. *Criminology, 40,* 553–577.

Kingsnorth, R., MacIntosh, R., & Wentworth, J. (1999). Sexual assault: The role of prior relationship and victim characteristics in case processing. *Justice Quarterly, 16,* 275–302.

Kinzl, J., Traweger, C., Guenther, V., & Biebl, W. (1994). Family background and sexual abuse associated with eating disorders. *American Journal of Psychiatry, 151,* 1127–1131.

Kitson, G. (1992). *Portrait of divorce: Adjustment to marital breakdown.* New York: Guilford Press.

Kitzmann, K., Gaylord, N., Holt, A., & Kenny, E. (2003). Child witnesses to domestic violence: A meta-analytic review. *Journal of Consulting and Clinical Psychology, 71,* 339–352.

Klein, A. (1996). Re-abuse in a population of court-restrained male batterers: Why restraining orders don't work. In E. Buzawa & C. Buzawa (Eds.), *Do arrests and restraining orders work?* (pp. 192–213). Thousand Oaks, CA: Sage.

Klein, C., & Helweg-Larsen, M. (2002). Perceived control and the optimistic bias: A meta-analytic review. *Psychology and Health, 17,* 437–446.

Klein, E., Campbell, J., Soler, J., & Ghez, M. (1997). *Ending domestic violence.* Thousand Oaks, CA: Sage.

Klein, H., & Pittman, D. (1989). Alcohol consumption and the perceived situational appropriateness of consuming different types of alcoholic beverages. *Alcohol and Alcoholism, 24,* 479–488.

Klerman, G., Leon, A., Wickramaratne, P., Warshaw, M., Mueller, T., Weissman, M., & Akiskal, H. (1996). The role of drug and alcohol abuse in recent increases in depression in the US. *Psychological Medicine, 26,* 343–351.

Knoester, C., & Booth, A. (2000). Barriers to divorce. *Journal of Family Issues, 21,* 78–99.

Kocot, T., & Goodman, L. (2003). The roles of coping and social support in battered women's mental health. *Violence Against Women, 9,* 323–346.

Koelega, H. (1995). Alcohol and vigilance performance: A review. *Psychopharmacology, 118,* 233–249.

Koerner, K., & Linehan, M. (2000). Research on dialectical behavior therapy for patients with borderline personality disorder. *Psychiatric Clinics of North America, 23,* 151–167.

Konradi, A. (1996a). Preparing to testify: Rape survivors negotiating the criminal justice process. *Gender and Society, 10,* 404–432.

Konradi, A. (1996b). Understanding rape survivors' preparations for court: Accounting for the influence of legal knowledge, cultural stereotypes, personal efficacy, and prosecutor contact. *Violence Against Women, 2,* 25–62.

Konradi, A. (1999). "I don't have to be afraid of you": Rape survivors' emotion management in court. *Symbolic Interaction, 22,* 45–77.

Konradi, A., & Burger, T. (2000). Having the last word: An examination of rape survivors' participation in sentencing. *Violence Against Women, 6,* 351–395.

Kornhauser, R. (1978). *Social sources of delinquency.* Chicago: University of Chicago Press.

Kornstein, S. (1997). Gender differences in depression: Implications for treatment. *Journal of Clinical Psychiatry, 58*(Suppl. 15), 12–18.

Kornstein, S., Schatzberg, A., Thase, M., Yonkers, K., McCullough, J., Keitner, G., et al. (2000). Gender differences in treatment response to sertraline versus imipramine in chronic depression. *American Journal of Psychiatry, 157,* 1445–1452.

Koss, M., Bailey, J., Yuan, N., Herrera, V., & Lichter, E. (2003). Depression and PTSD in survivors of male violence: Research and training initiatives to facilitate recovery. *Psychology of Women Quarterly, 27,* 130–142.

Koss, M., Dinero, T., Seibel, C., Cox, S. (1988). Stranger and acquaintance rape: Are there differences in the victim's experience? *Psychology of Women Quarterly, 12,* 1–24.

Koss, M., Figueredo, A., Bell, I., Tharan, M., & Tromp, S. (1996). Traumatic memory characteristics: A cross-validated mediational model of response to rape among employed women. *Journal of Abnormal Psychology, 105,* 421–432.

Koss, M., Figueredo, A., & Prince, R. (2002). Cognitive mediation of rape's mental, physical, and social health impact: Tests of four models in cross-sectional data. *Journal of Consulting and Clinical Psychology, 70,* 926–941.

Koss, M., Woodruff, W., & Koss, P. (1990). Relation of criminal victimization to health perceptions among women medical patients. *Journal of Consulting and Clinical Psychology, 58,* 147–152.

Kosterman, R., Hawkins, D., Guo, J., Catalano, R., & Abbott, R. (2000). The dynamics of alcohol and marijuana initiation: Patterns and predictors of first use in adolescence. *American Journal of Public Health, 90,* 360–366.

Kovac, S., Klapow, J., Kroenke, K., Spitzer, R., & Williams, J. (2003). Differing symptoms of abused versus nonabused women in obstetric-gynecology settings. *American Journal of Obstetric Gynecology, 188,* 707–713.

Kraemer, G. (1992). A psychobiological theory of attachment. *Behavioral and Brain Sciences, 15,* 493–541.

Krakow, B., Germain, A., Tandberg, D., Koss, M., Schrader, R., Hollifield, M., et al. (2000). Sleep breathing and sleep movement disorders masquerading as insomnia in sexual-assault survivors. *Comprehensive Psychiatry, 41,* 49–56.

Krakow, B., Hollifield, M., Johnston, L., Koss, M., Schrader, R., Warner, T., et al. (2001). Imagery rehearsal therapy for chronic nightmares in sexual assault survivors with posttraumatic stress disorder. *Journal of the American Medical Association, 286,* 537–545.

Krane, S., & Holick, M. (1998). Metabolic bone disease. In A. Fauci, E. Brunwald, K. Isselbacher, J. Wilson, J. Martin, D. Kasper, et al. (Eds.), *Harrison's principles of internal medicine* (14th ed., pp. 2247–2259). New York: McGraw-Hill.

Krause, E., Robins, C., & Lynch, T. (2000). A mediational model related sociotropy, ambivalence over emotional expression and eating disorder symptoms. *Psychology of Women Quarterly, 24,* 328–335.

Kreek, M. (2001). Drug addictions: Molecular and cellular endpoints. In V. Quiñones-Jenab (Ed.), *Annals of the New York Academy of Sciences: Vol. 937. The biological basis of cocaine addiction* (pp. 27–49). New York: New York Academy of Sciences.

Krieger, N., Sidney, S., & Coakley, E. (1999). Racial discrimination and skin color in the CARDIA study: Implications for public health research. *American Journal of Public Health, 88,* 1308–1313.

Krikorian, R., & Layton, B. (1998). Implicit memory in posttraumatic stress disorder with amnesia for the traumatic event. *Journal of Neuropsychiatry, 10,* 359–362.

Kripke, D., Garfinkel, L., Wingard, D., Klauber, M., & Marler, M. (2002). Mortality associated with sleep duration and insomnia. *Archives of General Psychiatry, 59,* 131–136.

Krishnan, S., Hilbert, J., & VanLeeuwen, D. (2001). Domestic violence and help-seeking behaviors among rural women. *Family and Community Health, 24,* 28–38.

Krishnan, S., Hilbert, J., VanLeeuwen, D., & Kolia, R. (1997). Documenting domestic violence among ethnically diverse populations: Results from a preliminary study. *Family Community Health, 20,* 32–48.

Krivo, L., & Peterson, R. (1996). Extremely disadvantaged neighborhoods and urban crime. *Social Forces, 75,* 619–650.

Krueger, R. Moffitt, T., Caspi, A., Bleske, A., & Silva, P. (1998). Assortative mating for antisocial behavior: Developmental and methodological implications. *Behavior Genetics, 28,* 173–186.

Kruttschnitt, C., McLaughlin, B., & Petrie, C. (Eds.). (2004). *Advancing the federal research agenda on violence against women.* Washington, DC: National Academies Press.

Kubany, E., Hill, E., & Owens, J. (2003). Cognitive trauma therapy for formerly battered women with PTSD (CTT-BW): Preliminary findings. *Journal of Traumatic Stress, 16,* 81–91.

Kuehner, C. (2003). Gender differences in unipolar depression: An update of epidemiological findings and possible explanations. *Acta Psychiatrica Scandinavica, 108,* 163–174.

Kurt, J. (1995). Stalking as a variant of domestic violence. *Bulletin of the American Academy of Psychiatry and the Law, 23,* 219–230.

Kurz, D. (1996). Separation, divorce, and woman abuse. *Violence Against Women, 2,* 63–81.

Kushner, M., Sher, K., & Beitman, B. (1990). The relation between alcohol problems and the anxiety disorders. *American Journal of Psychiatry, 147,* 685–695.

Kuyken, W., & Brewin, C. (1995). Autobiographical memory functioning in depression and reports of early abuse. *Journal of Abnormal Psychology, 104,* 585–591.

Kyriacou, D., Anglin, D., Taliaferro, E., Stone, S., Tubb, T., Linden, J., et al. (1999). Risk factors for injury to women from domestic violence. *New England Journal of Medicine, 341,* 1892–1898.

LaBar, K., & LeDoux, J. (2001) Coping with danger: The neural basis of defensive behavior and fearful feelings. In B. McEwen & H. Goodman (Eds.), *Handbook of physiology: A critical, comprehensive presentation of physiological knowledge and concepts* (pp. 139–178). New York: Oxford University Press.

Labouvie, E. (1996). Maturing out of substance use: Selection and self-correction. *Journal of Drug Issues, 26,* 457–476.

LaForge, K., & Kreek, M. (1999). Genetic contributions to protection from, or vulnerability to, addictive diseases. In L. Harris (Ed.), *Problems of drug dependence, 1999: Proceedings of the 61st annual scientific meeting, the College on Problems of Drug Dependence* (pp. 47–48). Washington, DC: National Institute on Drug Abuse, U.S. Department of Health and Human Services.

Lair, G. (1996). *Counseling the terminally ill: Sharing the journey.* Philadelphia: Taylor & Francis.

Lambert, M. (Ed.). (2004). *Bergin and Garfield's handbook of psychotherapy and behavior change* (5th ed.). New York: Wiley.

Lambert, M., & Ogles, B. (2004). The efficacy and effectiveness of psychotherapy. In M. Lambert (Ed.), *Bergin and Garfield's handbook of psychotherapy and behavior change* (5th ed., pp. 139–193). New York: Wiley.

Lambert, S., Brown, T., Phillips, C., & Ialongo, N. (2004). The relationship between perceptions of neighborhood characteristics and substance use among urban African American adolescents. *American Journal of Community Psychology, 34,* 205–218.

Lang, A., Rodgers, C., Laffaye, C., Satz, L., Dresselhaus, T., & Stein, M. (2003). Sexual trauma, posttraumatic stress disorder, and health behavior. *Sexual Trauma, 28,* 150–158.

Langan, P., & Levin, D. (2002). *Recidivism of prisoners released in 1994* (NCJ 193427). Washington, DC: U.S. Government Printing Office.

Langstrom, N. (2002). Long-term follow-up of criminal recidivism in young sex offenders: Temporal patterns and risk factors. *Psychology, Crime and Law, 8,* 41–58.

Larimer, M., Anderson, B., Baer, J., & Marlatt, G. (2000). An individual in context: Predictors of alcohol use and drinking problems among Greek and residence hall students. *Journal of Substance Abuse, 11,* 53–68.

Larimer, M., Lydum, A., Anderson, B., & Turner, A. (1999). Male and female recipients of unwanted sexual contact in a college student sample: Prevalence rates, alcohol use and depression symptoms. *Sex Roles, 40,* 295–308.

Latimer, W., Winters, K., Stinchfield, R., & Traver, R. (2000). Demographic, individual, and interpersonal predictors of adolescent alcohol and marijuana use following treatment. *Psychology of Addictive Behaviors, 14,* 162–173.

Laumakis, M., Margolin, G., & John, R. (1998). The emotional, cognitive, and coping responses of preadolescent children to different dimensions of marital conflict. In G. Holden, R. Geffner, & E. Jouriles (Eds.), *Children exposed to marital violence: Theory, research, and applied issues* (pp. 257–288). Washington, DC: American Psychological Association.

Laumann, E., Ellingson, S., Mahay, J., Paik, A., & Youm, Y. (Eds.). (2004). *The sexual organization of the city.* Chicago: University of Chicago Press.

Lauritsen, J., Laub, J., & Sampson, R. (1992). Conventional and delinquent activities: Implications for the prevention of violent victimization among adolescents. *Violence and Victims, 7,* 91–108.

Lauritsen, J., Sampson, R., & Laub, J. (1991). The link between offending and victimization among adolescents. *Criminology, 29,* 265–292.

Lauritsen, J., & White, N. (2001). Putting violence in its place: The influence of race, ethnicity, gender, and place on the risk for violence. *Criminology and Public Policy, 1,* 37–59.

LaVeist, T. (2000). On the study of race, racism, and health: A shift from description to explanation. *International Journal of Health Services, 30,* 217–219.

Laws, A. (1998). Sexual abuse. In E. Blechman & K. Brownell (Eds.), *Behavioral medicine and women: A comprehensive textbook* (pp. 470–474). New York: Guilford Press.

Lazarus, R. (1991). *Emotion and adaptation.* Oxford, England: Oxford University Press.

Lazarus, R. (1999). *Stress and emotion: A new synthesis.* New York: Springer Publishing Company.

Lazarus, R. (2001). Relational meaning and discrete emotions. In K. Scherer, A. Schorr, & T. Johnstone (Eds.), *Appraisal processes in emotion: Theory, methods, research* (pp. 37–67). New York: Oxford University Press.

Lazarus, R., & Folkman, S. (1984). *Stress, appraisal, and coping.* New York: Springer Publishing Company.

Leadley, K., Clark, C., & Caetano, R. (2000). Couples' drinking patterns, intimate partner violence, and alcohol-related partnership problems. *Journal of Substance Abuse, 11,* 253–263.

Leary, M. (1999). Making sense of self-esteem. *Current Directions in Psychological Science, 8,* 32–35.

Leary, M. (2003). The self and emotion: The role of self-reflection in the generation and regulation of affective experience. In R. Davidson, K. Scherer, & H. Goldsmith (Eds.), *Handbook of affective sciences* (pp 773–786). New York: Oxford University Press.

LeDoux, J. (2000). The amygdala and emotion: A view through fear. In J. P. Aggelton (Ed.), *The amygdala: A functional analysis* (2nd ed., pp. 289–310). New York: Oxford University Press.

Lee, C., Gavriel, H., Drummond, P., Richards, J., & Greenwald, R. (2002). Treatment of PTSD: Stress inoculation training with prolonged exposure compared to EMDR. *Journal of Clinical Psychology, 58,* 1071–1089.

Lee, M. (2000). Community cohesion and violent predatory victimization: A theoretical extension and cross-national test of opportunity theory. *Social Forces, 79,* 683–688.

Lee, R., & Robbins, S. (2000). Understanding social connectedness in college women and men. *Journal of Counseling & Development, 78,* 484–491.

Leeman, R., & Wapner, S. (2001). Some factors involved in alcohol consumption of first-year undergraduates. *Journal of Drug Education, 31,* 249–262.

Lefley, H., Scott, C., Llabre, M., & Hicks, D. (1993). Cultural beliefs about rape and victims' response in three ethnic groups. *American Journal of Orthopsychiatry, 63,* 623–632.

Leigh, B. (1990). The relationship of sex-related alcohol expectancies to alcohol consumption and sexual behavior. *British Journal of Addiction, 85,* 919–928.

Lemon, N. (2001). *Domestic violence law.* St. Paul, MN: West Group.

Leonard, K. (1999). Alcohol use and husband marital aggression among newlywed couples. In X. Arriaga & S. Oskamp (Eds.), *Violence in intimate relationships* (pp. 113–135). Thousand Oaks, CA: Sage.

Leonard, K., & Das Eiden, R. (1999). Husband's and wife's drinking: Unilateral or bilateral influences among newlyweds in a general population sample. *Journal of Studies on Alcohol, 13,* 130–138.

Leonard, K., Kearns, J., & Mudar, P. (2000). Peer networks among heavy, regular and infrequent drinkers prior to marriage. *Journal of Studies on Alcohol, 61,* 669–676.

Leonard, K., & Mudar, P. (2000). Alcohol use in the year before marriage: Alcohol expectancies and peer drinking as proximal influences on husband and wife alcohol involvement. *Alcoholism: Clinical and Experimental Research, 24,* 1666–1679.

Leonard, K., & Mudar, P. (2003). Peer and partner drinking and the transition to marriage: A longitudinal examination of selection and influence processes. *Psychology of Addictive Behavior, 17,* 115–125.

Leonard, K., & Mudar, P. (2004). Husbands' influence on wives' drinking: Testing a relationship motivation model in the early years of marriage. *Psychology of Addictive Behavior, 18,* 340–349.

Leonard, K., & Quigley, B. (1999). Drinking and marital aggression in newlyweds: An event-based analysis of drinking and the occurrence of husband marital aggression. *Journal of Studies on Alcohol, 60,* 537–545.

Lerner, C., & Kennedy, L. (2000). Stay–leave decision making in battered women: Trauma, coping, and self-efficacy. *Cognitive Therapy and Research, 24,* 215–232.

Lerner, M. (1980). *The belief in a just world.* New York: Plenum Press.

Leserman, J., Li, Z., Drossman, D., & Hu, J. (1998). Selected symptoms associated with sexual and physical abuse history among female patients with gastrointestinal disorders: The impact on subsequent health care visits. *Psychological Medicine, 28,* 417–425.

Leserman, J., Li, Z., Drossman, D., Toomey, T., Nachman, G., & Glogau, L. (1997). Impact of sexual and physical abuse dimensions on health status: Development of an abuse severity index. *Psychosomatic Medicine, 59,* 152–160.

Letourneau, E., Holmes, M., & Chasendunn-Roark, J. (1999). Gynecologic health consequences to victims of interpersonal violence. *Women's Health Issues, 9,* 115–120.

Levendosky, A., & Graham-Bermann, S. (2001). Parenting in battered women: The effects of domestic violence on women and their children. *Journal of Family Violence, 16,* 171–192.

Leventhal, T., & Brooks-Gunn, J. (2000). The neighborhoods they live in: The effects of neighborhood residence on child and adolescent outcomes. *Psychological Bulletin, 126,* 309–337.

Leventhal, T., & Brooks-Gunn, J. (2003a). Children and youth in neighborhood contexts. *Current Directions in Psychological Science, 12,* 27–31.

Leventhal, T., & Brooks-Gunn, J. (2003b). Moving to opportunity: An experimental study of neighborhood effects on mental health. *American Journal of Public Health, 93,* 1576–1582.

Levy, S., Wamboldt, F., & Fiese, B. (1997). Family-of-origin experiences and conflict resolution behaviors of young adult dating couples. *Family Process, 36,* 297–310.

Lewis, M., & Granic, I. (1999). Who put the self in self-organization? A clarification of terms and concepts for developmental psychopathology. *Development and Psychopathology, 11,* 365–374.

Lewis, M., & Rook, K. (1999). Social control in personal relationships: Impact on health behaviors and psychological distress. *Health Psychology, 18,* 63–71.

Li, L., Ford, J., & Moore, D. (2000). An exploratory study of violence, substance abuse, disability, and gender. *Social Behavior and Personality, 28,* 61–72.

Linehan, M. (1993). *Cognitive–behavioral treatment of borderline personality disorder.* New York: Guilford Press.

Linehan, M. (1999). Development, evaluation, and dissemination of effective psychosocial treatments: Levels of disorder, stages of care, and stages of treatment research. In M. Glantz & C. Hartel (Ed.), *Drug abuse: Origins and interventions* (pp. 367–394). Washington, DC: American Psychological Association.

Linehan, M., Armstrong, H., Suarez, A. Allmon, D., & Heard, H. (1991). Cognitive behavioral treatment of chronically parasuicidal borderline patients. *Archives of General Psychiatry, 48,* 1060–1064.

Linehan, M., Dimeff, L., Reynolds, S., Comtois, K., Welch, S., Heagerty, P., & Kivlahan, D. (2002). Dialectical behavior therapy versus comprehensive validation therapy plus 12-step for the treatment of opioid dependent women meeting criteria for borderline personality disorder. *Drug and Alcohol Dependence, 67,* 13–26.

Linehan, M., Heard, H., & Armstrong, H. (1993). Naturalistic follow-up of a behavioral treatment for chronically parasuicidal borderline patients. *Archives of General Psychiatry, 50,* 971–974.

Link, B. G., & Phelan, J. (1995). Social conditions as fundamental causes of disease. *Journal of Health and Social Behavior, Extra Issue,* 80–94.

Link, B. G., Phelan, J., Bresnahan, M., Stueve, A., Moore, R., & Susser, E. (1995). Lifetime and five-year prevalence of homelessness in the United States: New evidence on an old debate. *American Journal of Orthopsychiatry, 65,* 347–354.

Linton, S. (1997). A population-based study of the relationship between sexual abuse and back pain: Establishing a link. *Pain, 73,* 47–53.

Lira, L., Koss, M., & Russo, N. (1999). Mexican American women's definitions of rape and sexual abuse. *Hispanic Journal of Behavioral Sciences, 21,* 236–265.

Livingston, J., & Testa, M. (2000). Qualitative analysis of women's perceived vulnerability to sexual aggression in a hypothetical dating context. *Journal of Social and Personal Relationships, 17,* 729–741.

Locke, L., & Richman, C. (1999). Attitudes toward domestic violence: Race and gender issues. *Sex Roles: A Journal of Research, 40,* 227–239.

Lodico, M., Gruber, E., & DiClemente, R. (1996). Childhood sexual abuse and coercive sex among school-based adolescents in a Midwestern state. *Journal of Adolescent Health, 18,* 211–217.

Loewenstein, G., Weber, E., Hsee, C., & Welch, N. (2001). Risk as feelings. *Psychological Bulletin, 127,* 267–286.

Logan, T., Cole, J., Shannon, L., Medley, K., Rambo, N., Allen, J., et al. (2004, May 14). *Victimization and protective orders among Kentucky women.* Paper presented at the Statewide Coalition on Substance Abuse Meeting, Lexington, KY.

Logan, T., Cole, J., Shannon, L., & Walker, R. (in press). Relationship characteristics and protective orders among a diverse sample of women. *Journal of Family Violence.*

Logan, T., Cole, J., Shannon, L., & Walker, R. (2006). *Partner stalking victimization among women.* New York: Springer Publishing Company.

Logan, T., Evans, L., Stevenson, E., & Jordan, C. (2004). Barriers to services for rural and urban survivors of rape. *Journal of Interpersonal Violence, 20,* 591–616.

Logan, T., Leukefeld, C., & Walker, R. (2000). Stalking as a variant of domestic violence: Implications from young adults. *Violence and Victims, 15,* 91–111.

Logan, T., Nigoff, A., Jordan, C., & Walker, R. (2002). Stalker profiles with and without protective orders: Do protective orders make a difference in reoffending or criminal justice processing? *Violence and Victims, 17,* 541–554.

Logan, T., Shannon, L., & Cole, J. (in press). Stalking victimization in the context of intimate partner violence. *Violence and Victims.*

Logan, T., Shannon, L., & Walker, R. (2005). Protective orders in rural and urban areas: A multiple perspective study. *Violence Against Women, 11,* 876–911.

Logan, T., Stevenson, E., Evans, L., & Leukefeld, C. (2004). Rural and urban women's perceptions of barriers to health, mental health, and criminal justice services: Implications for victim services. *Violence and Victims, 19,* 37–62.

Logan, T., Walker, R., Cole, J., & Leukefeld, C. (2002). Victimization and substance use among women: Contributing factors, interventions, and implications. *Review of General Psychology, 6,* 325–397.

Logan, T., Walker, R., Jordan, C., & Campbell, J. (2004). An integrative review of separation and victimization among women: Consequences and implications. *Violence, Trauma, & Abuse, 5,* 143–193.

Logan, T., Walker, R., & Leukefeld, C. (2001). Urban, urban influenced, and rural differences among domestic violence arrestees in Kentucky. *Journal of Interpersonal Violence, 16,* 266–283.

Loring, M., & Smith, R. (1994). Health care barriers and interventions for battered women. *Public Health Reports, 109,* 328–338.

Lowe, R., Vedhara, K., Bennett, P., Brookes, E., Gale, L., Munnoch, K., et al. (2003). Emotion-related primary and secondary appraisals, adjustment and coping: Associations in women awaiting breast disease diagnosis. *British Journal of Health Psychology, 8,* 377–391.

Lown, E., & Vega, W. (2001). Intimate partner violence and health: Self-assessed health, chronic health, and somatic symptoms among Mexican American women. *Psychosomatic Medicine, 63,* 352–360.

Ludwig, J., Duncan, G., & Hirschfield, P. (2001). Urban poverty and juvenile crime: Evidence from a randomized housing-mobility experiment. *Quarterly Journal of Economics, 116,* 655–679.

Lundy, M., & Grossman, S. (2001). Clinical research and practice with battered women: What we know, what we need to know. *Trauma, Violence, & Abuse, 2,* 120–141.

Lutenbacher, M., Cohen, A., & Mitzel, J. (2003). Do we really help? Perspectives of abused women. *Public Health Nursing, 20,* 56–64.

Luthar, S., & Cicchetti, D. (2000). The construct of resilience: Implications for interventions and social policies. *Development and Psychopathology, 1,* 857–885.

Luthar, S., Cicchetti, D., & Becker, B. (2000). The construct of resilience: A critical evaluation and guidelines for future work. *Child Development, 71,* 543–562.

Lynch, J., Kaplan, G., & Shema, S. (1997). Cumulative impact of sustained economic hardship on physical, cognitive, psychological, and social functioning. *New England Journal of Medicine, 337,* 1889–1895.

Lynch, S., & Graham-Bermann, S. (2000). Woman abuse and self-affirmation. *Violence Against Women, 6,* 178–197.

Lynch, T., Robins, C., Morse, J., & Krause, E. (2001). A mediational model related affect intensity, emotion inhibition, and psychological distress. *Behavior Therapy, 32,* 519–536.

Lynch, W., Roth, M., & Carroll, M. (2002). Biological basis of sex differences in drug abuse: Preclinical and clinical studies. *Psychopharmacology, 164,* 121–137.

Lynn, R., & Friedman, L. (1998). Irritable bowel syndrome. In A. Fauci, E. Braunwald, K. Isselbacher, J. Wilson, J. Martin, D. Kasper, et al. (Eds.), *Harrison's principles of internal medicine* (14th ed., pp. 1646–1648). New York: McGraw-Hill.

Lyon, E. (1997). *Poverty, welfare and battered women: What does the research tell us?* Retrieved January 1, 2004, from http://www.vaw.umn.edu/documents/vawnet/welfare/welfare.html

Maccoby, E. (1990). Gender and relationships: A developmental account. *American Psychologist, 45,* 513–520.

Maccoby, E. (2000). Parenting and its effects on children: On reading and misreading behavior genetics. *Annual Review of Psychology, 51,* 1–27.

MacDonald, K., Zanna, M., & Fong, G. (1995). Decision making in altered states: Effects of alcohol on attitudes toward drinking and driving. *Journal of Personality and Social Psychology, 68,* 973–985.

Maciejewski, P., Prigerson, H., & Mazure, C. (2001). Sex differences in event-related risk for major depression. *Psychological Medicine, 31,* 593–604.

Maher, L. (1995). In the name of love: Women and initiation to illicit drugs. In R. E. Dobash, R. Dobash, & L. Noaks (Eds.), *Gender and crime* (pp. 132–166). Cardiff, Wales: University of Wales Press.

Mahoney, P. (1999). High rape chronicity and low rates of help-seeking among wife rape survivors in a nonclinical sample: Implications for research and practice. *Violence Against Women, 5,* 993–1016.

Maiden, P. (1997). Alcohol dependence and domestic violence: Incidence and treatment implications. *Alcoholism Treatment Quarterly, 15,* 31–50.

Maisto, S., Galizio, M., & Connors, G. (1995). *Drug use and abuse* (2nd ed.). Fort Worth, TX: Harcourt.

Maker, A., & Kemmelmeier, M. (1998). Long-term psychological consequences in women of witnessing parental physical conflict and experiencing abuse in childhood. *Journal of Interpersonal Violence, 13,* 574–590.

Malik, S., Sorenson, S., & Aneshensel, C. (1997). Community and dating violence among adolescents: Perpetration and victimization. *Journal of Adolescent Health, 21,* 291–302.

Malinosky-Rummell, R., & Hansen, D. (1993). Long-term consequences of childhood physical abuse. *Psychological Bulletin, 114,* 68–79.

Malmstrom, M., Sundquist, J., & Johansson, S. (1999). Neighborhood environment and self-reported health status: A multilevel analysis. *American Journal of Public Health, 89,* 1181–1186.

Mancoske, R., Standifer, D., & Cauley, C. (1994). The effectiveness of brief counseling services for battered women. *Research on Social Work Practice, 4,* 53–63.

Mare, R. (1991). Five decades of educational assortative mating. *American Sociological Review, 56,* 15–32.

Margolin, G., & Gordis, E. (2000). The effects of family and community violence on children. *Annual Review of Psychology, 51,* 445–479.

Margolin, G., Oliver, P., & Medina, A. (2001). Conceptual issues in understanding the relation between interparental conflict and child adjustment. In J. Grych & F. Finchman (Eds.), *Interparental conflict and child development* (pp. 9–38). New York: Cambridge University Press.

Marin, B. (1996). Cultural issues in HIV prevention for Latinos: Should we try to change gender roles? In S. Oskamp & S. Thompson (Eds.), *Understanding and preventing HIV risk behavior: Safer sex and drug use* (pp. 157–176). Thousand Oaks, CA: Sage.

Marin, N. (2003). HIV prevention in the Hispanic community: Sex, culture, and empowerment. *Journal of Transcultural Nursing, 14,* 186–192.

Marinelli-Casey, P., Domier, C., & Rawson, R. (2002). The gap between research and practice in substance abuse treatment. *Psychiatric Services, 53,* 984–987.

Marks, N. (1996). Flying solo at midlife: Gender, marital status, and psychological well-being. *Journal of Marriage and the Family, 58,* 917–932.

Marlatt, G., Baer, J., & Larimer, M. (1995). Preventing alcohol abuse in college students: A harm-reduction approach. In G. Boyd, J. Howard, & R. Zucker (Eds.), *Alcohol problems among adolescents: Current directions in prevention research* (pp. 147–172). Hillsdale, NJ: Erlbaum.

Marmot, M., Fuhrer, R., Ettner, S., Marks, N., Bumpass, L., & Ryff, C. (1998). Contribution of psychosocial factors to socioeconomic differences in health. *Milbank Quarterly, 76,* 403–448.

Marmot, M., Ryff, C., Bumpass, L., Shipley, M., & Marks, N. (1997). Social inequalities in health: Next questions and converging evidence. *Social Science and Medicine, 44,* 901–910.

Marsh, J., Cao, D., & D'Aunno, T. (2004). Gender differences in the impact of comprehensive services in substance abuse treatment. *Journal of Substance Abuse Treatment, 27,* 289–300.

Marshall, L. (1999). Effects of men's subtle and overt psychological abuse on low-income women. *Violence and Victims, 14,* 69–88.

Marshall, M., & Chassin, L. (2000). Peer influence on adolescent alcohol use: The moderating role of parental support and discipline. *Applied Developmental Science, 4,* 80–88.

Martin, M. (1997). Double your trouble: Dual arrest in family violence. *Journal of Family Violence, 12,* 139–157.

Martin, P., DiNitto, D., Byington, D., & Maxwell, M. (1998). Organizational and community transformation: The case of a rape crisis center. In M. Odom & J. Clay-Warner (Eds.), *Confronting rape and sexual assault* (pp. 231–246). Wilmington, DE: Scholarly Resources.

Martin, R., Rothrock, N., Leventhal, H., & Leventhal, E. (2003). Common sense models of illness: Implications for symptom perception and health related behavior. In J. Suls & K. Wallston (Eds.), *Social psychological foundations of health and illness* (pp. 199–225). Malden, MA: Blackwell.

Martin, S., Clark, K., Lynch, S., & Lawrence, K. (1999). Violence in the lives of pregnant teenage women: Associations with multiple substance use. *American Journal of Drug Alcohol Abuse, 25,* 425–440.

Martin, S., Kilgallen, B., Dee, D., Dawson, S., & Campbell, J. (1998). Women in prenatal care/ substance abuse treatment program: Links between domestic violence and mental health. *Maternal and Child Health Journal, 2,* 85–94.

Martin, S., Mackie, L., Kupper, L., Buescher, P., & Moracco, K. (2001). Physical abuse of women before, during, and after pregnancy. *Journal of the American Medical Association, 285,* 1581–1584.

Marx, B., Calhoun, K., Wilson, A., & Meyerson, L. (2001). Sexual revictimization prevention: An outcome evaluation. *Journal of Consulting and Clinical Psychology, 69,* 25–32.

Marx, B., Miranda, R., & Meyerson, L. (1999). Cognitive–behavioral treatment for rapists: Can we do better? *Clinical Psychology Review, 19,* 875–894.

Marx, B., Nichols-Anderson, C., Messman-Moore, T., Miranda, R., & Porter, C. (2000). Alcohol consumption, outcome expectancies, and victimization status among female college students. *Journal of Applied Social Psychology, 30,* 1056–1070.

Marx, B., & Sloan, D. (2002). The role of emotion in the psychological functioning of adult survivors of childhood sexual abuse. *Behavior Therapy, 33,* 563–577.

Maser, J., & Cloninger, C. (Eds.). (1990). *Comorbidity of mood and anxiety disorders.* Washington, DC: American Psychiatric Association.

Massart, F., Reginster, J., & Brandi, M. (2001). Genetics of menopause-associated diseases. *Maturitas, 40,* 103–116.

Max, W., Rice, D., Finkelstein, E., Bardwell, R., & Leadbetter, S. (2004). The economic toll of intimate partner violence against women in the United States. *Violence and Victims, 19,* 259–272.

Maxwell, C., Garner, J., & Fagan, J. (2001). *The effects of arrest on intimate partner violence: New evidence from the spouse assault replication program.* Washington, DC: U.S. Department of Justice, National Institute of Justice.

Maxwell, C., Robinson, A., & Post, L. (2003). The impact of race on the adjudication of sexual assault and other violent crimes. *Journal of Criminal Justice, 31*, 523–538.

Mayall, A., & Gold, S. (1995). Definitional issues and mediating variables in the sexual revictimization of women sexually abused as children. *Journal of Interpersonal Violence, 10*, 26–42.

Mayr, S., & Price, J. (1993). Co-dependency and myth. *Feminist Issues, 13*, 81–88.

Mays, V., & Cochran, S. (1988). Issues in the perception of AIDS risk and risk reduction by Black and Hispanic/Latina women. *American Psychologist, 43*, 949–957.

McCabe, S., Gotlib, I., & Martin, R. (2000). Cognitive vulnerability for depression: Deployment of attention as a function of history of depression and current mood state. *Cognitive Therapy and Research, 24*, 427–444.

McCann, U., Mertl, M., Eligulashvili, V., & Ricaurte, G. (1999). Cognitive performance in (±) 3,4-methylenedioxymethamphetamine (MDMA, "ecstasy") users: A controlled study. *Psychopharmacology, 143*, 417–425.

McCaul, M., Svikis, D., & Moore, R. (2001). Predictors of outpatient treatment retention: Patient versus substance use characteristics. *Drug and Alcohol Dependence, 62*, 9–17.

McCauley, J., Kern, D., Kolodner, K., Dill, L., Schroeder, A., DeChant, H., et al. (1995). The "battering syndrome": Prevalence and clinical characteristics of domestic violence in primary care internal medicine practices. *Annals of Internal Medicine, 123*, 737–746.

McCauley, J., Kern, D., Kolodner, K., Dill, L., Schroeder, A., DeChant, H., et al. (1997). Clinical characteristics of women with a history of childhood abuse: Unhealed wounds. *Journal of the American Medical Association, 277*, 1362–1368.

McCloskey, L. (2001). The "Medea complex" among men: The instrumental abuse of children to injure wives. *Violence and Victims, 16*, 19–37.

McCloskey, L., Figueredo, A., & Koss, M. (1995). The effects of systemic family violence on children's mental health. *Child Development, 66*, 1239–1261.

McCormick, J., Maric, A., Seto, M., & Barbaree, H. (1998). Relationship to victim predicts sentence length in sexual assault cases. *Journal of Interpersonal Violence, 13*, 413–420.

McCormick, R., & Smith, M. (1995). Aggression and hostility in substance abusers: The relationship to abuse patterns, coping styles, and relapse triggers. *Addictive Behaviors, 20*, 555–562.

McEwen, B. (2000). Allostasis and allostatic load: Implications for neuropsychopharmacology. *Neuropsychopharmacology, 22*, 108–124.

McEwen, B. (2003). Mood disorders and allostatic load. *Biological Psychiatry, 54*, 200–207.

McEwen, B., & Lasley, E. (2002). *The end of stress as we know it*. Washington, DC: Joseph Henry Press.

McEwen, B., & Sapolsky, R. (1995). Stress and cognitive function. *Current Opinion in Neurobiology, 5*, 205–216.

McFarlane, J., Campbell, J., & Watson, K. (2002). Intimate partner stalking and femicide: Urgent implications for women's safety. *Behavioral Sciences and the Law, 20*, 51–68.

McFarlane, J., Campbell, J., Wilt, S., Sachs, C., Ulrich, Y., & Xu, X. (1999). Stalking and intimate partner femicide. *Homicide Studies, 3*, 300–316.

McFarlane, J., Malecha, A., Gist, J., Watson, K., Batten, E., Hall, I., & Smith, S. (2002). An intervention to increase safety behaviors of abused women. *Nursing Research, 51, 6*, 347–354.

McFarlane, J., Malecha, A., Gist, J., Watson, K., Batten, E., Hall, I., & Smith, S. (2004). Protection orders and intimate partner violence: An 18-month study of 150 Black, Hispanic, and White women. *American Journal of Public Health, 94*, 613–618.

McFarlane, J., Soeken, K., & Wiist, W. (2000). An evaluation of interventions to decrease intimate partner violence victimization to pregnant women. *Public Health Nursing, 17*, 443–451.

McFarlane, J., Willson, P., Lemmey, D., & Malecha, A. (2000). Women filing assault charges on an intimate partner: Criminal justice outcome and future violence experienced. *Violence Against Women, 6*, 396–408.

McGregor, M., Du Mont, J., & Myhr, T. (2002). Sexual assault forensic examination: Is evidence related to successful prosecution? *Annals of Emergency Medicine, 39*, 639–647.

McGregor, M., Le, G., Marion, S., & Wiebe, E. (1999). Examination for sexual assault: Is the documentation of physical injury associated with the laying of charges? A retrospective cohort study. *Canadian Medical Association Journal, 160*, 1565–1569.

McGuire, M., & Troisi, A. (1998). *Darwinian psychiatry*. New York: Oxford University Press.

McKenna, F. (1993). It won't happen to me: Unrealistic optimism or illusion of control? *British Journal of Psychology, 84,* 39–40.

McKnight, L., & Loper, A. (2002). The effect of risk and resilience factors on the prediction of delinquency in adolescent girls. *School Psychology International, 23,* 186–198.

McKnight Investigators. (2003). Risk factors for the onset of eating disorders in adolescent girls: Results of the McKnight Longitudinal Risk Factor Study. *American Journal of Psychiatry, 160,* 248–254.

McLanahan, S., & Booth, K. (1989). Mother-only families: Problems, prospects, and politics. *Journal of Marriage and the Family, 51,* 557–580.

McLellan, A., Alterman, A., Metzger, D., Grissom, G., Woody, G., Luborsky, L., & O'Brien, C. (1994). Similarity of outcome predictors across opiate, cocaine, and alcohol treatments: Role of treatment services. *Journal of Counseling and Clinical Psychology, 62,* 1141–1158.

McLellan, A., Lewis, D., O'Brien, C., & Kleber, H. (2000). Drug dependence, a chronic medical illness: Implications for treatment, insurance, and outcomes research. *Journal of the American Medical Association, 284,* 1689–1695.

McLellan, A., Woody, G., & Metzger, D. (1996). Evaluating the effectiveness of addiction treatments: Reasonable expectations, appropriate comparisons. *Milbank Quarterly, 74,* 51–85.

McLeod, J. (1993). Spouse concordance for alcohol dependence and heavy drinking: Evidence from a community sample. *Alcoholism: Clinical and Experimental Research, 17,* 1146–1155.

McLoyd, V. (1990). The impact of economic hardship on Black families and children: Psychological distress, parenting, and socioemotional development. *Child Development, 61,* 311–346.

McLoyd, V. (1998). Socioeconomic disadvantage and child development. *American Psychologist, 53,* 185–204.

McLoyd, V., Jayaratne, T., Ceballo, R., & Borquez, J. (1994). Unemployment and work interruption among African American single mothers: Effects on parenting and adolescent socioemotional functioning. *Child Development, 65,* 562–589.

McNally, R. (1998). Experimental approaches to cognitive abnormality in posttraumatic stress disorder. *Clinical Psychology Review, 18,* 971–982.

McNally, R. (2003a). Psychological mechanisms in acute response to trauma. *Biological Psychiatry, 53,* 779–788.

McNally, R. (2003b). *Remembering trauma.* Cambridge, MA: Belknap Press.

McNally, R., Clancy, S., Schacter, D. L., & Pitman, R. (2000). Cognitive processing of trauma cues in adults reporting repressed, recovered, or continuous memories of childhood sexual abuse. *Journal of Abnormal Psychology, 109,* 355–359.

McNeal, C., & Amato, P. (1998). Parents' marital violence. *Journal of Family Issues, 19,* 123–140.

McNutt, L., Carlson, B., Persaud, M., & Postmus, J. (2002). Cumulative abuse experiences, physical health and health behaviors. *Annals of Epidemiology, 12,* 123–130.

McPherson, M., Smith-Lovin, L., & Cook, J. (2001). Birds of a feather: Homophily in social networks. *Annual Review of Sociology, 27,* 415–444.

Meadows, E., & Foa, E. (1998). Intrusion, arousal, and avoidance: Sexual trauma survivors. In V. Follette, J. Ruzek, & F. Abueg (Eds.), *Cognitive–behavioral therapies for trauma* (pp. 100–123). New York: Guilford Press.

Mears, D. (2003). Research and interventions to reduce domestic violence revictimization. *Trauma, Violence, & Abuse, 4,* 127–147.

Mears, D., Carlson, M., Holden, G., & Harris, S. (2001). Reducing domestic violence revictimization: The effects of individual and contextual factors and type of legal intervention. *Journal of Interpersonal Violence, 16,* 1260–1283.

Mechanic, M., Uhlmansiek, M., Weaver, T., & Resick, P. (2000). The impact of severe stalking experienced by acutely battered women: An examination of violence, psychological symptoms and strategic responding. *Violence and Victims, 15,* 443–458.

Mechanic, M., Weaver, T., & Resick, P. (2000). Intimate partner violence and stalking behavior: Exploration of patterns and correlates in a sample of acutely battered women. *Violence and Victims, 15,* 55–72.

Mellman, T., Bustamante, V., Fins, A., Pigeon, W., & Nolan, B. (2002). REM sleep and the early development of posttraumatic stress disorder. *American Journal of Psychiatry, 159,* 1696–1701.

Mellman, T., Clark, R., & Peacock, W. (2003). Prescribing patterns for patients with posttraumatic stress disorder. *Psychiatric Services, 54,* 1618–1621.

Melzack, R. (1999). Pain and stress: A new perspective. In R. Gatchel & D. Turk (Eds.), *Psychosocial factors in pain: Critical perspectives* (pp. 89–106). New York: Guilford Press.

Menard, A. (2001). Domestic violence and housing: Key policy and program challenges. *Violence Against Women, 7,* 707–720.

Menjivar, C., & Salcido, O. (2002). Immigrant women and domestic violence: Common experiences in different countries. *Gender and Society, 16,* 898–920.

Merikangas, K., Chakravarti, A., Moldin, S., Araj, H., Blangero, J., Burmeister, M., et al. (2002). Future of genetics of mood disorders research. *Biological Psychiatry, 52,* 457–477.

Merrill, K., Tolbert, V., & Wade, W. (2003). Effectiveness of cognitive therapy for depression in a community mental health center: A benchmarking study. *Journal of Counseling and Clinical Psychology, 71,* 404–409

Mertin, P., & Mohr, P. (2000). Incidence and correlates of posttraumatic stress disorder in Australian victims of domestic violence. *Journal of Family Violence, 15,* 411–422.

Mertin, P., & Mohr, P. (2001). A follow-up study of posttraumatic stress disorder, anxiety, and depression in Australian victims of domestic violence. *Violence and Victims, 16,* 645–654.

Merton, R. (1968). *Social theory and social structure.* New York: Free Press.

Messman-Moore, T., & Long, P. (2000). Child sexual abuse and revictimization in the form of adult sexual abuse, adult physical abuse, and adult psychological maltreatment. *Journal of Interpersonal Violence, 15,* 489–502.

Messman-Moore, T., & Long, P. (2002). Alcohol and substance use disorders as predictors of child to adult sexual revictimization in a sample of community women. *Violence and Victims, 17,* 319–340.

Messman-Moore, T., Long, P., & Siegfried, N. (2000). The revictimization of child sexual abuse survivors: An examination of the adjustment of college women with child sexual abuse, adult sexual assault, and adult physical abuse. *Child Maltreatment, 5,* 18–27.

Meyer, S., Vivian, D., & O'Leary, D. (1998). Men's sexual aggression in marriage: Couples report. *Violence Against Women, 4,* 415–435.

Miech, R., Caspi, A., Moffitt, T., Wright, B., & Silva, P. (1999). Low socioeconomic status and mental disorders: A longitudinal study of selection and causation during young adulthood. *American Journal of Sociology, 104,* 1096–1131.

Miethe, T., & Meier, R. (1990). Opportunity, choice, and criminal victimization: A test of a theoretical model. *Journal of Research in Crime and Delinquency, 27,* 243–266.

Mignon, S., & Holmes, W. (1995). Police response to mandatory arrest laws. *Crime and Delinquency, 41,* 430–442.

Mihalic, W., & Elliott, D. (1997). A social learning theory model of marital violence. *Journal of Family Violence, 12,* 21–47.

Miles-Doan, R. (1998). Violence between spouses and intimates: Does neighborhood context matter? *Social Forces, 77,* 623–645.

Milgram, S. (1974) *Obedience to authority.* New York: Harper & Row.

Miller, B. (2002). Family influences on adolescent sexual and contraceptive behavior. *Journal of Sex Research, 39,* 22–26.

Miller, B., Benson, B., & Galbraith, K. (2001). Family relationships and adolescent pregnancy risk: A research synthesis. *Developmental Review, 21,* 1–38.

Miller, B., Downs, W., & Testa, M. (1993). Interrelationships between victimization experiences and women's alcohol/drug use. *Journal of Studies on Alcohol, 11,* 109–117.

Miller, B., Monson, B., & Norton, M. (1995). The effects of forced sexual intercourse on White female adolescents. *Child Abuse and Neglect, 19,* 1289–1301.

Miller, J., & Krull, A. (1997). Controlling domestic violence: Victim resources and police intervention. In G. Kantor & J. Jasinski (Eds.), *Out of the darkness: Contemporary perspectives on family violence* (pp. 235–254). Thousand Oaks, CA: Sage.

Miller, J. (1986). *Toward a new psychology of women.* Boston: Beacon Press.

Miller, L., Burns, D., & Rothspan, S. (1995). Negotiating safer sex: The dynamics of African-American relationships. In P. Kalbfleisch & M. Cody (Eds.), *Gender, power, and communication in human relationships* (pp. 162–188). Hillsdale, NJ: Erlbaum.

Miller, N. (2001). Stalking investigation, law, public policy, and criminal prosecution as problem solver. In J. Davis (Ed.), *Stalking crimes and victim protection: Prevention, intervention, threat assessment, and case management* (pp. 387–425). Boca Raton, FL: CRC Press.

Miller, N., & Hoffman, N. (1995). Addictions treatment outcomes. *Alcoholism Treatment Quarterly, 12,* 41–55.

Miller, T., Cohen, M., & Wiersema, B. (1996). *The extent and costs of crime victimization: A new look* (NCJ 155281). Washington, DC: National Institute of Justice, U.S. Department of Justice.

Miller, T., Lestina, D., & Smith, G. (2001). Injury risk among medically identified alcohol and drug abusers. *Alcoholism: Clinical and Experimental Research, 25,* 54–59.

Millon, T. (1981). *Disorders of personality DSM–III: Axis II.* New York: Wiley.

Mills, L. (1998). Mandatory arrest and prosecution policies for domestic violence: A critical literature review and the case for more research to test victim empowerment approaches. *Criminal Justice and Behavior, 25,* 306–318.

Mineka, S., Rafaeli, E., & Yovel, I. (2003). Cognitive biases in emotional disorders: Informational processing and social–cognitive perspectives. In R. Davidson, K. Scherer, & H. Goldsmith (Eds.), *Handbook of affective sciences* (pp. 976–1009). New York: Oxford University Press.

Mirowsky, J., & Ross, C. (1989). Psychiatric diagnosis and reified measurement. *Journal of Health and Social Behavior, 30,* 11–25.

Mirowsky, J., & Ross, C. (2002). Measurement for a human science. *Journal of Health and Social Behavior, 43,* 152–170.

Mirowsky, J., & Ross, C. (2003). *Social causes of psychological distress* (2nd ed.). New York: Hawthorne.

Mirowsky, J., Ross, C., & Van Willigen, M. (1996). Instrumentalism in the land of opportunity: Socioeconomic causes and emotional consequences. *Social Psychology Quarterly, 59,* 322–337.

Misovich, S., Fisher, J., & Fisher, W. (1997). Close relationships and elevated HIV risk behavior: Evidence and possible underlying psychological processes. *Review of General Psychology, 1,* 72–107.

Mitchell, D., Angelone, D., Hirschman, R., Lilly, R., & Hall, G. (2002). Peer modeling and college men's sexually impositional behavior in the laboratory. *Journal of Sex Research, 39,* 326–333.

Modell, J. (1996). The uneasy engagement of human development and ethnography. In R. Jessor, A. Colby, & R. Shweder (Eds.), *Ethnography and human development: Context and meaning in social inquiry* (pp. 479–504). Chicago: University of Chicago Press.

Moffitt, T., & Caspi, A. (1999, July). *Findings about partner violence from the Dunedin multidisciplinary health and development study* (NCJ 170018). Washington, DC: National Institute of Justice.

Mohr, W., Lutz, M., Fantuzzo, J., & Perry, M. (2000). Children exposed to family violence: A review of empirical research from a developmental-ecological perspective. *Trauma, Violence, & Abuse, 1,* 264–283.

Molnar, B., Buka, S., & Kessler, R. (2001). Child sexual abuse and subsequent psychopathology: Results from the National Comorbidity Survey. *American Journal of Public Health, 91,* 753–761.

Monahan, K., & O'Leary, D. (1999). Head injury and battered women: An initial inquiry. *Health and Social Work, 24,* 269–280.

Monk-Turner, E. (2003). The benefits of medication: Experimental findings. *The Social Science Journal, 40,* 465–470.

Monson, C., Byrd, G., & Langhinrichsen-Rohling, J. (1996). To have and to hold: Perceptions of marital rape. *Journal of Interpersonal Violence, 11,* 410–424.

Monson, C., & Langhinrichsen-Rohling, J. (2002). Sexual and nonsexual dating violence perpetration: Testing an integrated perpetrator typology. *Violence and Victims, 17,* 403–428.

Montoya, I., Bell, D., Atkinson, J., Nagy, C., & Whitsett, D. (2002). Mental health, drug use, and the transition from welfare to work. *Journal of Behavioral and Health Services and Research, 29,* 144–156.

Moore, T., & Stuart, G. (2004). Illicit substance use and intimate partner violence among men in batterers' intervention. *Psychology of Addictive Behavior, 18,* 385–389.

Moracco, K., Runyan, C., & Butts, J. (1998). Femicide in North Carolina, 1991–1993. *Homicide Studies, 2,* 442–446.

Moran, P., & Eckenrode, J. (1991). Gender differences in the costs and benefits of peer relationship during adolescence. *Journal of Adolescent Research, 6,* 396–409.

Morgan, L. (1991). *After marriage ends: Economic consequences for mid-life women.* Newbury Park, CA: Sage.

Morgenstern, J., Keller, D., Morgan, T., McCrady, B., & Carroll, K. (2001). Manual-guided cognitive–behavioral therapy training: A promising method for disseminating empirically supported substance abuse treatments to the practice community. *Psychology of Addictive Behaviors, 15,* 83–88.

Moriarty, L., & Williams, J. (1996). Examining the relationship between routine activities theory and social disorganization: An analysis of property crime victimization. *American Journal of Criminal Justice, 21,* 43–59.

Morin, C., Rodrigue, S., & Ivers, H. (2003). Roles of stress, arousal, and coping skills in primary insomnia. *Psychosomatic Medicine, 65,* 259–267.

Morrill, A., Kasten, L., Urato, M., & Larson, M. (2001). Abuse, addiction, and depression as pathways to sexual risk in women and men with a history of substance abuse. *Journal of Substance Abuse, 13,* 169–184.

Morton, E., Runyan, C., Moracco, K., & Butts, J. (1998). Partner homicide–suicide involving female homicide victims: A population-based study in North Carolina, 1988–1992. *Violence and Victims, 13,* 91–106.

Mudar, P., Leonard, K., & Soltysinski, K. (2001). Discrepant substance use and marital functioning in newlywed couples. *Journal of Consulting and Clinical Psychology, 69,* 130–134.

Muehlenhard, C., Goggins, M., Jones, J., & Satterfield, A. (1991). Sexual violence and coercion in close relationships. In K. McKinney & S. Sprecher (Eds.), *Sexuality in close relationships* (pp. 155–175). Hillsdale, NJ: Erlbaum.

Mueser, K., Corrigan, P., Hilton, D., Tanzman, B., Schaub, A., Gingerich, S., et al. (2002). Illness management and recovery: A review of the research. *Community Psychiatry, 53,* 1272–1284.

Mulatu, M., & Schooler, C. (2002). Causal connection between socio-economic status and health: Reciprocal effects and mediating mechanisms. *Journal of Health and Social Behavior, 43,* 22–41.

Mumenthaler, M., Taylor, J., O'Hara, R., & Yesavage, J. (1999). Gender differences in moderate drinking effects. *Alcohol Research and Health, 23,* 55–61.

Muraven, M., Baumeister, R., & Tice, D. (1999). Longitudinal improvement of self-regulation through practice: Building self-control strength through repeated exercise. *Journal of Social Psychology, 139,* 446–457.

Muraven, M., Collins, R., & Nienhaus, K. (2002). Self-control and alcohol restraint: An initial application of the self-control strength model. *Psychology of Addictive Behaviors, 16,* 113–120.

Muraven, M., Tice, D., & Baumeister, R. (1998). Self-control as limited resource: Regulatory depletion patterns. *Journal of Personality and Social Psychology, 74,* 774–789.

Murphy, C., Musser, P., & Maton, K. (1998). Coordinated community intervention for domestic abusers: Intervention system involvement and criminal recidivism. *Journal of Family Violence, 13,* 263–284.

Murry, V., Smith, E., & Hill, N. (2001). Race, ethnicity, and culture in studies of families in context. *Journal of Marriage and Family, 63,* 911–914.

Musselman, D., Evans, D., & Nemeroff, C. (1998). The relationship of depression to cardiovascular disease: Epidemiology, biology, and treatment. *Archives of General Psychiatry, 55,* 580–592.

Mustaine, E. (1997). Victimization risks and routine activities: A theoretical examination using a gender-specific and domain-specific model. *American Journal of Criminal Justice, 22,* 41–70.

Mustaine, E., & Tewksbury, R. (1998). Specifying the role of alcohol in predatory victimization. *Deviant Behavior, 19,* 173–199.

Mustaine, E., & Tewksbury, R. (1999). A routine activity theory explanation for women's stalking victimizations. *Violence Against Women, 5,* 43–62.

Najavits, L. (2002). *Seeking safety: A treatment manual for PTSD and substance abuse.* New York: Guilford Press.

Najavits, L., Weiss, R., Shaw, S., & Muenz, L. (1998). "Seeking safety": Outcome of a new cognitive–behavioral psychotherapy for women with posttraumatic stress disorder and substance dependence. *Journal of Traumatic Stress, 11,* 437–456.

Naranjo, C., & Bremner, K. (1993). Behavioral correlates of alcohol intoxication. *Addiction, 88,* 31–41.

National Center for Injury Prevention and Control. (2003). *Costs of intimate partner violence against women in the United States.* Atlanta, GA: Centers for Disease Control and Prevention.

National Center on Addiction and Substance Abuse. (2000). *Missed opportunity: National survey of primary care physicians and patients on substance abuse* (pp. 651–670). New York: National Center on Addiction and Substance Abuse at Columbia University.

National Institute on Alcohol Abuse and Alcoholism. (1998). *Alcohol and sleep* (Alcohol Alert 41). Washington, DC: Department of Health and Human Services.

National Institute on Drug Abuse. (2001). *Prescription drugs: Abuse and addiction* (NIH Publication No. 01-4481). Washington, DC: U.S. Government Printing Office.

National Institute on Drug Abuse. (2003). *Drug use among racial/ethnic minorities revised.* Bethesda, MD: U.S. Department of Health and Human Services, National Institutes of Health, National Institute on Drug Abuse, Division of Epidemiology, Services & Prevention Branch.

National Institute of Justice. (1997). *A study of homicide in eight US cities: An NIJ intramural research project.* Washington, DC: U.S. Department of Justice.

National Research Council. (1993) *Understanding child abuse and neglect.* Washington, DC: National Academy Press.

Neighbors, H., Musick, M., & Williams, D. (1998). The African American minister as a source of help for serious personal crises: Bridge or barrier to mental health care? *Health Education and Behavior, 25,* 759–777.

Neville, H., Heppner, M., Oh, E., Spanierman, L., & Clark, M. (2004). General and culturally specific factors influencing black and white rape survivors' self-esteem. *Psychology of Women Quarterly, 28,* 83–94.

Newcomb, M., & Bentler, P. (1986). Cocaine use among adolescents: Longitudinal associations with social context, psychopathology, and use of other substances. *Addictive Behaviors, 11,* 263–273.

Newcomb, M., Vargas-Carmona, J., & Galaif, E. (1999). Drug problems and psychological distress among a community sample of adults: Predictors, consequences, or confound? *Journal of Community Psychology, 27,* 405–429.

Newmark, L., Harrell, A., & Salem, P. (1995). Domestic violence and empowerment in custody and visitation cases. *Family and Conciliation Courts Review, 33,* 30–62.

Nicastro, A., Cousins, A., & Spitzberg, B. (2000). The tactical face of stalking. *Journal of Criminal Justice, 28,* 69–82.

Nishino, S., Mishima, K., Mignot, E., & Dement, W. (2004). Sedative-hypnotics. In A. Schatzberg & C. Nemeroff (Eds.), *The American Psychiatric Publishing textbook of psychopharmacology* (3rd ed., pp. 651–670). Washington, DC: American Psychiatric Publishing.

Nishith, P., Mechanic, M., & Resick, P. (2000). Prior interpersonal trauma: The contribution to current PTSD symptoms in female rape victims. *Journal of Abnormal Psychology, 109,* 20–25.

Nolen-Hoeksema, S. (1995). Epidemiology and theories of gender differences in unipolar depression. In M. Seeman (Ed.), *Gender and psychopathology* (pp. 63–87). Washington, DC: American Psychiatric Association.

Norris, J., & Kerr, K. (1993). Alcohol and violent pornography: Responses to permissive and nonpermissive cues. *Journal of Studies on Alcohol, 11,* 118–127.

Norris, J., Nurius, P., & Dimeff, L. (1996). Through her eyes: Factors affecting women's perception of and resistance to acquaintance sexual aggression threat. *Psychology of Women Quarterly, 20,* 123–145.

Norris, J., Nurius, P., & Graham, T. (1999). When a date changes from fun to dangerous: Factors affecting women's ability to distinguish. *Violence Against Women, 5,* 230–250.

Norton, I., & Schauer, J. (1997). A hospital-based domestic violence group. *Psychiatric Services, 48,* 1186–1190.

Novacek, J., & Lazarus, R. (1990). The structure of personal commitments. *Journal of Personality, 58,* 693–715.

Nunes, E. V., & Levin, F. R. (2004). Treatment of depression in patients with alcohol or other drug dependence. *Journal of the American Medical Association, 291,* 1887–1896.

Nurius, P. (2000). Risk perception for acquaintance sexual aggression: A social cognitive perspective. *Aggression and Violent Behavior, 5,* 63–78.

Nurius, P., Furrey, J., & Berliner, L. (1992). Coping capacity among women with abusive partners. *Violence and Victims, 7,* 229–243.

Nurius, P., & Gaylord, J. (1998). Coping with threat from intimate sources: How self-protection relates to loss for women. In J. Harvey (Ed.), *Perspectives on personal and interpersonal loss: A sourcebook* (pp. 281–291). Ann Arbor, MI: Taylor & Francis.

Nurius, P., Macy, R., Bhuyan, R., Holt, V., Kernic, M., & Rivara, F. (2003). Contextualizing depression and physical functioning in battered women: Adding vulnerability and resources to the analysis. *Journal of Interpersonal Violence, 18,* 1411–1431.

Nurius, P., & Norris, J. (1996). A cognitive ecological model of women's response to male sexual coercion in dating. *Journal of Psychology & Human Sexuality, 8,* 117–139.

Nurius, P., Norris, J., Dimeff, L., & Graham, T. (1996). Expectations regarding acquaintance sexual aggression among sorority and fraternity members. *Sex Roles, 35,* 427–444.

Nurius, P., Norris, J., Young, D., Graham, T., & Gaylord, J. (2000). Interpreting and defensively responding to threat: Examining appraisals and coping with acquaintance sexual aggression. *Violence and Victims, 15,* 187–208.

Nussbaum, M. C. (2000). *Women and human development: The capabilities approach.* New York: Cambridge University Press.

Nyamathi, A., Bayley, L., Anderson, N., Keenan, C., & Leake, B. (1999). Perceived factors influencing the initiation of drugs and alcohol use among homeless women and reported consequences of use. *Women and Health, 29,* 99–114.

Nyamathi, A., Leake, B., & Gelberg, L. (2000). Sheltered versus nonsheltered homeless women: Differences in health, behavior, victimization, and utilization of care. *Journal of General Internal Medicine, 15,* 565–572.

Obert, J. L., Brown, A. H., Zweten, J., Christian, D., Delmhorst, J., Minsky, S., et al. (2005). When treatment meets research: Clinical perspectives from the CSAT Methamphetamine Treatment Project. *Journal of Substance Abuse Treatment, 28,* 231–238.

O'Brien, T. B., & DeLongis, A. (1996). The interactional context of problem-, emotion-, and relationship-focused coping: The role of the Big Five personality factors. *Journal of Personality, 64,* 775–813.

O'Connor, T., Hawkins, N., Dunn, J., Thorpe, K., & Golding, J. (1998). Family type and depression in pregnancy: Factors mediating risk in a community sample. *Journal of Marriage and the Family, 60,* 757–770.

O'Donnell, M., Creamer, M., & Pattison, P. (2004). Posttraumatic stress disorder and depression following trauma: Understanding comorbidity. *American Journal of Psychiatry, 161,* 1390–1396.

O'Farrell, T., & Murphy, C. (1995). Marital violence before and after alcoholism treatment. *Journal of Consulting and Clinical Psychology, 63,* 256–262.

O'Keefe, M. (1994). Racial/ethnic differences among battered women and their children. *Journal of Child and Family Studies, 3,* 283–305.

O'Keefe, M. (1998). Factors mediating the link between witnessing interparental violence and dating violence. *Journal of Family Violence, 13,* 39–57.

O'Neill, M., & Kerig, P. (2000). Attributions of self-blame and perceived control as moderators of adjustment in battered women. *Journal of Interpersonal Violence, 15,* 1036–1049.

Office of National Drug Control Policy. (2001). *The economic costs of drug abuse in the United States, 1992–1998.* (NCJ 190636). Washington, DC: Executive Office of the President.

Ohayon, M., & Schatzberg, A. (2003). Using chronic pain to predict depressive morbidity in the general population. *Archives of General Psychiatry, 60,* 39–47.

Olasov Rothbaum, B., Meadows, E., Resick, P., & Foy, D. (2000). Cognitive–behavioral therapy. In E. Foa, T. Keane, & M. Friedman (Eds.), *Effective treatments for PTSD* (pp. 60–105). New York: Guilford Press.

Oliver, J., & Brough, P. (2002). Cognitive appraisal, negative affectivity and psychological well-being. *New Zealand Journal of Psychology, 31,* 2–7.

Olson, D., & Stalans, L. (2001). Violent offenders on probation: Profile, sentence, and outcome differences among domestic violence and other violent probationers. *Violence Against Women, 7,* 1164–1185.

Oquendo, M., Friend, J., Halberstam, B., Brodsky, B., Burke, A., Grunebaum, M., et al. (2003). Association of comorbid posttraumatic stress disorder and major depression with greater risk for suicidal behavior. *American Journal of Psychiatry, 160,* 580–582.

Ornduff, S., Kelsey, R., & O'Leary, D. (2001). Childhood physical abuse, personality, and adult relationship violence: A model of vulnerability to victimization. *American Journal of Orthopsychiatry, 71,* 322–331.

Orth, U. (2003). Punishment goals of crime victims. *Law and Human Behavior, 27,* 173–186.

Orth, U., & Maercker, A. (2004). Do trials of perpetrators retraumatize crime victims? *Journal of Interpersonal Violence, 19,* 212–227.

Ouimette, P., Brown, P., & Najavits, L. (1998). Course and treatment of patients with both substance abuse and posttraumatic stress disorders. *Addictive Behaviors, 23,* 785–795.

Owens, M., & Nemeroff, C. (1993). The role of corioctropin-releasing factor in the pathophysiology of affective and anxiety disorders: Laboratory and clinical studies. *CIBA Foundation Symposium, 172,* 296–308.

Ozer, E., Best, S., Lipsey, T., & Weiss, D. (2003). Predictors of posttraumatic stress disorder and symptoms in adults: A meta-analysis. *Psychological Bulletin, 129,* 52–73.

Padgett, D., Struening, E., Andrews, H., & Pittman, J. (1995). Predictors of emergency room use by homeless adults in New York City: The influence of predisposing, enabling, and need factors. *Social Science and Medicine, 41,* 547–557.

Pagelow, D. (1984). *Family violence.* New York: Praeger.

Palarea, R., Zona, M., Lane, J., & Langhinrichsen-Rohling, J. (1999). The dangerous nature of stalking: Threats, violence and associated risk factors. *Behavioral Sciences and the Law, 17,* 269–283.

Panksepp, J. (1998). *Affective neuroscience: The foundations of human and animal emotions.* New York: Oxford University Press.

Panksepp, J. (2003, October 10). Feeling the pain of social loss. *Science, 302,* 237–239.

Pape, K., & Arias, I. (2000). The role of perceptions and attributions in battered women's intentions to permanently end their violent relationships. *Cognitive Therapy and Research, 24,* 201–214.

Parillo, K., Freeman, R., Collier, K., & Young, P. (2001). Association between early sexual abuse and adult HIV—Risky sexual behaviors among community-recruited women. *Child Abuse and Neglect, 25,* 335–346.

Paris, J. (1997). Childhood trauma as an etiological factor in the personality disorders. *Journal of Personality Disorders, 11,* 34–49.

Paris, J. (2002). Implications of long-term outcome research for the management of patients with borderline personality disorder. *Harvard Review of Psychiatry, 10,* 315–323.

Paris, J., & Braverman, S. (1995). Successful and unsuccessful marriages in borderline patients. *Journal of the American Academy of Psychoanalysis, 23,* 153–156.

Parker, B., McFarlane, J., Soeken, K., Silva, C., & Reel, S. (1999). Testing an intervention to prevent further abuse to pregnant women. *Research in Nursing and Health, 22,* 59–66.

Parkinson, B. (1997). Untangling the appraisal–emotion connection. *Personality and Social Psychology Review, 1,* 62–79.

Parks, K. (2000). An event-based analysis of aggression women experience in bars. *Psychology of Addictive Behaviors, 14,* 102–110.

Parks, K., & Miller, B. (1997). Bar victimization of women. *Psychology of Women Quarterly, 21,* 509–525.

Parks, K., Miller, B., Collins, L., & Zetes-Zanatta, L. (1998). Women's descriptions of drinking in bars: Reasons and risks. *Sex Roles, 38,* 701–717.

Parks, K., & Zetes-Zanatta, L. (1999). Women's bar-related victimization: Refining and testing a conceptual model. *Aggressive Behavior, 25,* 349–364.

Parry, B. (2000). Hormonal basis of mood disorders in women. In E. Frank (Ed.), *Gender and its effects on psychopathology* (pp. 3–21). Washington, DC: American Psychiatric Press.

Parsons, T. (1951). *The social system.* New York: Free Press.

Passik, S., & Portenoy, R. (1998). Substance abuse issues. In M. Ashburn & L. Rice (Eds.), *The management of pain* (pp. 51–61) Philadelphia: Churchill Livingstone.

Pate, A., & Hamilton, E. (1992). Formal and informal deterrents to domestic violence: The Dade County spouse assault experiment. *American Sociology Review, 57,* 691–697.

Patrick, L. (2002) Eating disorders: A review of the literature with emphasis on medical complications and clinical nutrition. *Alternative Medicine Review, 7,* 184–193.

Pearlin, L. (1989). The sociological study of stress. *Journal of Health and Social Behavior, 30,* 241–256.

Pearlin, L. (1999a). Stress and mental health: A conceptual overview. In A Horwitz & T. Scheid (Eds.), *A handbook for the study of mental health* (pp. 161–175). New York: Cambridge University Press.

Pearlin, L. (1999b). The stress process revisited: Reflections on concepts and their interrelationships. In C. Aneshensel & J. Phelan (Eds.), *Handbook of the sociology of mental health* (pp. 395–415). Dordrecht, the Netherlands: Kluwer Academic.

Pearlin, L., Lieberman, M., Menaghan, E., & Mullen, J. (1981). The stress process. *Journal of Health and Social Behavior, 22,* 337–356.

Pederson, C., Maurer, S., Kaminski, P., Zander, K., Peters, C., Stokes-Crowe, L., & Osborn, R. (2004). Hippocampal volume and memory performance in a community-based sample of women with posttraumatic stress disorder secondary to child abuse. *Journal of Traumatic Stress, 17,* 37–40.

Pelcovitz, D., Kaplan, S., DeRosa, R., Mandel, F., & Salzinger, S. (2000). Psychiatric disorders in adolescents exposed to domestic violence and physical abuse. *American Journal of Orthopsychiatry, 70,* 360–369.

Pence, E. (2001). Advocacy on behalf of battered women. In C. Renzetti, J. Edleson, & R. Bergen (Eds.), *Sourcebook on violence against women* (pp. 329–343). Thousand Oaks, CA: Sage.

Penninx, B., Beekman, A., Honig, A., Deeg, D., Schoevers, R., van Eijk, J., & van Tilburg, W. (2001). Depression and cardiac mortality: Results from a community-based longitudinal study. *Archives of General Psychiatry, 58,* 221–227.

Peplau, L. (2003). Human sexuality: How do men and women differ? *Current Directions in Psychological Science, 12,* 37–40.

Perez, D. (2000). The relationship between physical abuse, sexual victimization, and adolescent illicit drug use. *Journal of Drug Issues, 30,* 641–662.

Perilla, J. (1999). Domestic violence as a human rights issue: The case of immigrant Latinos. *Hispanic Journal of Behavioral Sciences, 21,* 107–133.

Perkins, W. (1999). Stress-motivated drinking in collegiate and postcollegiate young adulthood: Life course and gender patterns. *Journal of Studies on Alcohol, 60,* 219–227.

Perrin, S., Van Hasselt, V., Basilio, I., & Hersen, M. (1996). Assessing the effects of violence on women in battering relationships with the Keane MMPI-PTSD scale. *Journal of Traumatic Stress, 9,* 805–816.

Petersen, R., Gazmararian, J., & Clark, K. (2001). Partner violence: Implications for health and community settings. *Women's Health Issues, 11,* 116–125.

Peterson, J., Rothfleisch, J., Zelazo, P., & Pihl, R. (1990). Acute alcohol intoxication and cognitive functioning. *Journal of Studies on Alcohol, 51,* 114–122.

Petronis, K., & Anthony, J. (2000). Perceived risk of cocaine use and experience with cocaine: Do they cluster within US neighborhoods and cities? *Drug and Alcohol Dependence, 57,* 183–192.

Phillips, L., Quirk, R., Rosenfeld, B., & O'Connor, M. (2004). Is it stalking? Perceptions of stalking among college undergraduates. *Criminal Justice and Behavior, 31,* 73–96.

Pike, K., Walsh, B., Vitousek, K., Wilson, G., & Bauer, J. (2003). Cognitive behavioral therapy in the posthospitalization treatment of anorexia nervosa. *American Journal of Psychiatry, 160,* 2046–2049.

Pillow, D., Barrera, M., & Chassin, L. (1998). Using cluster analysis to assess the effects of stressful life events: Probing the impact of parental alcoholism on child stress and substance use. *Journal of Community Psychology, 26,* 361–380.

Pincus, T., & Williams, A. (1999). Models and measurements of depression in chronic pain. *Journal of Psychosomatic Research, 47,* 211–219.

Placios, W., Urmann, C., Newel, R., & Hamilton, N. (1999). Developing a sociological framework for dually diagnosed women. *Journal of Substance Abuse Treatment, 1–2,* 91–102.

Planalp, S., & Fitness, J. (1999). Thinking/feeling about social and personal relationships. *Journal of Social and Personal Relationships, 16,* 731–750.

Plested, B., Smitham, D., Thurman, P., Oetting, E., & Edwards, R. (1999). Readiness for drug use prevention in rural minority communities. *Substance Use and Misuse, 43,* 521–544.

Plichta, S. (1992). The effects of woman abuse on health care utilization and health status: A literature review. *Women's Health Institute, 2,* 154–163.

Plichta, S. (1996). Violence and abuse: Implications for women's health. In M. Falik & K. Collins (Eds.), *Women's health: The Commonwealth Fund survey* (pp. 238–270). Baltimore: Johns Hopkins University Press.

Plichta, S., & Falik, M. (2001). Prevalence of violence and its implications for women's health. *Women's Health Issues, 11,* 244–258.

Plichta, S., & Weisman, C. (1995). Spouse or partner abuse, use of health services, and unmet need for medical care in U.S. women. *Journal of Women's Health, 4,* 45–53.

Ploghaus, A., Tracey, I., Gati, J., Clare, S., Menon, R., Matthews, P., & Rawlins, J. (1999, June 18). Dissociating pain from its anticipation in the human brain. *Science, 284,* 1979–1981.

Poincaré, H. (1952). *Science and hypothesis.* Mineola, NY: Dover. (Original work published 1905)

Polaschek, D., & King, L. (2002). Rehabilitating rapists: Reconsidering the issues. *Australian Psychologist, 37,* 215–221.

Polaschek, D., Ward, T., & Hudson, S. (1997). Rape and rapists: Theory and treatment. *Clinical Psychology Review, 17,* 117–144.

Pollack, H., Danziger, S., Seefeldt, K., & Jayakody, R. (2002). Substance use among welfare recipients: Trends and policy responses. *Social Service Review, 76,* 256–274.

Polusny, M., & Follette, V. (1995). Long-term correlates of child sexual abuse: Theory and review of the empirical literature. *Applied and Preventive Psychology, 4,* 143–166.

Polusny, M., Rosenthal, M., Aban, I., & Follette, V. (2004). Experiential avoidance as a mediator of the effects of adolescent sexual victimization on negative adult outcomes. *Violence and Victims, 19,* 109–120.

Pope, H., Gruber, A., Hudson, J., Huestis, M., & Yugelun-Todd, D. (2001). Neuropsychological performance in long-term cannabis users. *Archives of General Psychiatry, 58,* 909–915.

Pope, H., Gruber, A., & Yurgelun-Todd, D. (1995). The residual neuropsychological effects of cannabis: The current status of research. *Drug and Alcohol Dependence, 38,* 25–34.

Poulos, A., Gertz, M., Pankratz, S., & Post-White, J. (2001). Pain, mood disturbance, and quality of life in patients with multiple myeloma. *Oncology Nursing Forum, 28,* 1163–1170

Pratt, M., Prancer, M., Hunsberger, B., & Manchester, J. (1990). Reasoning about the self and relationships in maturity: An integrative complexity analysis of individual differences. *Journal of Personality and Social Psychology, 59,* 575–581.

Prochaska, J., DiClemente, C., & Norcross, J. (1992). In search of how people change: Applications to addictive behaviors. *American Psychologist, 47,* 1102–1114.

Proulx, J., Pellerin, B., Paradis, Y., McKibben, A., Aubut, J., & Ouimet, M. (1997). Static and dynamic predictors of recidivism in sexual aggressors. *Sexual Abuse: Journal of Research and Treatment, 9,* 7–27.

Ptacek, J. (1999). *Battered women in the courtroom: The power of judicial response.* Boston: Northeastern University Press.

Purdie, V., & Downey, G. (2000). Rejection sensitivity and adolescent girls' vulnerability to relationship-centered difficulties. *Child Maltreatment, 5,* 338–349.

Putnam, F. (2003). Ten-year research update review: Child sexual abuse. *Journal of the American Academy of Child and Adolescent Psychiatry, 42,* 269–278.

Puzone, C. (2000). National trends in intimate partner homicide: United States, 1976–1995. *Violence Against Women, 6,* 409–418.

Raj, A., & Silverman, J. (2002). Violence against immigrant women: The roles of culture, context, and legal immigrant status on intimate partner violence. *Violence Against Women, 8,* 367–398.

Ramsay, J., Richardson, J., Carter, Y., Davidson, L., & Feder, G. (2002). Should health professionals screen women for domestic violence? Systematic review. *British Medical Journal, 325,* 1–13.

Randall, M., & Haskell, L. (1995). Sexual violence in women's lives. *Violence Against Women, 1,* 6–31.

Rankin, B., & Quane, J. (2000). Neighborhood poverty and the social isolation of inner-city African American families. *Social Forces, 79,* 139–164.

Rapaport, M., Judd, L., Schettler, P., Yonkers, K., Thase, M., Kupfer, D., et al. (2002). A descriptive analysis of minor depression. *American Journal of Psychiatry, 159,* 637–643.

Ratner, P. (1993). The incidence of wife abuse and mental health status in abused wives in Edmonton, Alberta. *Canada Journal of Public Health, 84,* 246–249.

Read, J., Agar, K., Argyle, N., & Aderhold, V. (2003). Sexual and physical abuse during childhood and adulthood as predictors of hallucinations, delusions and thought disorder. *Psychology and Psychotherapy: Theory, Research and Practice, 76,* 1–22.

Reardon, S., & Buka, S. (2002). Differences in onset and persistence of substance abuse and dependence among Whites, Blacks, and Hispanics. *Public Health Reports, 117*(Suppl. 1), S51–S59.

Rees, V., & Heather, N. (1995). Individual differences and cue reactivity. In D. Drummond, S. Tiffany, S. Glautier, & B. Remington (Eds.), *Addictive behaviour: Cue exposure theory and practice* (pp. 99–118). New York: Wiley.

Regehr, C., Regehr, G., & Bradford, J. (1998). A model for predicting depression in victims of rape. *Journal of the American Academy of Psychiatry and the Law, 26,* 595–605.

Regier, D., Farmer, M., Rae, D., Locke, B., Keith, S., Judd, L., & Goodwin, F. (1990). Comorbidity of mental disorders with alcohol and other drug abuse. *Journal of the American Medical Association, 264,* 2511–2518.

Reinecke, M., Ryan, N., & DuBois, D. (1998). Cognitive–behavioral therapy of depression and depressive symptoms during adolescence: A review and meta-analysis. *Journal of the American Academy of Child and Adolescent Psychiatry, 37,* 26–34.

Reitzel-Jaffe, D., & Wolfe, D. (2001). Predictors of relationship abuse among young men. *Journal of Interpersonal Violence, 16,* 99–115.

Ren, X., Amick, B., & Williams, D. (1999). Racial/ethnic disparities in health: The interplay between discrimination and socioeconomic status. *Ethnicity and Disease, 9,* 151–165.

Rennison, C. (2002). *Rape and sexual assault: Reporting to police and medical attention, 1992–2000* (NCJ 194530). Washington, DC: U.S. Department of Justice, Office of Justice Programs.

Rennison, C., & Planty, M. (2003). Nonlethal intimate partner violence: Examining race, gender, and income patterns. *Violence and Victims, 18,* 433–443.

Repetti, R., Taylor, S., & Seeman, T. (2002). Risky families: Family social environments and the mental and physical health of offspring. *Psychological Bulletin, 128,* 330–366.

Resick, P. (1993). The psychological impact of rape. *Journal of Interpersonal Violence, 8,* 223–255.

Resick, P., Nishith, P., Weaver, T., Astin, M., & Feuer, C. (2002). A comparison of cognitive-processing therapy with prolonged exposure and waiting condition for the treatment of chronic posttraumatic stress disorder in female rape victims. *Journal of Consulting and Clinical Psychology, 70,* 867–879.

Resick, P., & Schnicke, M. (1993). *Cognitive processing therapy for rape victims: A treatment manual.* Thousand Oaks, CA: Sage.

Resnick, H., Acierno, R., Holmes, M., Dammeyer, M., & Kilpatrick, D. (2000). Emergency evaluation and intervention with female victims of rape and other violence. *Journal of Clinical Psychology, 56,* 1317–1333.

Resnick, H., Acierno, R., Holmes, M., Kilpatrick, D., & Jager, N. (1999). Prevention of post-rape psychopathology: Preliminary findings of a controlled acute rape treatment study. *Journal of Anxiety Disorders, 13,* 359–370.

Resnick, H., Acierno, R., & Kilpatrick, D. (1997). Health impact of interpersonal violence: 2. Medical and mental health outcomes. *Behavioral Medicine, 23,* 65–78.

Resnick, H., Holmes, M., Kilpatrick, D., Clum, G., Acierno, R., Best, C., & Saunders, B. (2000). Predictors of post-rape medical care in a national sample of women. *American Journal of Preventive Medicine, 19,* 214–219.

Resnick, H., Yehuda, R., Pitman, R., & Foy, D. (1995). Effect of previous trauma on acute plasma cortisol level following rape. *American Journal of Psychiatry, 152,* 1675–1677.

Reyna, V. (2004). How people make decisions that involve risk: A dual-processes approach. *Current Directions in Psychological Science, 13,* 60–66.

Reyna, V., & Adam, M. (2003). Fuzzy-trace theory, risk communication, and product labeling in sexually transmitted diseases. *Risk Analysis, 23,* 325–342.

Rhodes, K., & Levinson, W. (2003). Interventions for intimate partner violence against women: Clinical applications. *Journal of the American Medical Association, 289,* 601–605.

Ricca, V., Mannucci, E., Zucchi, T., Rotella, C., & Faravelli, C. (2000). Cognitive–behavioral therapy for bulimia nervosa and binge eating disorder: A review. *Psychotherapy and Psychosomatics, 69,* 287–295.

Richardson, J., Coid, J., Petruckevitch, A., Chung, W., Moorey, S., & Feder, G. (2002). Identifying domestic violence: Cross sectional study in primary care. *British Medical Journal, 324,* 274–277.

Richman, K. (2002). Women, poverty, and domestic violence: Perceptions of court and legal aid effectiveness. *Sociological Inquiry, 72,* 318–344.

Riger, S., Raja, S., & Camacho, J. (2002). The radiating impact of intimate partner violence. *Journal of Interpersonal Violence, 17,* 184–205.

Riggs, D., Kilpatrick, D., & Resnick, H. (1992). Long-term psychological distress associated with marital rape and aggravated assault: A comparison to other crime victims. *Journal of Family Violence, 7,* 283–296.

Riggs, D., Rothbaum, B., & Foa, E. (1995). A prospective examination of symptoms of posttraumatic stress disorder in victims of nonsexual assault. *Journal of Interpersonal Violence, 10,* 201–214.

Riggs, D., Rukstalis, M., Volpicelli, J., Kalmanson, D., & Foa, E. (2003). Demographic and social adjustment characteristics of patients with comorbid posttraumatic stress disorder and alcohol dependence: Potential pitfalls to PTSD treatment. *Addictive Behaviors, 28,* 1717–1730.

Ringel, Y., Sperber, A., & Drossman, D. (2001). Irritable bowel syndrome. *Annual Review of Medicine, 52,* 319–338.

Ringwalt, C., Greene, J., & Robertson, M. (1998). Familial backgrounds and risk behaviors of youth with thrownaway experiences. *Journal of Adolescence, 21,* 241–252.

Rini, C., Dunkel-Schetter, C., Wadhwa, P., & Sandman, C. (1999). Psychological adaptation and birth outcomes: The role of personal resources, stress, and sociocultural context in pregnancy. *Health Psychology, 18,* 333–345.

Ritzer, G. (1999). *Classical sociological theory* (3rd ed.). Boston: McGraw-Hill.

Rivier, C. (1993). Acute interactions between cytokine and alcohol on ACTH and corticosterone secretion in rats. *Alcohol Clinical and Experimental Research, 17,* 946–950.

Rivier, C. (2000). Effects of alcohol on the neuroendocrine system. In A. Noronha, M. Eckardt, & K. Warren (Eds.), *Review of NIAAA's neuroscience and behavioral research portfolio* (NIAAA Research Monograph No. 34; pp. 61–81). Washington, DC: U.S. Department of Health and Human Services.

Robbennolt, J. (2000). Outcome severity and judgments of "responsibility": A meta-analytic review. *Journal of Applied Social Psychology, 30,* 2575–2609.

Roberts, A., & Yeager, K. (2004). (Eds.) *Evidence-based practice manual: Research and outcome measures in health and human services.* New York: Oxford University Press.

Roberts, L., & Leonard, K. (1997). Gender differences and similarities in the alcohol and marriage relationship. In R. Wilsnack & S. Wilsnack (Eds.), *Gender and alcohol: Individual and social perspectives* (pp. 289–311). New Brunswick, NJ: Rutgers Center of Alcohol Studies.

Roberts, L., & Leonard, K. (1998). An empirical typology of drinking partnerships and their relationship to marital functioning and drinking consequences. *Journal of Marriage and the Family, 60,* 515–526.

Roberts, T., & Nolen-Hoeksema, S. (1989). Sex differences in reactions to evaluative feedback. *Sex Roles, 21,* 725–747.

Roberts, T., & Nolen-Hoeksema, S. (1994). Gender comparisons in responsiveness to others' evaluations in achievement settings. *Psychology of Women Quarterly, 18,* 221–240.

Robins, L., & Regier, D. (Eds.). (1991). *Psychiatric disorders in America: The epidemiologic catchment area study.* New York: Free Press.

Robinson, A., & Chandek, M. (2000). The domestic violence arrest decision: Examining demographic, attitudinal, and situational variables. *Crime and Delinquency, 46,* 18–37.

Rodgers, K., & Roberts, G. (1995). Women's non-spousal multiple victimization: A test of the routine activities theory. *Canadian Journal of Criminology, 37,* 363–391.

Rodriguez, M., Bauer, H., McLoughlin, E., & Grumbach, K. (1999). Screening and intervention for intimate partner abuse: Practices and attitudes of primary care physicians. *Journal of the American Medical Association, 282,* 468–474.

Rodriguez, M., Sheldon, W., Bauer, H., & Perez-Stable, E. (2001). The factors associated with disclosure of intimate partner abuse to clinicians. *Journal of Family Practice, 50,* 338–344.

Rogers, R., Everitt, B., Baldacchino, A., Blackshaw, A., Swainson, R., Wynne, K., et al. (1999). Dissociable deficits in the decision-making cognition of chronic amphetamine abusers, opiate abusers, patients with focal damage to prefrontal cortex, and tryptophan-depleted normal volunteers: Evidence for monoaminergic mechanisms. *Neuropsychopharmacology, 20,* 322–339.

Roizen, J. (1997). Epidemiological issues in alcohol related violence. In M. Galanter (Ed.), *Recent developments in alcoholism* (Vol. 13, pp. 7–40). New York: Plenum Press.

Rollstin, A., & Kern, J. (1998). Correlates of battered women's psychological distress: Severity of abuse and duration of the postabuse period. *Psychological Reports, 82,* 387–394.

Roodman, A., & Clum, G. (2001). Revictimization rates and method variance: A meta-analysis. *Clinical Psychology Review, 21,* 183–204.

Rose, L., Campbell, J., & Kub, J. (2000). The role of social support and family relationships in women's responses to battering. *Health Care for Women International, 21,* 27–39.

Roseman, I. (2001). A model of appraisal in the emotion system: Integrating theory, research, and applications. In K. Scherer, A. Schorr, & T. Johnstone (Eds.), *Appraisal processes in emotion: Theory, methods, research* (pp. 68–91). New York: Oxford University Press.

Roseman, I., & Smith, C. (2001). Appraisal theory: Overview, assumptions, varieties, controversies. In K. Scherer, A. Schorr, & T. Johnstone (Eds.), *Appraisal processes in emotion: Theory, methods, research* (pp. 3–19). New York: Oxford University Press.

Rosenbaum, J., Reynolds, L., & Deluca, S. (2002). How do places matter? The geography of opportunity, self-efficacy and a look inside the black box of residential mobility. *Housing Studies, 17,* 71–82.

Rosenberg, M. (1979). *Conceiving the self.* New York: Basic Books.

Rosenfeld, B. (2003). Recidivism in stalking and obsessional harassment. *Law and Human Behavior, 27,* 251–265.

Rosenfeld, B. (2004). Violence risk factors in stalking and obsessional harassment: A review and preliminary meta-analysis. *Criminal Justice and Behavior, 31,* 9–36.

Rosenfeld, R., & Decker, S. (1999). Are arrest statistics a valid measure of illicit drug use? The relationship between criminal justice and public health indicators of cocaine, heroin, and marijuana use. *Justice Quarterly, 16,* 685–699.

Ross, C. (1995). Reconceptualizing marital status as a continuum of social attachment. *Journal of Marriage and the Family, 57,* 129–134.

Ross, C., & Mirowsky, J. (1989). Explaining the social patterns of depression: Control and problem solving—or support and talking? *Journal of Health and Social Behavior, 30,* 206–219.

Ross, C., & Mirowsky, J. (2001). Neighborhood disadvantage, disorder, and health. *Journal of Health and Social Behavior, 42,* 258–276.

Ross, C., Mirowsky, J., & Pribesh, S. (2001). Powerlessness and the amplification of threat: Neighborhood disadvantage, disorder, and mistrust. *American Sociological Review, 66,* 568–591.

Ross, S. (1996) Risk of physical abuse to children of spouse abusing parents. *Child Abuse & Neglect, 20,* 589–598.

Rothbaum, B. (1997). A controlled study of eye movement desensitization and reprocessing in the treatment of posttraumatic stress disorder. *Bulletin of the Menninger Clinic, 61,* 317–335.

Rothbaum, B., Foa, E., Riggs, D., Murdock, T., & Walsh, W. (1992). A prospective examination of post-traumatic stress disorder in rape victims. *Journal of Traumatic Stress, 5,* 455–475.

Rotter, J. (1966). Generalized expectancies of internal versus external control of reinforcements. *Psychological Monographs, 80,* 1–28.

Roy, A., DeJong, J., Lamparski, D., George, T., & Linnoila, M. (1991). Depression among alcoholics: Relationship to clinical and cerebrospinal fluid variables. *Archives of General Psychiatry, 48,* 428–432.

Rozin, P. (2003). Introduction: Evolutionary and cultural perspectives on affect. In R. Davidson, K. Scherer, & H. Goldsmith (Eds.), *Handbook of affective sciences* (pp 839–851). New York: Oxford University Press.

Ruback, R. (1994). Advice to crime victims: Effects of crime, victim, and advisor factors. *Criminal Justice and Behavior, 21,* 423–442.

Ruback, R., Menard, K., Outlaw, M., & Shaffer, J. (1999). Normative advice to campus crime victims: Effects of gender, age, and alcohol. *Violence and Victims, 14,* 381–396.

Ruble, D., Greulich, F., Pomerantz, E., & Gochberg, B. (1993). The role of gender-related processes in the development of sex differences in self-evaluation and depression. *Journal of Affective Disorders, 29,* 97–128.

Ruiz, R., Fullerton, J., Brown, C., & Dudley, D. (2002). Predicting risk of preterm birth: The roles of stress, clinical risk factors, and corticotrophin-releasing hormone. *Biological Research for Nursing, 4,* 54–64.

Rumstein-McKean, O., & Hunsley, J. (2001). Interpersonal and family functioning of female survivors of childhood sexual abuse. *Clinical Psychology Review, 21,* 471–490.

Rusbult, C., & Martz, J. (1995). Remaining in an abusive relationship: An investment model analysis of nonvoluntary dependence. *Personality and Social Psychology Bulletin, 21*, 558–571.

Russell, D. (1990). *Rape in marriage*. Indianapolis: Indiana University Press.

Rutter, M. (1987). Psychosocial resilience and protective mechanisms. *American Journal of Orthopsychiatry, 57*, 316–331.

Rutter, M. (1990). Psychosocial resilience and protective mechanisms. In J. Rolf, A. Masten, D. Cicchetti, K. Nuechterlein, & S. Weintraub (Eds.), *Risk and protective factors in the development of psychopathology* (pp. 181–214). New York: Cambridge University Press.

Ruzek, J., Polusny, M., & Abueg, F. (1998). Assessment and treatment of concurrent posttraumatic stress disorder and substance abuse. In V. Follette, J. Ruzek, & F. Abueg (Eds.), *Cognitive–behavioral therapies for trauma* (pp. 226–255). New York: Guilford Press.

Ryan, K., Kilmer, R., Cauce, A., Watanabe, H., & Hoyt, D. (2000). Psychological consequences of child maltreatment in homeless adolescents: Untangling the unique effects of maltreatment and family environment. *Child Abuse & Neglect, 24*, 333–352.

Sabatelli, R., & Bartle-Haring, S. (2003). Family-of-origin experiences and adjustment in married couples. *Journal of Marriage and Family, 65*, 159–169.

Sabo, A. (1997). Etiological significance of associations between childhood trauma and borderline personality disorder: Conceptual and clinical implications. *Journal of Personality Disorders, 11*, 50–70.

Sabourin, T., Infante, D., & Rudd, J. (1993). Verbal aggression in marriages: A comparison of violent, distressed but nonviolent, and nondistressed couples. *Human Communication Research, 20*, 245–267.

Sackett, L., & Saunders, D. (1999). The impact of different forms of psychological abuse on battered women. *Violence and Victims, 14*, 105–117.

Saladin, M., Drobes, D., Coffey, S., Dansky, B., Brady, K., & Kilpatrick, D. (2003). PTSD symptom severity as a predictor of cue-elicited drug craving in victims of violent crime. *Addictive Behaviors, 28*, 1611–1629.

Salazar, L., & Cook, S. (2002). Violence against women: Is psychology part of the problem or the solution? A current analysis of the psychological research from 1990 through 1999. *Journal of Community and Applied Social Psychology, 12*, 410–421.

Salomon, A., Bassuk, S., & Huntington, N. (2002). The relationship between intimate partner violence and the use of addictive substances in poor and homeless single mothers. *Violence Against Women, 8*, 785–815.

Saltzman, L., & Mercy, J. (1993). Assaults between intimates: The range of relationship involved. In A. Wilson (Ed.), *Homicide: The victim / offender connection*. Cincinnati, OH: Anderson.

Sampson, R. (1991). Linking the micro- and macrolevel dimensions of community social organization. *Social Forces, 70*, 43–64.

Sampson, R. (1997, August 15). Neighborhoods and violent crime: A multilevel study of collective efficacy. *Science, 277*, 918–924.

Sampson, R., Morenoff, J., & Gannon-Rowley, T. (2002). Assessing "neighborhood effects": Social processes and new directions in research. *Annual Review of Sociology, 28*, 443–478.

Sampson, R., & Raudenbush, S. (1999). Systematic social observation of public spaces: A new look at disorder in urban neighborhoods. *American Journal of Sociology, 105*, 603–651.

Sanathara, V., Gardner, C., Prescott, C., & Kendler, K. (2003). Interpersonal dependence and major depression: Aetiological inter-relationship and gender differences. *Psychological Medicine, 33*, 927–931.

Sandman, C., Wadhwa, P., Glynn, L., Chicz-DeMet, A., Porto, M., & Garite, T. (1999). Corticotropin-releasing hormone and fetal response in human pregnancy. In C. A. Sandman, F. L. Strand, B. Beckwith, B. M. Chronwall, F. W. Flynn, & R. J. Nachman (Eds.), *Annals of the New York Academy of Sciences: Vol. 897. Neuropeptides: Structure and function in biology and behavior* (pp. 66–75). New York: New York Academy of Sciences.

Sansone, R., Wiederman, M., & Sansone, L. (1998). Borderline personality symptomatology, experience of multiple types of trauma, and health care utilization among women in a primary care setting. *Journal of Clinical Psychiatry, 59*, 108–111.

Sapolsky, R. (1990). Glucocorticoids, hippocampal damage and the glutamatergic synapse. In P. Coleman, G. Higgins, & C. Phelps (Eds.), *Molecular and cellular mechanisms of neuronal plasticity in normal aging and Alzheimer's disease: Progress in brain research* (Vol. 86, pp. 13–23). St. Louis, MO: Elsevier Science.

Sapolsky, R. (1996, August 9). Why stress is bad for your brain. *Science, 273,* 749–750.

Sapolsky, R. (2000). Glucocorticoids and hippocampal atrophy in neuropsychiatric disorders. *Archives of General Psychiatry, 57,* 925–935.

Sapolsky, R., Alberts, S., & Altman, J. (1997). Hypercortisolism associated with subordinace or social isolation among wild baboons. *Archives of General Psychiatry, 54,* 1137–1143.

Sapolsky, R., Romero, L., & Munck, A. (2000). How do glucocorticoids influence stress responses? Integrating permissive, suppressive, stimulatory, and preparative actions. *Endocrine Reviews, 21,* 55–89.

Sappington, A., Pharr, R., Tunstall, A., & Rickert, E. (1997). Relationships among child abuse, date abuse, and psychological problems. *Journal of Clinical Psychology, 53,* 319–329.

Saunders, B., Kilpatrick, D., Hanson, R., Resnick, H., & Walker, M. (1999). Prevalence, case characteristics, and long-term psychological correlates of child rape among women: A national survey. *Child Maltreatment, 4,* 187–200.

Saunders, D. (1994). Posttraumatic stress symptom profiles of battered women: A comparison of survivors in two settings. *Violence and Victims, 9,* 31–44.

Saunders, R. (1998). The legal perspective on stalking. In J. Meloy (Ed.), *The psychology of stalking: Clinical and forensic perspectives* (pp. 25–49). San Diego, CA: Academic Press.

Saxe, L., Kadushin, C., Beveridge, A., Livert, D., Tighe, E., Rindskopf, D., et al. (2001). The visibility of illicit drugs: Implications for community-based drug control strategies. *American Journal of Public Health, 91,* 1987–1994.

Sayette, M. (1999). Does drinking reduce stress? *Alcohol Research and Health, 23,* 250–255.

Schaaf, K., & McCanne, T. (1998). Relationship of child sexual, physical, and combined sexual and physical abuse to adult victimization and posttraumatic stress disorder. *Child Abuse and Neglect, 22,* 1119–1133.

Schacter, S., & Singer, S. (1962). Cognitive, social, and physiological determinants of emotional state. *Psychological Review, 69,* 379–399.

Schafer, J., Caetano, R., & Clark, C. (1998). Rates of intimate partner violence in the United States. *American Journal of Public Health, 88,* 11, 1702–1704.

Scheck, M., Schaeffer, J., & Gillette, C. (1998). Brief psychological intervention with traumatized young women: The efficacy of eye movement desensitization and reprocessing. *Journal of Traumatic Stress, 11,* 25–44.

Scheier, L., Botvin, G., Griffin, K., & Diaz, T. (2000). Dynamic growth models of self-esteem and adolescent alcohol use. *Journal of Early Adolescence, 20,* 178–209.

Scherer, K. (2001). Appraisal considered as a process of multilevel sequential checking. In K. Scherer, A. Schorr, & T. Johnstone (Eds.), *Appraisal processes in emotion: Theory, methods, research* (pp. 92–120). New York: Oxford University Press.

Schmidt, J., & Sherman, L. (1996). Does arrest deter domestic violence? In E. Buzawa & C. Buzawa (Eds.), *Do arrests and restraining orders work?* (pp. 43–53). Thousand Oaks, CA: Sage.

Schmidt, L., & McCarty, D. (2000). Welfare reform and the changing landscape of substance abuser services for low-income women. *Alcoholism: Clinical and Experimental Research, 24,* 1298–1311.

Schober, R., & Annis, H. (1996). Barriers to help-seeking for change in drinking: A gender-focused review of the literature. *Addictive Behaviors, 21,* 81–92.

Schoon, I., Sacker, A., & Bartley, M. (2003). Socio-economic adversity and psychosocial adjustment: A developmental–contextual perspective. *Social Science and Medicine, 57,* 1001–1015.

Schubot, D. (2001). Date rape prevalence among female high school students in a rural Midwestern state during 1993, 1995, and 1997. *Journal of Interpersonal Violence, 16,* 291–296.

Schuckit, M. (1992). A clinical model of genetic influences in alcohol dependence. *Journal of Studies on Alcohol, 55,* 5–17.

Schuller, R., & Stewart, A. (2000). Police responses to sexual assault complaints: The role of perpetrator/complainant intoxication. *Law and Human Behavior, 24,* 535–551.

Schumaker, J., Fals-Stewart, W., & Leonard, K. (2003). Domestic violence treatment referrals for men seeking alcohol treatment. *Journal of Substance Abuse Treatment, 24,* 279–283.

Schwalbe, M., & Staples, C. (1991). Gender differences in sources of self-esteem. *Social Psychology Quarterly, 54,* 158–168.

Schwartz, M., & DeKeseredy, W. (1997). *Sexual assault on the college campus: The role of male peer support.* Thousand Oaks, CA: Sage.

Schwartz, M., & DeKeseredy, W. (2000). Aggregation bias and woman abuse: Variations by male peer support, region, language, and school type. *Child Development, 71,* 555–565.

Schwartz, M., DeKeseredy, W., Tait, D., & Alvi, S. (2001). Male peer support and a feminist routine activities theory: Understanding sexual assault on the college campus. *Justice Quarterly, 18,* 623–649.

Schwartz, M., & Nogrady, C. (1996). Fraternity membership, rape myths, and sexual aggression on a college campus. *Violence Against Women, 2,* 148–162.

Schwartz, M., & Pitts, V. (1995). Exploring a feminist routine activities approach to explaining sexual assault. *Justice Quarterly, 12,* 9–31.

Scott, K., Schafer, J., & Greenfield, T. (1999). The role of alcohol in physical assault perpetration and victimization. *Journal of Studies on Alcohol, 60,* 528–536.

Scott Collins, K., Schoen, C., Joseph, S., Duchon, L., Simantov, E., & Yellowitz, M. (1999). *Health concerns across a woman's lifespan: The Commonwealth Fund 1998 survey of women's health.* New York: The Commonwealth Fund.

Seeman, M. (1983). Alienation motifs in contemporary theorizing: The hidden continuity of classic themes. *Social Psychology Quarterly, 46,* 171–184.

Seligman, M. (1975). *Helplessness.* San Francisco: Freeman.

Seligman, M., & Csikszentmihalyi, M. (2000). Positive psychology: An introduction. *American Psychologist, 55,* 5–14.

Selye, H. (1956). *The stress of life.* New York: McGraw-Hill.

Selye, H. (1974). *Stress without distress.* New York: Harper & Row.

Selye, H. (1982). History and present status of the stress concept. In L. Goldberger & S. Breznitz (Eds.), *Handbook of stress: Theoretical and clinical aspects* (pp. 7–17). New York: Free Press.

Selye, H. (1991). History and present status of the stress concept. In A. Monat & R. Lazarus (Eds.), *Stress and coping: An anthology* (3rd ed., pp. 21–35). New York: Columbia University Press.

Seto, M., & Barbaree, H. (1995). The role of alcohol in sexual aggression. *Clinical Psychology Review, 15,* 545–566.

Sev'er, A. (1997). Recent or imminent separation and intimate violence against women. *Violence Against Women, 3,* 566–589.

Shalansky, C., Ericksen, J., & Henderson, A. (1999). Abused women and child custody: The ongoing exposure to abusive ex-partners. *Journal of Advanced Nursing, 29,* 416–425.

Shalev, A. (2002). Acute stress reactions in adults. *Biological Psychiatry, 51,* 532–543.

Shalev, A., Yehuda, R., & McFarlane, A. (Eds.). (2000). *International handbook of human response to trauma.* New York: Kluwer Academic/Plenum.

Shapiro, D., Barkham, M., Rees, A., Hardy, G., Reynolds, S., & Startup, M. (1994). Effects of treatment duration and severity of depression on the effectiveness of cognitive-behavioral and psychodynamic–interpersonal psychotherapy. *Journal of Counseling and Clinical Psychology, 62,* 522–534.

Shapiro, F. (1989). Eye movement desensitization: A new treatment for post-traumatic stress disorder. *Journal of Behavior Therapy and Experimental Psychiatry, 20,* 211–217.

Shapiro, F. (1995). *Eye movement desensitization and reprocessing.* New York: Guilford Press.

Sharps, P., & Campbell, J. (1999). Health consequences for victims of violence in intimate relationships. In X. Arriaga & S. Oskamp (Eds.), *Violence in intimate partner relationships* (pp. 163–180). Thousand Oaks, CA: Sage.

Shavelson, R., Hubner, J., & Stanton, G. (1976). Self-concept: Validation of construct interpretations. *Review of Educational Research, 46,* 407–441.

Shaver, J., Johnston, S., Lentz, M., & Landis, C. (2002). Stress exposure, psychological distress, and physiological stress activation in midlife women with insomnia. *Psychosomatic Medicine, 64,* 793–802.

Shaw, C. (1999). A framework for the study of coping, illness behavior and outcomes. *Journal of Advanced Nursing, 29,* 1246–1255.

Shea, M., Zlotnick, C., & Weisberg, R. (1999). Commonality and specificity of personality disorder profiles in subjects with trauma histories. *Journal of Personality Disorders, 13,* 199–210.

Sher, K., Bartholow, B., & Nanda, S. (2001). Short- and long-term effects of fraternity and sorority membership on heavy drinking: A social norms perspective. *Psychology of Addictive Behaviors, 15,* 42–51.

Sheridan, L., Blaauw, E., & Davies, G. (2003). Stalking: Knowns and unknowns. *Trauma, Violence, & Abuse, 4,* 148–162.

Sheridan, L., & Davies, G. (2001). Violence and the prior victim–stalker relationship. *Clinical Behavior and Mental Health, 11,* 102–116.

Sheridan, L., Gillett, R., Davies, G., Blaauw, E., & Patel, D. (2003). "There's no smoke without fire": Are male ex-partners perceived as more "entitled" to stalk than acquaintance or stranger stalkers? *British Journal of Psychology, 94,* 87–98.

Sherman, L., & Berk, R. (1984). The specific deterrence effects of arrest for domestic violence. *American Sociological Review, 49,* 261–272.

Sherman, L., Schmidt, J., Rogan, D., Smith, D., Gartin, P., Cohn, E., et al. (1992). The variable effects of arrest on criminal careers: The Milwaukee domestic violence experiment. *Journal of Criminal Law and Criminology, 83,* 137–169.

Shields, G., Baer, J., Leininger, K., Marlow, J., & DeKeyser, P. (1998). Interdisciplinary health care and female victims of domestic violence. *Social Work in Health Care, 27,* 27–48.

Shively, C. (1998). Social stress and disease susceptibility in female monkeys. *Psychological Science Agenda, 11,* 6–7.

Shuchter, S., Downs, N., & Zisook, S. (1996). *Biologically informed psychotherapy for depression.* New York: Guilford Press.

Siegel, J., Golding, J., Stein, J., Burnam, M., & Sorenson, S. (1990). Reactions to sexual activity: A community study. *Journal of Interpersonal Violence, 5,* 229–246.

Siegel, J., & Williams, L. (2003). Risk factors for sexual victimization of women—Results from a prospective study. *Violence Against Women, 9,* 902–930.

Siemer, M. (2001). Mood-specific effects on appraisal and emotion judgments. *Cognitions and Emotion, 15,* 453–485.

Silverman, A., Reinherz, H., & Giaconia, R. (1996). The long-term sequelae of child and adolescent abuse: A longitudinal community study. *Child Abuse & Neglect, 20,* 709–723.

Silverman, J., & Williamson, G. (1997). Social ecology and entitlements involved in battering by heterosexual college males: Contributions of family and peers. *Violence and Victims, 12,* 147–164.

Simon, G., Vonkorff, M., Barlow, W., Pabiniak, C., & Wagner, E. (1996). Predictors of chronic benzodiazepine use in a health maintenance organization sample. *Journal of Clinical Epidemiology, 49,* 1067–1073.

Simon, L. (1996). Legal treatment of the victim–offender relationship in crimes of violence. *Journal of Interpersonal Violence, 11,* 94–106.

Simon, T., Anderson, M., Thompson, M., Crosby, A., Shelley, G., & Sacks, J. (2001). Attitudinal acceptance of intimate partner violence among U.S. adults. *Violence and Victims 16,* 115–126.

Simoni-Wastila, L. (1998). Gender and psychotropic drug use. *Medical Care, 36,* 88–94.

Simoni-Wastila, L. (2000). The use of abusable prescription drugs: The role of gender. *Journal of Women's Health and Gender-Based Medicine, 9,* 289–297.

Simons, A., Gordon, J., Monroe, S., & Thase, M. (1995). Toward an integration of psychologic, social, and biologic factors in depression: Effects on outcome and course of cognitive therapy. *Journal of Consulting and Clinical Psychology, 63,* 369–377.

Simpson, D., & Brown, B. (Eds.). (2002). Transferring research to practice [Special issue]. *Journal of Substance Abuse Treatment, 22*(4).

Singareddy, R., & Balon, R. (2002). Sleep in posttraumatic stress disorder. *Annals of Clinical Psychiatry, 14,* 183–190.

Sinha, R., & Rounsaville, B. (2002). Sex differences in depressed substance abusers. *Journal of Clinical Psychiatry, 63,* 616–627.

Skodol, A., & Bender, D. (2003). Why are women diagnosed borderline more than men? *Psychiatric Quarterly, 74,* 349–360.

Skodol, A., Gunderson, J., Pfohl, B., Widiger, T., Livesley, W., & Siever, L. (2002). The borderline diagnosis I: Psychopathology comorbidity, and personality structure. *Biological Psychiatry, 51,* 936–950.

Skodol, A., Stout, R., McGlashan, T., Grilo, C., Gunderson, J., Shae, M., et al. (1999). Co-occurrence of mood and personality disorders: A report from the Collaborative Longitudinal Personality Disorders Study (CLPS). *Depression and Anxiety, 10,* 175–182.

Slesinger, D., Archer, R., & Duane, W. (2002). MMPI-2 characteristics in a chronic pain population. *Assessment, 9,* 406–414.

Sloan, L. (1995). Revictimization by polygraph: The practice of polygraphing survivors of sexual assault. *Medicine and Law, 14,* 255–267.

Small, M., & Newman, K. (2001). Urban poverty after *The Truly Disadvantaged*: The rediscovery of the family, the neighborhood, and culture. *Annual Review of Sociology, 27,* 23–45.

Smith, A. (2000). It's my decision, isn't it? *Violence Against Women, 6,* 1384–1402.

Smith, B., & Marsh, J. (2002). Client-service matching in substance abuse treatment for women with children. *Journal of Substance Abuse Treatment, 22,* 161–168.

Smith, C., & Kirby, L. (2001). Affect and cognitive appraisal processes. In J. Forgas (Ed.), *Handbook of affect and social cognition* (pp. 75–92). Mahwah, NJ: Erlbaum.

Smith, D., & Germolec, D. (1999). Introduction to immunology and autoimmunity. *Environmental Health Perspectives, 107*(Suppl. 5), 661–665.

Smith, G., Kohn, S., Savage-Stevens, Finch, J., Ingate, R., & Lim, Y. (2000). The effects of interpersonal and personal agency on perceived control and psychological well-being in adulthood. *Gerontologist, 40,* 458–468.

Smith, H., & Betz, N. (2002). An examination of efficacy and esteem pathways to depression in young adulthood. *Journal of Counseling Psychology, 49,* 438–448.

Smith, P., Danis, M., & Helmick, L. (1998). Changing the health care response to battered women: A health education approach. *Family and Community Health, 20,* 1–18.

Smith, P., Smith, J., & Earp, J. (1999). Beyond the measurement trap: A reconstructed conceptualization and measurement of women battering. *Psychology of Women Quarterly, 23,* 177–193.

Smith, P., White, J., & Holland, L. (2003). A longitudinal perspective on dating violence among adolescent and college-age women. *American Journal of Public Health, 93,* 1104–1109.

Smith, T. (1994). Attitudes toward sexual permissiveness: Trends, correlates, and behavioral connections. In A. Rossi (Ed.), *Sexuality across the life course* (pp. 63–97). Chicago: University of Chicago Press.

Sobo, E. (1993). Inner-city women and AIDS: The psychosocial benefits of unsafe sex. *Culture, Medicine, and Psychiatry, 17,* 455–485.

Sobo, E. (1995). Finance, romance, social support and condom use among impoverished inner-city women. *Human Organization, 54,* 115–128.

Solomon, E., & Heide, K. (2005). The biology of trauma: Implications for treatment. *Journal of Interpersonal Violence, 20,* 51–60.

Solomon, S., Gerrity, E., & Muff, A. (1992). Efficacy of treatments for posttraumatic stress disorder. *Journal of the American Medical Association, 268,* 633–638.

Sommers, M., Schafer, J., Zink, T., Hutson, L., & Hillard, P. (2001). Injury patterns in women resulting from sexual assault. *Trauma, Violence, & Abuse, 2,* 240–258.

Sorensen, J., Rawson, R., Guydish, J., & Zweben, J. (Eds.). (2003). *Drug abuse treatment through collaboration: Practice and research partnerships that work.* Washington, DC: American Psychological Association.

Sorenson, S. (1996). Violence against women: Examining ethnic differences and commonalities. *Evaluation Review, 20,* 123–145.

Sorenson, S., Upchurch, D., & Shen, H. (1996). Violence and injury in marital arguments: Risk patterns and gender differences. *American Journal of Public Health, 86,* 35–40.

South, S. (2001). Time-dependent effects of wives' employment on marital dissolution. *American Sociological Review, 66,* 226–245.

South, S., & Lloyd, K. (1995). Spousal alternatives and marital dissolution. *American Sociological Review, 60,* 21–35.

South, S., Trent, K., & Shen, Y. (2001). Changing partners: Toward a macrostructural-opportunity theory of marital dissolution. *Journal of Marriage and Family, 63,* 743–754.

Sparks, R. (1982). *Research on victims of crime.* Washington, DC: U.S. Government Printing Office.

Spears, J., & Spohn, C. (1997). The effect of evidence factors and victim characteristics on prosecutors' charging decisions in sexual assault cases. *Justice Quarterly, 14,* 501–524.

Spitzberg, B. (2002). The tactical topography of stalking victimization and management. *Trauma, Violence, & Abuse, 3,* 261–288.

Spitzberg, B., & Rhea, J. (1999). Obsessive relational intrusion and sexual coercion victimization. *Journal of Interpersonal Violence, 14,* 3–20.

Spohn, C., Beichner, D., & Davis-Frenzel, E. (2001). Prosecutorial justifications for sexual assault case rejection: Guarding the "gateway to justice." *Social Problems, 48,* 206–235.

Spohn, C., & Holleran, D. (2001). Prosecuting sexual assault: A comparison of charging decisions in sexual assault cases involving strangers, acquaintances, and intimate partners. *Justice Quarterly, 18,* 651–688.

Spohn, C., & Spears, J. (1996). The effect of offender and victim characteristics on sexual assault case processing decisions. *Justice Quarterly, 13,* 649–679.

Springer, C., Britt, T., & Schlenker, B. (1998). Codependency: Clarifying the construct. *Journal of Mental Health Counseling, 20,* 141–152.

Squire, L. (1987). *Memory and brain.* New York: Oxford University Press.

Squire, L., & Knowlton, B. (1995). Memory, hippocampus, and brain systems. In M. Gazzaniga (Ed.), *The cognitive neurosciences* (pp. 825–838). Cambridge, MA: MIT Press.

Stark, E. (1996). Mandatory arrest: A reply to its critics. In E. Buzawa & C. Buzawa (Eds.), *Do arrests and restraining orders work?* (pp. 115–149). Thousand Oaks, CA: Sage.

Stark, E., & Flitcraft, A. (1996). *Women at risk: Domestic violence and women's health.* Thousand Oaks, CA: Sage.

Stark, R. (1987). Deviant places: A theory of the ecology of crime. *Criminology, 25,* 893–909.

Staton, M., Leukefeld, C., & Logan, T. (2001). Health service utilization and victimization among incarcerated female substance abusers. *Substance Use and Misuse, 36,* 713–732.

Staveteig, S., & Wigton, A. (2000). *Racial and ethnic disparities: Key findings from the National Survey of America's Families.* New York: Urban Institute.

Stein, M., & Barrett-Connor, E. (2000). Sexual assault and physical health: Findings from a population-based study of older adults. *Psychosomatic Medicine, 62,* 838–843.

Stein, M., & Cyr, M. (1997). Women and substance abuse. *Medical Clinics of North America, 81,* 979–998.

Sterk-Elifson, C. (1994). Sexuality among African-American women. In A. Rossi (Ed.), *Sexuality across the life course* (pp. 99–126). Chicago: University of Chicago Press.

Sterling, P., & Eyer, J. (1988). Allostasis: A new paradigm to explain arousal pathology. In S. Fisher & J. Reason (Eds.), *Handbook of life stress, cognition, and health* (pp. 629–649). New York: Wiley.

Stermac, L., Del Bove, G., & Addison, M. (2001). Violence, injury, and presentation patterns in spousal sexual assaults. *Violence Against Women, 7,* 1218–1233.

Stermac, L., Reist, D., Addison, M., & Millar, G. (2002). Childhood risk factors for women's sexual victimization. *Journal of Interpersonal Violence, 17,* 647–670.

Stets, J. (1990). Verbal and physical aggression in marriage. *Journal of Marriage and the Family, 52,* 501–514.

Stewart, A., & Maddren, K. (1997). Police officers' judgments of blame in family violence: The impact of gender and alcohol. *Sex Roles, 37,* 921–936.

Stewart, S. (1996). Alcohol abuse in individual exposed to trauma: A critical review. *Psychological Bulletin, 120,* 1, 83–112.

Stewart, S., & Conrod, P. (2003). Psychosocial models of functional associations between posttraumatic stress disorder and substance use disorder. In P. Ouimette & P. Brown (Eds.), *Trauma and substance abuse: Causes, consequences, and treatment of comorbid disorders* (pp. 29–71). Washington, DC: American Psychiatric Press.

Stewart, S., Zvolensky, M., & Eifert, G. (2002). The relations of anxiety sensitivity, experiential avoidance, and alexithymic coping to young adults' motivations for drinking. *Behavior Modification, 26,* 274–296.

Stewart, W., Ricci, J., Chee, E., Hahn, S., & Morganstein, D. (2003). Cost of lost productive work time among US workers with depression. *Journal of the American Medical Association, 289,* 3135–3144.

Stith, S., Rosen, K., & McCollum, E. (2003). Effectiveness of couples treatment for spouse abuse. *Journal of Marital and Family Therapy, 29,* 407–426.

Stith, S., Rosen, K., Middleton, K., Busch, A., Lundeberg, K., & Carlton, R. (2000). The intergenerational transmission of spouse abuse: A meta-analysis. *Journal of Marriage and the Family, 62,* 640–654.

Straight, E., Harper, F., & Arias, I. (2003). The impact of partner psychological abuse on health behaviors and health status in college women. *Journal of Interpersonal Violence, 18,* 1035–1054.

Straus, M., & Gelles, R. (Eds.). (1990). *Physical violence in American families: Risk factors and adaptation to violence in 8,145 families.* New Brunswick, NJ: Transaction.

Straus, M., Hamby, S., Boney-McCoy, S., & Sugarman, D. (1996). The revised conflict tactics scales (CTS2): Development and preliminary psychometric data. *Journal of Family Issues, 17,* 283–316.

Straus, M., & Smith, C. (1990). Violence in Hispanic families in the United States: Incidence rates and structural interpretations. In M. Straus & R. Gelles (Eds.), *Physical violence in American families: Risk factors and adaptations to violence in 8,145 families* (pp. 341–368). New Brunswick, NJ: Transaction.

Street, A., & Arias, I. (2001). Psychological abuse and posttraumatic stress disorder in battered women: Examining the roles of shame and guilt. *Violence and Victims, 16,* 65–78.

Strickland, T., Mena, I., Villanueva-Meyer, J., Miller, B., Cummings, J., Mehringer, C., et al. (1993). Cerebral perfusion and neuropsychological consequences of chronic cocaine use. *Journal of Neuropsychiatry and Clinical Neuroscience, 5,* 419–427.

Strober, M., Freeman, R., Lampert, C., Diamond, J., & Kaye, W. (2000). Controlled family study of anorexia nervosa and bulimia nervosa: Evidence of shared liability and transmission of partial syndromes. *American Journal of Psychiatry, 157,* 393–401.

Substance Abuse and Mental Health Services Administration. (1997). *Substance use among women in the United States* (DHHS Publication No. SMA 97-3162). Rockville, MD: U.S. Government Printing Office.

Substance Abuse and Mental Health Services Administration. (2000). *Summary of findings from the 1999 National Household Survey on Drug Abuse.* Rockville, MD: U.S. Government Printing Office.

Substance Abuse and Mental Health Services Administration. (2001a). *Summary of findings from the 2000 National Household Survey on Drug Abuse.* Rockville, MD: U.S. Government Printing Office.

Substance Abuse and Mental Health Services Administration. (2001b). *Risk and protective factors for adolescent drug use: Findings from the 1997 National Household Survey on Drug Abuse.* Rockville, MD: U.S. Government Printing Office.

Substance Abuse and Mental Health Services Administration. (2001c). *Mental health: Culture, race, and ethnicity—A supplement to mental health: A report to the surgeon general.* Rockville, MD: U.S. Department of Health and Human Services.

Substance Abuse and Mental Health Services Administration. (2002, January). *The National Household Survey on Drug Abuse (NHSDA) report: Neighborhood characteristics and youth marijuana use.* Retrieved September, 9, 2003, from http://www.oas.samhsa.gov/2k1/neighbor/neighbor.htm

Sudderth, L. (1998). "It'll come right back at me": The interactional context of discussing rape with others. *Violence Against Women, 4,* 572–595.

Sullivan, C., & Bybee, D. (1999). Reducing violence using community-based advocacy for women with abusive partners. *Journal of Consulting and Clinical Psychology, 67,* 43–53.

Sullivan, C., & Gillum, T. (2001). Shelters and other community-based services for battered women and their children. In C. Renzetti, J. Edleson, & R. Bergen (Eds.), *Sourcebook on violence against women* (pp. 227–241). Thousand Oaks, CA: Sage.

Sullivan, G., & Strongman, K. (2003). Vacillating and mixed emotions: A conceptual–discursive perspective on contemporary emotion and cognitive appraisal theories through examples of pride. *Journal for the Theory of Social Behavior, 33,* 203–226.

Sullivan, P. (1995). Mortality in anorexia nervosa. *American Journal of Psychiatry, 152,* 1073–1074.

Sullivan, P., Neale, J., & Kendler, K. (2000). Genetic epidemiology of major depression: Review and meta-analysis. *American Journal of Psychiatry, 157,* 1552–1562.

Suls, J., & Green, P. (2003). Pluralistic ignorance and college student perceptions of gender-specific alcohol norms. *Health Psychology, 22,* 479–486.

Suls, J., Martin, R., & Wheeler, L. (2002). Social comparison: Why, with whom, and with what effect? *Current Directions in Psychological Science, 11,* 159–163.

Surrey, J. (1991). The "self-in-relation": A theory of women's development. In J. Jordan, A. Kaplan, J. Miller, I. Stiver, & J. Surrey (Eds.), *Women's growth in connection: Writings from the Stone Center* (pp. 51–66). New York: Guilford Press.

Susman, S., Dent, C., McAdams, L., Stacy, A., Burton, D., & Flay, B. (1994). Group self-identification and adolescent cigarette smoking: A 1-year prospective study. *Journal of Abnormal Psychology, 103,* 576–580.

Sussman, L., Robins, L., & Earls, F. (1987). Treatment-seeking for depression by Black and White Americans. *Social Science and Medicine, 24,* 187–196.

Svarstad, B., Cleary, P., Mechanic, D., & Robers, P. (1987). Gender differences in the acquisition of prescribed drugs: An epidemiological study. *Medical Care, 25,* 1089–1098.

Swartz, M., Blazer, D., George, L., & Winfield, I. (1990). Estimating the prevalence of borderline personality disorder in the community. *Journal of Personality Disorders, 4,* 257–272.

Swearingen, C., Moyer, A., & Finney, J. (2003). Alcoholism treatment outcome studies, 1970–1998: An expanded look at the nature of the research. *Addictive Behaviors, 28,* 415–436.

Swendsen, J., Conway, K., Rounsaville, B., & Merikangas, K. (2003). Are personality traits familial risk factors for substance use disorders? Results of a controlled family study. *American Journal of Psychiatry, 159,* 1760–1766.

Swendsen, J., & Merikangas, K. (2000). The comorbidity of substance use and depression. *Clinical Psychology Review, 20,* 173–189.

Szeszko, P., Goldberg, E., Gunduz-Bruce, H., Ashtari, M., Robinson, D., Malhotra, A., et al. (2003). Smaller anterior hippocampal formation volume in antipsychotic-naïve patients with first-episode schizophrenia. *American Journal of Psychiatry, 160,* 2190–2197.

Tafet, G., & Bernardini, R. (2003). Psychoneuroendicronological links between chronic stress and depression. *Progress in Neuro-Psychopharmacology and Biological Psychiatry, 27,* 893–903.

Talley, N., & Jones, B. (1998). Is the association between irritable bowel syndrome and abuse explained by neuroticism? A population based study. *Gut, 42,* 47–53.

Talley, N., & Koloski, N. (2000). Irritable bowel syndrome. In M. Goldman & M. Hatch (Eds.), *Women and health* (pp. 1098–1109). New York: Academic Press.

Tamres, L., Janicki, D., & Helgeson, V. (2002). Sex differences in coping behavior: A meta-analytic review and an examination of relative coping. *Personality and Social Psychology Review, 6,* 2–30.

Tan, C., Basta, J., Sullivan, C., & Davidson, W. (1995). The role of social support in the lives of women exiting domestic violence shelters. *Journal of Interpersonal Violence, 10,* 437–451.

Taylor, B., Davis, R., & Maxwell, C. (2001). The effects of a group batterer treatment program: A randomized experiment in Brooklyn. *Justice Quarterly, 18,* 171–201.

Taylor, J. (2002). "The straw that broke the camel's back:" African American women's strategies for disengaging from abusive relationships. In C. West (Ed.), *Violence in the lives of Black women: Battered black and blue* (pp. 79–94). New York: Haworth Press.

Taylor, R., Jason, L., & Jahn, S. (2003). Chronic fatigue and sociodemographic characteristics as predictors of psychiatric disorders in a community-based sample. *Psychosomatic Medicine, 65,* 896–901.

Taylor, R., Mann, A., White, N., & Goldberg, D. (2000). Attachment style in patients with unexplained physical complaints. *Psychological Medicine, 30,* 931–941.

Taylor, S., & Brown, J. (1991). Illusion and well-being: A social psychological perspective on mental health. *Psychological Bulletin, 103,* 193–210.

Taylor, S., Klein, L., Lewis, B., Gruenewald, T., Gurung, R., & Updegraff, J. (2000). Biobehavioral responses to stress in females: Tend-and-befriend, not fight-or-flight. *Psychological Review, 107,* 411–429.

Taylor, S., Repetti, R., & Seeman, T. (1997). Health psychology: What is an unhealthy environment and how does it get under the skin? *Annual Review of Psychology, 48,* 411–448.

Taylor, S., Thordarson, D., Maxfield, L., Fedoroff, I., Lovell, K., & Ogrodniczuk, J. (2003). Comparative efficacy, speed, and adverse effects of three PTSD treatments: Exposure therapy, EMDR, and relaxation training. *Journal of Consulting and Clinical Psychology, 71,* 330–338.

Terrell, E. (1997). Street life: Aggravated and sexual assaults among homeless and runaway adolescents. *Youth & Society, 28,* 267–291.

Testa, M. (2004). The role of substance use in male-to-female physical and sexual violence: A brief review and recommendations for future research. *Journal of Interpersonal Violence, 19,* 1494–1505.

Testa, M., & Dermen, K. (1999). The differential correlates of sexual coercion and rape. *Journal of Interpersonal Violence, 14,* 548–562.

Testa, M., & Livingston, J. (2000). Alcohol and sexual aggression: Reciprocal relationships over time in a sample of high-risk women. *Journal of Interpersonal Violence, 15,* 413–427.

Testa, M., Livingston, J., & Leonard, K. (2003). Women's substance use and experiences of intimate partner violence: A longitudinal investigation among a community sample. *Addictive Behaviors, 28,* 1649–1664.

Testa, M., Miller, B., Downs, W., & Panek, D. (1992). The moderating impact of social support following childhood sexual abuse. *Violence and Victims, 7,* 173–186.

Testa, M., & Parks, K. (1996). The role of women's alcohol consumption in sexual victimization. *Aggression and Violent Behavior, 1,* 217–234.

Thakkar, R., & McCanne, T. (2000). The effects of daily stressors on physical health in women with and without a childhood history of sexual abuse. *Child Abuse and Neglect, 24,* 209–221.

Thase, M., Dube, S., Bowler, K., Howland, R., Myers, J., Friedman, E., & Jarrett, D. (1996). Hypothalamic–pituitary–adrenocortical activity and response to cognitive behavior therapy in unmedicated, hospitalized depressed patients. *American Journal of Psychiatry, 153,* 886–891.

Thomas, C., & Corcoran, J. (2001). Empirically based marital and family intervention for alcohol abuse: A review. *Research on Social Work Practice, 11,* 549–575.

Thompson, M., Arias, I., Basile, K., & Desai, S. (2002). The association between childhood physical and sexual victimization and health problems in adulthood in a national representative sample of women. *Journal of Interpersonal Violence, 17,* 1115–1129.

Thompson, M., Kaslow, N., Kingree, J., Rashid, A., Puett, R., Jacobs, D., & Matthews, A. (2000). Partner violence, social support, and distress among inner-city African American women. *American Journal of Community Psychology, 28,* 127–143.

THRIVEnet Story of the Month—December 1999. (1999). Retrieved December 29, 2004, from http://www.thrivenet.com/stories/stories99/stry9912.html

Tice, D., Bratslavsky, E., & Baumeister, R. (2001). Emotional distress regulation takes precedence over impulse control: If you feel bad, do it! *Journal of Personality and Social Psychology, 80,* 53–67.

Tiet, Q., Bird, H., Davies, M., Hoven, C., Cohen, P., Jensen, P., & Goodman, S. (1998). Adverse life events and resilience. *Journal of the American Academy of Child and Adolescent Psychiatry, 37,* 1191–1201.

Tjaden, P., & Thoennes, N. (1998). *Stalking in America: Findings from the National Violence Against Women Survey* (NCJ 169592). Washington, DC: National Institute of Justice and Centers for Disease Control and Prevention.

Tjaden, P., & Thoennes, N. (2000a). *Full report of the prevalence, incidence, and consequences of violence against women* (NCJ 183781). Washington, DC: National Institute of Justice, Office of Justice Programs, U.S. Department of Justice.

Tjaden, P., & Thoennes, N. (2000b). *Extent, nature and consequences of intimate partner violence* (NCJ 181867). Washington, DC: National Institute of Justice, Office of Justice Programs, U.S. Department of Justice.

Tjaden, P., & Thoennes, N. (2000c). The role of stalking in domestic violence crime reports generated by the Colorado Springs Police Department. *Violence and Victims, 15,* 427–441.

Tjaden, P., & Thoennes, N. (2000d). Prevalence and consequences of male-to-female and female-to-male intimate partner violence as measured by the National Violence Against Women Survey. *Violence Against Women, 6,* 142–161.

Tolman, R., & Raphael, J. (2000). A review of research on welfare and domestic violence. *Journal of Social Issues, 56,* 655–682.

Tolman, R., & Weiscz, A. (1995). Coordinated community intervention for domestic violence: The effects of arrest and prosecution on recidivism of woman abuse perpetrators. *Crime and Delinquency, 41,* 481–495.

Tomaka, J., Blascovich, J., Kibler, J., & Ernst, J. (1997). Cognitive and physiological antecedents of threat and challenge appraisal. *Journal of Personality and Social Psychology, 73,* 63–72.

Tomaka, J., Palacios, R., Schneider, K., Colotla, M., Concha, J., & Herrald, M. (1999). Assertiveness predicts threat and challenge reactions to potential stress among women. *Journal of Personality and Social Psychology, 76,* 1008–1021.

Toner, B., & Akman, D. (2000). Gender role and irritable bowel syndrome: Literature review and hypothesis. *American Journal of Gastroenterology, 95,* 11–16.

Toner, B., Segal, Z., Emmott, S., & Myran, D. (2000). *Cognitive–behavioral treatment of irritable bowel syndrome: The brain–gut connection*. New York: Guilford Press.

Torres, S. (1991). A comparison of wife abuse between two cultures: Perceptions, attitudes, nature, and extent. *Journal of Mental Health Nursing, 12,* 113–131.

Trull, T. (2001). Structural relations between borderline personality disorder features and putative etiological correlates. *Journal of Abnormal Psychology, 110,* 471–481.

Trull, T., Widiger, T., & Burr, R. (2001). A structured interview for the assessment of the five factor model of personality: Facet-level relations to the Axis II personality disorders. *Journal of Personality, 69,* 175–198.

Truman-Schram, D., Cann, A., Calhoun, L., & Vanwallendael, L. (2000). Leaving an abusive dating relationship: An investment model comparison of women who stay versus women who leave. *Journal of Social and Clinical Psychology, 19,* 161–183.

Tsigos, C., & Chrousos, G. (1996). Stress, endocrine manifestations, and diseases. In C. Cooper (Ed.), *Handbook of stress, medicine, and health* (pp. 61–85). New York: CRC Press.

Tsuaung, M., & Faraone, S. (1990). *The genetics of mood disorders*. Baltimore: Johns Hopkins University Press.

Tuel, B., & Russell, R. (1998). Self-esteem and depression in battered women: A comparison of lesbian and heterosexual survivors. *Violence Against Women, 4,* 344–362.

Turner, R. (1999). Social support and coping. In A. Horwitz & T. Scheid (Eds.), *A handbook for the study of mental health: Social contexts, theories, and systems* (pp. 198–210). New York: Cambridge University Press.

Turner, R., Lloyd, D., & Roszell, P. (1999). Personal resources and the social distribution of depression. *American Journal of Community Psychology, 27,* 643–672.

Turner, R., Sorenson, A., & Turner, J. (2000). Social contingencies in mental health: A seven-year follow-up study of teenage mothers. *Journal of Marriage and the Family, 62,* 777–791.

Turner, R., & Wheaton, B. (1997). Checklist measurement of stressful life events. In S. Cohen, R. Kessler, & L. Gordon (Eds.), *Measuring stress: A guide for health and social scientists* (pp. 29–58). New York: Oxford University Press.

Turner, R., Wheaton, B., & Lloyd, D. (1995). The epidemiology of social stress. *American Sociological Review, 60,* 104–125.

Tutty, L. (1999). Residents' views of the efficacy of shelters services for assaulted women. *Violence Against Women, 5,* 898–926.

Tutty, L., Bidgood, B., & Rothery, M. (1996). Evaluating the effect of group process and client variables in support groups for battered women. *Research on Social Work Practice, 6,* 308–324.

Tyler, K., Hoyt, D., & Whitbeck, L. (2000). The effects of early sexual abuse on later sexual victimization among female homeless and runaway adolescents. *Journal of Interpersonal Violence, 15,* 235–251.

Tyler, K., Hoyt, D., Whitbeck, L., & Cauce, A. (2001). The impact of childhood sexual abuse on later sexual victimization among runaway youth. *Journal of Research on Adolescence, 11,* 151–176.

Uchino, B., Cacioppo, J., & Kiecolt-Glaser, J. (1996). The relationship between social support and physiological processes: A review with emphasis on underlying mechanisms and implications for health. *Psychological Bulletin, 119,* 488–531.

Uchino, B., Uno, D., & Holt-Lunstad, J. (1999). Social support, physiological processes, and health. *Current Directions in Psychological Science, 8,* 145–148.

Ulbrich, P., & Stockdale, J. (2002). Making family planning clinics an empowerment zone for rural battered women. In C. Reyes, W. Rudman, & C. Hewitt (Eds.), *Domestic violence and health care: Policies and prevention* (pp. 83–100). New York: Haworth Press.

Ullman, S. (1996). Social reactions, coping strategies, and self-blame attributions in adjustment to sexual assault. *Psychology of Women Quarterly, 20,* 505–526.

Ullman, S. (1999). Social support and recovery from sexual assault: A review. *Aggression and Violent Behavior, 4,* 343–358.

Ullman, S., & Filipas, H. (2001). Correlates of formal and informal support seeking in sexual assault victims. *Journal of Interpersonal Violence, 16,* 1028–1047.

Ullman, S., & Siegel, J. (1993). Victim–offender relationship and sexual assault. *Violence and Victims, 8,* 121–134.

Ullman, S., & Siegel, J. (1995). Sexual assault, social reactions, and physical health. *Women's Health, 1,* 289–308.

Urry, H., Nitsehke, J., Dolski, I., Jackson, D., Dalton, K., Mueller, C., et al. (2004). Making a life worth living: Neural correlates of well-being. *Psychological Science, 15,* 367–372.

U.S. Department of Health and Human Services, Administration on Children, Youth and Families. (2003). *Child maltreatment 2001.* Washington, DC: U.S. Government Printing Office.

U. S. Department of Justice. (1997). *Sex differences in violent victimization, 1994: Bureau of Justice Statistics special report* (NCJ 178247). Washington, DC: Office of Justice Programs.

U. S. Department of Justice. (2000). *Intimate partner violence: Bureau of Justice Statistics special report* (NCJ 178247). Washington, DC: Office of Justice Programs.

Uziel-Miller, N., & Lyons, J. (2000). Specialized substance abuse treatment for women and their children: An analysis of program design. *Journal of Substance Abuse Treatment, 19,* 355–367.

Vaiva, G., Thomas, P. Ducrocq, F., Fontaine, M., Boss, V., Devos, P., et al. (2003). Low posttrauma GABA levels as a predictive factor in the development of acute posttraumatic stress disorder. *Biological Psychiatry, 55,* 250–254.

Vakili, K., Pillay, S., Lafer, B., Fava, M., Rensaw, P., Bonello-Cintron, C., & Yurgelun-Todd, D. (2000). Hippocampal volume in primary unipolar major depression: A magnetic resonance imaging study. *Biological Psychiatry, 47,* 1087–1090.

Valenstein, M., Taylor, K., Austin, K., Kales, H., McCarthy, J., & Blow, F. (2004). Benzodiazepine use among depressed patients treated in mental health settings. *American Journal of Psychiatry, 161,* 654–661.

Valentiner, D., Foa, E., Riggs, D., & Gershuny, B. (1996). Coping strategies of posttraumatic stress disorder in female victims of sexual and nonsexual assault. *Journal of Abnormal Psychology, 105,* 455–458.

Valera, E., & Berenbaum, H. (2003). Brain injury in battered women. *Journal of Consulting and Clinical Psychology, 71,* 797–804.

Van Cauter, E., & Spiegel, K. (1999). Sleep as a mediator of the relationship between socioeconomic status and health: A hypothesis. In N. Adler, M. Marmot, B. McEwen, & J. Steward (Eds.), *Socioeconomic status and health in industrial nations: Social, psychological, and biological pathways* (pp. 254–261). New York: New York Academy of Sciences.

van der Kolk, B. (1996a). The body keeps the score: Approaches to the psychobiology of posttraumatic stress disorder. In B. van der Kolk, A. McFarlane, & L. Weisaeth (Eds.), *Traumatic stress: The effects of overwhelming experience on mind, body, and society* (pp. 214–243). New York: Guilford Press.

van der Kolk, B. (1996b). The complexity of adaptation to trauma: Self-regulations, stimulus discrimination, and characterlogical development. In B. van der Kolk, A. McFarlane, & L. Weisaeth (Eds.), *Traumatic stress: The effects of overwhelming experience on mind, body, and society* (pp. 182–213). New York: Guilford Press.

van der Kolk, B. (1997). Trauma and memory. In P. Appelbaum, L. Uyehara, & M. Elin (Eds.), *Trauma and memory* (pp. 3–27). New York: Oxford University Press.

van der Kolk, B., & Fisler, R. (1994). Childhood abuse and neglect and loss of self-regulation. *Bulletin of the Menninger Clinic, 58,* 145–168.

van der Kolk, B., Pelcovitz, D., Roth, S. Mandel, F., McFarlane, A., & Herman, J. (1996). Dissociation, somatization, and affect dysregulation: The complexity of adaptation to trauma. *American Journal of Psychiatry, 153,* 83–93.

van der Kolk, B., Perry, C., & Herman, J. (1991). Childhood origins of self-destructive behavior. *American Journal of Psychiatry, 148,* 1665–1671.

van der Kolk, B., van der Hart, O., & Marmar, C. (1996). Dissociation and information processing in posttraumatic stress disorder. In B. van der Kolk, A. McFarlane, & L. Weisaeth (Eds.), *Traumatic stress: The effects of overwhelming experience on mind, body, and society* (pp. 303–332). New York: Guilford Press.

Van Hightower, N., & Gorton, J. (2002). A case study of community-based responses to rural woman battering. *Violence Against Women, 8,* 845–872.

Van Houdenhove, B., Neerinckx, E., Lysens, R., Vertommen, H., Van Houdenhove, L., Onghena, P., et al. (2001). Victimization in chronic fatigue syndrome and fibromyalgia in tertiary care: A controlled study on prevalence and characteristics. *Psychosomatics, 42,* 21–28.

Ventura, L., & Davis, G. (2005). Domestic violence: Court case conviction and recidivism. *Violence Against Women, 11,* 255–277.

Viki, G., & Abrams, D. (2002). But she was unfaithful: Benevolent sexism and reactions to rape victims who violate traditional gender role expectations. *Sex Roles, 47,* 289–293.

Vines, S., Gupta, S., Whiteside, T., Dostal-Johnson, D., & Hummler-Davis, A. (2003). The relationship between chronic pain, immune function, depression, and health behaviors. *Biological Research for Nursing, 5,* 18–29.

Vogel, L., & Marshall, L. (2001). PTSD symptoms and partner abuse: Low income women at risk. *Journal of Traumatic Stress, 14,* 569–584.

Vohs, K., & Heatherton, T. (2000). Self-regulatory failure: A resource-depletion approach. *Psychological Science, 11,* 249–254.

Vonk, M., Bordnick, P., & Graap, K. (2004). Cognitive–behavioral therapy with posttraumatic stress disorder: An evidence-based approach. In A. Roberts & K. Yeager (Eds.), *Evidence-based practice manual: Research and outcome measures in health and human services* (pp. 303–312). New York: Oxford University Press.

Von Korff, M., & Lin, E. (2002). Pain and depression in primary care: Research findings from the Center for Health Studies, Group Health Cooperative. *Journal of Psychosomatic Research, 52,* 313–314.

Vythilingam, M., Heim, C., Newport, J., Miller, A., Anderson, E., Bronen, R., et al. (2002). Childhood trauma associated with smaller hippocampal volume in women with major depression. *American Journal of Psychiatry, 159,* 2072–2080.

Wadhwa, P., Glynn, L., Hobel, C., Garite, T., Porto, M., Chicz-DeMet, A., et al. (2002). Behavioral perinatology: Biobehavioral processes in human fetal development. *Regulatory Peptides, 108,* 149–157.

Wadman, M., & Muelleman, R. (1999). Domestic violence homicides: Emergency department use before victimization. *American Journal of Emergency Medicine, 17,* 689–691.

Wager, T., Rilling, J., Smith, E., Sokolik, A., Casey, K., Davidson, R., et al. (2004, February 20). Placebo-induced changes in fMRI in the anticipation and experience of pain. *Science, 303,* 1162–1167.

Wagner, U., Gais, S., Haider, H., Verleger, R., & Born, J. (2004, January 22). Sleep inspires insight. *Nature, 427,* 352–355.

Walker, E., Katon, W., Russo, J., Ciechanowski, P., Newman, E., & Wagner, A. (2003). Health care costs associated with posttraumatic stress disorder symptoms in women. *Archives of General Psychiatry, 60,* 369–374.

Walker, E., Keegan, D., Sullivan, G., Gardner, M., Berstein, D., & Katon, W. (1997). Psychosocial factors in fibromyalgia compared with rheumatoid arthritis: II. Sexual, physical, and emotional abuse and neglect. *Psychosomatic Medicine, 59,* 572–577.

Walker, R., Logan, T., & Shannon, L. (2004, March). *Disturbed sleep and victimization among women.* Paper presented at the Second World Congress on Women's Mental Health, Washington, DC.

Wall, A., McKee, S., & Hinson, R. (2000). Assessing variation in alcohol outcome expectancies across the environmental context: An examination of the situational-specificity hypothesis. *Psychology of Addictive Behaviors, 14,* 367–375.

Wall, A., McKee, S., Hinson, R., & Goldstein, A. (2001). Examining alcohol outcome expectancies in laboratory and naturalistic bar settings: A within-subject experimental analysis. *Psychology of Addictive Behaviors, 15,* 219–226.

Wallace, J. (1999). The social ecology of addiction: Race, risk, and resilience. *Pediatrics, 103,* 1122–1127.

Wallace, J., Bachman, J., O'Malley, P., & Johnston, L. (1995). Racial/ethnic differences in adolescent drug use: Exploring possible explanations. In G. Botvin, S. Schinke, & M. Orlandi (Eds.), *Drug abuse prevention with multiethnic youth* (pp. 59–80). Thousand Oaks, CA: Sage.

Wallace, J., & Muroff, J. (2002). Preventing substance abuse among African American children and youth: Race differences in risk factor exposure and vulnerability. *Journal of Primary Prevention, 22,* 235–261.

Walls, H., & Brownlie, A. (1985). *Drink, drugs, and driving* (2nd ed.). London: Sweet & Maxwell.

Walsh, B., Fairburn, C., Mickley, D., Sysko, R., & Parides, M. (2004). Treatment of bulimia nervosa in a primary care setting. *American Journal of Psychiatry, 161,* 556–561.

Wand, G. (2000). The hypothalamic–pituitary–adrenal axis: Changes and risk for alcoholism. In A. Noronha, M. Eckardt, & K. Warren (Eds.), *Review of NIAAA's neuroscience and behavioral research portfolio* (NIAAA Research Monograph No. 34; pp. 397–416). Washington, DC: U.S. Department of Health and Human Services.

Warner, B., & Coomer, B. (2003). Neighborhood drug arrest rates: Are they a valid indicator of drug activity? A research note. *Journal of Research in Crime and Delinquency, 40,* 123–138.

Wasco, S. (2003). Conceptualizing the harm done by rape: Applications of trauma theory to experiences of sexual assault. *Trauma, Violence, & Abuse, 4,* 309–322.

Wasco, S., Campbell, R., Howard, A., Mason, G., Staggs, S., Schewe, P., & Riger, S. (2004). A statewide evaluation of services provided to rape survivors. *Journal of Interpersonal Violence, 19,* 252–263.

Wathen, C., & MacMillan, H. (2003). Interventions for violence against women: Scientific review. *Journal of the American Medical Association, 289,* 589–599.

Websdale, N. (1999). *Understanding domestic homicide.* Boston: Northeastern University Press.

Webster, D. (1990). Women and depression (alias codependency). *Family Community Health, 13,* 58–66.

Wegner, D. (2002). *The illusion of conscious will.* Cambridge, MA: MIT Press.

Weisberg, R., Bruce, S., Machan, J., Kessler, R., Culpepper, L., & Keller, M. (2002). Nonpsychiatric illness among primary care patients with trauma histories and posttraumatic stress disorder. *Psychiatric Services, 53,* 848–854.

Weiss, E., Longhurst, J., & Mazure, C. (1999). Childhood sexual abuse as a risk factor for depression in women: Psychosocial and neurobiological correlates. *American Journal of Psychiatry, 156,* 816–828.

Weiss, R., Griffin, M., & Mirin, S. (1992). Drug abuse as self-medication for depression: An empirical study. *American Journal of Drug and Alcohol Abuse, 18,* 121–129.

Weissman, M., Bland, R., Joyce, P., Newman, S., Wells, J., & Wittchen, H. (1993). Sex differences in rates of depression: Cross-national perspectives. *Journal of Affective Disorders, 29,* 77–84.

Weissman, M., Greenwald, S., Nino-Murcia, G., & Dement, W. (1997). The morbidity of insomnia uncomplicated by psychiatric disorders. *General Hospital Psychiatry, 19,* 245–250.

Weissman, M., Warner, V., Wickramaratne, P., Moreau, D., & Olfson, M. (1997). Offspring of depressed parents: 10 years later. *Archives of General Psychiatry, 54,* 932–394.

Weissman, M., Wickramaratne, P., Adams, P., Lish, J., Horwath, E. Charney, D., et al. (1993). The relationship between panic disorder and major depression: A new family study. *Archives of General Psychiatry, 50,* 767–771.

Weisstein, N. (1971). *Psychology constructs the female; or, the fantasy life of the male psychologist (with some attention to the fantasies of his friends, the male biologist and the male anthropologist).* Summerville, MA: New England Free Press.

Weisz, A. (1999). Legal advocacy for domestic violence survivors: The power of an informative relationship. *Families in Society, 80,* 2138–140.

Weisz, A. (2002). Prosecution of batterers: Views of African American battered women. *Violence and Victims, 17,* 19–34.

Welch, S., & Fairburn, C. (1996). Childhood sexual and physical abuse as risk factors for the development of bulimia nervosa: A community-based case control study. *Child Abuse & Neglect, 20,* 633–642.

Wells, K. (2001). Prosecuting those who stalk: A prosecutor's legal perspective and viewpoint. In J. Davis (Ed.), *Stalking crimes and victim protection: Prevention, intervention, threat assessment, and case management* (pp. 427–456). Boca Raton, FL: CRC Press.

Werner, E., & Smith, R. (1992). *Overcoming the odds: High risk children from birth to adulthood.* Ithaca, NY: Cornell University Press.

West, C., Kaufman Kantor, G., & Jasinski, J. (1998). Sociodemographic predictors and cultural barriers to help-seeking behaviors by Latina and Anglo American battered women. *Violence and Victims, 13,* 361–375.

West, C., Williams, L., & Siegel, J. (2000). Adult sexual revictimization among black women sexually abused in childhood: A prospective examination of serious consequences of abuse. *Child Maltreatment, 5,* 49–57.

Westen, D., & Morrison, K. (2001). A multidimensional meta-analysis of treatments for depression, panic, and generalized anxiety disorder: An empirical examination of the status of empirically supported therapies. *Journal of Consulting and Clinical Psychology, 69,* 875–899.

Westermeyer, J., Eames, S., & Nugent, S. (1998). Comorbid dysthymia and substance disorder: Treatment history and cost. *American Journal of Psychiatry, 155,* 1556–1560.

Whatley, M. (1996). Victim characteristics influencing attributions of responsibility to rape victims: A meta-analysis. *Aggression and Violent Behavior, 1,* 81–95.

Wheaton, B. (1980). The sociogenesis of psychological disorder: An attributional theory. *Journal of Health and Social Behavior, 21,* 100–124.

Wheaton, B. (1997). The nature of chronic stress. In B. Gottlieb (Ed.), *Coping with chronic stress* (pp. 43–73). New York: Plenum Press.

Wheaton, B. (1999). The nature of stressors. In A. Horwitz & T. Scheid (Eds.), *A handbook for the study of mental health* (pp. 176–197). New York: Cambridge University Press.

Whitbeck, L., Hoyt, D., & Yoder, K. (1999). A risk-amplification model of victimization and depressive symptoms among runaway and homeless adolescents. *American Journal of Community Psychology, 27,* 273–285.

White, B., & Kurpius, S. (1999). Attitudes toward rape victims: Effects of gender and professional status. *Journal of Interpersonal Violence, 14,* 989–995.

White, H., Johnson, V., & Buyske, S. (2000). Parental modeling and parenting behavior effects on offspring alcohol and cigarette use: A growth curve analysis. *Journal of Substance Abuse, 12,* 287–310.

White, L., & Booth, A. (1991). Divorce over the life course: The role of marital happiness. *Journal of Family Issues, 12,* 5–21.

Whitehead, W. E. (1999). Patient subgroups in irritable bowel syndrome that can be defined by symptom evaluation and physical examination. *American Journal of Medicine, 8,* 33S–40S.

Whitmire, L., Harlow, L., Quina, K., & Morokoff, P. (1999). *Childhood trauma and HIV: Women at risk.* Ann Arbor, MI: Taylor & Francis.

Wiederman, M., Sansone, R., & Sansone, L. (1999). Obesity among sexually abused women: An adaptive function for some? *Women and Health, 29,* 89–100.

Wiist, W., & McFarlane, J. (1998) Utilization of police by abused pregnant Hispanic women. *Violence Against Women, 4,* 677–693.

Wild, T. (2002). Personal drinking and sociocultural drinking norms: A representative population study. *Journal of Studies on Alcohol, 63,* 469–475.

Williams, D. (2000). Race, stress, and mental health. In C. Hogue, M. Hargraves, & K. Scott-Collins (Eds.). *Minority health in America* (pp. 209–243). Baltimore: Johns Hopkins University Press.

Williams, D., Yu, Y., Jackson, J., & Anderson, N. (1997). Racial differences in physical and mental health: Socio-economic status, stress and discrimination. *Journal of Health Psychology, 2,* 335–351.

Willoughby, S., Hailey, B., Mulkana, S., & Rowe, J. (2002). The effect of laboratory-induced depressed mood state on responses to pain. *Behavioral Medicine, 28,* 23–31.

Wills, T., & Cleary, S. (1999). Peer and adolescent substance use among 6th–9th graders: Latent growth analyses of influence versus selection mechanisms. *Health Psychology, 18,* 453–463.

Wills, T., & Filer, M. (1996). Stress-coping model of adolescent substance use. In T. Ollendick & R. Prinz (Eds.), *Advances in clinical and child psychology* (Vol. 18, pp. 91–132). New York: Plenum Press.

Wills, T., & Hirky, E. (1996). Coping and substance abuse: A theoretical model and review of the evidence. In M. Zeidner & N. Endler (Eds.), *Handbook of coping: Theory, research, and application* (pp. 297–302). New York: Wiley.

Wills, T., & Yaeger, A. (2003). Family factors and adolescent substance use: Models and mechanisms. *Current Directions in Psychological Science, 12,* 222–226.

Willson, P., McFarlane, J., Lemmey, D., & Malecha, A. (2001). Referring abused women: Does police assistance decrease abuse? *Clinical Nursing Research, 10,* 69–81.

Wilsnack, S., Vogeltanz, N., Klassen, A., & Harris, T. (1997). Childhood sexual abuse and women's substance abuse: National survey findings. *Journal of Studies on Alcohol, 58,* 264–271.

Wilson, A., Calhoun, K., & Bernat, J. (1999). Risk recognition and trauma-related symptoms among sexually revictimized women. *Journal of Consulting and Clinical Psychology, 67,* 705–710.

Wilson, A., Calhoun, K., & McNair, L. (2002). Alcohol consumption and expectancies among sexually coercive college men. *Journal of Interpersonal Violence, 17,* 1145–1159.

Wilson, D., & Lipsey, M. (2003). The role of method in treatment effectiveness research: Evidence from meta-analysis. In A. Kazdin (Ed.), *Methodological issues and strategies in clinical research* (3rd ed., pp. 589–616). Washington, DC: American Psychological Association.

Wilson, G. (1996). Manual-based treatments: The clinical application of research findings. *Behavior Research Therapy, 34,* 295–314.

Wilson, M., & Daly, M. (1993). Spousal homicide risk and estrangement. *Violence and Victims, 8,* 3–16.

Wilson, M., Johnson, H., & Daly, M. (1995). Lethal and non-lethal violence against wives. *Canadian Journal of Criminology, 37,* 331–361.

Wilson, S., Becker, L., & Tinker, R. (1995). Eye movement desensitization and reprocessing (EMDR) treatment for psychologically traumatized individuals. *Journal of Consulting and Clinical Psychology, 63,* 928–937.

Wilson, W. (1987). *The truly disadvantaged: The inner city, the underclass, and public policy.* Chicago: University of Chicago Press.

Wilson, W. (1996). *When work disappears: The world of the urban poor.* New York: Knopf.

Wilt, S., & Olson, S. (1996). Prevalence of domestic violence in the United States. *Journal of the American Medical Women's Association, 51,* 77–82.

Wilton, R. (2003). Poverty and mental health: A quantitative study of residential care facility tenants. *Community Mental Health Journal, 39,* 139–156.

Windle, M. (2000). Parental, sibling, and peer influences on adolescent substance use and alcohol problems. *Applied Developmental Science, 4,* 98–110.

Windle, M. (1994). Substance use, risky behaviors, and victimization among a U.S. national adolescent sample. *Adolescence, 89,* 175–182.

Windle, M. (1997). Mate similarity, heavy substance use and family history of problem drinking among young adult women. *Journal of Studies on Alcohol, 58,* 573–587.

Wingood, G., DiClemente, R., & Raj, A. (2000). Adverse consequences of intimate partner abuse among women in non-urban domestic violence shelters. *American Journal of Preventive Medicine, 19,* 270–275.

Winhusen, T., & Kropp, F. (2003). Psychosocial treatments for women with substance use disorders. *Obstetrics and Gynecological Clinics of North America, 30,* 483–499.

Winkel, F., Blaauw, E., & Wisman, F. (1999). Dissociation-focused victim support and coping with traumatic memory: An empirical search for evidence sustaining the effectiveness of downward comparison based interventions. *International Journal of Victimology, 6,* 179–200.

Winterer, G., & Goldman, D. (2003). Genetics of human prefrontal function. *Brain Research Reviews, 43,* 134–163.

Winters, J., Fals-Stewart, W. O'Farrell, T., Birchler, G., & Kelley, M. (2002). Behavioral couples therapy for female substance-abusing patients: Effects on substance use and relationship adjustment. *Journal of Consulting and Clinical Psychology, 70,* 344–355.

Wisner, C., Gilmer, T., Saltzman, L., & Zink, T. (1999). Intimate partner violence against women: Do victims cost health plans more? *Journal of Family Practice, 48,* 439–443.

Woldoff, R. (2002). The effects of local stressors on neighborhood attachment. *Social Forces, 81,* 87–116.

Wolf, M., Holt, V., Kernic, M., & Rivara, F. (2000). Who gets protection orders for intimate partner violence? *American Journal of Preventive Medicine, 19,* 286–291.

Wolf, M., Ly, U., Hobart, M., & Kernic, M. (2003). Barriers to seeking police help for intimate partner violence. *Journal of Family Violence, 18,* 121–129.

Wolfinger, N. (1999). Trends in the intergenerational transmission of divorce. *Demography, 36,* 415–420.

Wolfinger, N. (2000). Beyond the intergenerational transmission of divorce: Do people replicate the patterns of marital instability they grew up with? *Journal of Family Issues, 21,* 1061–1086.

Wolfinger, N. (2001). The effects of family structure of origin on offspring cohabitation duration. *Sociological Inquiry, 71,* 3, 293–313.

Wolkstein, E., & Spiller, H. (1998). Providing vocational services to clients in substance abuse rehabilitation. *Directions in Rehabilitation Counseling, 9,* 65–78.

Wong, C., & Yehuda, R. (2002). Sex differences in posttraumatic stress disorder. In F. Lewis-Hall, T. Williams, J. Panetta, & J. Herrera (Eds.), *Psychiatric illness in women* (pp. 57–98). Washington, DC: American Psychiatric Press.

Wood, J. (1989). Theory and research concerning social comparisons of personal attributes. *Psychological Bulletin, 106,* 231–248.

Woodward, L., & Fergusson, D. (2000). Childhood and adolescent predictors of physical assault: A prospective longitudinal study. *Criminology, 38,* 233–261.

Wooldredge, J., & Thistlethwaite, A. (2002). Reconsidering domestic violence recidivism: Conditioned effects of legal controls by individual and aggregate levels of stake in conformity. *Journal of Quantitative Criminology, 18,* 45–70.

Worden, P. (2000). The changing boundaries of the criminal justice system: Redefining the problem and the response in domestic violence. In C. Friel (Ed.), *Criminal justice 2000. Vol. 2: Boundary changes in criminal justice organizations* (pp. 215–266). Washington, DC: National Institute of Justice.

Wright, P., & Wright, K. (1991). Codependency: Addictive love, adjustive relating, or both? *Contemporary Family Therapy, 13,* 435–454.

Wuest, J., Ford-Gilboe, M., Merritt-Gray, M., & Berman, H. (2003). Intrusion: The central problem for family health promotion among children and single mothers after leaving an abusive partner. *Qualitative Health Research, 13,* 597–622.

X, L. (1999). Accomplishing the impossible. An advocate's notes from the successful campaign to make marital and date rape a crime in all 50 U.S. states and other countries. *Violence Against Women, 5,* 1064–1081.

Yama, M., Fogas, B., Teegarden, L., & Hastings, B. (1993). Childhood sexual abuse and parental alcoholism: Interactive effects in adult women. *American Journal of Orthopsychiatry, 63,* 300–305.

Yehuda, R. (1999). Biological factors associated with susceptibility to posttraumatic stress disorder. *Canadian Journal of Psychiatry, 44,* 34–39.

Yehuda, R., Levengood, R., Schmeidler, J., Wilson, S., Guo, L., & Gerber, D. (1996). Increased pituitary activation following metyrapone administration in post-traumatic stress disorder. *Psychoneuroendocrinology, 21,* 1–16.

Yehuda, R., McFarlane, A., & Shalev, A. (1998). Predicting the development of posttraumatic stress disorder from the acute response to a traumatic event. *Biological Psychiatry, 44,* 1305–1313.

Young, A., Klap, R., Sherbourne, C., & Wells, K. (2001). The quality of care for depressive and anxiety disorders in the United States. *Archives of General Psychiatry, 58,* 55–61.

Zador, P. (1991). Alcohol-related relative risk of fatal driver injuries in relation to driver age and sex. *Journal of Studies on Alcohol, 52,* 302–310.

Zanarini, M., Frankenburg, F., Dubo, E., Sickel, A., Trikha, A., Levin, A., & Reynolds, V. (1998). Axis I comorbidity of borderline personality disorder. *American Journal of Psychiatry, 155,* 1733–1739.

Zanarini, M., Frankenburg, F., Hennen, J., Reich, D., & Silk, K. (2004). Axis I comorbidity in patients with borderline personality disorder: 6-year follow-up and prediction of time to remission. *American Journal of Psychiatry, 161,* 2108–2114.

Zanarini, M., Williams, A., Lewis, R., Reich, R., Vera, S., Marion, M., et al. (1997). Reported pathological childhood experiences associated with the development of borderline personality disorder. *American Journal of Psychiatry, 154,* 1101–1106.

Zhang, L., Welte, J., & Wieczorek, W. (2001). Deviant lifestyle and crime victimization. *Journal of Criminal Justice, 29,* 133–143.

Zimbardo, P., & Leippe, M. (1991). *The psychology of attitude change and social influence.* New York: McGraw-Hill.

Zlotnick, C., Franklin, C., & Zimmerman, M. (2002). Is comorbidity of posttraumatic stress disorder and borderline personality disorder related to greater pathology and impairment? *American Journal of Psychiatry, 159,* 1940–1943.

Zlotnick, C., Najavits, L., Rohsenow, D., & Johnson, D. (2003). A cognitive–behavioral treatment for incarcerated women with substance abuse disorder and posttraumatic stress disorder: Findings from a pilot study. *Journal of Substance Abuse Treatment, 25,* 99–105.

Zoellner, L., Feeny, N., Alvarez, J., Watlington, C., O'Neill, M., Zager, R., & Foa, E. (2000). Factors associated with completion of the restraining order process in female victims of partner violence. *Journal of Interpersonal Violence, 15,* 1081–1099.

Zoellner, L., Feeny, N., Fitzgibbons, L., & Foa, E. (1999). Response of African American and Caucasian women to cognitive behavioral therapy for PTSD. *Behavior Therapy, 30,* 581–595.

Zoellner, L., Goodwin, M., & Foa, E. (2000). PTSD severity and health perceptions in female victims of sexual assault. *Journal of Traumatic Stress, 13,* 635–649.

Zucker, R., Ellis, D., Fitzgerald, H., Bingham, C., & Sanford, K. (1996). Other evidence for at least two alcoholisms: II. Life course variation in antisociality and heterogeneity of alcoholic outcome. *Development and Psychopathology, 8,* 831–848.

Zuckerman, D. (1989). Stress, self-esteem, and mental health: How does gender make a difference? *Sex Roles, 20,* 429–444.

Zweig, J., Barber, B., & Eccles, J. (1997). Sexual coercion and well-being in young adulthood: Comparisons by gender and college status. *Journal of Interpersonal Violence, 12,* 291–308.

Zweig, J., Crockett, L., Sayer, A., & Vicary, J. (1999). A longitudinal examination of the consequences of sexual victimization for rural young adult women. *Journal of Sex Research, 36,* 396–409.

Author Index

Subject Index

About the Authors

TK Logan, PhD, is an associate professor at the University of Kentucky Department of Behavioral Science, with appointments in psychology, psychiatry, sociology, and social work as well as the Center on Drug and Alcohol Research. Dr. Logan is also a grant reviewer for the National Institutes of Health. Funded by the National Institute on Drug Abuse and by the National Institute on Alcohol Abuse and Alcoholism, she has studied intimate partner violence and partner sexual assault, examining a wide range of contributing factors and outcomes. Her recent research focuses on stalking and aims to shed light on cultural differences in victimization and community responses. Dr. Logan has published extensively on partner violence, sexual assault, substance abuse, and drug courts.

Robert Walker, MSW, LCSW, is an assistant professor of psychiatry at the University of Kentucky Center on Drug and Alcohol Research with conjoint appointments in social work and behavioral science and has taught psychopathology as well as research. He has over 25 years of experience as a clinician and clinical supervisor and has developed clinical services for a wide array of clinical problems, including partner violence. He has been a coinvestigator on partner violence studies and an evaluator of substance abuse treatment programs in rural and inner-city programs. He is the principal investigator for the Kentucky Treatment Outcome Study. He has published articles on substance abuse, brain injury, domestic violence, ethics, and personality disorders.

Carol E. Jordan, MS, is director of the University of Kentucky Center for Research on Violence Against Women and holds faculty appointments in the Department of Psychology and the College of Social Work. Her writing and research interests include the nexus of mental health and criminal justice, particularly as it relates to the experience of women. She has authored numerous articles and coauthored two books on victimization and mental-health-related practice implications. Ms. Jordan has 20 years of experience in public policy, legislative advocacy, and the development of programs addressing intimate partner violence, rape, and stalking. Her work has been recognized by numerous national and state organizations and legislative bodies.

Carl G. Leukefeld, DSW, is professor and chair of behavioral science and director of the Center on Drug and Alcohol Research at the University of Kentucky. He was a commissioned officer and chief health services officer in the U.S. Public Health Service, including assignments to the National Institute on Drug Abuse. He has presented and written more than 175 articles and chapters and has written or edited 17 books and monographs on treatment, criminal justice, prevention, and AIDS. His current projects are supported by the National Institutes of Health, the National Science Foundation, and private industry. His research interests include judicial sanctions, drug abuse treatment, the delivery of rural services, and HIV.